Yale Egyptological Studies 12

Cult and Ritual in Persian Period Egypt

Yale Egyptological Studies

Yale Egyptological Studies 12

Cult and Ritual in Persian Period Egypt

An Analysis of the Decoration of the Cult Chapels of the Temple of Hibis at Kharga Oasis

Fatma Talaat Ismail

Yale Egyptology New Haven, CT

Yale Egyptological Studies 12

ISBN 978-1-950343-09-6 (paperback)
ISBN 978-1-950343-11-9 (PDF eBook)

Library of Congress Cataloging-in-Publication Data

Names: Ismail, Fatma Talaat, author.
Title: Cult and ritual in Persian Period Egypt : an analysis of the decoration of the cult chapels of the Temple of Hibis at Kharga Oasis / Fatma Talaat Ismail.
Description: New Haven, CT : Yale Egyptology, [2019] | Series: Yale egyptological studies ; 12 | Includes bibliographical references and index. | In English; includes text in Ancient Egyptian (transcribed) with parallel English translation. | Summary: "Ancient Egyptian temple walls expressed royal and political ideologies, reflected the ancient Egyptian secular and spiritual world order, supplied a medium for the reenactments of assorted myths, and implied a metaphor for the universe. The Temple of Hibis is one of the most important temples from Late Period Egypt. Despite the conventional overall architecture plan of the temple, it exhibits numerous particularities. While the more prominent parts of the temple, such as the sanctuary, have been studied by numerous scholars, in other areas the decoration schemes remain largely unexplained. This book focuses on the decorative schemes of several chapels in the earlier part of the temple, chapels that were either established and/or were decorated during the first Persian Period (525–404 BCE). These chapels were located around the main sanctuary A, but have rarely been the subject of scholarly discussions. It concentrates on a few chapels of the Temple of Hibis: chapels F and G to the south of sanctuary A on the first level of the temple and all the decorated chapels, E1, E2, H1, and H2, on the second level of the temple. Each chapter begins with a brief description of the scenes and their basic layout and a complete translation of the accompanying texts. A more in-depth analysis regarding both text and image follows in the commentary. It includes the analysis of the different aspects of the gods, their origins, and the development of their cults that are significant to the scenes and to each other. Also discussed are their coherence, any aspects that are especially emphasized, and any other information that could be gleaned from the whole scene. The analysis tries to detail the specific composition that makes up the mosaic of the picture, wall, or room. Attention is paid to both the scenic arrangement and the hieroglyphic inscriptions, as the interpretation of one would be meaningless without the other. Attention is given to investigating the general function of the different rooms by means of their decoration and by identifying the patterns or important themes generated by the layout of the scenes. The results are summarized in the last chapter. A number of line drawings have been inserted into the text beside a described scene as an aid to the reader"-- Provided by publisher.
Identifiers: LCCN 2019031028 (print) | LCCN 2019031029 (ebook) | ISBN 9781950343096 (paperback) | ISBN 9781950343119 (PDF eBook)
Subjects: LCSH: Temple of Hibis (Egypt) | Temples, Egyptian--Egypt--Kharga (Oasis) | Art, Egyptian--Egypt--Kharga (Oasis) | Religious art--Egypt--Kharga (Oasis) | Kharga (Egypt : Oasis)--Antiquities.
Classification: LCC DT73.K5 I76 2019 (print) | LCC DT73.K5 (ebook) | DDC 932/.3--dc23
LC record available at https://lccn.loc.gov/2019031028
LC ebook record available at https://lccn.loc.gov/2019031029

Typeset in Minion Pro and Warnock Pro.

Printed in the United States of America on acid-free paper.

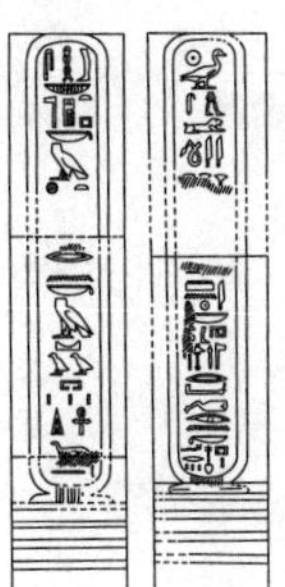

Contents

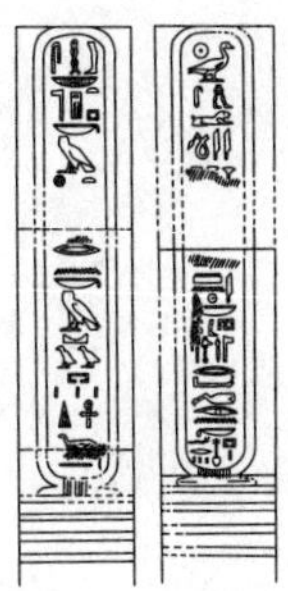

List of Illustrations

FIGURES

PLATES

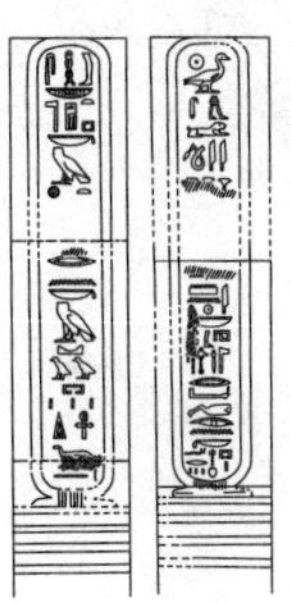

Acknowledgements

First and foremost, I acknowledge and express my gratitude and admiration for my former advisers Dr. Betsy Bryan and Dr. Richard Jasnow of the Department of Near Eastern Studies at Johns Hopkins University. They have helped me complete the writing of the original manuscript of this book as a PhD thesis, as well as updating it in its current format. They have graciously availed me of their time and guidance every step of the way. Furthermore, I will always appreciate what incredible advisors and great people they are.

Special heatfelt thanks to Dr. John Darnell, Dr. Hans-W. Fischer-Elfert and Dr. David Klotz for sending early drafts of their articles and for their insightful suggestions and observations. I acknowledge the works of previous scholars who laid the foundation for our knowledge of the Hibis material, most notably, Dr. Eugene Cruz-Uribe and the Hibis Publication by the Metropolitan Museum. Dr. Edwin Krupp, Director of the Griffith Observatory, reviewed a draft of my discussion on astronomy related to the decanal representations on the roof of Hibis and gave helpful feedback and references. These scholars, as well as the cited authors in the following pages, must share the credit for anything that is worthwhile in this work, but they cannot be liable for anything that is erroneous.

During the course of my work, I was supported in part by academic grants from the Egyptian Ministry of Higher Education under the auspices of the Egyptian Educational Bureau, Washington D.C.; the American Research Center in Egypt, supported by the U.S. State Department Bureau of Education and Cultural Affairs, via the Council for Overseas Research Centers; the Near Eastern Studies Department at Johns Hopkins, the Dean's Teaching Fellowship, and the J. Brien Graduate Student Assistance Fund.

Permission to conduct research in Egypt was generously granted by the Supreme Council of Antiquities of Egypt and the former Secretary General Dr. Zahi Hawass. I acknowledge with gratitude the cooperation and assistance of officials of the Supreme Council of Antiquities at the various temple sites, in particular the essential advice and support given by the Inspectorate at Kharga: Mr. Bahgat Ibrahim, Director for Antiquities of Kharga; Mr. Magdy Hussein, Chief Inspector for Antiquities of Kharga; Mr. Ibrahim Refaat, Chief Inspector for Antiquities of Hibis Temple; Mr. Bahaa el Din Zakaria, Chief Conservator; and Mr. Ahmad Mostafa, Inspector of Hibis Temple. Mr. Refaat and Mr. Zakaria facilitated and organized trips to the other archaeological sites in Kharga; their generosity and dedication in the long and hot Kharga summer season are most appreciated.

My greatest debt, one that I can never repay, is to my parents, Dr. Talaat Ismail and Mrs. Zeinab Abdel-Shahid, whose encouragement and many sacrifices made it possible for me to complete my studies while enjoying the privilege of raising a family. They and my three beautiful girls, Mahey, Laila, and Farrah, are the cornerstones of my life.

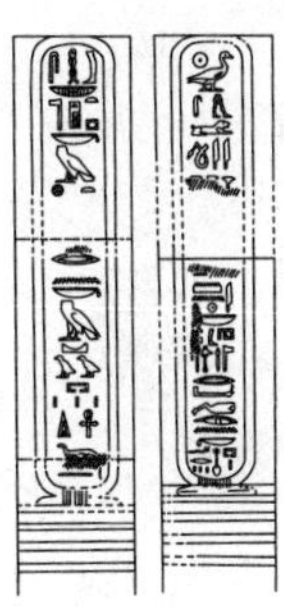

Abbreviations

BIBLIOGRAPHICAL ABBREVIATIONS

ÄAT	Ägypten und Altes Testament, Wiesbaden (until 2013) and Münster.
ADAIK	Abhandlungen des Deutschen Archäologischen Instituts, Abteilung Kairo.
AJSL	*The American Journal of Semitic Languages and Literatures*, Chicago.
ASAE	*Annales du Service des Antiquités de l'Égypte*, Cairo.
BdE	Bibliothèque d'Étude, Cairo.
BES	*Bulletin of the Egyptological Seminar*, New York.
BIFAO	*Bulletin de l'Institut Français d'Archéologie Orientale*, Cairo.
BiOr	*Bibliotheca Orientalis*, Leiden.
BSEG	*Bulletin de la Société d'Égyptologie, Genève*, Geneva.
BSFE	*Bulletin de la Société Française d'Égyptologie*, Paris.
BSPABA	*Bollettino della Società Piemontese di Archeologia e Belle Arti*, Turin.
CdÉ	*Chronique d'Égypte*, Brussels.
CRIPEL	*Cahier de Recherche de l'Institut de Papyrologie et d'Égyptologie de Lille*
CT	A. de Buck, *The Egyptian Coffin Texts*, 7 vols. OIP 34, 49, 64, 67, 73, 81 and 87. Chicago: The University of Chicago Press, 1935–1961.
D Mammisis	F. Daumas, *Les Mammisis de Dendera*. Cairo: IFAO, 1959.
D	E. Chassinat and F. Daumas, *Le temple de Dendera*, 11 vols. Cairo: IFAO, 1934–2000.
DE	*Discussions in Egyptology*, Oxford.
E Mammisis	E. Chassinat, *Le Mammisis d'Edfou*. MIFAO 16. Cairo: IFAO, 1939.
E	Le Marquis de Rochemonteix, *Le temple d'Edfou I*. MMAF 10. Cairo: IFAO, 1897; E. Chassinat, *Le temple d'Edfou II–XIV*. MMAF 11 and 20–31. Cairo: IFAO, 1918–1928; S. Cauville and D. Devauchelle, *Le temple d'Edfou XV*. MMAF 32. Cairo: IFAO, 1985.
EAT	O. Neugebauer and R. Parker, *Egyptian Astronomical Texts*, 3 vols. Published for Brown University Press, Providence, Rhode Island by Lund Humphries, London, England, 1960–1969.
Enchoria	*Enchoria. Zeitschrift für Demotistik und Koptologie*, Wiesbaden.
Esna V	S. Sauneron, *Les fêtes religieuses d'Esna aux derniers siécles du Paganisme*. Cairo: IFAO, 1962.
Esna	S. Sauneron, *Le temple d'Esna*, II-IV. Cairo: IFAO, 1963–1975.

EVO	*Egitto e Vicino Oriente. Rivista della sezione orientalistica dell'Istituto di Storia Antica. Università degli Studi di Pisa*, Pisa.
FIFAO	Fouilles de l'Institut Français d'Archéologie Orientale du Caire, Cairo.
GM	*Göttinger Miszellen*, Göttingen
Gutbub, Ko	A. Gutbub, *Kôm Ombo*, I. Cairo: IFAO, 1995.
HÄB	Hildesheimer Ägyptologische Beiträge, Hildesheim.
IFAO	Institut Français d'Archéologie Orientale.
JARCE	*Journal of the American Research Center in Egypt*, Cambridge (MA) / Boston / Princeton / New York.
JNES	*Journal of Near Eastern Studies: The Journal of the Department of Oriental Languages and Civilizations of the University of Chicago*, Chicago.
JSSEA	*The Journal of the Society of the Study of Egyptian Antiquities*, Toronto.
Kom Ombos	J. de Morgan, *Kom Ombos. Catalogue des monuments et inscriptions de l'Égypte antique*, II–III. Vienna: Adolphe Holzhausen, 1895–1909.
LÄ	W. Helck and E. Otto (eds.), *Lexikon der Ägyptologie.* Wiesbaden: Harrassowitz, 1975-98.
LingAeg	*Lingua Aegyptia. Journal of Egyptian Language Studies*, Göttingen.
MÄS	Münchner ägyptologische Studien, Berlin and Munich.
MDAIK	*Mitteilungen des Deutschen Archäologischen Instituts, Abteilung Kairo*, Berlin / Wiesbaden / Mainz.
Medinet Habu	The Epigraphic Survey, *Medinet Habu*, 8 vols. OIP 8, 9, 23, 51, 83, 84, 93, and 94. Chicago: Oriental Institute of the University of Chicago, 1930–70.
MEEF	Memoir of the Egypt Exploration Fund, London.
MIFAO	Mémoires publiés par les membres de l'Institut Français d'Archéologie Orientale du Caire, Cairo.
MIO	*Mitteilungen des Instituts für Orientforschung*, Berlin.
MMAF	Mémoires publiés par les membres de la Mission Archéologique Française au Caire, Cairo.
Numen	*Numen: International Review for the History of Religions*, Leiden.
OBO	Orbis Biblicus et Orientalis, Fribourg.
OIP	Oriental Institute Publications, Chicago.
OLA	Orientalia Lovaniensa Analecta, Leuven.
OMRO	*Oudheidkundige mededelingen uit het Rijksmuseum van Oudheden*, Leiden.
Opet	C. de Wit, *Les inscriptions du temple d'Opet, à Karnak.* Bibliotheca Aegyptiaca XI–XIII. Brussels: Fondation Égyptologique Reine Élisabeth, 1958–1968.
Philae II	H. Junker and E. Winter, *Das Geburtshaus des Tempels der Isis in Philae.* Vienna: Hermann Böhlaus Nachfolger, 1965.
PM	B. Porter, R. L. B. Moss, and J. Málek, *Topographical Bibliography of Ancient Egyptian Hieroglyphic Texts, Reliefs, and Paintings*, 8 vols. Oxford: Griffith Institute, Ashmolean Museum, 1978.
PSBA	*Proceedings of the Society of Biblical Archaeology*, London.

PT — K. Sethe, *Die altägyptischen Pyramidentexte, nach den Papierabdrücken und Photographien des Berliner Museums, neu herausgegeben und erläutert.* Hildesheim: Georg Olms Verlagsbuchhandlung, 1960.

RdE — *Revue d'Égyptologie*, Paris.

RecTrav — *Recueil de travaux relatifs à la philologie et à l'archéologie égyptiennes et assyriennes*, Institut Français d'Archéologie Orientale, Cairo.

SAOC — Studies in Ancient Oriental Civilization, Chicago.

SAK — *Studien zur altägyptischen Kultur*, Hamburg.

VA — *Varia Aegyptiaca*, San Antonio.

Wb. — A. Erman and H. Grapow, *Das Wörterbuch der ägyptischen Sprache*, 5 vols. Berlin: Akademie-Verlag, 1926–1931.

YES — Yale Egyptological Studies, New Haven.

ZÄS — *Zeitschrift für ägyptische Sprache and Altertumskunde*, Leipzig / Berlin.

GENERAL ABBREVIATIONS

ed(s).	editor(s)
pl(s).	plate(s)
vol(s).	volume(s)
col(s).	column(s)
reg.	register
p(p).	page(s)
cf.	compare
esp.	especially
fig(s).	figure(s)
n.	note
CG	Prefix for registration number of object in the *Catalogue Général des Antiquitiés Égyptiennes du Musee du Caire.*

SYMBOLS

[ ]	Square brackets denote a restored word or words.
< >	Angled brackets denote words or suffixes omitted in the original.
( )	Round brackets denote words supplied to bring out the sense.
{ }	encloses a scribal error.
////	denotes destruction on the wall or that the inscription is not clear or is erased
( )¦	denotes a cartouche.
(...)¦	denotes an empty cartouche.
[ ]¦	denotes a Serekh.
[...]¦	denotes an empty Serekh.

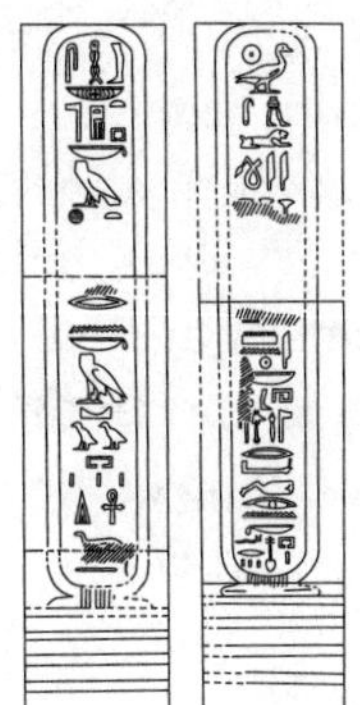

1
Introduction

Ancient Egyptian temples were the most distinctive cultural institutions of the land. Despite domestic and foreign upheavals, their decorations expressed and preserved the country's religious culture through the centuries. These multifaceted complexes served a wide range of functions: they were centers for national and local religious festivals, daily and seasonal ritual cults, economic exchange, and theological development. The temple walls expressed royal and political ideologies, reflected the ancient Egyptian secular and spiritual world order, supplied a medium for the reenactments of assorted myths, and implied a metaphor for the universe.

The temples, which interacted with both the divine and human spheres, were called "God's houses" or "*ḥwwt nṯr*;" they were directly built for the benefit of the gods but with substantial cultic connections between the king and the deities. Even though commoners were excluded from the temple activities, they realized that their prosperity depended on the temple "working." Outside the temple premises, commoners used the sites as entertainment venues, especially around national festivities and as pilgrimage sites.[1] Though the temples were prohibited to the majority of the people, they were "machines" that benefitted the whole society.[2]

Thus, temple decoration presents a central perspective into many aspects of the ancient Egyptian belief system. However, interpreting temple decoration is as complex as the temples themselves. With their prolific reliefs and inscriptions, the temples contained a variety of themes, iconographical details, and architectural elements that challenge scholars to explain their meanings against the background of the social and political conditions of the time. Most temple scenes present only short speeches and labels for text that do not usually form single meaningful units with their vignettes. In only a few places temple walls clearly indicate narratives or sequences of scenes relating to a single ritual.

Scholars have used several modes for interpreting temple decoration. Different interpretation methodologies have coexisted with no apparent incompatibility problems. The emphasis on the interrelation between text, image, and architecture as a fundamental ingredient in trying to decipher a scene's meaning is already a given principle that is used

1 Van der Plas, "Tempel in Ägypten," pp. 249ff, where he also suggested that the people would have been attracted to the colorfulness of the temple decorations. The Roman governors in the Kharga Oasis found the gateways of the Temple of Hibis a convenient medium for their important civil announcements, see p. 12 below.

2 Quirke, *Ancient Egyptian Religion*, p. 70.

in the context of New Kingdom[3] and Greco-Roman temples.[4] In general, two theoretical apparatuses were developed to analyze temple decoration: the *Raumfunktion* and the *grammaire du temple. Raumfunktion* is understood as both the symbolic as well as the cultic purpose of the space that is determined by the specific arrangements of the wall decoration and architecture.[5] The principle of *grammaire du temple* is used to refer to the logical balance of the distribution of the overall orientation and organization of the contents of each wall.[6] However, Traunecker, for example, warned against depending solely on the *grammaire du temple* in analyzing temple scenes:

> La restitution de la «grammaires des temples» est une entreprise difficile. S'il est évident que la composition du décor est en rapport avec la fonction de la pièce, il est souvent difficile d'estimer l'influence des rites célébrés, des allusions mythologiques, ou encore des éléments théologiques d'opportunité. De plus, le commentateur moderne ne prend en compte que l'auteur du décor et s'accommode à l'idée d'un récepteur idéal et immuable, reflet figé du décorateur antique. Mais si l'on considère le décor d'un temple comme une sorte de texte, il faut non seulement se pencher sur sa grammaire mais aussi s'interroger sur le contexte de sa création. Qui a conçu ce «texte des temples», comment, pourquoi et pour qui?[7]

As Traunecker hinted, one's understanding of temple scenes should combine a response to the context of their creation, taking into consideration the intentions of the original

3 For example, see the papers in Dorman and Bryan, *Sacred Space and Sacred Function in Ancient Thebes*; Refai, *Untersuchungen zum Bildprogramm der grossen Säulensäle in den thebanischen Tempeln des Neuen Reiches*; el-Sharkawy, *Der Amun-Tempel von Karnak. Die Funktion der Grossen Säulenhalle, erschlossen aus der Analyse der Dekoration ihrer Innenwände.*

4 For example, Labrique, *Stylistique et Théologie à Edfou*; Cauville, *Essai sur la théologie du temple d'Horus à Edfou*; Cauville, *La Théologie d'Osiris à Edfou*; Derchain-Urtel, "Die Bild- und Textgestaltung in Esna — eine "Rettungsaktion;" Vassilika, *Ptolemaic Philae.*

5 J. Spiegel was the first to suggest that every architectural and decoration detail has a relationship with the intended function of the space, Spiegel, "Das Auferstehungritual der Unaspyramide," esp. pp. 430–439.This *Raumfunktion* relation was later applied on New Kingdom temples in the pioneer study by Arnold, *Wandrelief und Raumfunktion in ägyptischen Tempeln des neuen Reiches,* and later amplified by the works of Gundlach; see for examples papers in *Ägyptische Tempel — Struktur, Funktion und Programm,* and in *Ägyptologische Tempeltagung*, series 1–8, and Recklinghausen and Stadler, *Kultorte: Mythen, Wissenschaft und Alltag in den Tempeln Ägyptens.*

6 The term was coined by Derchain, "Un manuel de géographie liturgique à Edfou," pp. 31–44; Derchain, "Réflexions sur la décoration des pylônes,"pp. 17–24. See also Gutbub, "Remarques sur quelques règles observées dans l'architecture, la décoration et les inscriptions des temples de Basse Epoque," pp. 123–135; Winter, "Weitere Beobachtungen zur 'Grammaire du Temple' in der griechisch-römischen Zeit," pp. 61–76; Cauville, "Une règle de la grammaire du temple," pp. 51–84.

7 Traunecker, "Observations sur le Décor des temples Égyptiens," pp. 83ff. See also Traunecker, "De l'hiérophanie au temple," pp. 303–317.

designer of the scenes. The modern interpreter's objectivity or subjectivity when considering relevant religious and Egyptological data will affect the outcome of the interpretation. More importantly, an interpreter of meaning of ancient Egyptian temples must be aware of the many layers inherent in the temple decoration itself, or what came to be called *Dekorationsachsen:* "Decoration Semantic stratum or layerings."[8] Because of the accumulation of millennia of praxis and traditions, the temple became "a world of giant metaphors,"[9] heavily intertwined with often contradicting complexities of mythology. Each wall scene served as a premodern changing billboard that delivered many messages simultaneously, a fact that has often obstructed attempts to find coherence between the different scenes, even when each detail is carefully analyzed.

Every Egyptian temple is unique; its design was not done haphazardly, but was, instead, premeditated. It contained pre-doctored formulae that automatically pushed its agenda.[10] Knowledge was certainly behind the choice of the individual scene components. As with a musical composition that combines already widely known notes, every composition has its unique sound. The designer had a wide repertoire of images at his disposal, so that he was able to choose and thereby make a personal statement about fashions of the time and the ideology of the society. Although the decoration might seem repetitive, standardized, or coming from stock formulae, they can be defragmented, recollected, and reinterpreted in new light.

The word *iconography* comes from the Greek meaning "image writing" or "writing in image." Examining iconography and meaning of the temple decoration is thus based on *reading* these images by identifying the figures, understanding the accompanying text, and deciphering the ritual actions involved. Only after this initial process and sorting out the usual and characteristic features can one hope to extract meaning by "rewriting" the scene, detangling each subsequent layer of interaction between the characters, texts, actions, and architectural settings.[11]

I chose to analyze the decoration of one of the most important temples from Late Period Egypt, the Temple of Hibis. Despite the conventional overall architecture plan of the Hibis Temple (see pl. 3), it exhibits numerous particularities. Among Egyptologists, the Hibis Temple is famous for the iconic colorful relief in hypostyle hall B of the god

8 Gundlach, "Das Dekorationsprogramm der Tempel von Abu Simbel und Ihre kultische und königsideologische Funktion," pp. 47–71.

9 Wilkinson, *Complete Temples*, p. 76. For the symbolism of the temple see Wilkinson, *Symbol and Magic in Egyptian Art*, pp. 27–29, 36ff.

10 For interesting comments about who supported temple building and the roles of kings in this process, see recent article by Kockelmann and Pfeiffer, "Betrachtungen zur Dedikation von Tempeln und Tempelteilen in ptolemäischer und römischer Zeit," pp. 93–104.

11 In his influential 1939 work *Studies in Iconology*, Panofsky detailed his idea of three levels of art-historical understanding to the visual arts: a basic understanding of the subject matter, a secondary level that takes into consideration the subject cultural and iconographic facts, and a third level of identifying the intrinsic meaning of the subject as a whole. He suggested the term "iconology" to refer to studies that concern themselves with the analysis of the meaning of works of art rather than its form and identification; however, the term iconography is still the more popular term to refer to both the identification and meaning of art historical material; Panofsky, *Studies in Iconology; Humanistic Themes in the Art of the Renaissance.*

Seth in his role as assistant to the sun god, killing the dangerous Apophis serpent that threatened the Maat, or order of the universe (see pls. 6 and 7).[12]

The temple is also famous for the main sanctuary or "holy of the holies." The unusually intense compendia of more than 650 deities represented on the crowded walls of the main sanctuary have sparked the interest of many scholars (see pls. 8 and 9), but the sanctuary has not yet received a dedicated study. Cruz-Uribe understood the multitudes of scenes of the sanctuary to be an inventory or "geographical list" of all the gods of Egypt.[13] Myśliwiec described them as:

> Another puzzle for historians of religion.... The walls of this small, narrow room are completely covered with a series of mythological scenes that are small in size, rich in content. What is unusual about this "stop-action film" with its hundred of frames lies not only in its richness but also in its iconographic originality and in the incomprehensibility of many of the motifs. As a whole, it seems to be a series of scenes illustrating abbreviated episodes selected from or even torn out of the context of various myths...only a few of the figures represented here are familiar from other sources, and even these confirm the eclectic character of the decoration as a whole....[14]

But other parts of the Temple of Hibis are equally unusual. The walls of the different parts of the temple are covered with ritualistic scenes, both carved and painted, containing some unique motifs and very complex symbols. In the absence of the traditional mighty smiting scenes on the exterior facade, one enters into a realm of uninterrupted sacred dialogue between the deities and the king. No other human is represented besides the king, except for the semi-godly priest Iunmutef. The vignettes provide unprecedented information on the theologies of the various locales in Egypt—information that we would otherwise learn only from the later texts in the Ptolemaic temples.

Although scholars have studied the inscribed lengthy texts on the temple walls,[15] the decoration schemes remain largely unexplained.[16] Sternberg-El-Hotabi and Kessler concentrated on a few registers of the sanctuary, focusing on the gods associated with the

12 Davies, *The Temple of Hibis*, Part 3, pl. 43. For the possible association of this god with Seth in Dakhla Oasis, see Kaper, "A Painting of the Gods of Dakhla in the Temple of Ismant el-Kharab," pp. 208–211, and Guermeur, *Les cultes d'Amon hors de Thèbes: recherches de géographie religieuse*, pp. 435–440. This scene is regarded as a precursor of the motif of St. George and the dragon; see Myśliwiec, *The Twilight of Ancient Egypt*, pp. 140ff; Abdel-Rahman, "Amun-nakht Fighting against an Enemy in Dakhla Oasis: A Rock Drawing in Wadi al-Gemal" pp. 13–22.

13 Cruz-Uribe, *Hibis Temple Project I*, pp. 192ff.

14 Myśliwiec, *The Twilight of Ancient Egypt*, p. 142.

15 Lorton, "The Invocation Hymn at the Temple of Hibis," pp. 159–217; Klotz, *Adoration of the Ram: Five Hymns to Amun-Re from Hibis Temple*; Derchain, "Review of C. Thiers, Tôd. Les inscriptions du temple ptolémaïque et romain, II ," p. 543, pls. 32–33; Assmann, *Liturgische Lieder an den Sonnengott*, pp. 168–186 (Text II 1).

16 As Žabkar says, "[The Hibis Temple] is full of lore as yet unexplored;" Žabkar, *Apedemak, Lion God of Meroe*, p. 114.

Heracleopolitan and the Hermopolitan cult centers, respectively, and tried to show their various cultic manifestations.[17] Osing ventured outside the sanctuary, dealing briefly with the Osiris chapels to the north of the sanctuary, chapels K to K2, and their connection to the Osiris chapels on the roof.[18] However, he concluded that such connections couldn't be clearly determined: "Genaueres läßt sich hierzu jedoch derzeit nicht ermitteln."[19]

I chose to focus on the decorative schemes of several chapels in the earlier part of the temple, chapels that were either established and/or were decorated during the first Persian Period (525–404 BCE)[20] These chapels were located around the main sanctuary A, but have rarely been the subject of scholarly discussions. Authors have consistently and briefly described them as containing lesser-known deities[21] or as failing to exhibit "any remarkable features of plan or constructions."[22]

The brief comments about these chapels encouraged me to try to explain the meaningful set of choices the ancient theologians made in incorporating those so-called "minor deities" who, by their mere presence, no doubt introduced important theological elements to the temple's overall doctrine. In contrast to the universal character of the decoration of the main sanctuary, those of the surrounding rooms emphasized the temple's dogma through well-spaced depictions. Besides their potential in yielding significant information and providing access to understanding the particularities of the main sanctuary, the analysis of these chapels shows the distinguished local *Kultlandschaft* or "cultic landscape" of Hibis.[23]

This book concentrates on a few chapels of the Temple of Hibis: chapels F and G to the south of sanctuary A on the first level of the temple and all the decorated chapels, E1, E2, H1, and H2, on the second level of the temple (see pl. 10). Each chapter begins with a brief description of the scenes and their basic layout and a complete translation of the accompanying texts. A more in-depth analysis regarding both text and image follows in the commentary. It includes the analysis of the different aspects of the gods, their origins, and the development of their cults that are significant to the scenes and to each other. Also discussed are their coherence, any aspects that are especially emphasized, and any other information that could be gleaned from the whole scene. The analysis tries to detail the specific composition that makes up the mosaic of the picture, wall, or room.

---

17 Sternberg-El-Hotabi, "Die 'Götterliste' des Sanktuars im Hibis-Tempel von El-Chargeh," pp. 239–254; Kessler, "Hermopolitanische Götterformen im Hibis-Tempel," pp. 211–223. See also Sternberg-El-Hotabi, "Der Raum M im Hibistemple von El Charga," pp. 597–623; Sternberg-El-Hotabi, "Der Hibistempel in der Oase El Charga," pp. 527–547; Wahlberg, "Representations of Hathor and Mut in the Hibis Temple," pp. 69–75.

18 Osing, "Zur Anlage und Dekoration des Tempels von Hibis," pp. 751–767; Osing, "Zu den Osiris-Räumen in Tempel von Hibis," pp. 511–516.

19 Osing, "Zu den Osiris-Räumen in Tempel von Hibis," p. 515.

20 For discussion of the date of the earlier part of the temple, see p. 12 below.

21 Osing, "Zur Anlage und Dekoration des Tempels von Hibis," p. 754, described these deities as "eine Gruppe weniger bedeutender Götter."

22 Winlock, *The Temple of Hibis*, Part 1, p. 12.

23 For this term see Ullmann, "Thebes: Origins of a Ritual Landscape," pp. 3–25.

In this present interpretive effort, attention is paid to both the scenic arrangement and the hieroglyphic inscriptions, as the interpretation of one would be meaningless without the other. Attention is given to investigating the general function of the different rooms by means of their decoration and by identifying the patterns or important themes generated by the layout of the scenes. The results are summarized in the last chapter. A number of line drawings have been inserted into the text beside a described scene as an aid to the reader. Whole groups of scenes are reserved for the plates at the end.

In treating enigmatic words in foreign text, a translator should consider the context and avoid simply imposing a narrow translation. An interpreter should do the same with any mysterious scene that poses problems regarding meanings. By investigating the specific and the general compositions of the wall on which such scenes are located, the interpreter can unravel both apparent and hidden meanings. It may be insufficient to view each scene separately from the others, as the meaning of one scene or theme can sometimes extend over and beyond the physical limits of the register walls or rooms. It is through connecting the scenes that we understand and apprehend greater meanings. References to the adjoining rooms (J, K1–2, I, L), hypostyle hall B, hypostyle hall M, and the sanctuary will be included in the final analysis of the chosen chapels. The scenes on the doorways and their reveals will also be specially examined. Most of the chosen chapels offer a good opportunity for detecting the category of scenes that could be called *Blickpunktsbild,* or visual focus,[24] from which one can deduce the emphasis the theologian directly or indirectly indicated.

Some parts of the discussion might seem denser in the *apparatus criticus* than others. Sometimes I could not successfully grapple with meaning without thoroughly investigating a specific iconographic detail or a specific phraseology. In other cases, I tried to avoid dwelling on variable details such as the royal regalia or purely traditional epithets or set phrases.

One last word must be said of the use of the supporting texts. Full attention is given to the comparative materials from within the Temple of Hibis itself, but when this was not possible, other iconographic parallels, related ritual episodes, and texts from both earlier and later time periods were used and compared to clarify and expand understanding of the different scenes. In her study of the religious symbols of the 21st Dynasty, Goff differentiated between a "vertical method," by which separate symbols are studied through a series of periods and cultures, and a "horizontal method" of studying symbols confined to a specific period. She preferred the horizontal method and illustrated how the vertical method may be deceiving.[25] Even though I attempt to be selective and focus specially on the texts and reliefs most close to the time period being studied, I must accept both methods to gain a wider spectrum, especially in such a period that has limited comparative material. In deciphering the more important aspects of a figure, Hornung encouraged us to use the "widest and most balanced range of sources, and to let the center of gravity lie at a point determined by the availability of source material."[26]

24 Arnold, *Wandrelief und Raumfunktion in ägyptischen Tempeln des Neuen Reiches*, p. 128.

25 Goff, *Symbols of Ancient Egypt in the Late Period: The Twenty-First Dynasty*, pp. 1, 9ff.

26 Hornung, *Einführung in die Ägyptologie*, p. 60, quoted from Baines, "R. T. Rundle Clark's Papers on the Iconography of Osiris," p. 286.

THE TEMPLE OF HIBIS: ITS SITE, EXCAVATION, CONSTRUCTION, AND DATE.

The Hibis Temple is located in the center of the city of Hibis, in the Kharga Oasis, in the midst of attractive panoramic fields and a palm grove (see pl. 2). In antiquity, the ancient Egyptians called Kharga Oasis "The Great Oasis." This appellation still holds true today; Kharga is the largest Egyptian oasis. Located in the western desert of Egypt, 175 miles west of Luxor, 430 miles south of Cairo, in the New Valley Governorate, the beautiful oasis measures about a half-mile wide, but extends more than 70 miles from north to south. The Kharga Oasis is partially surrounded by natural geographic barriers that have brought it both good and bad fortune (see pl. 12). Gebel el Tarif frames the northwest of the oasis, from which an impassable sea of sand dunes extends to the south. The rocky waste of Gebel el Teir is also a large hill rising east of Gebel el Taref into a limestone-capped plateau. To the south, the oasis is almost plain, with cultivable soil that depends on the fresh water coming from the numerous drilled wells.[27] Various rulers took advantage of its strategic location to erect long-lived fortresses at several locations. In addition to the significant Pharaonic and Greco-Roman sites scattered about its premises, the Kharga Oasis has considerable prehistoric remains,[28] as well as an impressive Coptic necropolis.[29] Although the oasis that housed the temple was isolated, it was far from being detached. The combination of hills and mountains on one side and fertile agricultural land on the other drew settlers, traders, and even refugees throughout ancient times. People who inhabited the oasis came from all over the region and brought their various religious traditions, an interaction that must have enhanced the life and culture of the area.

The Temple of Hibis sits at advantageous geographical and historical crossroads. Geographically, it was located in the city of Hibis, which was a major city in the Kharga Oasis (see pl. 13), and which perhaps acted as its fortified capital. The city is situated at the southern end of the foothills of the Gebel el Teir. Hibis, estimated to be about 1,000 meters north to south and 1,200 meters east to west, was the center of the ancient trade routes located between the Nile Valley, the Egyptian and Libyan oases further to the east, and the famous southern markets in the Sudan and Ethiopia. Historically, the major parts of the temple belong to the Persian Period, the time of Darius the Great, about 510 BCE. This temple is almost the only considerably well-preserved temple that survived from the period 1100–300 BCE. Of that period, nothing in the Delta or in Thebes compares or even comes close to the Hibis Temple for its beautiful state of preservation. Where most of its contemporary sacred buildings are now reduced to piles of inscribed building blocks, the Temple of Hibis has miraculously withstood environmental weathering, a shifting

27 For the history and geography of the Kharga Oasis see Vivian, *The Western Desert of Egypt: An Explorer's Handbook*, pp. 117–129; Aufrère, *L'Egypte restituée. [Tome II], Sites et temples des déserts, de la naissance de la civilisation pharaonique à l'époque gréco-romaine*, pp. 78–113; Willeitner, *Die ägyptischen Oasen: Städte, Tempel und Gräber in der libyschen Wüste*, pp. 4–20, 22ff.

28 Caton-Thompson, *Kharga Oasis in Prehistory*.

29 Fakhry, *The Necropolis of El-Bagawāt in Kharga Oasis*; Kaufmann, *Ein altchristliches Pompeji in der libyschen Wüste: Die Nekropolis der "grossen Oase."*

foundation, and an earthquake. It has resisted centuries of pillage and vandalism in later occupations: the nomads who used it to stable their animals, Christian iconoclasts,[30] quarry miners,[31] and early treasure seekers.

Currently, the temple has been stabilized against the rising water table, thanks to a rehabilitation project under the auspices of the Supreme Council of Antiquities and the Arab Contractors Company, who are conserving the temple *in situ* by several measures, including erecting a filtration wall around the temple, thereby abandoning a previous plan to remove the temple. In 2007, for the first time in more than a decade, the temple stood free of the scaffolding that had been placed there when plans for moving it were first made.[32]

Perhaps the French traveler Poncet was the first western traveler to mention the temple, during the late 17th to early 18th centuries.[33] However, European travelers of the early 19th century are known to have visited the oasis, because they left abundant graffiti on the temple walls. Most important of these early travelers were Cailliaud, the French mineralogist, who left graffiti claiming that he was the first European to discover the temple,[34] Schweinfurth,[35] and Rohlfs.[36] Other important visitors left short descriptions of the temple, including Hoskins,[37] Beadnell,[38] and Brugsch.[39] The Metropolitan Museum of Art was the first to scientifically study the temple, and Norman Davies' work there contributed to the folio-size publication of *The Temple of Hibis* in 1953, which provided outlined drawings of the decoration and a few photographs.[40] Winlock described the excavation and the architecture of the temple,[41] while Evelyn White and Oliver published

30 For the later church, see Winlock, *The Temple of Hibis*, Part 1, p. 45.

31 Before the Metropolitan Museum expedition, a Frenchman called Ayme, serving under Mohamed Ali, used the temple as a quarry for his alum factory; Winlock, *The Temple of Hibis*, Part 1, p. 18.

32 Some white marks that the surveyors made in preparation for its move still mask some scenes, but it is hoped that by following the process of fine restoration the scenes will be much clearer. Some restoration patches done by SCA have been conducted in the inner rooms, where remains of the cooking fires of later occupation have almost covered the walls with a heavy black layer. The results shown by the courtesy of the restorers working for the Arab contractors were astounding.

33 Poncet, *A Voyage to Æthiopia, Made in the Years 1698, 1699, and 1700*; Veryard and Favard-Meeks, *Voyages en Egypte pendant les années 1678–1701*, pp. XVIII–XXIV, 201–218

34 Cailliaud and Jomard, *Travels in the Oasis of Thebes, and in the Deserts Situated East and West of the Thebaid, In the Years 1815, 16, 17, and 18.*

35 Schweinfurth, *Notizen zur Kenntniss der Oase El-Chargeh.*

36 Rohlfs and Alfred von Zittel, *Drei Monate in der Libyschen Wüste.*

37 Hoskins, *Visit to the Great Oasis of the Libyan Desert; With an Account, Ancient and Modern, of the Oasis of Amun, and the Other Oases Now Under the Dominion of the Pasha of Egypt.*

38 Beadnell, *An Egyptian Oasis; An Account of the Oasis of Kharga in the Libyan Desert, with Special Reference to Its History, Physical Geography, and Water-Supply.*

39 Brugsch, *Reise nach der grossen Oase El Khargeh in der libyschen Wüste: Beschreibung ihrer Denkmäler und wissenschaftliche Untersuchungen über das Vorkommen der Oasen in den altägyptischen Inschriften auf Stein und Papyrus.*

40 Davies, *The Temple of Hibis*, Part 3.

41 Winlock, *The Temple of Hibis*, Part 1.

the Greek inscriptions.[42] With a grant from the National Endowment for the Humanities, Cruz-Uribe began his epigraphic survey of the Hibis Temple in three successive seasons from the fall of 1984 to the summer of 1986.[43] He intended to complete Davies' work toward a more comprehensive graphic description of the temple with a complete translation and commentary regarding the inscriptions. He finished translating the inscriptions, but the analysis of the different aspects of the religious concepts of the temple and its mythology were not completed as he had wished.[44] However, he provided a base of work for scholars interested in studying any part of the temple. His main volume includes the complete translation of the temple wall inscriptions, new line drawings of the scenes not included in the Davies volumes, and a helpful list of the hieroglyphic signs used in the inscriptions.[45] He then published his second volume titled *The Demotic Graffiti*.[46] Recently, he published his third volume that deals with the figurative graffiti found in the Temple of Hibis.[47]

In general, the temple measures about 27 by 62 meters. The walls are about 6 meters high (see pl. 3). The temple is made of local sandstone, but its quarry has not been located. The temple texts suggest that the construction material came from more exotic locations; the king is said to have built it from beautiful white stone of Meskat and to have erected its Libyan cedar portals (inlaid) with Asian bronze.[48] The temple's facade appears to have been constantly changed because of subsequent additions, but it seems that it was never intended to receive a pylon. As with many Egyptian temples, the Hibis Temple has gone through several building phases: under the Persian Period, the 30th Dynasty, the Ptolemies, and finally with Roman additions. The dates of the later parts of the temple are less controversial than the date of the earlier parts, as will be discussed below.

The earlier temple includes the area from sanctuary A to hypostyle hall M and the upper level of the temple, an area that measures about 16 by 24 meters (see pls. 4 and 5). Many architectural elements that once were part of the sanctuary are missing; its west wall was originally intended to be shaped as a false door, but later was masked before the rest of the walls were decorated.[49] In the center of the sanctuary, a narrow engraved line still visible on the floor suggests that a very thin wall once divided the sanctuary in two. Hoskins described the existence of shallow jambs, sill, and lintel, but Winlock found

---

42 Evelyn White and Oliver, *The Temple of Hibis*, Part 2.

43 Cruz-Uribe, "Hibis Temple Project: Preliminary Report, 1985–1986 and Summer 1986 Field Seasons," pp. 215–230; Cruz-Uribe, "The Hibis Temple Project. 1984–1985 Field Season, Preliminary Report," pp. 157–166.

44 Cruz-Uribe, "The Hibis Temple Project. 1984–1985 Field Season, Preliminary Report," p. 166.

45 Cruz-Uribe, *Hibis Temple Project I*.

46 Cruz-Uribe, "The Demotic Graffiti From Gebel Teir," pp. 79–86.

47 Cruz-Uribe, *Hibis Temple Project III, The Graffiti from the Temple Precinct*.

48 Davies, *The Temple of Hibis*, Part 3, pl. 29, (dado inscription in hypostyle hall M), and pl. 44 (exterior frieze inscription), pl. 48 (exterior frieze inscription) adds electrum to its material, and pl. 50 (south wall) repeated its erection of white stone of Meskat, the identity of which is still unknown.

49 One should note that this feature was found by Baraize during his restoration; Winlock, *The Temple of Hibis*, Part 1, p. 9.

only fragments of these architectural features.[50] Unfortunately, these elements have not been photographed.[51] The sanctuary is carved in coarse raised relief with some details that are only indicated by outline and hard to see in regular light, especially the bottom registers. No traces of color remain (see pls. 8 and 9).

Scholars agree that the Temple of Hibis was dedicated to the god Amun of Hibis or Amunebis in his many forms, together with his triad. However, we have ample evidence for other cults, such as Osiris and his triad, Seth, and Re Horakhty. The sanctuary alone has about 650 images of different gods and goddesses of ancient Egypt, representing almost all of the significant deities of the ancient Egyptian religious pantheon. This is an obvious break with the earlier tradition of New Kingdom temples, where we usually have the king making offerings to the main deity of the temple depicted on a large scale. The decoration of the main sanctuary reflects unusual expansiveness in their accounts of the various deities.

The sanctuary opens into hypostyle hall B, which Arnold called "a hall of the table of offerings,"[52] perhaps because of the offering tables to the triad of Amunebis depicted on its walls. Hypostyle hall B has sunken relief painted mostly with vivid colors still remaining, especially on the top registers. Four columns in hypostyle hall B were never finished, as the capitals were left half-carved and their decoration on the shafts was only painted. Beside the main sanctuary, hypostyle hall B leads to six side chapels arranged around its south, west, and north walls (see pl. 11). On the west side, chapel L is clearly a room for the royal cult, where the scenes show various images of the celebration of the king's enthronement and legitimacy. Its decoration is executed in coarse raised relief, with few traces of color. Its roof seems to have suffered some damage, where later restorers, perhaps in the time of Nectanebo or even later,[53] constructed a single column to support it. A doorway in the northwest corner of the hypostyle hall leads to a series of decorated spaces: chapels K and K2, connected by a stairway, K1. Chapel K and stairway K1 are in shallow sunken relief, whereas chapel K2 is in raised relief. These chapels are connected with the cult of Osiris. On the north side of hypostyle hall B are two other small chapels: the lower parts of chapel J are in sunken relief, the upper parts are in raised relief, and chapel I is undecorated. Chapels F and G are built south of hypostyle hall B, and their decoration is done in shallow sunken relief with few traces of color. Chapel G in particular shows damage: a heavy layer of black on its walls indicates cooking fire that perhaps occurred when it was used as a kitchen during its later Coptic occupation. This book mainly focuses on the last two chapels on the south side of hypostyle hall B:

---

50 Hoskins, *Visit to the Great Oasis of the Libyan Desert*, p. 107; Winlock, *The Temple of Hibis*, Part 1, p. 9.

51 Davies gives some description of the decoration that he labels as "Jambs of Intrusive Doorway" inside the sanctuary, but he does not mention where he saw them or their exact location. He adds that the missing portions of the north jamb are "said to be in Cairo Museum" (Livre d'entrée no. 44262), but so far they cannot be traced;" Davies, *The Temple of Hibis*, Part 3, p. 14.

52 Arnold, *Temples of the Last Pharaohs*, p. 77.

53 Cruz-Uribe dates these restoration efforts to the Ptolemaic Period; Cruz-Uribe, "The Ancient Reconstruction of Hibis Temple," pp. 247–262.

chapels F and G, as well as the decorated roof chapels. However, most of the earlier part of the temple will be discussed in comparison with these chapels.

Two undecorated stairways, E and H, in the southwest and the southeast corners of hypostyle hall B, respectively, lead to the upper floor of the temple, which consists of an extensive series of relatively small cult rooms. In the doorsill of stairway E, a trap door, C, leads to a series of undecorated crypts, C1 and C2, below the temple level. Directly above them, two undecorated crypts, D1 and D2, are reached through another trap door, D, cut in the wall opposite the same doorway E[54] (see pl. 17). The roof chapels mainly consist of two complexes. On the east side are chapels H1 and H2, divided only by a thin partition wall, which is missing. A wooden roof may have covered chapel H2. Both chapels are separated from chapels E1 and E2 by the undecorated open area H3. On the west side of the roof, chapel E1 takes the form of a porch with two side pilasters. Its roof might have been supported by one column, but both roof and column are now destroyed. Opposite to chapel E1 is chapel E2, whose east wall is the only wall still standing. Both chapels are bordered in the north by two undecorated open courts, E3 and E4, which lead to the rest of the undecorated temple roof.

Hypostyle hall B is followed by hypostyle hall M, which probably formed the original entrance facade of the earlier temple. It consists of a broad but narrow pronaos with four papyrus bundle columns and screen walls at the front, and another four columns in the center of the hall. The decoration of hypostyle hall M is in shallow sunken relief, except on the doorways leading to hypostyle hall B and the top parts of the wall with the sky signs, but overall it shows a very fine carving with well-cut hieroglyphs. The exterior belongs to the earlier temple, as the cartouches of Darius are neatly inscribed all over its decoration. These are depicted in large scale with raised relief and elaborate details, with even some color remaining.

During the 29th Dynasty, perhaps under King Achoris,[55] a third hypostyle hall was built, hypostyle hall N, which included twelve columns. The west side of this hypostyle hall is formed by the east exterior wall of hypostyle hall M and is thus part of the additions of Darius the Great. The scenes on these sections were executed in the best style of the early temple, with considerable details in sunken relief. The rest of hypostyle hall N is undecorated. The name of King Nectanebo II is inscribed throughout the beautifully decorated portico Q at the front of the temple.[56] This portico consisted of screen walls with four doorways and four columns at each corner. Most of the decoration of portico Q is in raised relief. This same 30th Dynasty addition included some modifications and repairs to the earlier temple.[57]

---

54 Winlock, *The Temple of Hibis*, Part 1, 10, pls. XXXII, XXXIII, XXXVII.

55 The discovery of some parts of a pair of statues belonging to King Achoris confirms the date of this hypostyle hall; see Cruz-Uribe, "Hibis Temple Project: Preliminary Report, 1985–1986 and Summer 1986 Field Seasons," pp. 220–225, figs. 4 and 5; Arnold, *Temples of the Last Pharaohs*, p. 79.

56 Winlock, *The Temple of Hibis*, Part 1, pp. 26ff.

57 For discussion of the repairs in the Hibis Temple, see Cruz-Uribe, "The Ancient Reconstruction of Hibis Temple," pp. 247–262.

The temple was also fronted by three gateways that still stand in relatively good shape. The first, which belongs to the earlier Persian temple, is called the Inner Gateway. Its interior is decorated in shallow sunken relief with small figures, and some color remains, while the exterior is in large-scale raised relief, with a considerable amount of preserved color. The second gate, called the Great Gateway, is decorated with one panel of raised relief. The third gateway is called the Outer Gateway. These two latter gates date to Greco-Roman times, and they are famous for their use as "bulletin boards" by the Roman governors of the oasis, starting from the first century CE.[58] These rulers left inscriptions indicating that the oasis was an important economic center with considerable revenue.

The temple ended finally with the quay, which consisted of a square platform that once stood at the edge of the ancient lake. An avenue of sphinxes seems to have extended from the front of the portico to the quay. Winlock discovered the bases of five sphinxes but only two of the actual sphinxes.[59] However, the SCA and the Arab Contractors recently discovered a third sphinx during the consolidation of the temple. None of these sphinxes are inscribed. Two seem to have had a human head over a lion's body, while the third had a ram's head on a lion's body. These, together with the obelisks, might belong to the same time as the portico, around the 30th Dynasty. About 800 scattered blocks are collected to the north of the temple, varying in size but in good condition. Some have worked surfaces and others have decorations that are yet to be investigated.[60]

As mentioned before, scholars have argued about the date of the earlier temple. The overwhelming number of cartouches of the Persian King Darius carved and/or painted throughout the earlier temple's interior and exterior walls can effortlessly point to a relatively reliable date of the earlier temple's decoration and perhaps even its erection. However, Winlock suggested that a change of plan in the erection of the rear wall of the sanctuary—from a false door to a plain design—might indicate a building phase previous to the Persian Period, dating it to perhaps the 26th Dynasty.[61] Winlock also mentioned an interesting representation on the right of the east door of hypostyle hall B.[62] The scene represents a priest censing a figure of the king, who appears to be coming out of the royal palace and followed by several nome emblems. Above the king is an enigmatic Horus name of "*Mnḫ-ib*." Because Darius did not receive a Horus

58 Winlock, *The Temple of Hibis*, Part 1, pp. 36–37; Evelyn White and Oliver, *The Temple of Hibis*, Part 2, nos.1–6.

59 Winlock, *The Temple of Hibis*, Part 1, pp. 36–37.

60 Cruz-Uribe, "Hibis Temple Project. 1984–1985 Field Season, Preliminary Report," pp. 160–162 attributes them mostly to a Ptolemaic date.

61 It is interesting that Winlock's idea of this "false door" and all the arguments that followed derived from a photograph of a niched architectural design, taken by Baraize while reconsolidating the west wall of the sanctuary in 1920. This niched feature was long gone before Winlock came to the site, see Winlock, *The Temple of Hibis*, Part 1, p. 9.

62 Davies, *The Temple of Hibis*, Part 3, pl. 13, east wall of hypostyle hall B.

name during his reign,[63] this Horus name was taken as a reference to the preceding dynasty's King Psamtik II.[64]

In any case, Winlock maintained the most reasonable date of the building and decoration of the temple to be the Persian Period.[65] In addition to reiterating the attestation of the *Mnḫ-ib* Horus name of Darius, Cruz-Uribe added to his evidence supporting a Saite date a superficial change in art style between some parts of the temples, especially on the decoration on the reveals of the doorways. This led Cruz-Uribe to suggest that most of the building was constructed and even received most of the decoration during the Saite period.[66] Pierre Briant expressed doubt about Cruz-Uribe's reconstruction,[67] and one can also add a few new thoughts against a 26th Dynasty date, at least in regard to the decoration.

This mention of *Mnḫ-ib* was attested only once throughout the temple and may have been indeed a legitimate Horus name for King Darius that unfortunately has not been discovered elsewhere.[68] This occurrence might have been an on-the-spot decision on the part of the decorators who might have worked previously under the former Saite rulers. This novelty in treating King Darius' name is seen also in the making of his own prenomen. Although King Darius' name is spelled consistently throughout the temple as *Darius*, he has three prenomens in the Temple of Hibis: *Nṯr nfr mry ʾImn Rʿ nb Hbt nṯr ʿ3 wsr ḫpš* "The Good God, Beloved of Amun-Re, Lord of Hibis, the Great God, Strong of Arm;" *Mry ʾImn Rʿ* "Beloved of Amun Re;" and *Stwt Rʿ* "He who was caused to resemble Re."[69]

As evidence for a 26th Dynasty date for the decoration of the earlier temple, Cruz-Uribe wrote,

> An examination of the cartouches of the king shows the following; all of the cartouches of Darius appear to have been painted in and not carved except in certain areas. Darius's cartouche was carved on the reveals of the doorways to rooms F, G, H, and J and also on the interior screen walls between M and N, on the door jambs and reveals of the door between M and N, on the west

63 See von Beckerath, *Handbuch der Ägyptischen Königsnamen*, pp. 113–114; Cruz-Uribe, "Hibis Temple Project. 1984–1985 Field Season, Preliminary Report," p. 164; Cruz-Uribe, "Hibis Temple Project: Preliminary Report, 1985–1986 and Summer 1986 Field Seasons," p. 226.

64 Winlock, *The Temple of Hibis*, Part 1, p. 6.

65 Winlock, *The Temple of Hibis*, Part 1, pp. vii, 5-9.

66 Cruz-Uribe, "Hibis Temple Project. 1984–1985 Field Season, Preliminary Report," pp. 164–165; Cruz-Uribe, "Hibis Temple Project: Preliminary Report, 1985–1986 and Summer 1986 Field Seasons," pp. 225–230, fig. 12. A recent article tries to dismiss the temple of Hibis altogether from the contributions of Darius in Egypt, suggesting that the cartouches of Darius are likely a form of date stamp that "were added very much as an urgent afterthought," Lloyd, "Darius I in Egypt: Suez and Hibis," pp. 99–115, especially 107–111.

67 Briant, *Histoire de l'Empire perse: de Cyrus à Alexandre*, pp. 973-974.

68 The Horus name appears in other places in the earlier temple but they are only blank or destroyed.

69 Winlock, *The Temple of Hibis*, Part 1, p. 7.

> wall of N, and on the exterior of the temple. One possible reason for this phenomenon is that Darius had not built those sections and simply filled his name into blank or painted cartouches.[70]

The reconstruction of Cruz-Uribe assumes that all the cartouches of Darius in the earlier part of the temple have been carved or painted over already-existing inscribed or blank cartouches of an earlier 26th Dynasty king. The numerous cartouches of Darius from hypostyle hall M to the inner sanctuary show no evidence of recutting, reworking, or repainting on the surface. Recarvers would have most likely neglected several examples of very tiny cartouches that are written inside the sanctuary as well as on the upper level of the temple. These cartouches are more likely to show any remains of manipulation, if indeed they were reworked. It is also hard to believe that the decorators who occupied themselves with representing these scenes that appear "custom made" to suit the ruler's ideology, legitimacy, piety, and authorship would leave blank cartouches, a practice that is mostly attested from a much later date inside the Greco-Roman temples.

Problematic is the idea that the decoration of the reveals of the doors belonged to a later period than the rest of the decoration inside the chapel where the reveals led. Based on the underpinning theology analyzed from the decoration of some of these chapels studied in this book, one is compelled to believe that the reveals, jambs, and interior decoration belonged to a single decoration phase, usually forming a coherent and uniform design.[71] By the same token, one can refute the distinction in time between the decoration of the chapels E1 and E2, and between the chapels H1 and H2 on the roof.[72] As will be shown below, the decoration of both chapels corresponds to one cycle of thought that most probably took place in one decoration phase.

Examining the decoration of the earlier part of the temple shows that although it may appear that different artistic styles were used, it is mainly because of slightly different levels of skill in execution. It is not unusual to see the best decorative work occupying the most visually important parts of ancient Egyptian temples, such as the entrance doorways and reveals. Hypostyle hall M, where several texts are executed in finer reliefs with well-cut hieroglyphs, presents important hymns that show many theological associations to the text and decoration of the other less skillfully done parts inside the earlier temple. It seems that the work was constantly in progress; changed or unfinished elements are evident in several aspects. For example, after hypostyle hall B was built, its design was changed to accommodate a wider area for stairway H. Thus the front of doorway H protruded into hypostyle hall B. To avoid an awkward design or perhaps for symmetry, the front of chapel I also protruded into the hypostyle hall.[73] The columns of hypostyle hall B were never finished as well. In hypostyle hall M, amid fairly elaborately

70 Cruz-Uribe, "The Hibis Temple Project. 1984–1985 Field Season, Preliminary Report," p. 164.

71 As evident in the doorway of hypostyle hall B leading to the doorway E and the doorway to chapel G, see pp. 81ff and 176ff.

72 Contra the suggestion of Cruz-Uribe, "Hibis Temple Project: Preliminary Report, 1985–1986 and Summer 1986 Field Seasons," pp. 228–229 that the decoration of E1 and E2 was Saite work, while that of H1 and H2 was later done under the Persian King Darius I.

73 Winlock, *The Temple of Hibis*, Part 1, p. 12.

carved and completed decoration, the only unfinished scene from the earlier temple strangely remains on the southernmost bay of the east wall.[74] The scene represents the king, Amun, and Amunet outlined only in faint red paint. The western front of hypostyle hall M consisted of screen walls between two rows of columns. However, the two end screen walls were heightened with detached blocks, raising the screen walls into towers, after the carving of the decoration on the end capitals was almost finished.[75]

Differences in style can also be, as Winlock suggested, due to "difference in lighting and scale…and passage of time."[76] Contrary to the older view that the name of Darius, spelled constantly in Hibis as *Ntaryush*, indicates that the *terminus ad quem* for his involvement in the Hibis Temple is to be set after his 25th regnal year, giving a date between 510–490 BCE,[77] Cruz-Uribe was able to show, in a separate article, the invalidity of this theory regarding the orthography of the name of King Darius.[78] The new theory allows more flexibility regarding the date of the Persian activity in Hibis. Thus, Darius I could have started the activities inside this temple very early in his reign, allowing a longer time span, which could help explain iconographical changes and alterations in architectural and artistic style.

The only tangible dated evidence of a pre-Persian date does not come from the earlier temple but from the nearby Southern Building I. To the south of the Hibis Temple, outside the temenos wall, two buildings were labeled as South Buildings I and II[79] They were built on an opposite axis to that of the temple. Of the first building only the foundation blocks remain, and few walls are standing from the second building. A fragment of a dish with the name of King Apries of the 26th Dynasty was found inside South Building I. However, both buildings seem to belong to an earlier building phase, as the level of the top of the foundations was below that of the earlier Temple of Hibis[80] and thus was not contemporaneous with the earlier temple. Recently, another confident source was found that dates a previous building phase to the current Hibis Temple. As the Arab Contractors and the SCA were digging non-archaeological trenches to test the temple's substructure, three decorated blocks with inscriptions and reliefs were found in a trench in hypostyle hall M (see pls. 14–16). Unfortunately, based on the remaining decoration, no date can be confirmed. Cruz-Uribe suggested that one block is early 26th Dynasty.[81] More firm evidence of an original temple must wait for more discoveries of these blocks, hopefully one with an inscribed cartouche. Even if these blocks belonged to the preceding Saite Dynasty, their existence as foundation blocks to the current temple and the fact that they

74 Davies, *The Temple of Hibis*, Part 3, pl. 35; Cruz-Uribe, "The Hibis Temple Project. 1984–1985 Field Season, Preliminary Report," p. 165.

75 Winlock, *The Temple of Hibis*, Part 1, pp. 14–15.

76 Winlock, *The Temple of Hibis*, Part 1, p. 8.

77 Winlock, *The Temple of Hibis*, Part 1, p. 9; Posener, *La première domination Perse en Egypte*, p. 161.

78 Cruz-Uribe, "The Writing of the Name of King Darius," pp. 5–10.

79 Winlock, *The Temple of Hibis*, Part 1, pp. 5ff, pl. XXX.

80 Winlock, *The Temple of Hibis*, Part 1, p. 5.

81 Cruz-Uribe, "The Foundation of Hibis Temple," p. 76, figs. 8 and 9. The other two blocks were discovered after his visit to the temple.

do not link to any architectural settings inside the current temple may confirm that the Persian rulers razed an earlier building of the Saite rulers and rebuilt and decorated it as the temple that stands today.

Many datable monuments in the name of Darius, either referring to Darius I or II,[82] are found throughout Egypt, from Memphis,[83] Sinai,[84] Tell Basta,[85] Busiris,[86] El Minia,[87] Wadi Hammammat,[88] Karnak,[89] Edfu,[90] and El Kab.[91] However, in no other place in Egypt were the Persian activities so apparent as in the Oasis of Kharga. Besides the extensive attestation of the Temple of Hibis, the name of Darius is clearly written inside the main sanctuary of the Temple of El Ghuita[92] and the Temple of Ain Manawir,[93] surpassing the number of any other attestation of pre-Ptolemaic rulers in the entire oasis. To deny that Darius participated in the original building or even in the additions to this central temple of the oasis is an argument that is thus very difficult to sustain.

---

82 No solid evidence supports the identity of either Darius I or II as the king named in the Hibis Temple. Winlock prefers Darius I. However, Kienitz and Friedrich, *Die politische Geschichte Ägyptens vom 7. bis zum 4. Jahrhundert vor der Zeitwende*, pp. 73–74, and Van Wijngaarden, "Der Hibistempel in der Oase El-Chargeh," pp. 69–70, suggest Darius II.

83 Posner, *La première domination Perse en Egypte: recueil d'inscriptions hiéroglyphiques*, pp. 30–35, pls. II–III (The Apis Stelae).

84 Posner, *La première domination Perse en Egypte: recueil d'inscriptions hiéroglyphiques*, pp. 48–87; Parker, "Darius and his Egyptian Campaign," pp. 373–377.

85 Naville, *Bubastis*, p. 62, tells of his purchase of a tablet from a *fellah* that was inscribed with the name of Darius on one side and on the other Mahes *nb pḥty*, which he later gave to the Gizah Museum.

86 Arnold, *Temples of the Last Pharaohs*, p. 92.

87 Myśliwiec, *The Twilight of Ancient Egypt*, pp. 144ff, pls. V–VIB.

88 Posner, *La première domination Perse en Egypte: recueil d'inscriptions hiéroglyphiques*, pp. 88–116; Goyon, *Nouvelles inscriptions rupestres du Wadi Hammamat*, pp. 118–120.

89 Traunecker, "Un document nouveau sur Darius Ier à Karnak," pp. 209–213.

90 Meeks, *Le grand texte des donations au temple d'Edfou*, pp. 133–135.

91 Arnold, *Temples of the Last Pharaohs*, p. 92.

92 Cruz-Uribe in http://www.cais soas.com/CAIS/History/hakhamaneshian/persians_at_qasr_el_Ghieta.htm.; Darnell, "The Antiquity of Ghueita Temple," pp. 29–40.

93 Wuttmann et al., "Premier rapport préliminaire des travaux sur le site de 'Ayn Manawir (oasis de Kharga)," pp. 385–451; Chauveau, "Les archives d'un temple des oasis au temps des Perses," pp. 32–47. The names of Artaxerxes I and Darius II occur most frequently among the numerous Demotic ostraca found at the site.

2

Chapel F

1. DESCRIPTION

Chapel F is located to the south of the main sanctuary A. It opens onto hypostyle hall B, through a doorway, from the north. It is decorated in shallow sunken relief. The few traces of color remaining suggest that it was painted at some point. The registers of the scenes are framed horizontally by star motifs.[1]

THE DOORWAY — LINTEL OF DOOR TO CHAPEL F

Figure 1: Lintel of door to chapel F
(after Davies, *The Temple of Hibis*, Part 3, detail from pl. 12).

The remaining decoration of this lintel shows Behdet as a winged solar disk with two uraei. Each uraeus has an *ankh* sign hanging as a pendant from its body.

THE INSCRIPTION

Register I

Left of the winged sun disk

Bḥdt nṯr ꜥꜣ nb pt sꜣb šwty

"Behdet, great god, lord of heaven, variegated of feathers."

Register II

Sꜣ Rꜥ nb/// di ꜥnḫ ḏ[t]

"Son of Re, lord of///, given life forev[er]"

1 For the publication of this chapel and its doorway see Winlock, *The Temple of Hibis*, Part 1, p. 12, pls. XXXIII, XXXVI, XXXVII; Davies, *The Temple of Hibis*, Part 3, p. 19, pls. 12 and 17; Cruz-Uribe, *Hibis Temple Project I*, pp. 65, 79–82.

THE DOORWAY — THE REVEALS OF THE DOOR TO CHAPEL F[2]

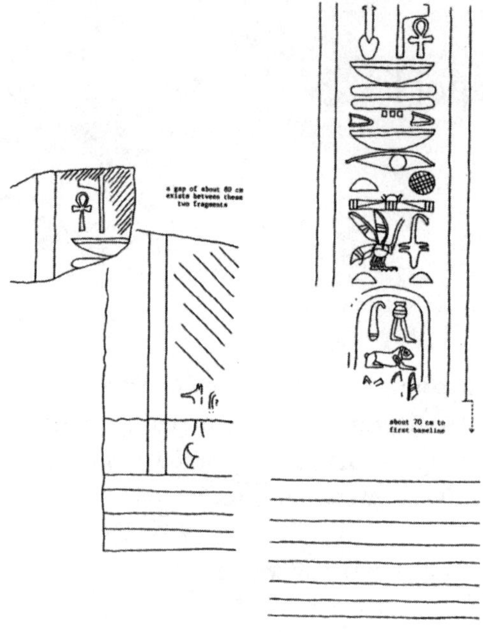

Figure 2: West and east reveals of door to chapel F (after Cruz-Uribe, *Hibis Temple Project I*, pl. 17A).

WEST REVEAL

///ꜥnḫ nṯr [nfr] nb t[ꜣwy]///wsr [ḫpš]

"Live the [good] god, lord of the two l[ands]///powerful of [strength]."

EAST REVEAL

ꜥnḫ nṯr nfr nb tꜣwy nb irt ḫt nsw tꜣwy (Dry[š])¦,///

"Live the good god, lord of the two lands, lord of cult act, king of Egypt, (Dariu[s])¦,///"

2 The plates of the inscriptions on the west and east reveals of door to chapel F are not included in Davies' publication. They were drawn by Cruz-Uribe in Cruz-Uribe, *Hibis Temple Project I*, pl. 17A.

THE DOORWAY — EAST JAMB OF DOOR TO CHAPEL F[3]

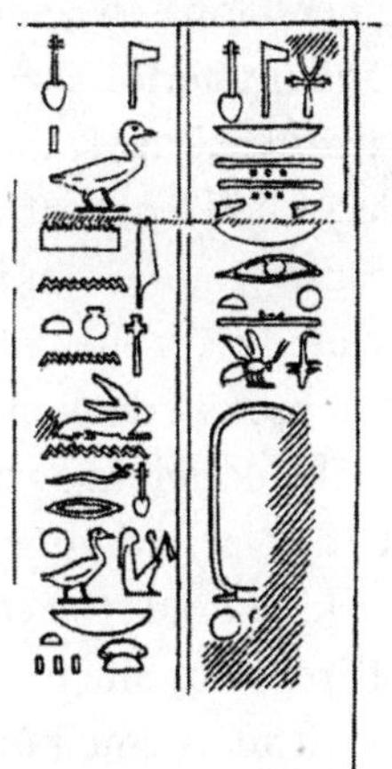

Figure 3: East jamb of door to chapel F
(after Davies, *The Temple of Hibis,* Part 3, detail from pl. 12).

THE INSCRIPTION

ꜥnḫ nṯr nfr nb t3wy nb irt ḫt nsw biti (…)¦, [*s3*] *Rꜥ/// nṯr nfr s3 'Imn nḏt Wn nfr s3 Rꜥ nb ḫꜥwt///*

"Live the good god, lord of the two lands, lord of cult act, king of Egypt, (…)¦ [son of] Re […]. Good god, son of Amun, protector of Wennefer, son of Re, lord of appearances […]."

EAST WALL — REGISTER I

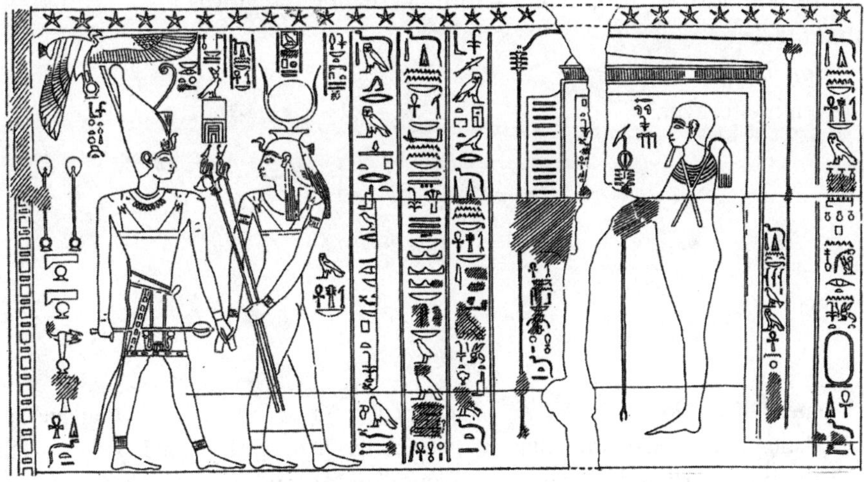

Figure 4: East wall of chapel F, Register I
(after Davies, *The Temple of Hibis,* Part 3, detail from pl. 17).

3 The west jamb is unfortunately destroyed.

The wings of the vulture goddess Nekhbet dominate the left corner of the top register of the east wall. She holds the *shen* sign in her talons. In a vertical column at the far left is a collection of some of the common, yet still mysterious, symbols connected with the *Heb Sed* festivities and other rites and rituals.[4] The king stands with his left foot advanced; he is wearing a short tight kilt with a decorated front sash ending with two cobras with solar disks on top of their heads. He wears a wrap-around two-strap shirt and an ox tail. His knee-length garment can be associated with the coronation robe or the *Heb Sed* robe.[5] He is adorned with two anklets, a broad collar, and possibly two bracelets and one armlet. Most importantly, he wears the double crown with the uraeus on the brow. In this image the king is represented in a solarized guise of Atum, who is depicted in the top register of the adjacent wall. The king holds the ceremonial mace with his right hand, while Hathor gently holds his other hand. She is wearing an ankle-length dress with two straps, a broad collar, and two armlets. She holds two papyrus staffs topped with cobras that represent Upper and Lower Egypt. One cobra wears the white crown and one wears the red crown. She wears the Hathoric headdress: a solar disk with the horns of a cow atop a modius that had been worn by goddesses since the New Kingdom. She leads the king to the shrine of Ptah, her feet facing right but her head turned toward the king. Ptah is in his usual mummified form, wearing the skull cap and holding the composite *was*, *ankh*, and *djed* staff. He stands inside a shrine with an open door. The shrine stands within another structure with a curved roof that seems to be supported by two poles. The front pole ends with an architectural element in the shape of a *djed* symbol, while the rear pole has a partially obliterated papyrus symbol.

THE INSCRIPTION

Above the King

Nṯr nfr nb tȝwy nb irt ḫt Ḥr […].

"Good god, lord of the two lands, lord of cult act, the Horus […]."

Behind the King[6]

Di ꜥnḫ ḏt

"Given life forever."

4 For a general discussion of these symbols see Spencer, "Two Enigmatic Hieroglyphs and their Relation to the Sed-Festival," pp. 52–55; Egberts, *Quest of Meaning*, I, pp. 64–65; Kees, "Nachlese zum Opfertanz des ägyptischen Königs," pp. 61–72; Bomhard, *The Naos of the Decades*, p. 230. See the new treatment for the *Heb Sed* in Hornung and Staehelin, *Neue Studien zum Sedfest*, for the relief representations of the *Heb Sed* scene see pp. 49–76.

5 Larson, "The Heb-Sed Robe and the 'Ceremonial Robe' of Tut'ankhamun," p. 181.

6 Below the *Heb Sed* symbols.

Below the Vulture

Nḫbt ḥḏt nḫn ꜣwt-[ʿ]

"Nekhbet, the White one of Hierakonpolis,[7] long of [talon][8]"

Above Hathor[9]

Ḥwt -ḥr n[*b.t*] *p tꜣwy nh.t rst nbt pt tꜣwy.*

"Hathor, la[dy] of Pe, of the two lands and of the southern sycamore, lady of the sky and of the two lands.[10]"

In Front of Hathor

Ḏd mdw di n<*ỉ*> *n.k ʿnḫ wꜣs nb*

"Words spoken: it is to <you> that I have given all life and dominion."

Behind Hathor

(1) *Ḏd mdw m r* <*.i* > *m ḥtp r st wr mꜣ k ỉt.k ptḥ rsy* [*ỉnb*] *f*[11] *ẖnm. f ṯ*/////[12] *m ʿnḫ ḏd wꜣs nb* (2) *Ḏd mdw di n.*<*ỉ*> *n.k ʿnḫ wꜣs nb di n.*< *ỉ*> *n.k tꜣwy tꜣ mḥw tꜣ šmʿw nb tꜣwy nb ḫꜣswt nb s*//// *wḥm* ///[*di*] *ʿnḫ mi Rʿ* (3) *Bs m*[13] *ḥwt wrt*[14] *ḏd mdw di n.* (*ỉ*) *n.k ʿnḫ ḏd wꜣs nb* /////// *nsw biti ḥr st Ḥr ḏt*

"(1) Words spoken: come to(wards) me in peace to the great place that you might see your father, Ptah, south of his [wall]. May he endow you with all life, stability and dominion. (2) Words spoken: it is to <you> that I have given all life and dominion. It is to <you> that I have given the two lands, Upper and Lower Egypt, all lands, all foreign lands and all […] in ///Repeating ///[given] life like Re. (3) Introduction of the king to the great temple. It is to <you> that I have given all life, stability and dominion, ////[as] king of Upper and Lower Egypt upon the seat of Horus forever."

---

7 The title of "the White one of Hierakonpolis" and "long of talon" are common titles for the Goddess Nekhbet as well as other deities, see *Wb.* III, pp. 210, 20–22; 211, 2; Leitz, *Lexikon*, II, p. 5.

8 Cruz-Uribe, *Hibis Temple Project I*, p.79, n. 251, reads *nb fʿg*, lady of Fag, based on a collation of the wall. The line drawings and the inspection of the wall do not confirm that reading; however, Nekhbet bears the three titles of "the White one of Hierakonpolis," "long of talon," and "lady of Fag" together in the neighboring chapel G: Davies, *The Temple of Hibis*, Part 3, p. 18 (East wall, register II).

9 The first line of inscription is actually surmounted by Hathor's two horns.

10 *nht rst Wb.* II, p. 282. Hathor appears with the first three titles together only in Hibis: Leitz, *Lexikon*, IV, p. 48. The last title of *nbt pt tꜣwy* is equally uncommon, with only one other occurrence in Naville, *The Temple of Deir El Bahari*, IV, pl. 93; Leitz, *Lexikon*, IV, p. 51.

11 Signs collated from other occurrences.

12 Cruz-Uribe, *Hibis Temple Project I*, p. 79 suggested that the inscriptions continue under Hathor's left arm.

13 Kruchten, *Les annales des prêtres de Karnak (XXI-XXIIImes dynasties) et autres textes contemporains relatifs à l'initiation des prêtres d'Amon*, pp. 149 ff.

14 *Bs(t) m ḥwt wrt* is written opposite to the norm of direction of the rest of the inscriptions in the same line. This might indicate the phrase's importance to the scene, functioning as a label for the following ritual.

In Front of the Shrine

[Di͗ n.i͗ n.k] ꜥnḫ wꜣs nb snb nb ꜣwt ib mi Rꜥ ḏt

"[It is to you that I have given] all life and dominion, all health and joy like Re forever."

In Front of Ptah

Pt(ḥ) rsy [inb].f [di͗] ꜥnḫ wꜣs ꜥꜣ pḥty nsw nṯrw

"Pta[h], south of his [wall], who [gives] life and dominion, great of strength, king of the gods."

Behind Ptah

Ḏd mdw di <n.i͗ >n.k rnpwt ḥr m ꜥnḫ/////

"Words spoken: it is to you that < I > have given the years of Horus in life ///"

Column Behind Shrine

Ḏd mdw di n <i͗> n.k ꜥnḫ ḏd wꜣs nb m ḥsw mnw pn nfr wꜥb i͗rt n nsw biti (…)| di ꜥnḫ ḏt.

"Words spoken: it is to you that < I > have given all life, stability and dominion as reward for this beautiful and pure monument that the king of Egypt, (…)|, given life forever, made."

EAST WALL — REGISTER II

Figure 5: East wall of chapel F, Register II
(after Davies, *The Temple of Hibis*, Part 3, detail from pl. 17).

The scene depicts the king offering a bouquet to Hw and three other deities. In the upper left corner is a sun disk surmounted by the two cobras, the symbol of the solar god Behdet. The sun disk is placed above the king, designating him as the earthly representative of the sun god. The king is striding and has both of his arms raised in front of him to present the flowers to the gods. His figure is somewhat damaged, but we still can see that he wears a false beard, a loose kilt, and a solarized *atef* crown set atop a round wig. The *abu* bouquet is depicted as open lotus blooms and closed buds, although this designation more commonly means "lettuce." The solarization of the king's participation may have influenced the representation of the bouquet. The gods are all in striding positions. They are each beardless, wear the two-strap garment, hold the *ankh* sign with the left hand (where the left hand is not obliterated by surface damage) at the side of the left leg, and hold the *was* scepter out before the body with the right hand. Hw, conventionally understood as "Utterance," is the first figure facing the king. He is a ram-headed human figure with downward horns like Amun, and is wearing a pleated knee-length garment. Sia is the second god, another ram-headed human figure with downward horns and wearing a plain garment with a bull's tail. Third is the human-headed god Ir.[15] Fourth is a baboon-headed figure identified in the inscription as Sedjem.

THE INSCRIPTION

In Front of the Solar Disk Behdet

Bḥdt nṯr ꜥ3 nb pt s3b šwty

"Behdet, great god, lord of heaven, variegated of feathers."

Above the King

Nsw biti nb t3wy (…)¦ nb irt ḫt (…)¦ di ꜥnḫ ḏt

"King of Upper and Lower Egypt, lord of the two lands, (…)¦, lord of cult act…)¦, given life forever."

Below the Hand of the King

Rdi ꜥbw n Ḫw

"Giving floral bouquet to Hw."

Above the First Figure (Hw)

ḏd mdw in Iw nṯr ꜥ3 ḥr ib Hbt

"Words spoken by Hw, great god who dwells in Hibis."

Above the Second Figure (Sia)

Ḏd mdw in Si3 ḥr ib Hbt

"Words spoken by Sia, who dwells in Hibis."

Above the Third Figure (Ir)

Ḏd mdw in ꞽIr nṯr ꜥ3 nb Hbt

"Words spoken by Ir (seeing), great god, lord of Hibis."

Above the Fourth Figure (Sedjem)

Ḏd mdw in Sḏm nṯr ꜥ3 ḥr ib Hbt

"Words spoken by Sedjem (hearing), great god, who dwells in Hibis."

---

15 The traces of a sun disk over his head are identified by Cruz-Uribe, *Hibis Temple Project I*, p. 80, n. 259, as damage marks and not a true disk representation. Although there are no other representations of Ir with a sun disk, personal inspection of the wall reveals that the circle on the wall on top of his head was intended as a true sun disk and that the destruction on the wall seems to have carefully followed the outline of his disk. This is a repeated pattern of the destruction on several scenes on the walls of Hibis, especially in chapels F, G, and J.

SOUTH WALL — REGISTER I

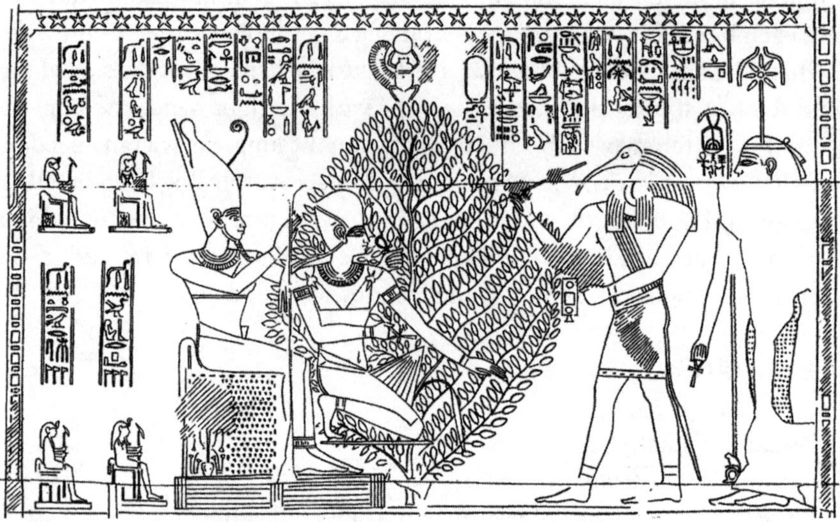

Figure 6: South wall of chapel F, Register I
(after Davies, *The Temple of Hibis*, Part 3, detail from pl. 17)

The main tableau of this register is the crowning of the king by Atum and the writing of the king's names and annals on the Ished tree. The Ished occupies the center of the register, and is surmounted by a winged scarab pushing the solar disk toward the top of the register. The king kneels on a ground line placed artificially at the ankle height of the seated figure of Atum. He wears a knee-length kilt with a starched apron in front of which is his bent bull tail. He wears the blue crown with the uraeus in the front. He holds the *ankh* sign pointed toward Thoth with his right hand, while his left arm is extended outward with the palm down. Atum is seated on a low-backed throne, decorated on the side with the Sema-Tawey sign. The throne rests on a mat that elevates him above the ground level. He wears his usual double crown and curved beard. He fixes the crown on the king's head with his right hand while giving the *ankh* sign to the king in front of his nose with his left hand, confirming his coronation and bestowing life on him simultaneously. Behind Atum are the miniature figures of four deities on thrones. Shu is seated before his consort Tefnut behind Atum's crown, while their children Geb and Nut are seated below them behind Atum's throne. Each deity is represented holding a *was* scepter. Each has a uraeus on the brow, and the male deities are bearded. In front of the king, to the right of the register, are the two deities of writing: ibis-headed Thoth and Seshat. Thoth is represented in his usual attire: a short garment with one strap of cloth across his chest that usually holds his scribal kit. In this instance, he has his scribal equipment in front of him just touching his clenched hand, and he is writing with a reed pen on the leaves of the tree. Seshat stands behind Thoth, but her figure is greatly damaged. The remaining traces suggest that she was wearing the panther skin attire,[16] but the vital part where it ends with the claw over her ankles is missing. Her headdress is an important iconographic element that can be used for dating. Originally, it

16 This type of dress is seen in association with her function as the goddess granting the regeneration of the king, Budde, *Die Göttin Seschat*, p. 225.

consisted of a short staff surmounted by a five- or seven-petaled star or rosette and a pair of feathers. After the 18th dynasty, when she was given the new name of Sefkhet-Abwy (literally the "seven horned"), the two feathers changed into two horns, surmounting the seven-petaled rosette.[17] She holds the *renpet* palm branch sign with the composite symbol of the Millions of *Heb Sed* sign dangling from its top. The emblems of the *hefen* frog and the *shen* sign are represented on the bottom of the *renpet* year palm branch.

THE INSCRIPTION

Above the King

Nsw bỉtỉ (...)¦ <dỉ> ꜥnẖ ḏt

"King of Upper and Lower Egypt (...)¦ < given> life forever."

Above Thoth

Ḏd mdw ỉn Ḏḥwty ꜥꜣ ꜥꜣ[18] *nb ẖmnw spẖr*[19] *<ỉ> <n>.k*[20] *gnw.k m ỉšd*[21]*///m ḥwt*[22] *wr m ỉwnw*

"Words spoken by Thoth the twice great, lord of Hermopolis: may <I> inscribe <for> you your annals on the Ished tree in the great temple in Heliopolis."

In Front of Seshat

Ḏd mdw ỉn Sšꜣt wrt nb <t> sšw dỉ n.<ỉ> < n>.k ḥḥ m ꜥnẖ ḏd wꜣs nb ḥfnw n rnpwt m ḥtp

"Word spoken by Seshat the great, the lady of documents: <I> have given <to> you infinity of all life, stability, and dominion and hundred of thousands of years in peace."

In Front of Atum Re Horakhty

Ḏd mdw ỉn Jtm Rꜥ Ḥr ꜣẖty nṯr ꜥꜣ nb ỉwnw ḥr ỉb Hbt dỉ n <ỉ> n.k ꜥnẖ wꜣs nb rf ẖnty.k sꜣ mry.j

"Words spoken by Atum Re Horakhty, great god, lord of Heliopolis, who dwells in Hibis: <I> have indeed given to you all life and dominion that is in front of you, O my beloved son."

Above the Four Miniature Deities[23]

Above the figure at the top right (God Shu)

Ḏd mdw ỉn Šw sꜣ Rꜥ

"Words spoken by Shu, son of Re."

---

17 For the detailed iconography of Seshat see Budde, *Die Göttin Seschat*, pp. 29ff.

18 A common title of Thoth, *Wb.* I, pp. 163; see Quaegebeur, "Thoth-Hermès, le dieu le plus grand!," pp. 525–544.

19 Prospective *sḏm.f spẖr, Wb.* IV, p. 106, "to inscribe, register."

20 The sign appears as the *nb*, but it makes sense to take it as *k*.

21 The signs following the Ished tree appear to be , the meaning of which is unclear.

22 Cruz-Uribe, *Hibis Temple Project I*, p. 81, n. 265, says that the sign of the man inside the house appears to be a variant of IFAO list; p. 69.5–10, for *ḥwt*.

23 It is interesting that the artist was careful enough to emphasize the femininity of Nut and Tefnut by indicating the tripartite hair wig on the front. He treated the bodies of the other male deities differently by representing the curved beards.

Above the figure at the top left (Goddess Tefnut)
Ḏd mdw in Tfnwt s3t Rꜥ
"Words spoken by Tefnut, daughter of Re."
Above the figure at the bottom right (God Geb)
Ḏd mdw in Gb rpꜥty nṯrw
"Words spoken by Geb, prince of the gods."
Above the figure at the bottom left (Goddess Nut)
Ḏd mdw in Nwt wrt ms nṯrw
"Words spoken by Nut, the great, who bore the gods."

SOUTH WALL — REGISTER II

Figure 7: South wall of chapel F, Register II
(after Davies, *The Temple of Hibis*, Part 3, detail from pl. 17)

This register may be divided into two main scenes, each marked by the representation of the king under the image of the solar disk Behdet. The scene to the right includes Behdet in his usual solar disk form above the head of the king. The solar disk has two uraei and each has an *ankh* sign suspended from its body. The king is wearing a knee-length kilt with a starched triangular apron and a sash flanked by cobras. His *nemes* headdress has an attached uraeus. He holds a mace and a long staff with his left hand. His right hand is positioned in a gesture of adoration toward the falcon-headed Montu, who is facing the king but separated from him by two columns of text. Montu presents the king with a scimitar that is embellished with a ram or falcon head on which rests a solar disk and a uraeus. Montu holds the *ankh* sign in his left hand, and his left arm is slightly extended toward the king. He wears a pleated kilt with an ox tail behind and a headdress that combines two tall plumes and the solar disk.

The other half of the register is occupied by the king again with the solar disk of Behdet above him. Here the king is represented with the double crown and the ureaus at its front. He holds Khepri's hands on his left side and Re Horakhty's hand on his right. Both the king and Khepri face Re Horakhty who presents the *ankh* sign to the king's nose. Khepri is in human form with the scarab on his human head as a headdress, while the falcon-headed Re Horakhty has the solar disk, encircled with the uraeus, on his head.

THE INSCRIPTION

Below Behdet

Bḥdt nṯr ꜥꜣ nb pt

"Behdet, great god, lord of heaven."

Above the King on the Right Side

[Nṯr] nfr nb tꜣwy ( )¦[24] *nb i͗rt ḫt* (...)T *[di͗ ꜥnḫ] snb ḏt*

"Good [god], lord of the two lands (...)¦, lord of cult act (...)¦ [given life] and health forever."

The Speech of Montu[25]

Ḏd mdw i͗n Mnṯw nṯr ꜥꜣ ḥr i͗b Hbt n sꜣ.f mr.f di͗ <n.i͗> n.k nḫtw r tꜣ nb ḫꜣswt nb w[ꜥ]f[26]*// šnty.k*[27] *n s[ꜣ] ꜣst [mi͗] Rꜥ ḏt*

"Words spoken by Montu, great god who dwells in Hibis to his son whom he loves: <I> give to you victories against all lands, all foreign lands that you might c[ur]b // your enemies for the son of Isis [like] Re forever."

The Speech of Khepri [28]

Ḏd mdw i͗n Ḫpri͗ di͗ n <i͗> n.k ꜥnḫ ḏd wꜣs nb snb ḥb ꜣwt i͗b ḥꜣ.k ///

"Words spoken by Khepri: <I> give to you all life, stability, dominion and all health, feasts and joy of heart behind you///"

Above the King on the Left Side

Nsw bi͗ti͗ (...)¦ *sꜣ Rꜥ* (...)¦ *di͗ ꜥnḫ mi͗ Rꜥ ḏt*

"King of Upper and Lower Egypt (...)¦ son of Re (...)¦ given life like Re forever"

Above Re Horakhty

Ḏd mdw i͗n Rꜥ Ḥr ꜣḫty ḥwnw.f ẖnty.k m ꜥnḫ ẖnm.k st.k m ꜥnḫ ḏd wꜣs nb

"Words spoken by Re Horakhty: His son is before you in life that you may endow your place with all life, stability and dominion."

---

24 The cartouche has one unclear sign.

25 This speech begins with the two short lines of inscription above Montu, and then continues to the long vertical line of inscription facing the opposite direction in front of Montu. The speech ends with the short line of inscriptions under the hand of the king.

26 *wꜥf* in *Wb.* I, p. 285, 1–10.

27 Cruz-Uribe, *Hibis Temple Project I*, p. 81, n. 267 reads *nb* for *k*, translating this sentence as "all that the sun disk encircles for Horus son of Isis." However, it is reasonable to reconstruct this as *šnty.k* "your enemies," *Wb.* IV, p. 520, 3–7.

28 This speech begins with the central line, continuing to the left, then to the right.

WEST WALL — REGISTER I

Figure 8: West wall of chapel F, Register I
(after Davies, *The Temple of Hibis*, Part 3, detail from pl. 17)

The king is at the far right of the scene under the protection of the solar disk of Behdet. He wears a kilt with a starched triangular apron, a sash, and an ox tail. He offers a conical loaf of white bread to the seated figure of Amun, followed by the standing figures of Mut, Khonsu, and Sakhmet. A considerable portion of Amun is destroyed, but it can still be seen that he is seated, wearing his two tall plumes and holding the *was* scepter with his right hand. Behind him is Mut, his consort, wearing the double crown combined with the vulture headdress. Khonsu is in mummified form, standing on a rectangular base or plinth. He has the crescent moon, the full lunar disk, and a uraeus on his head. He has a side-lock and a curved beard and holds the long *was-ankh-djed* scepter, the *heka* crook, and the *nekhekh* flail with both hands. Behind the Theban Triad stands the lioness-headed goddess Sakhmet with a solar disk and uraeus on her head. She is holding a papyrus scepter with her left hand and the *ankh* sign hangs down at her side from her right hand.

THE INSCRIPTION

Beside the Sun Disk with the Two Uraeus

Bḥdt nṯr ꜥꜣ nb pt sꜣb šwty

"Behdet, great god, lord of heaven, variegated of feathers."

Below the Hand of the King

Sḳr tꜣ [*ḥḏ*] [29] *n ỉt.f Imn Rꜥ nṯr ꜥꜣ nb Hb*[*t*]

"Consecrating the [white] bread to his father, Amun Re, great god, lord of Hibi[s]."

29 *sḳr* is best translated here as "to consecrate" rather than "to present;" see *Wb*. IV, p. 320, 7, 9–10. The representation of the king offering bread confirms the reading of *tꜣ- ḥḏ*. This act represents the important ritual of "consecrating the white bread." According to Wilson, *Lexicon*, pp. 939–940 and 1116–1117, this ritual appeared since at least the Middle Kingdom. In our scene, the king is holding the white bread in one hand while raising the other hand

In Front of the King

Nṯr nfr nb tꜣwy (...)¦ *nb irt ḫt* (...)¦ *di ꜥnḫ mi Rꜥ ḏt*

" Good god, lord of the two lands (...)¦ lord of cult act (...)¦ given life like Re forever."

In Front Of Amun Re

Ḏd mdw in Ꞽmn Rꜥ wsr ḫpš nṯr ꜥꜣ nb Hbt irt n.f di ꜥnḫ mi Rꜥ ḏt

"Words spoken by Amun Re, powerful of strength, the great god, lord of Hibis, doing for him 'given life like Re forever.'"

Above Mut

Ḏd mdw in Mwt irt Rꜥ ḥr ib Hbt

"Words spoken by Mut, the eye of Re who dwells in Hibis."

In Front Of Khonsu

Ḏd mdw in Ḫnsw ḥr ib Hbt

"Words spoken by Khonsu who dwells in Hibis."

In front of Sakhmet

Ḏd mdw in Sḫmt ꜥꜣt mr<t> Ptḥ

"Words spoken by Sakhmet, the great one, beloved of Ptah."

WEST WALL — REGISTER II

Figure 9: West wall of chapel F, Register II
(after Davies, *The Temple of Hibis*, Part 3, detail from pl. 17)

In this scene the king, whose figure is largely destroyed, stands below the figure of a falcon and presents a *nw* wine jar to a seated god wearing the *hemhem* crown. The king has a uraeus at his brow. The deity's figure is lost except for his crown and the base for his throne that takes the form of the *mr* or canal sign. Three goddesses stand behind the seated deity facing the king. Hathor is standing behind the seated god, wearing her elaborate crown of two tall feathers and a solar disk between two small horns connected to a vulture headdress by a modius. She holds the *was* scepter in front of her body with

before his face in adoration. This conforms with the norm of representations of the ritual; see ibid.

her left hand and the *ankh* sign hangs at her side from her other hand. Nebet Hetepet (written with the gold sign) follows Hathor. Her headdress consists of a naos-shaped sistrum with a uraeus at the center and two curls. Another female deity follows, wearing the uraeus; her name is written as Iusaas.

THE INSCRIPTION

Above the Falcon

[Bḥdt] s3b [šwty] ḏi ʿnḫ mi Rʿ ḏt[30]

"[Behdet], variegated of [feathers], given life like Re forever."

In Front of the King

Nṯr nfr nb t3wy (…)¦ s3 Rʿ (…)¦ di ʿnḫ mi Rʿ ḏt

"Good god, lord of the two lands (…)¦ son of Re (…)¦ given life like Re forever."

Above the First God

Ḏ[d mdw i] n /// nb t3wy nṯr ʿ3 ḫnt ///ḥr ib Hbt [31]

"[Words] spok[en b]y /// lord of the two lands, great god, foremost of /// who dwells in Hibis."

In Front of Hathor

Ḏd mdw in Ḥwt-ḥr nbt nn-[nswt]/// ḥr ib Hbt dj [n.j n.k ʿnḫ ḏd]/ snb.nb?

"Words spoken by Hath[or] lady of Heracl[eopolis] /// who dwells in Hibis: I have given [to you all life, stability] and health?"

In Front of Nebet Hetepet

Ḏd mdw in Nbt Ḥtpt ḥr ib Hbt.

"Words spoken by Nebet Hetepet who dwells in Hibis."

In Front of Iusaas

Ḏd mdw in ʿsst ḥr ib Hbt

"Words spoken by Iusaas who dwells in Hibis."

2. COMMENTARY

EAST WALL — REGISTER I

The decoration of this register is divided into two main scenes by three long inscription lines. The scene on the left represents Hathor leading the king toward the shrine of Ptah represented on the right. Her stance conveys a sense of motion and emphasizes her intermediate role of leading the king to Ptah. On the right, Ptah is standing inside his double shrines in his traditional mummiform guise, facing the king who is coming toward him. From the initial description, it appears to be an introduction scene, where Hathor introduces the king to Ptah, but investigating the iconographical details of the

30 *ḏt* is located below the tail of the falcon.

31 Cruz-Uribe, *Hibis Temple Project I*, p. 82 adds the name of Amun Re, foremost in [Karnak]. In light of the discussion of the identity of this god, as explained below, this reconstruction is questionable.

figures' gestures, epithets, and their relationship to other nearby scenes can offer more insights to the identification of the scene.

The east wall shows a ceremony that probably took place in Memphis. The connection to Memphis is indicated through several points in the register. Beside the obvious association of Ptah *rsy inb.f*, "south of his wall," with the Memphite region,[32] Hathor's title of "Lady of the Southern Sycamore" was a deliberate choice associating her with the Memphite area. Hathor and Ptah appear frequently as a pair; the designation of one usually follows the other accordingly, expressing an attribution to a specific location.[33] In Papyrus Harris I, Ptah "south of his wall" would sail in his river barge to visit his daughter Hathor of the Southern Sycamore and, specifically, "on the south of Inbu," in other words, Memphis.[34] Whether or not Hathor was depicted as Ptah's daughter, she was clearly associated with his "south of his wall" form in Memphis.[35]

In this register, Hathor encourages the king to enter the *st wrt* "the great seat" to see his father Ptah "south of his wall." Originally the term *st wrt* referred to the throne of a god or a king, but in the 18th Dynasty, the range of its use expanded considerably. It was employed in reference to the barque shrine, the god's shrine, the sanctuary of the temple, various halls in the temple, and even as a designation for the entire temple.[36] One learns about the *st wrt* in reference to Ptah more specifically from New Kingdom sources. The *st wrt* was an important part of the Temple of Ptah in Memphis. Regarding the new Temple of Ptah, the king states: "its monuments were sculpted and established with labor. Its towers were of stone, approaching heaven. Its 'Great Seat' (*st wrt*) was enlarged like a 'Great House,' having a door of gold like the double doors of heaven."[37] In the Memphite theology, "Ptah upon the Great Seat (*Ptḥ ḥr st wrt*)" is the first form of Ptah in a list enumerating his different forms.[38] The location of Ptah's *st wrt* is most likely in the domain of his main temple in the Memphite area that was also strongly connected to the celebration of the *Heb Sed* festivals. Since the Ramesside Period, Ptah together with his assimilated form of Ptah Tatenen were among the gods frequently associated with

32 Holmberg, *The God Ptah*, pp. 204ff.

33 For example, in Karnak, Ptah was worshipped together with Hathor, "The Ruler of Thebes;" in Serabit el Khadim in Sinai, Ptah was worshipped together with Hathor "The Mistress of the Malachite." See Holmberg, *The God Ptah*, pp. 191–193 and 226.

34 Erichsen, *Papyrus Harris I*, p. 55; Breasted, *Ancient Records of Egypt*, IV, §331.

35 Gardiner, *The Wilbour Papyrus*, II, p. 176, n. 4; Schafik, *Beiträge zum Hathorkult*, pp. 4–5; Mahmud, *A New Temple for Hathor at Memphis*, p. 20 n. 71. On the geographical information and construction of their cult centers see Kitchen, "Towards a Reconstruction of Ramesside Memphis," pp. 87ff. For the problems of locating the Temple of the god Ptah, see Malek, "The Temples at Memphis," p. 90.

36 Kuhlmann, *Der Thron im alten Ägypten. Untersuchungen zu Semantik, Ikonographie und Symbolik eines Herrschaftszeichens*, pp. 29–32; Spencer, *The Egyptian Temple. A Lexicographical Study*, pp. 108–114.

37 Erichsen, *Papyrus Harris I*, pl. 45, l. 15–16; Breasted, *Ancient Records of Egypt*, IV, pp. 163–164, §311.

38 Clagett, *Ancient Egyptian Science I*, p. 309.

the royal jubilee feast.[39] This feast might have been alluded to in this register, because its symbols are depicted behind the king.

Among the rites of the royal accession, according to the liturgical composition of the Papyrus Brooklyn 47.218.50, was a ceremony labeled as "The Ceremony of the Great Throne (*st wrt*)." [40] These rites seem to have taken place in a specific location in the Helio-Memphite region, especially because "allusions to the intermediate role of the king between Re and Ptah-Tatenen" are frequently repeated.[41] The connection of Ptah's *st wrt* to the *Heb Sed* celebration and the royal coronation continued to grow during the Late Period through the Roman Period.[42]

The representation of Ptah inside two shrines in the vignette of the first register of the east wall of chapel F is uncommon. In fact, this is the only representation of its kind from the Temple of Hibis. Ptah is more frequently seated or standing on a podium or base alone, or inside an open or closed shrine. The outer shrine of Ptah on register I of the eastern wall has a vaulted roof and symbols of the papyrus plant and the *djed* pillar decorating its corners. These symbols may have been chosen in reference to the jubilee hall of Ptah at Memphis, where the *djed* column was raised as part of the *Heb Sed* festivities.[43] These two marked shrines could also symbolize the two locations indicated in the surrounding text: the "*st wrt*" and the "*ḥwt wrt*."

The format of the scene in register I is in keeping with that of the "Royal Introduction" (*bs nyswt*) into the temple. Directly in front of the shrine of Ptah, almost in the middle of the scene, the label reads *bs nyswt m ḥwt wrt*.[44] The hieroglyphs are facing the opposite direction of the remainder of the text, including hieroglyphs in the same line of the inscription. This unique occurrence emphasizes the significance of the text not only to this scene, but also to the other scenes of the room.

The verb *bsi* in such usage carries more meaning than the basic rendering "to enter." It signifies not only movement from one place to another, but also the elevation of status and the achievement of Maat. Kruchten explained the use of *bsi* to mark a ceremonial initiation between two different worlds: from the chaotic to the organized, from the profane to the sacred, or from the world of the dead to the world of the living. [45] Although Kruchten did not discuss this example from chapel F of Hibis Temple, he discussed similar examples to the "royal initiation" (*bs*(*t*) *nyswt*). Most of the royal initiation texts imply the

---

39 Holmberg, *The God Ptah*, pp. 87ff.

40 Goyon, *Confirmation du pouvoir royal au nouvel an. [Brooklyn Museum 47.218.50]*.

41 Goyon, *Confirmation du pouvoir royal au nouvel an. [Brooklyn Museum 47.218.50]*, pp. 15–16.

42 Myśliwiec, "Ramesside Traditions in the Arts of the Third Intermediate Period," pp. 111–112.

43 Pinch, *Egyptian Mythology: A Guide to the Gods, Goddesses, and Traditions of Ancient Egypt*, p. 128. The *djed* pillar was connected with Ptah as a symbol for stability and duration, before its connection to Osiris: Altenmüller, "Djed-Pfeiler," cols. 1101–1102; Koemoth, "Le rite de redresser Osiris," p. 160.

44 This format was the subject of study of chapter III and IV of Kruchten, *Les annales des prêtres de Karnak (XXI–XXIIImes dynasties) et autres textes contemporains relatifs à l'initiation des prêtres d'Amon*, who examined a corpus of over forty documents constituting the Annals of the Amun priests at Karnak in the 21st–23rd dynasties, discovered by Legrain in 1900.

45 Kruchten, *Les annales des prêtres de Karnak (XXI–XXIIImes dynasties)* , pp. 149 ff.

royal accession to the throne, and they are usually associated with the coronation of the pharaoh. The king enters into the presence of the gods who will endow him with kingship. These are frequently creator gods such as Amun, Re, Atum, and, as in this case, Ptah.

The significance of this ceremonial initiation is intensified by Hathor's enthusiastic invitation to the king and heightened by the sacred space of Ptah's double shrine. This may refer to a unique moment that may mark an important rite or a step in a series of rites preceded by *Heb Sed* festivities or another type of ceremony that required the *Heb Sed* regalia. This rite in turn may have been followed by the royal coronation on the south wall. According to Papyrus Harris, under the heading of "Praise of Ptah:" "leading the king to his great throne (*st wrt*) in his name: king of the two lands. I am your son whom you have installed (*bs*) as king in the place of my father in peace. I follow you; your plans are before me."[46]

The single line of inscription behind the shrines of Ptah reveals a formulaic yet important piece of information regarding Ptah's role in this particular stanza. The inscription reads: "Words spoken. It is to you that I have given all life, stability and dominion through (or better, on account of) the praises of this beautiful and pure monument (*mnw pn*) which the king of Egypt, (....)|, given life forever, made." Most probably, this *mnw pn* refers here to the Temple of Hibis. The king is hereby coming to receive the blessings of the god perhaps as a reward for this *mnw pn*, "this monument," whose creation is likewise connected to Ptah's control and oversight. This scene exhibits an underlying association to a preliminary stage of the temple foundation. Investigation of the association of Ptah with the construction of temples in general and of the Temple at Hibis in particular will prove most valuable in extracting the meaning of this scene, as well as the meaning of the scene on the second register below.

Ptah's most distinguished feature was his position as patron of all craftsmen. This association with manufacturing led to his extraordinary position in Egyptian religion, particularly in connection with the major temple-building activity of the New Kingdom. During the New Kingdom, he was widely acknowledged as a creator god.[47] This theme is reflected in the Memphite Theology and in various hymns.[48] In references to his taking part in building or manufacturing animate or inanimate objects, he is usually entrusted with the earlier planning or designing. When he came in close association with Khnum,[49] both had distinguishable roles in the manufacturing process. An example may be found in the inscription in room C of the Temple of Seti I at Abydos: "Ptah is the designer of the king's body while Khnum is forming the king's limbs on a potter's wheel."[50]

46 Breasted, *Ancient Records of Egypt*, IV, p. 163; Lichtheim, *Ancient Egyptian Literature*, I, pp. 50ff; Erichsen, *Papyrus Harris I*, pl. 44, l. 17–18.

47 For Ptah's veneration as a creator god see Berlandini, "Ptah-démiurge et l'exalation du ciel," pp. 9–41.

48 Holmberg, *The God Ptah*, pp. 31ff, 47–49

49 Ptah was even called Khnum in the hymn to Ptah found in Berlin Papyrus 3048, dating to the time of Ramesses VI; see Assmann, *Ägyptische Hymnen und Gebete*, pp. 322–333, 589–592; Clagett, *Ancient Egyptian Science. A Source Book*, I, Doc. II.7d, who suggests "the fashioner" for translating Khnum.

50 Holmberg, *The God Ptah*, pp. 46–47. A fragment of a stone block of a temple on Elephantine inscribed with a prayer to Imhotep, son of Ptah, is written under Ptah's double name of

This role is confirmed by the attestation of Ptah's participation in the so-called "Temple Foundation Ceremony." These scenes represent the ritual actions performed by the king, who is sometimes assisted by one or more divinities, pertaining to the physical or symbolic construction of the temple, depicted as early as the Second Dynasty.[51] However, these scenes became relatively well-defined in the Ptolemaic temples, especially at Edfu, Dendera, Philae, and Kom Ombo.[52] Ptah is frequently depicted participating in these ceremonies, and he usually has the epithet "south of his wall."[53] He is also depicted in scenes connected with the initial planning and layout of the temple, as reflected in chapel F where the preliminary phase of ritual activity essential to the start of the building process probably took place. His acceptance, praises, and control formed commission to inaugurate the work.[54] A preliminary stage where the king decided to build the temple and took councel from the gods must have taken place before the commencement of the construction including the fixed steps of stretching out the cord, leveling the soil, marking out the site with a baton, and setting up the four walls correctly. In the Temple of Qurna, Ptah announces the start of the active building of the Temple of Seti I.[55] A reference to a comparably early stage in the "stretching of the cord" ceremony can be extracted from the building inscription at Edfu: "Stretching (the measuring cord) in the Great Seat (*st wrt*), the sages and Thoth plotting its halls while burning incense, its foundation being exact from afore time, the builder gods building, he who is south of his wall (a reference to Ptah) controlling (the work), the Ogdoad rejoicing round about it."[56] On the exterior of the sanctuary wall in Edfu, Ptah *rsy inb.f* is described as the director (*ḥr ḫrp*) of the work of the temple construction.[57]

In fact, Ptah is depicted at Hibis as the decorator par excellence in connection with the process of building the temple. In hypostyle hall M, the north reveal of the gateway to hypostyle hall B, as part of a dedicatory statement mentioning the name of the temple and that King Darius built it for his father Amun-Re [lord of Hibis, great god, powerful of strength], continues to state more basic facts about the temple: "It is Seshat who constructed its walls, formed as beneficent works of eternity. It is Resyinebef (Ptah) who decorated its

Tatenen-Khnum; Laskowska-Kusztal, "Imhotep d'Elephantine," pp. 281–287. The relationship between Ptah and Imhotep and their depiction together in scenes related to the scene in chapel F will be discussed below.

51 On the earliest representation of such scenes see Engelbach, "A Foundation Scene of the Second Dynasty," pp. 183–184.

52 Weinstein, *Foundation Deposits in Ancient Egypt*, p. 3.

53 Though very briefly, Budde mentioned this association of Ptah's epithet of "south of his wall" in relation to the "stretching the cord" ritual; Budde, *Die Göttin Seschat*, p. 180.

54 In such scenes, Ptah, seated or standing in his shrine, usually with his epithet *rsy inb.f*, "south of his wall," is led or introduced by Hathor or Sakhmet. In addition, he is represented giving praises to the king while a mention of a certain monument is sometimes alluded to in the surrounding inscriptions.

55 *PM* II, 411, p. 43; Arnold, *Wandrelief und Raumfunktion in ägyptischen Tempeln des neuen Reiches*, pp. 7, 75; El-Adly, *Das Gründungs- und Weiheritual des Ägyptischen Tempels von der frühgeschichtlichen Zeit bis zum Ende des Neuen Reiches*, pp. 204–205.

56 After David, *Religious Ritual at Abydos*, p. 214; De Wit, "Inscriptions dédicatoires du temple d'Edfou," p. 287.

57 Budde, *Die Göttin Seschat*, p. 180, n. 255; *E.* I, 65, 17–18 (*rsy inb.f ḥr ḫrp k3t.f*).

scenes. There is not another sovereign like Pharaoh, king of Egypt, lord of the two lands, (Darius)¦."[58] This statement is also repeated on the exterior of the temple walls,[59] where, as well as in register I, Ptah is portrayed in his capacity as the divine interior designer of Hibis.

These early rites, which can be called "temple conception," may have been incorporated within the preliminary rites of the "stretching the cord" when the king departs the palace or arrives at the site of the new temple. In contrast to the final rites[60] of the "stretching of the cord," the preliminary rites of the foundation ceremony unfortunately remain unexplored. Scholars have confined the early rites to the placing of the foundation deposits and the departure of the king from the palace to the site of the ceremony.[61] The initial action, when the king decided to build a monument, when the symbolic conception of the temple was born, and when the plan or design was determined has not been investigated. It is interesting to note that among the early foundation rituals in Edfu, Hathor is the divinity that greets the king at the ceremony site where she invites him to "enter the *st wrt* to stretch the cord."[62]

Additional "temple conception" scenes include a group of scenes and texts associating Ptah with Imhotep and Amenhotep, son of Hapu.[63]. They reflect the relationship between temple foundation rituals and the two famous architects. Such scenes exhibit similar motifs to the scenes in chapel F; Ptah is always the main deity of the scene, either standing or seated in his shrine and usually preceded by Hathor.[64] The connection of the city of Memphis to its patron deity Ptah, its patron sage Imhotep, and the formation of the temple decoration schemes is illustrated in the "Building Texts" of the Ptolemaic temples. They are an important source of information regarding the temple building process. According to these texts, the ancient Egyptians believed that the plans of the temples were devised according to very old divine books drawn by Imhotep and delivered to Memphis.[65] In the Late Period, when Imhotep was worshipped as a god, he was considered the "son of Ptah" and was especially associated with his epithet of "Ptah south of his wall." A text in the Ptolemaic chamber inside the Hatshepsut Temple at Deir el

58 Davies, *The Temple of Hibis*, Part 3, pl. 29; Cruz-Uribe, *Hibis Temple Project I*, p. 114.

59 Davies, *The Temple of Hibis*, Part 3, pl. 50; Cruz-Uribe, *Hibis Temple Project I*, p. 155.

60 The final rites of the purification of the temple, its consecration, and final dedication to its lord have been carefully studied by scholars like Blackman and Fairman who managed to show that, at least in Edfu, there was a connection between the rites associated with the consecration of the temple and the Opening of the Mouth ceremony; Blackman and Fairman, "The Consecration of an Egyptian Temple according to the Use of Edfu," pp. 75–91; Weinstein, *Foundation Deposits in Ancient Egypt*, pp. 14–16.

61 Weinstein, *Foundation Deposits in Ancient Egypt*, pp. 7–8ff.

62 Weinstein, *Foundation Deposits in Ancient Egypt*, p. 9.

63 Wildung, *Imhotep und Amenhotep. Gottwerdung im Alten Ägypten*, especially pp. 204, 212ff and 223.

64 Wildung, *Imhotep und Amenhotep*, pls. XLVI (from Ptolemaic Temple of Ptah in Karnak, hypostyle hall, north wall) and L (exterior east wall of Ptolemaic Temple of Ptah in Karnak).

65 These texts are discussed in detail in Reymond, *The Mythical Origin of the Egyptian Temple*; Winter, "A Reconsideration of the Newly Discovered Building Inscription on the Temple of Denderah," pp. 75–85; Sethe, *Imhotep: Der Asklepios der Aegypter*, pp. 15–18. See also Quack, "Der historische Abschnitt des Buches vom Tempel," pp. 267–278; Quack, "Das Buch vom Tempel und verwandte Texte: Ein Vorbericht," pp. 1–20.

Bahari mentions the "restoration of the monument (*mnw*) of his king…done by the son of him who is south of his wall…Imhotep the great son of Ptah."[66] In the Temple of Ptah at Karnak, a hymn to Imhotep states that Imhotep renews his father's creation.[67] The discussion of the rest of the wall will provide further evidence for the aforementioned theory on the meanings behind the scenes on this register.

EAST WALL — REGISTER II

In the second register of the east wall, the king stands and wears his composite *atef* crown. The *abu* bouquet he offers to the double pair of the gods Hw, Sia, Ir, and Sedjem lies freely between his open palms. These gods were considered among the minor deities from ancient Egypt, and little information is known about their significance. This, together with the fact that the scene contains a minimum amount of textual evidence, makes it important to discuss somewhat in detail Hw and Sia in terms of their relationship to the other pair, Ir and Sedjem, the other scene of Ptah on the top register, and the scene of the Ished tree on the south wall. Their exact combination and relationship to the surrounding other deities adds an important dimension to their identification.

The first pair, Hw and Sia, belonged to the group of gods called "Begriffsgötter" or "conceptual gods" who personified the concepts of "authorative or creative utterance" and "perception, discernment, insight or understanding," respectively.[68] They balance each other in that "Sia is complementary to Hw but where Hw is done by the mouth, Sia is the action of the heart; Hw is active where what is perceived is 'spoken' and Sia is passive where what will be spoken is perceived."[69] They correlate closely to creation in the Heliopolitan and the Memphite theologies and are thus associated with the main creator gods Atum, Re, and Ptah. From their early attestation in the Old Kingdom, they were associated with Re; Sia appears in the Pyramid Texts §§ 267–268 as the knowing one on the right of Re while Hw would have taken Re's left side.[70] They are often shown with other gods accompanying the sun god in his barque.[71] In the Pyramid Texts and in the Books of the Dead, where knowledge of all things is required for the survival of the deceased king, many texts confirm the king's control and possession of Sia and Hw, as in Pyramid Text § 300, where it is said that the Great One lays down his office before the dead king who "takes hold of Hw and gains control over Sia,"[72] thus acquiring "the power of uttering commands."[73]

66 Wildung, *Imhotep und Amenhotep*, p. 221; *PM* II, p. 367 (145[g]–[h]); Naville, *Deir el Bahari* V, pl. 148.

67 Lichtheim, *Ancient Egyptian Literature*, III, p. 106.

68 Otto, "Altägyptischer Polytheismus," p. 255; Gugliemi, "Personifikationen," p. 982.

69 Wilson, *Lexicon*, p. 795.

70 Ringgren, *Word and Wisdom: Studies in the Hypostatization of Divine Qualities and Functions in the Ancient Near East*, pp. 9–10, citing Sethe, *Übersetzung und Kommentar* I, p. 273.

71 Ringgren, *Word and Wisdom*, pp. 17ff.

72 Similar statements exist in Pyramid Texts §§ 307, 755, 697, 806, 411 (in the last two examples Sia does not have the determinative for god.) Also see Book of the Dead Chapters 174 and 17; see Ringgren, *Word and Wisdom*, pp. 10ff.

73 Gardiner, "Some Personifications," p. 51.

The Heliopolitan association of this pair of deities is indicated in several texts. However, during the Persian Period, it is stated specifically in a papyrus that Horus is "Excellent of Hw and Sia…in the council of gods, borne at Heliopolis" (*mnḫ n ḥw siꜣ…<m>ḏꜣḏꜣ.t ir m Ỉwnw*).[74] Hw and Sia were connected first to the Heliopolitan cosmogony but linked, at least in principle, to Ptah as indicated in the Memphite Theology mentioned below.

The second pair of deities, Ir, "seeing," and Sedjem, "hearing," did not appear until the 18th or 19th Dynasty.[75] They later joined the first pair, Hw and Sia, as the gods of the temple during the time of Ramesses II.[76] Since their early attestation, this pair is most frequently associated with Thoth and Seshat, as the wisdom and knowledge discerned from seeing and hearing. The arm of the seeing god (*ꜥ n Ỉr*) was a designation of the scribal palette.[77] They were referred to as the eyes and ears of Re in the Temple of Edfu.[78] At the Temple of Dendera, they are associated with the sun god where "seeing" is called "the right (eye) of Re, illuminating all lands with his rays," and "hearing" is called "hearing all things, reviser of all the country."[79] Sedjem and Ir are also connected to the temple foundation, perhaps encouraged by their link to Thoth and Seshat, who were the main performers in such ceremonies. According to the Coffin Texts, Seshat was in charge of building the mansions of the gods and was assisted by the gods of sight and hearing.[80]

The order of the representations of the four gods in the Hibis Temple reflects their known status in the Egyptian tradition. As in most of his attestations, Hw is leading the row of the four gods. In the Mammisi of Kom Ombo, Hw is behind the born deity, and Sia is behind them.[81] In the ritual of Amenhotep I, the following text is addressed to the king: "the hearts of the gods revive when they see you, Sia following you and Hw in front of him."[82] Sedjem is always mentioned behind Ir, especially in the fables of the birds of seeing and hearing, where they were registering the booty.[83] They are in the same order when they are mentioned in the Temple of Edfu; in one instance the king is presenting Maat to a row of deities, including these four.[84] In another instance, they are abbreviated into two divinities: Hw-Sia and Ir-Sedjem.[85] The Temple of Dendera has a

---

74 Ringgren, *Word and Wisdom*, p. 20; Daressy, "Décret d'Amon en faveur d'Osiris," p. 220.

75 Brunner-Traut, "Der Sehgott und der Hörgott in Literatur und Theologie," p. 127. A representation of a figure who may have been holding a palette with the remains of the combined name *Ỉr-Sḏm* ( ) appears in the New Kingdom Temple of Amun Re, on the door of the 4th pylon of Karnak (Barguet, *Temple d'Amon-Re*, 97, pl. XIIIB); however, their first confirmed attestation is found in the New Kingdom Temple of Abydos under Seti I; ibid., p. 127, nn. 7–9.

76 Brunner-Traut, "Der Sehgott und der Hörgott in Literatur und Theologie," pp. 127ff.

77 Cauville, "A propos des désignations de la palette de scribe," p. 185; Clère, *La porte d'Évergète à Karnak*, p. 59, pl. 22.

78 *E* I, p. 508, 2; *E* I, p. 521, 14; *E* VIII, p. 122, 16; *E Mammisis*, p. 42, 16.

79 *D* III, pl. 12 h.

80 Spell 709; Faulkner, *Coffin Texts*, II, p. 268.

81 *Kom Ombos*, p. 30, 2.

82 Ringgren, *Word and Wisdom*, p. 21 (Papyrus Chester Beatty IX, 9, 4f and Pap. Brit. Mus. III pl. 54)

83 Brunner-Traut, "Der Sehgott und der Hörgott in Literatur und Theologie," pp. 128ff.

84 *E* III, p. 291, 13. See also *E* III, pl. 59.

85 *E* X, pl. 89; *E* IV, p. 310, 1–7.

scene representing the procession of the Hermopolitan Ogdoad, Hw, Sia, the king, and the queen, Ir, Sedjem, Thoth, and Maat.[86]

This scene on the second register of the east wall of chapel F, however, may be a rare indication of worship devoted to them in an ancient Egyptian temple in general and the elevated status they enjoyed at the Hibis Temple in particular, as the king specifically presents the offering directly to them. Their iconography in this register is unique. Hw and Sia are sometimes represented with falcon heads; however, the representation here of the gods with ram heads for the first time might reflect an influence of Theban theology. Ir is almost always represented in fully human form. His representation with the now-destroyed sun disk can link him to the solar theology. Sedjem was sometimes represented with the head of a bull or a cow but appears here in Hibis for the first time with the head of a baboon, an iconography which links him to Thoth. The offering of the *abu* bouquet, which was connected to the fertility of Min,[87] might also reflect the association of Hw and Sia with the fertility of the solar god, who created them from drops of blood from his phallus.[88] This is perhaps intended to assimilate the creation concepts inherent in the solar link to these deities and in the usual recipients of the *abu* offering.

All in all, the existence of this group of four gods, and in particular this instance in the Temple of Hibis, probably reflects their role in the accomplishment of the divine will. They seem to represent the four sensory means of gaining knowledge from hearing, seeing, perception, and finally utterance, and collectively report to the creator god, helping him in the final realization of physical and abstract creation.[89] These gods are carefully selected to fill a double capacity in this chapel. On one hand, they are associated with the crowning of the king and the Heliopolitan theology. They appear in many scenes of the king's coronation, especially in the Ptolemaic temples. One interesting example comes from the Temple of Edfu, where the crowning of the king took place in front of a gathering of divinities that included most of the divinities that are represented on the different walls of this chapel F; among those divinities were Hw and Sia who are giving millions of *Heb Sed* symbols, Montu who is offering the king a scimitar, Thoth who gives the symbol of the red crown beside the prominent double figures of Seshat.[90] These four gods also represent the royal dominance over the two parts of the country and its uni-

86 *D* III, p. 87, pl. 200.

87 Germer, "Die Bedeutung des Lattichs als Pflanze des Min," pp. 85–87.

88 Ringgren, *Word and Wisdom*, p. 17

89 The gods Hw and Sia are frequently connected with the magician god Heka or the goddess Maat as tools of achievement; Ringgren, *Word and Wisdom*, pp. 9–52. Sometimes these deities are connected with the curing process; see Kákosy, "A New Source of Egyptian Mythology and Iconography," p. 624, who refers to an example of the healing statue of Horus Cippus or the so called Tyszkiewicz statue that bears the figures of Hw and Sia, as evidence for "tangible evidence that abstract concepts were not alien to healing statues;" Hornung, "Götterworte im Alten Ägypten," pp. 159–186.

90 Budde, *Die Göttin Seschat*, pp. 104–105, Dok. 134, fig. 16; also see Dok. 138, fig. 17, pls. 10 and 12, fig.1. Other examples come from the Temple of Karnak; Clère, *La Porte d'Evergète*, pl. 41, the Temple of Philae, *PM* VI, pp. 231 (a) and (b); 236, 5 (c–d). See also Brunner-Traut, "Der Sehgott und der Hörgott in Literatur und Theologie," pp. 137–138.

fication. Hw and Sia sometimes tie the knot of the Sema-Tawey sign, representing the unification between the two halves of the country; they are occasionally designated as the generals or *mr mšꜥ* of Upper and Lower Egypt, respectively.[91] Even among their early representations in Medinet Habu, Ir and Sedjem were depicted in front of the shrines of *Pr wr* of Upper Egypt and *Pr nw* of Lower Egypt, respectively.[92]

On the other hand, they are likely to be involved in the pious act of the king in the building of the temple for the gods, assisting Ptah who appears in the top register and Seshat who appears on the nearby south wall in its conception by interjecting the power of the creative word and will. The Memphite Theology is of great interest in this regard. It elaborates on how Ptah created the whole world by his heart and tongue.[93] In a hymn to Ptah found in Berlin Papyrus 3048, "the most extensive of the New Kingdom documents which refer to the creative activity of Ptah," he is described as the one who created the earth according to the plans of his heart, while another document says "your mouth has engendered and your hands have fashioned."[94] This aspect of planning is met also in Papyrus Harris, which mentions that he made the sky by means of his heart, (*ỉr pt m kꜣ m ib.f*)[95] This following excerpt from the same papyrus expresses several elements in the Hibis scene: "Praise of Ptah…leading the king to his great throne (*st wrt*) in his name: king of the two lands. I am your son whom you have installed (*bs*) as king in the place of my father in peace. I follow you; your plans are before me."[96] Note that the king is led to the *st wrt*, being initiated (*bs*) as the sole king who follows Ptah's plans. Such notion of planning is expressed by the character of those four personified divine qualities represented by the four gods in the second register of chapel F, especially Hw and Sia,[97] and adds some weight to the above reference to an early stage of "temple conception" as deduced from the first register.

Many inscriptions stress that Sia is particularly entrusted with the making and the organization of the Egyptian temple.[98] The Temple of Edfu has a scene of the foundation ritual with the king and Seshat. She announces the stretching of the cord in the precinct of the temple, while the inscription above the king says "the good god who knows the *merkhet* as the god of knowledge (Sia), who divides the ball like Seshat, long live the good god who established the two chapels, who stretched the cord in the temple, divided the ball in the cities and nomes, who turned (on the potter's wheel) what was decayed in the

91 Ringgren, *Word and Wisdom*, pp. 10–11; Schott, "Falke, Geier und Ibis als Krönungsboten," pp. 55ff; *D* II, p. 101, 7.

92 *PM* II, p. 491 (54)(J), published in *Medinet Habu* V, pl. 251.

93 Allen, *Genesis in Egypt. The Philosophy of Ancient Egyptian Creation Accounts*, pp. 42–47, 59–60.

94 Clagett, *Ancient Egyptian Science. A Source Book*, I, pp. 306ff, 551, 571; Assman, *Ägyptische Hymnen und Gebete*, pp. 322–333, 589–592.

95 Erichsen, *Papyrus Harris I*, l. 10–11 (pl. 44, 4).

96 Breasted, *Ancient Records of Egypt*, IV, p. 163.

97 Bilolo, "La notion du 'progrès historique' au cours du IIIe millénaire. Contribution à la philosophie pharaonique de l'histoire," pp. 90ff.

98 Cauville, "Les inscriptions dédicatoires du temple d'Hathor à Dendera," p. 99; Leitz, *Lexikon*, VI, p. 162; *E* VI, p. 186, 4; *E* VI, p. 183, 7 and 8; *E* VII, p. 185, 15.

temples and organized the house of his father."[99] The walls of the Temple of Dendera are inscribed (*sphr*) with the formula (*šsꜣw*) of Sia and carved (*ḫt*) by the hand of Tatenen.[100] In another place in the same temple, it is stated that "the great powers (*sḫmw wrw*) are carved inside the (*wꜥrt-ḫpr-ḫꜣt*) (room D in Dendera) according to the excellent plans of Sia.[101]

The Berlin Leather Roll is an administrative document that reports King Sesostris' decision to build a temple in Heliopolis. It gives abundant statements on the early foundation and planning process of the monument. In particular, it emphasizes the roles of Hw and Sia in this early phase of temple construction.[102] This register thus functions symbolically as a two-dimensional representation of the ideas inherent in the previously cited texts that these four divine concepts serve as the basis for the creative power of Ptah, which is realized by the intelligible expression of the deed by Hw. The recitation of the texts in the top register that mention this deed as "*mnw*" would activate this creation course of action.

SOUTH WALL — REGISTER I

The south wall of chapel F depicts important features of the divine munificence to the kingship of the ruler. In the first register, the king is wearing the kilt, kneeling on a base in front of Atum Re Horakhty, the chief divinity in the local pantheon of Heliopolis. Atum Re Horakhty is fixing the blue crown on the king's head in a gesture similar to that of Khnum, while creating people on his potter's wheel, in front of him.

In front of the king, another important feature of kingship is taking place, that is, the writing of the king's name on the Ished tree—an important part of the coronation ceremony in ancient Egypt.[103] Thoth is writing on the leaves of the tree and saying that he is writing the annals of the king on the Ished tree in the great temple of Heliopolis. Seshat, who is represented in his following, is giving the king infinity of all life, stability, and dominion, and hundreds of thousands of years in peace.

The four miniature figures of the deities behind Atum Re Horakhty represent the four offspring of the Heliopolitan deity, perhabs as witnesses to the royal coronation. The existence of these four divinities beside the Ished is a novel motif that has no parallel in any of the Ished tree scenes.[104]

---

99 *E* III, p. 114; Montet, "Le rituel de fondation des temples égyptiens," p. 80; also see other examples on pp. 81 and 95.

100 *D* I, p. 31, 9. In many other instances, it is repeated that the walls are inscribed with the texts (*šnw*) of Sia: *D* I, p. 32, 8; *D* II, p. 208, 7; *D* IV, p. 112, 1; *D* V, p. 59, 8; *D* V, p. 109, 6; Leitz, *Lexikon*, VI, p. 165.

101 *D* II, p. 73, 6.

102 Buck, "The Building Inscription of the Berlin Leather Roll," pp. 48–57; El-Adly, "Die Berliner Lederhandschrift (pBerlin 3029)," pp. 6–18; Piccato, "The Berlin Leather Roll and the Egyptian Sense of History," pp. 137–159, who argues that the text is a New Kingdom composition with a Middle Kingdom setting.

103 Myśliwiec, *Eighteenth Dynasty before the Amarna Period*, pp. 12–14.

104 Myśliwiec, *Studien zum Gott Atum*, p. 353.

The representation of Thoth, Seshat, and the connection to the royal coronation ceremony by Atum started in the New Kingdom.[105] However, this combination of Atum's crowning of the king, the Ished tree, and the king's kneeling inside it bears strong Ramesside influences.[106] Two Ramesside representations provide an almost direct parallel to the iconography used in the Hibis scene. The first representation occurs on the second pylon of the Temple of Amun at Karnak.[107] Two parallel scenes of King Ramesses II are depicted on opposite north and south walls of the doorway to the hypostyle hall. The king kneels inside the Ished tree before Atum on the north side with the double crown and human face, while on the south side is the falcon-headed Re Horakhty. On both sides, the king is wearing the blue crown and is facing the enthroned god who is giving him the symbol of many *Sed* Festivals. Behind the king stands a divinity who is writing the king's name on the leaves of the Ished tree; on the north side it is Seshat, on the south side it is Thoth. Inside the Temple of the Ramesseum is another relevant scene, located on the west wall of the "Astronomical Room."[108] Seshat and Thoth are writing the king's name. The king is sitting on a low-backed throne in front of them inside the Ished tree. Behind Ramesses II is Atum with the double crown and the human head, writing the king's names on the leaves of the tree.

As for the representation of the scarab on top of the Ished tree, the Temple of Amada provides the only other representation that is like this one.[109] Amada also provides an exact pose of Re Horakhty Atum affixing the double crown on the king's head. Thutmosis IV is kneeling inside the Ished tree in front of Re Horakhty Atum, whose head is destroyed but seems to have been a falcon head. Both the king and the god are on a platform supported by the lowest branch of the tree. Thoth is writing the names and annals of the king on the Ished tree. From the remaining inscription of Re Horakhty Atum is the statement: "Hundred thousand (of) *Sed* Festivals upon earth." Different styles exist in the depiction of the winged scarab in the two scenes. In the Temple of Amada, the wings of the scarab are more stylized like a "fly wing," rather than the "bird wing" in the Hibis example. The scarab beetle is known for rolling a ball of dung in front of it. This ball is used by the female scarab as a nest to lay her eggs and feed the newly hatched scarabs until they mature and emerge from the ball. For the ancient Egyptians, this image of the scarab rolling its ball was an important symbol of rebirth. The scarab is thus reinforcing the solar theology in this representation by reflecting the idea of the eternal rebirth of the sun, indicated by the sun disk in front of him. In the Temple of Amada, the scarab has the cartouche of the king attached to his hind legs, while in Hibis the whole tree is

---

105 Budde, *Die Göttin Seschat*, p. 153.

106 See Helck, "Ramessidische Inschriften aus Karnak," examples on pp. 118ff. See also Myśliwiec, "Ramesside Traditions in the Arts of the Third Intermediate Period," pp. 108–126.

107 *PM* II, p. 42 (g) and (h) III, 2; Seele, *The Coregency of Ramesses II with Seti I*, fig.14; Myśliwiec, *Studien zum Gott Atum*, pp. 350ff, pl. 86.

108 *PM* II, p. 440 (25); Helck, "Ramessidische Inschriften aus Karnak," p. 120; Budde, *Die Göttin Seschat*, Dok. 51, pl. 9, fig.1.

109 *PM* VII, p. 68 (16)–(17); Gauthier, *Le temple d'Amada*, pl. XXXVII(B), pp. 165–167; Aly, Abdel-Hamid, and Dewachter, *Le temple d'Amada*, C7; Myśliwiec, *Studien zum Gott Atum*, pp. 349ff.

attached to him. Besides representing the king as the manifestation of the sun god, this might further reflect the idea that the name of the king or the names and annals inscribed on the whole tree will exist eternally, as the sun is reborn daily.

Seshat carries the title of *nbt sšw*, "lady of documents," in this register in chapel F, reflecting her official role in the king's domain. Her instrumental skills in the necessary meticulous actions involved in the physical construction and decoration of the ancient Egyptian temple seem to have made her closely associated with the keeping of the sacred writings and the records of the king, the writing of his name and annals on the Ished tree, and the king's coronation in general. The scene of "writing the king's name on the Ished tree" is known from the 18th dynasty onward but had its origin in much earlier beliefs.[110] In many of the Ished tree scenes the writing of the name in the tree is accompanied by the giving of the *Heb Sed* festival.[111] While the inscription does not mention the *Heb Sed* festivities in this chapel, it might be indicated by the *Heb Sed* symbols behind the king on the first register of the east wall. The east wall, as discussed earlier, provides references to an early ritual of the temple foundation that together with the *Heb Sed* ceremonies was part of the coronation rituals of the king. The top registers of the east and south walls of this chapel seem to be combined into one unique scene on a door of Merenptah from Memphis.[112] Ptah in his mummiform image is represented inside his shrine. King Merenptah is standing in front of the shrine and between them are many *Heb Sed* signs. This scene is unique in that Ptah is holding the symbols of Seshat and using the pen decorated with her five-petal flower to write the annals of the king on the *renpet* sign.

Seshat's speech, as written inside the stairway passage of the Temple of Seti I at Abydos, provides important information on the relationship between this goddess and the surrounding representations in this Hibis chapel. She is describing the foundation of the temple in perhaps our earliest and most complete representation of such a ceremony, despite no depiction of the "stretching of the cord." She narrates the ground operation of the temple, incorporating all the gods that helped in the construction; Ptah is described as the master of the building and Sia and Hw are mentioned. The speech is followed by a reference to the *Heb Sed* festivities.[113]

Inside hypostyle hall B of the Temple of Hibis, a scene of Seshat offers a different iconography. She is in front of the king and wears a long garment and only a five-petal rosette on her head.[114] She is clearly depicted in a foundation ceremony, pounding the stakes into the ground. The inscription between the king and Seshat is reconstructed as follows: "[driving in the Stake] for his father, Amun Re, lord of Hibis, great god, powerful of strength."[115] This scene occurs directly below the royal procession from the palace in front

110 Helck, "Ramessidische Inschriften aus Karnak," pp. 117–140; Welvaert, "On the Origin of the Ished-Scene," p. 101.

111 Helck, "Ramessidische Inschriften aus Karnak," pp. 133–140.

112 Budde, *Die Göttin Seschat*, p. 180, pl. 6.

113 David, *Religious Ritual at Abydos*, p. 69; Bastin, "De la fondation d'un temple," pp. 9–24; El-Adly, *Das Gründungs- und Weiheritual des Ägyptischen Tempels*, pp. 205–211; El-Sabban, *Temple Festival Calendars of Ancient Egypt*, pp. 48–49.

114 Davies, *The Temple of Hibis*, Part 3, pl. 13.

115 Cruz-Uribe, *Hibis Temple Project I*, p. 69.

of the Temple of Ptah, as indicated by the different standards accompanying the king and the inscription "royal procession from the palace, being content in the Temple of Ptah."[116] This may in fact be a reference to the early role of Seshat in such foundation ceremonies and the close relationship to Ptah. The scene is not far from depictions of Atum "lord of the two lands and Heliopolis" and Nebet Hetepet,[117] who are also represented on the west wall of chapel F. Located on the east wall of hypostyle hall B, the scene as a whole is on the section of the wall that is close to the door to chapel F.

According to the analysis of the east and south wall decorations, these scenes may belong to a group of early rites relating to the planning and creation of temples, which can be termed "temple conception." Besides having the *st wrt* as common ground,[118] both series of scenes of the "stretching of the cord" and the "temple conception" are closely related to the *Heb Sed* festival and the coronation ceremony. The gods almost always give the king "millions of *Heb Sed* festivals" in a nearby scene or text, usually succeeded by the crowning or the writing of the annals on the Ished tree. This is especially apparent in such Ramesside temples as the Temple of Medinet Habu,[119] the Temple of Abydos,[120] and the Temple of Derr.

This latter temple in Lower Nubia, built by Ramesses II and dedicated to the solar deity Re,[121] provides us with some interesting scenes that resemble not only our scene on the east wall but also the whole cycle of rites and the scheme of decoration of Room F. The

116 South of door, register II; Cruz-Uribe, *Hibis Temple Project I*, p. 69.

117 North of door, register IV, Cruz-Uribe, *Hibis Temple Project I*, p. 68.

118 See the examples of Hathor leading the king to the "*st wrt*;" sometimes the king declares that he is "taking the good way toward the '*st wrt*' in order to found the temple of Horakhty;" Montet, "Le rituel de fondation des temples égyptiens," pp. 74–100.

119 In Medinet Habu, two scenes reflect this fact. In the second court, west colonnade, the king is giving an offering to Ptah who is accompanied by Sakhmet in place of Hathor. Behind the king is Seshat giving him the sign of millions of jubilees between the two *renpet* signs; *Medinet Habu*, VI, pl.376. In room 23, west wall, north of the doorway, Ramesses III is offering flowers of Papyrus and Lotus to Ptah, seated in his elaborate double shrine. Ptah is preceded by Sakhmet. Nefertum is standing behind the king, in the same manner as Seshat in the previous scene, giving the king many signs of millions of *Sed* festivals piled between the two *renpet* signs. The inscription above Ptah says that he, Ptah *rsy inb.f*, is giving him millions of *Heb Sed* festivals like Re. Unfortunately, there is a break after this line of inscription but we can still read */// mnw rd* (may your monument endure or [for] your endured monument); *Medinet Habu*, VI, pl. 458; For further examples of this type of scene, see Nelson and Murnane, *The Great Hypostyle Hall at Karnak*, I, Part 1, pl. 235. For an example with Hathor in place of Sakhmet, see Clère, *La porte d'Évergète*, pl. 28. In that scene, the king is offering a pectoral in the shape of a temple with the figures of Amun, Mut, and Khonsu inside it.

120 In the temple of Seti I at Abydos, in the second hypostyle hall between doors IIWb and IIIWb, Ptah is seated in front of the king in a shrine decorated with a row of uraei on top. The king is kneeling in front of Ptah and offers him the sign of millions of jubilees. Ptah reciprocates by inscribing a tablet or drawing on the sign of millions of jubilees itself. Re Horakhty is behind the king, writing the king's jubilees on the Ished tree; Calvery and Gardiner, *The Temple of King Sethos I at Abydos*, IV, pl. 35.

121 Blackman, *The Temple of Derr*, pp. 2ff.

Second Pillared hall of the temple shows a series of important scenes.[122] After the king has been ushered in to enter the temple of his father (*bs nswy(t) r ḥwt nṯr n i͗t.f*) (scene III, west wall) in the presence of Atum, Iusaas, and Horakhty, Re Horakhty declares: "O son of my body whom I love, lord of the two lands, Usermare-Setepnre! O my son wide is your love for me I rejoiced when I behold what you have done (scene II, east wall). The reward for doing beneficial acts is eternal jubilees (*mꜣ (i͗) i͗r n.k i͗sw n i͗r ꜣḫw ḏt m ḥb sd*). This royal action is clearly stated on the north wall: the king has erected a boat-shrine in the Temple of Derr. Over the procession of the king and the priests carrying the boat shrine, the king is described as *nṯr nfr i͗r mnw m pr i͗t.f*, "The good god, he has made a monument, namely the house of his father." On the east wall, Osiris, Khentamenty, and Weret Hekau are presented as well as the four seated miniature deities: Shu, Tefnut, Montu, and Atum. The king offers *nw* jars to Amon Re in his phallic form with two *abu* plants behind him. Seshat is giving the jubilee sign to the king (scene II, west wall). Ptah is on the north wall, while Sakhmet, beloved of Ptah, accompanies him. In front of Ptah is an Ished tree. Behind the tree is Thoth who holds a *renpet* and millions of jubilee signs. Thoth marks with his reed pen on the leaves of the Ished tree "...your name is established upon the Persea tree by the writing of my fingers. I speak as your father Ptah Tatenen has commanded. You are given millions of years, hundreds of thousands of jubilees like Re forever. ... I have given you the years of Atum eternally." Ptah says, "I have given you my duration as king, like Re every day." Sakhmet says, "I have given you the duration of Re, jubilees as Horakhty, like Re every day."

SOUTH WALL — REGISTER II

The king is represented twice in this register. On the right side, he wears the *nemes* headdress in front of the falcon-headed Montu, who is giving him the scimitar decorated with a ram's head on which rests a solar disk. On the left, the king wears the double crown and holds Khepri's hands to his left and Re Horakhty's hand to his right. Re Horakhty is extending life to the king's nostrils. Khepri is represented with the scarab on his human head, while Re Horakhty is shown with the solar disk, encircled with the uraeus, on his falcon head.

Montu gives a ceremonial scimitar to the king, symbolizing vigor over all lands as the inscription in front of the king on the right side confirms: *di͗ <n.i͗> n.k nḫtw r tꜣ nb ẖꜣswt nbw*, "<I> give to you victories against all lands, all foreign lands." Khepri promises the king *di͗ n <i͗> n.k ꜥnḫ ḏd wꜣs nb snb ḥb ꜣwt i͗b*, "<I> give to you all life, stability, dominion, and all health, feasts and joy of heart." Re Horakhty at the left of the register makes an important reference to the "place" or "*st.*" The inscription states: *ḥwnw.f ẖnty.k m ꜥnḫ ẖnm.k st.k m ꜥnḫ ḏd wꜣs nb*, "his son is before you in life that you may endow your place with all life, stability and dominion." Such a "place" may refer to the seat of governance of the king or the Temple of Hibis that the king erected for the gods. The latter suggestion seems quite possible, considering the other temple references reflected from the other registers discussed in the same chapel.

---

122 Blackman, *The Temple of Derr*, pls. XXVIII–XLIV.

The iconography of the victory-scimitar is unique. The lower part is curved in the shape of a bent stem of a lotus flower, rather than the usual sharply curved blade of the scimitar, while the upper part takes the shape of a ram's head or falcon's head, a uraeus and sun disk on its head, and is exaggerated in height.[123] Actual examples of the lotus flower as a handle to the scimitar appear since at least the 19th Dynasty,[124] coinciding with the culmination of the "triumph scene," where a deity gives the king the *khepesh* scimitar saying: "Take for yourself the *khepesh*!" to defeat the enemies.[125] However, the earlier specimens have no examples of the upper part of a falcon's or ram's head. The extension of the upper part of the animal's head in the Hibis example might suggest its function as a sheath or it might actually be the handle to the scimitar, while the lower body of the scimitar is the sheath.[126] The combination of the different parts of the Hibis example of the scimitar appears later in the Ptolemaic temples, sometimes near scenes of the crowning of the king and the Ished tree.[127]

The ideology of the victorious king is reinforced not only by the representation of the scimitar, its symbolism, and the inscription accompanying the scenes, but also by the choice of Montu, who is primarily a war god whose patronage of the victory of King Montuhotep II of the 11th dynasty elevated his status until the end of Egyptian civilization.[128] Montu is especially associated with such scenes of giving the *khepesh* scimitar to the king. A scene on an ivory wristlet representing Thutmosis IV holding a captive by the hair and facing Montu Re who is giving him the scimitar is considered to be the first representation where the god is portrayed taking an "active role" in front of the "triumph scene" of the king.[129] The text attached to the deity says: "Take for yourself the *khepesh* scimitar, O Good God, that you may smite the heads of every foreign land."[130] Montu Re appears again on the chariot of the same king in his tomb: Montu is giving the scimitar to the king who is shooting arrows against foreign enemies.[131] Such scenes showing the giving of the scimitar to the king appear on both royal and private stelae of the New Kingdom,[132] and frequentely indicate a simultaneous giving and rewarding interaction

123 The iconography of these heads seems to correspond to the heads of the dedicating deities who usually are either ram-headed, such as Amun Re and Khnum, or falcon-headed, such as Montu, Horus, and Re Horakhty; see Schulman, "Take for Yourself the Sword," figs. 1–18. Also compare the usual type of the scimitar in the New Kingdom, as exemplified by the scenes in Medinet Habu of Ramesses III receiving the scimitar; *Medinet Habu*, I, pl. 23.

124 See examples in Petrie, *Tools and Weapons*, pl. XXVII, nos. 192–200.

125 Galán, *Victory and Border*, p. 71.

126 An example of the animal's head used as a handle to a dagger is found in Karnak; see Lubicz, "The Temples of Karnak," p. 630, pl. 190. See also Petrie, *Tools and Weapons*, pl. XXV, example 63.

127 For example, *E* X pl. CLXIX; *E* IX, pl. XXIXA; *E*, IX, pl. XXIB; *E* X, pl. CXVII.

128 Werner, *The God Montu*, I, p. 54.

129 Berlin 21685; Galán, *Victory and Border*, p. 72. For a discussion of this wristlet, see Bryan, *The Reign of Thutmose IV*, pp. 162–163 (9.2).

130 Ibid.

131 Galán, *Victory and Border*, p. 72, n. 391; Carter-Newberry, *The Tomb of Thoutmosis IV*, pl. 10, 12.

132 Schulman, "Take for Yourself the Sword," pp. 267ff.

between the king and the god. In this scene on the south wall of chapel F in Hibis, the act of rewarding the king with the victory scimitar can be seen as an exchange for his pious involvement in the building of the Temple of Hibis, which is surmised from the other scenes on the walls of this chapel. Building the temple could equally be a grant offering in response to receiving the victory scimitar. One of the architraves at Luxor refers to Amenhotep III as "beloved son of Amun who makes endowments in return for his *khepesh*."[133]

Since together with the god Atum, who is represented on the top register, the god Montu formed a "Götterpaar" or "divine pair" that was used iconographically to represent Upper and Lower Egypt,[134] one may speculate that this wall reflects the affirmation of the king's authority in both Lower Egypt, attested from the top scene, and Upper Egypt, attested from the lower scene.

The scene on the left portrays the king in the middle between Re Horakhty and Khepri. Re Horakhty, who represents another solar emphasis, is depicted in his common form as a falcon-headed god with the solar disk and the uraeus enveloping the disk on his head. Khepri, as in the rest of his representation in the Temple of Hibis, is shown in his less-frequent completely human form with the scarab on his head.[135] In this register, there is an interesting correspondence between image and text. The inscription on the right side of the register declares the king as the son of Montu. The inscription on the left side above Re Horakhty states "His son is before you in life that you may endow your place with life stability and dominion." Thus, Re Horakhty seems to be addressing Khepri. The mention of "His son" is a reference to the king as the son of Montu, who is indeed shown in the scene "before" Khepri. On the west exterior jamb of Portico Q of the Temple of Hibis, an inscription describes that because the king walks with Khepri and Re Horakhty, "stability may be upon all of your routines. Your illumination of the two lands (will) not cease...."[136]

Note the reciprocal reference or, as noted by M. Minas-Nerpel, a "wechselseitiger Bezug" between the two scenes: Khepri is standing directly on the same axis as that of the winged scarab of the above register, while the king wearing the double crown of Upper and Lower Egypt is beneath Atum, who is wearing the same regalia as the king but faces the other direction.[137]

In this scene from chapel F and in the Temple of Hibis in general, Khepri stresses a solar association, as evident from his representation with the other Heliopolitan deities on this wall. Such an association of Khepri with the solar realm is rarely attested in the Late Period. M. Minas-Nerpel wrote: "Einzige deutliche Ausnahme ist der Hibis-Tempel von Charga aus der Zeit Dareios' I. mit seinen vielfältigen Sonnengottszenen,

133 Galán, *Victory and Border*, p. 72.

134 Werner, *The God Montu*, pp. 237ff.

135 For the other two representations of Khepri, see Davies, *The Temple of Hibis*, Part 3, pls. 53, 55. The iconography of this god is discussed in Minas-Nerpel, *Der Gott Chepri*, pp. 471–473.

136 Davies, *The Temple of Hibis*, Part 3, pl. 68; Cruz-Uribe, *Hibis Temple Project I*, p. 179.

137 Minas-Nerpel, *Der Gott Chepri*, pp. 392–393.

dem Amunhymnus und auch den hybriden Gottheiten im Sanktuar, die oft mit Käferleib gebildet sind."[138]

WEST WALL — REGISTER I

In the first register of the west wall of chapel F, the king is consecrating (*sḳr tꜣ ḥḏ*) the white bread to the Theban triad of Amun Re, followed by Sakhmet. The first figure of Amun is destroyed, but the inscription as well as his iconography are clearly indicative of him. He is seated with his two tall plumes on a rectangular base. He is followed by his Theban triad of Mut and Khonsu, followed by Sakhmet. Mut, his consort, with her double crown and vulture headdress, is followed by Khonsu, who is represented in his mummified form with the solar disk on his head. He has the side-lock and curved beard, and he holds the long *was-ankh-djed* scepter, the *heka* crook, and the *nekhekh* flail, and stands on a rectangular base. Sakhmet with a solar disk on her leonine head holds a scepter with her left hand and the *ankh* sign with her right hand. Several scenes inside the Temple of Hibis show Amun in an upper register, joined by Osiris in the bottom register. This seems to be the case in this chapel, as discussed below.

WEST WALL — REGISTER II

The figure of the king and the first deity are largely destroyed, but the remaining hand of the king with the *nw* jar suggests that the scene was part of a wine-offering ritual. The scene of the king offering wine contained in these two small round jars is a very familiar one on the walls of temples, especially during the Ptolemaic Period.[139] In the Temple of Hibis, this offering is also common among the wall representations, perhaps because in antiquity Kharga was a major production site for wine, known as the "green eye of Horus."[140] The offering of wine is mainly a placation by the king to appease the gods so that they provide him with peace, rulership, and the destruction of his enemies.[141]

Unfortunately, the identity of the first figure cannot be confirmed on evidence of the remaining inscription. However, based on the few remaining traces of iconography of the decoration, one may suggest the figure of Osiris or a hypostasis of him, as discussed below. He is most probably seated with crossed hands, holding his insignia of the flail and the crook between his crossed hands on his chest. Above the remaining traces of his bent elbow is a pointed carved line, most probably the beginning of horizontal ram's horns as part of the elaborate *hemhem* crown. The throne of this deity is resting on a base in the form of the *mr* or canal sign, which is an unusual base decoration. Hathor is represented next, with two tall feathers and a miniature version of the Hathoric crown

138 Minas-Nerpel, *Der Gott Chepri*, p. 395ff. See also pp. 298–299, 306 for his association with the Amun hymn in the Hibis Temple.

139 Dils, "Wine for Pouring and Purification in Ancient Egypt," p. 111.

140 Dils, "Wine for Pouring and Purification in Ancient Egypt," pp. 118–121.

141 Dils, "Wine for Pouring and Purification in Ancient Egypt," p. 11; Götte, "Eine Individualcharakteristik Ptolemäischer Herrscher anhand der Epitheta-Sequenzen beim Weinopfer," pp. 63–80.

with the two horns between the sun disk in the middle. This crown lies on her tripartite wig and vulture headdress. She holds the *was* scepter with her left hand and the *ankh* in the other. According to the remaining inscription, she might have been represented as Hathor of Heracleopolis, as the sign of the seated child and the city (*niwt*) sign suggest *nn-nswt*, or Heracleopolis.

Two main goddesses of the Heliopolitan region are following Hathor. First is Nebet Hetepet, whose name means "lady of offerings" or "lady of satisfaction." She wears a crown in the shape of a naos-shaped sistrum with a uraeus and a solar disk at the center. Iusaas, whose name means "She is great when she comes," is similarly represented in a complete human form wearing a uraeus at her brow but no crown. These two goddesses belonged to the Heliopolitan theology, where they were primarily attributed to Atum as the hands that enabled his masturbation while bringing the world into existence.[142] There also seems to have been a cult established for their worship in the same region.[143] In their representations in the ancient Egyptian temples, they are usually entrusted with giving the king a long lifespan equal to that of Geb and Atum, along with millions of *Heb Sed* celebrations.[144] In the Temple of Amada, where a close parallel for the representation of the Ished tree and the coronation of the king on the south wall of chapel F has been found, a scene that represents Iusaas and Nebet Hetepet occurs beside a text that mentions that King Thutmosis III established a monument for his father Re Horakhty.[145]

The goddesses' occurrence beside Hathor perhaps underscores a deeper sexual connotation. They were considered a hypostasis of Hathor, closely associated with her fertility and aportropaic aspects.[146] Iconographically, their representations are also influenced by the Hathoric image. Nebet Hetepet usually appears with the Hathoric crown or, as in this case, the sistrum of Hathor.[147] Iusaas usually appears with the same iconography as that of Hathor, similar to Nebet Hetepet, but she also appears with the scarab on her

142 The major study on these two goddesses was done by Vandier, "Iousâas et (Hathor)-Nébet-Hétépet," pp. 55–146; Vandier, "Iousâas et (Hathor)-Nébet-Hétépet. Deuxième article," pp. 89–176; Vandier, "Iousâas et (Hathor)-Nébet-Hétépet. Troisième article," pp. 67–142; Vandier, "Iousâas et (Hathor)-Nébet-Hétépet. Quatrième article," pp. 135–148. See also Refai, "Nebet-Hetepet, Iusas und Temet, Die Weiblichen Komplemente des Atum," pp. 89–94.

143 El-Banna, "Une stèle inédite d'un prêtre-ouâb d'Hathor-Nébet-Hétépet," pp. 7–20; Vandier, "Iousâas et (Hathor)-Nébet-Hétépet," pp. 135–148.

144 Vandier, "Iousâas et (Hathor)-Nébet-Hétépet," pp. 79ff.

145 Gauthier, *Le temple d'Amada*, pp. 73, 148–149, pls. 15, 34A, 35B; Vandier "Iousâas et (Hathor)-Nébet-Hétépet," pp. 78–79.

146 Karlshausen, "Une perruque divine du Nouvel Empire: la coiffure à volants," pp. 53–173; Vandier, "Iousâas et (Hathor)-Nébet-Hétépet. Troisième article," pp. 67–142, 117ff; Derchain, "Hathor Quadrifrons. Recherches sur la syntaxe d'un mythe égyptien," pp. 50–53.

147 Beside this representation, Nebet Hetepet is depicted in hypostyle hall B and inside the sanctuary, together with other figures from the Heliopolitan region, including Iusaas; see Davies, The Temple of Hibis, Part 3, pl.3 register VI, figure 5 and pl.10, east jamb of door to J.

head inside the sanctuary in the Temple of Hibis.[148] Her representation without headgear is not unusual, but seems to appear only in a later period.[149]

The identification of the destroyed figure of the deity at the beginning of the register is important to understanding the overall meaning of the scenes on this wall. The remaining inscriptions above the figure of this deity can be translated as follows: *Ḏ[d mdw ỉ] n /// nb tꜣwy nṯr ꜥꜣ ḫnt ///ḥr ib Hbt*, "[words] spok[en b]y /// lord of the two lands, the great god foremost of /// who dwells in Hibis." However, some scholars have added *ḏ[d mdw ỉ] n /// nb [nswt] tꜣwy nṯr ꜥꜣ ḫnt [ipt swt] ḥr ib Hbt*, "[words] spok[en b]y /// lord of the [thrones] (of) the two lands, the great god foremost [of Karnak] who dwells in Hibis."[150] The outline in Davies' publication provides no evidence for this reading, nor does the personal collation of the wall. I believe that this proposed reconstruction was influenced by the author's preconceived theory of the identification of the god as Amun. Thus, identifying the god must rest on other criteria.

The iconography of the figure seems to tilt the balance toward Osiris more than Amun. Three main features are clear in the representation: the base of the throne takes the shape of a *mr* sign of a lake, the figure was most probably mummiform, and the elaborate *hemhem* crown seems to consist of three *atef* crowns, with two uraei, two ram's horns, and three to six solar disks.[151] The *hemhem* crown first appeared under Akhenaten as an alternative to the *atef* crown and seems to have developed between the 18th and 21st dynasties.[152] Only one example of Amun appears with similar depiction. In that example, he is in front of King Ramesses II in Karnak, together with his triad of Mut and Khonsu.[153] He stands in his traditional anthropomorphic image with no indication of a mummiform shape, on a rectangular base, under which run streams of water that continue under the feet of the following deities. He is represented with the *hemhem* crown, but only as an "added element" to his traditional crown of the distinct two feathers, with ram horns, cow horns, and Amun's horns.[154]

Osiris appears numerous times with the *hemhem* crown as well as its original prototype, the *atef* crown.[155] The association of Osiris with water is evident from his aspect of resurrection and renewal, as he was responsible for and identified with the annual inundation of the Nile.[156] For example, in the Papyrus of Hunefer, Osiris in a mummiform position is preceded by Isis and Nephthys, wearing the *atef* crown, with the crook and flail in his hands. The inscription mentions his usual epithet of *ḫnti-imntt* or "foremost of the westerners." Moreover, he is depicted seated on a base in the form of a lake of water.

---

148 Davies, *The Temple of Hibis*, Part 3, pl. 3, VI.

149 As in *E* I, p. 201, 14; *E* IX, pl. 24a.

150 Davies, *The Temple of Hibis*, Part 3, pl. 17; Cruz-Uribe, *Hibis Temple Project I*, p. 82.

151 Collier, *The Crowns of Pharaoh: Their Development and Significance in Ancient Egyptian Kingship*, pp. 41–42.

152 See Collier, *The Crowns of Pharaoh*, table 7 on p. 52.

153 For this unique representation of Amun, see Gabolde, "L'inondation sous les pieds d'Amon," pp. 235–258.

154 Collier, *The Crowns of Pharaoh*, p. 96; Nelson, *Hypostyle Hall*, pl. 36.

155 Collier, *The Crowns of Pharaoh*, pp. 41ff.

156 Pécoil, "Les sources mythiques du Nil et le cycle de la crue," pp. 7–110.

From this base sprouts a lotus flower; on top stand four miniature mummiform deities, perhaps the Four Sons of Horus.[157]

In the later Greco-Roman temples, the *hemhem* crown reappears and seems to be often associated with primordial-solar deities who were a developed form of the child-god Horus, like Mandulis, Harsomtus, and Arsaphes. Mandulis, for example, appears in anthropomorphic form or as a human-headed bird, often wearing the *hemhem* crown and sometimes squatting on a lotus flower over a pedestal taking the form of a similar *mr* sign.[158] Harsomtus, or "Horus Sema-Tawey," was also closely connected with the *hemhem* crown, especially in the Temple of Edfu.[159] He was the son of Hathor[160] and took part in the coronation ceremony of the king.[161] He was related to Somtus, the child god of Heracleopolis Magna, or Ihnasia.[162] Both of these gods were represented as a newly born sun on a lotus flower. The relationship with water and thus with the *mr* sign of the scene in chapel F might stem from Harsomtus' origin who, as a serpent, came out from the *nwn*.[163] Besides Osiris, other deities also wore this crown, especially Re Horakhty. In the Temple of Derr, he wears the *hemhem* crown, while his consort bears the title of [hieroglyphs], which could be "lady of Heracleopolis,"[164] similar to the title of the following goddess in the Hibis scene.

Another important god that belonged to that group of primordial solar gods is Heryshef, or Arsaphes, whose name means "he who is upon his lake."[165] He emerged from the first primeval water as a creator god and was associated with the Ba of Re and the Ba of Osiris.[166] Heryshef was usually represented as a ram-headed mummiform deity. His strong association with Osiris in particular might have led to his depiction with the

157 Budge, *Osiris and the Egyptian Resurrection*, p. 1, figure on p. 20. This motive was most popular during the New Kingdom, represented with variation especially on Memphite stelae depicting Osiris; Berlandini, "Varia Memphitica VI. La stèle de Parâherounemyef," p. 42, n.3.

158 Gauthier, *Le temple de Kalabchah. Les temples immergés de la Nubie*, pl. xxxv (in the pro-cella, north wall, second register, second tableau). For the iconography of Mandoulis, see Desroches-Noblecourt, "Les zélateurs de Mandoulis et les maitres de Ballana et de Qustul," pp. 203ff, pls. i–viii, Hofmann, "Miszellen zu einigen meroitischen Götterdarstellungen," pp. 43–44.

159 For example *E* I, p. 572, 11; *E* IX, pl. 38; *E* II, p. 203, 3; *E* IX, pl. xliiia.

160 Gestermann, "Hathor, Harsomtus und *Mnṯw-ḥtp.w* II.," pp. 763–776; El-Kordy, "Deux études sur Harsomtous," pp. 171–186.

161 Louant, "Harsomtus the Child, Son of Horus of Edfu, and the Triple Confirmation of the Royal Power," pp. 225–250.

162 Quaegebeur, "Somtous l'Enfant sur le lotus," pp. 113–121.

163 Morenz and Schubert, *Der Gott auf der Blume. Eine ägyptische Kosmogonie und ihre weltweite Bildwirkung*, pp. 37ff.

164 Blackman, *The Temple of Derr*, pl. v (first pillared hall, north wall, scene VII).

165 Vandier, "Iousâas et (Hathor)-Nébet-Hétépet. Troisième article," pp. 111–112 is the first scholar to point out this association of the figure with the god Heryshef, but he still labels the figure as Amun Re; he says: "mais il est probable qu' Amon est, ici, en dépit de son titre, très proche de Hérichef."

166 Altenmüller, " Harsaphes," cols. 1015–1018.

hemhem crown. Not only can he be connected to this scene based on the iconographical evidence, but also through a strong theological connection to the following figure of Hathor of Heracleopolis Magna, the city that was his major cult center.[167] The same city is closely connected with the coronation of Osiris.[168] Heryshef seems to have played an important part in the king's accession to the throne as well. This is apparent from the autobiography of Somtutefnakht who witnessed the second Persian Period.[169] In this text, Somtutefnakht asserts that he has been summoned back to Egypt by a dream-vision of Heryshef who also aided Alexander the Great in attaining the throne of Egypt and defeating the Persians.[170]

Besides this debatable occurrence in chapel F, Heryshef is attested, though mostly in name,[171] a few times in the Hibis Temple. Most importantly, his name is found inside chapel L, which is mainly reserved for the representations of the kingship scenes, the unification of the two lands under the king, and the divinity of the king. On the main inscription of the north wall, several acclamations or hymns (*ḥknw*) are recited for many divinities. Among them is Heryshef, who is described as "the powerful one, foremost of Abydos nome."[172] This inscription reveals the important close association of Osiris and Heryshef in the Hibis Temple and their position in the king's coronation ceremonies.

Significant evidence for this identification of the enigmatic figure as Heryshef comes from other sources where some of the deities of the second register of the west wall occur together. In the Temple of Ramesses III at Karnak, the king offers *nw* jars to Heryshef and Hathor Nebet Hetepet.[173] Ram-headed Heryshef is seated with the *atef* crown and the epithets *nsw tꜣwy nṯr ꜥꜣ nb pt*, "king of the two lands, the great god, lord of heaven." Hathor Nebet Hetepet stands behind him with the Hathoric crown, and she bears the title *ỉrt Rꜥ*, "the eye of Re." The name of Hathor of Heracleopolis appears next to that of

167 Mokhtar, "Relations between Ihnasya and Memphis during the Ramesside Period," pp. 105–107. For the importance of this city, see Kees, *Ancient Egypt: A Cultural Topography*, "Heracleoplolis and the Fayum," pp. 213–230.

168 Kees, "Totenbuchstudien: Ein Mythus vom Königtum des Osiris in Herakleopolis aus dem Totenbuch Kap. 175," p. 65; Goyon, "Le cérémonial pour faire sortir Sokaris. Papyrus Louvre I. 3079, col. 112–114," p. 91, n. 25.

169 His autobiography is inscribed on a stela found in the Temple of Isis at Pompei, currently in the Naples Museum, no. 1035, Lichtheim, *Ancient Egyptian Literature*, III, pp. 41–44.

170 Lichtheim, *Ancient Egyptian Literature*, III, pp. 41–44.

171 One exception might be a mummiform standing figure with a ram's head and double crown on top of a pair of horizontal horns in the sanctuary. There is no inscription to suggest his identity as Heryshef except that he is grouped together with other deities from the Heracleopolitan region (Davies, T*he Temple of Hibis*, Part 3, pl. 3, register II, fig. 11) and not far from the representation of the goddesses Nebet Hetepet and Iusaas, and may be also in Davies, *The Temple of Hibis*, Part 3, pl 5, south reveal, register I, fig. 3.

172 Davies, *The Temple of Hibis*, Part 3, p. 23, pl. 27 (line 12 from left); Cruz-Uribe, *Hibis Temple Project I*, p. 109. These hymns may have been recited by the king or his representative Iunmutef, who are depicted on the east wall, after his proclamation as divine king on the first registers of the chapel; see Davies, *The Temple of Hibis*, Part 3, pls. 26–27.

173 Nelson, *Reliefs and Inscriptions at Karnak*, II, pl. 97.

Nebet Hetepet in Papyrus Bremner-Rhind, in a ceremony of the feast of Sokar.[174] Just like Osiris,[175] Heryshef was connected to the city of Heliopolis. He bears the title "foremost one (*ḫnt*) of Heliopolis" since the time of Osorkon I in Bubastis.[176] In that scene in Bubastis, the inscription records "what the majesty of the king donated to the temple of his father Re Horakhty," which included a chapel in gold, statues, sphinx statues of lapis lazuli, and a chapel of 100,000 *deben* presented to Hathor Nebet Hetepet.[177] Similar to the composition in chapel F, Heryshef appears in the Temple of Abu Simbel as an intermediate deity between the representation of Hathor of Heliopolis on one side and Ptah of the *st wrt* on the other.[178] In this register, the god seems to assimilate the identity of Heryshef into an Osirian character to best suit the overall composition of the west wall and the whole of the chapel F. This god reinforces the interpretation of the room as relating to the celebrations of the king's coronation among other memorializations of the Memphite and Heliopolitan festivities.

A beautiful stela in the Cairo Museum (JE 3299), dating to the 20th dynasty,[179] provides valuable evidence of such representations of the two gods in one scene, as indicated by both inscription and iconography. Parâherounemyef, the owner of the stela, and his wife are adoring Osiris who is seated on his throne in his mummified form, holding the crook and flail. He wears an elaborate *atef* crown with a uraeus and ram horns. The base of his throne might have been understood as a pool of water, because a lotus flower carrying the four mummified small-scale divinities emerges from under his feet, from that base, in a manner similar to the previously mentioned scene of Osiris in the Payprus of Hunefer. Osiris is followed by the two protectresses Isis and Nephthys, according to the inscriptions above them, but their iconography is assimilated into that of Hathor. Their distinctive emblems are minimized and placed as a motif in the center of the Hathoric crown of the solar disk between the two cow's horns.[180] The inscription in front of Osiris is revealing as to the meaning of this specific iconography. The main inscription of the first register of the stela mentions a hymn to Osiris that begins: "Adoration to Osiris, foremost of the west, Wennefer, lord of eternity, great god who came from the *nwn*, divine falcon, king of the gods, lord of power, great of respect, lord of the great *atef* crowns in

174 Faulkner, *The Papyrus Bremner-Rhind*, pp. 35–41, cols. 19, 22, with parallel in Papyrus Louvre I. 3079, col. 113, II: Goyon, "Le cérémonial pour faire sortir Sokaris. Papyrus Louvre I. 3079, cols. 112–114," pp. 78–79.

175 For a general review of the literature on Osiris and the city of Heliopolis, see El-Banna, "A propos des aspects Héliopolitains d'Osiris," pp. 101–126.

176 Naville, *The Festival-Hall of Osorkon II. in the Great Temple of Bubastis*, pl. 51, G. 2, 1.4, p. 61; Vandier, "Iousâas et (Hathor)-Nébet-Hétépet," pp. 75, 93, n. 4 (document BXXXVI).

177 Naville, *The Festival-Hall of Osorkon II. in the Great Temple of Bubastis*, pl. 51, G. 2, 1.4, p. 61; Vandier, "Iousâas et (Hathor)-Nébet-Hétépet," pp. 75, 93, n. 4 (document BXXXVI).

178 Gundlach, "Das Dekorationsprogramm der Tempel von Abu Simbel und ihre kultische und königsideologische Funktion,"p. 63, fig. 2.

179 Berlandini, "Varia Memphitica VI. La stèle de Parâherounemyef," pl. XL.

180 Nephthys is indicated only by a silhouette behind Isis. This makes their image appear as one Hathorian goddess. Mariette did not recognize her image in the early publication of the stela; Mariette, *Monuments divers recueillis en Égypte et en Nubie*, pl. 61.

Heracleopolis...."[181] Both the inscription and the vignette combine the elements of Osiris with the coming from the *nwn* or primeval ocean, the association with the *atef* crown, and, more importantly, to the city of Heracleopolis where Heryshef was its lord. The syncretism of Isis and Nephthys into Hathor may be a further reference to the goddess Hathor of Heracleopolis.

The overwhelming Osirian attributes of Heryshef during that time, building on New Kingdom religious thought, might have been the impetus of the later emergence and increased popularity of similar deities in the Greco-Roman temples, such as Mandulis, Harsomtus, and Harpokrates who, besides having a solar origin, were closely connected with the Osirian triad and the city of Ihnasia, or Heracleopolis.[182] This reveals one of the most valuable aspects of the Temple of Hibis as a link between the theological tradition of the earlier Pharaonic Period, especially of the Ramesside Period, and the later Greco-Roman tradition.

181 Berlandini, "Varia Memphitica VI. La stèle de Parâherounemyef," pp. 52ff.

182 For studies on these deities see papers in Budde, *Kindgötter im Ägypten der griechisch-römischen Zeit: Zeugnisse aus Stadt und Tempel als Spiegel des interkulturellen Kontakts.*

3
Chapel G

1. DESCRIPTION

Chapel G is located to the south of hypostyle hall B between chapels F and H. The decoration of this chapel, like its neighbor chapel F, is in shallow sunken relief but exhibits greater detail and more remaining color.[1]

THE DOORWAY — LINTEL OF DOOR TO CHAPEL G

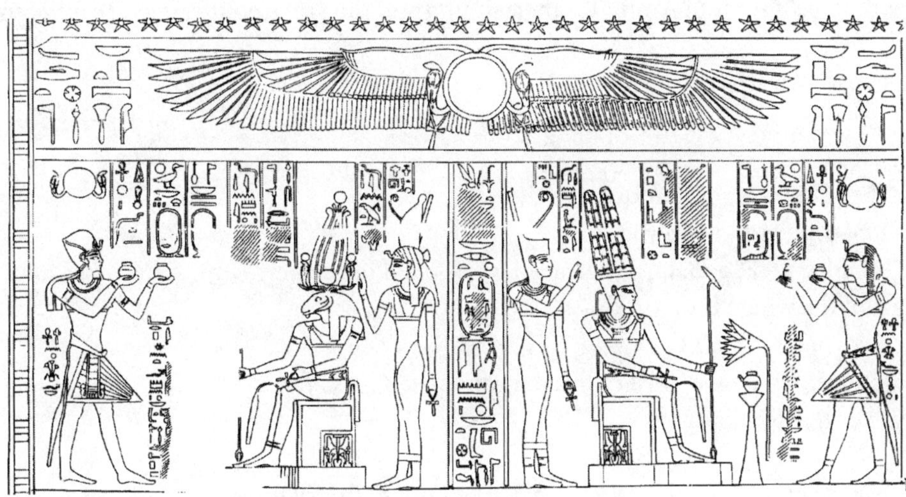

Figure 10: Lintel of door to chapel G
(after Davies, *The Temple of Hibis*, Part 3, detail from pl. 12)

Although the doorway of the neighboring chapel F is mostly destroyed, that of chapel G is completely preserved. The lintel is divided into two registers, framed at the top by the star-filled extended *pt* sign of the sky. In the upper register, Behdet is depicted as a solar disk with extended wings. Two uraei flank the solar disk and each has a pendant *ankh* sign. The lower register of the lintel is comprised of two almost mirror-image compositions, similar to the main vignettes on the lintel decoration to the other chapels around the sanctuary. On this lintel the king is offering wine to Amun Re who is seated on a throne.

1 For the publication of this chapel and its doorway see Winlock, *The Temple of Hibis*, Part 1, p. 12, pls. XXXIII, XXXVI, XXXVII; Davies, *The Temple of Hibis*, Part 3, p. 19, pls. 12 and 18; Cruz-Uribe, *Hibis Temple Project I*, pp. 64–65, 82–85.

A standing female deity behind the throne is raising one hand in a protection gesture and holding a pendant *ankh* sign at her side with her other hand. These two scenes vary in the iconography of the crowns of the king, the head and crown of the god Amun Re, and the iconography and identification of the goddesses. On the right side, the king is represented under the protection of the solar disk, with one uraeus wearing the crown of Upper Egypt and one uraeus wearing the crown of Lower Egypt. The king wears the *nemes* headdress and a belted kilt with a starched, pleated, triangular apron, a sash, and an ox tail. He offers two *nw* wine jars to the seated Amun Re, who is represented with a human head. Amun Re has a curved beard and wears a crown that consists of a modius topped by two tall feathers. Amunet of Karnak is represented behind the seated figure of Amun Re. A *nemset* jar atop a libation table and a large open lotus flower with the bloom bent toward Amun Re are depicted between the figure of the king and the god. On the left, the king wears the blue crown and stands under the protection of the solar disk with the two uncrowned uraei. He wears a belted kilt with a starched, pleated, triangular apron, an ox tail, and an elaborate sash terminating in two uraei with solar disks. He offers two *nw* wine jars to a ram-headed Amun Re seated on a throne. Mut stands behind the throne. The nearby lintel of the door to staircase E depicts a similar scene, except that the figures of Amun Re are standing and the types of offerings are different.[2]

THE INSCRIPTION

Register I

Right of the winged sun disk

Bḥdt nṯr ꜥꜣ nb pt sꜣb šwty

"Behdet, great god, lord of heaven, variegated of feathers."

Left of the winged sun disk

Bḥdt nṯr ꜥꜣ nb pt sꜣb šwty

"Behdet, great god, lord of heaven, variegated of feathers."

Register II, Right Side

Above the king

Nṯr nfr nb tꜣwy (///Hbt)¦ sꜣ Rꜥ nb ḫꜥwt (…)¦ di ꜥnḫ ḏt mi Rꜥ

"Good god, lord of the two lands, (///Hibis)¦, son of Re, lord of appearances, (…)¦, given life like Re forever."

Behind the king

Sꜣ ꜥnḫ ḥꜣ.f nb mi Rꜥ

"All protection and life behind him like Re."

In front of the king

Ḥnk irp n it.f Imn [Rꜥ] nb nswt tꜣwy

"Presenting wine to his father, Amun [Re], lord of the thrones of the two lands."

Above Amun Re

Ḏ[d mdw]///[nb n]swt tꜣw[y] ḫnt Ipt swt

"Wo[rds Spoken] /// lord of the thrones of the t[wo] lands, foremost of Karnak."

2 See p. 147 below.

Above Amunet

Ḏd mdw in ꞽImnt nb[t] ꞽIpt swt

"Words spoken by Amunet, lady of Karnak."

Register II, Left Side

Above the king

Nṯr nfr nb tꜣwy (...)| sꜣ Rꜥ nb ḫꜥwt ([Dry]š)| di ꜥnḫ ḏt mi Rꜥ

"Good god, lord of the two lands, (...)|, son of Re, lord of appearances ([Dariu]s)| given life like Re forever."

Behind the king

Sꜣ ꜥnḫ ḥꜣ.f nb

"All protection and life behind him."

In front of the king

Ḥnk irp n it.f ꞽImn Rꜥ nb Hbt nṯr ꜥꜣ wsr [ḫp]š

"Presenting wine to his father Amun Re, lord of Hibis, great god, powerful of [stre]ngth."

Above Amun Re

Ḏd mdw in ꞽImn Rꜥ/// nṯr ꜥꜣ wsr ḫpš

"Words spoken by Amun Re, /// great god, powerful of strength."

Above Mut

Ḏd mdw in Mwt ḥr ib Hbt

"Words spoken by Mut, who dwells in Hibis."

The central line of inscription

Nsw biti nb [tꜣwy] nb irt ḫt (Dryš)| mry ꞽImn Rꜥ nb Hbt nṯr ꜥꜣ wsr ḫpš

"King of Egypt, lord [of the two lands], lord of cult act, (Darius)|, beloved of Amun Re, lord of Hibis, great god, powerful of strength."

THE DOORWAY — JAMBS OF DOOR TO CHAPEL G

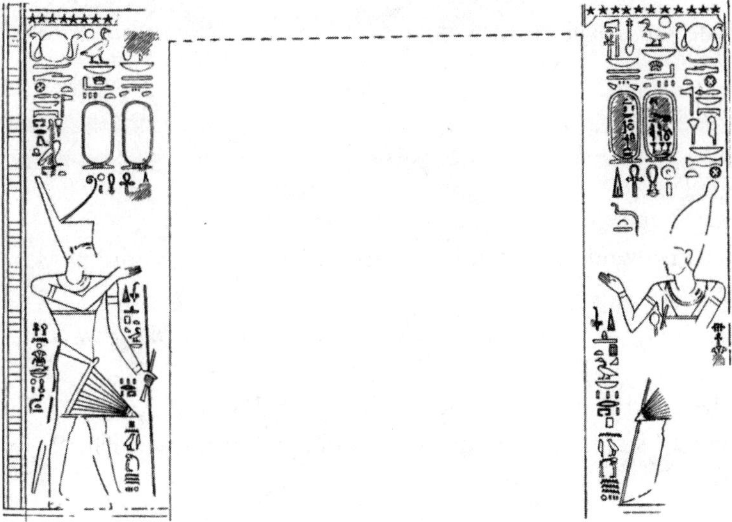

Figure 11: Jambs of door to chapel G
(after Davies, The Temple of Hibis, Part 3, detail from pl. 12)

Each of the two jambs of the door to chapel G represents a standing figure of king Darius surrounded by his names and epithets, making a *Hetep-di-nsw* offering to the purified ones who enter this chapel. On the left jamb, the king wears the red crown of Lower Egypt and a belted kilt with a starched, pleated, triangular apron. He holds his staff and mace with one hand, while raising the other hand in an offering gesture. The same features are repeated on the right jamb, except that he wears the white crown of Upper Egypt. Both representations of the king are depicted under the protection of Behdet who is represented as a solar disk with two uraei.

LEFT JAMB OF DOOR TO CHAPEL G

THE INSCRIPTION

Below sun disk

Bḥdt nṯr ꜥꜣ nb pt sꜣb šwty pri m ꜣḫt

"Behdet, great god, lord of heaven, vareigated of feathers, who goes forth from the horizon."

Above the king

[*Nṯr*] *nfr nb tꜣwy* (…)¦*sꜣ Rꜥ nb ḫꜥwt* (…)¦ *d*[*i*] *ꜥnḫ mi Rꜥ ḏt*

"Good [god], lord of the two lands, (…)¦, gi[ven] life like Re forever."

Behind the king

Sꜣ ꜥnḫ ḥꜣ.f nb mi Rꜥ ḏt

"All protection and life behind him like Re forever."

In front of the king

Ḥtp di nsw ꜥḳ nbw r pr pn iw wꜥbw wꜥbw wꜥbw wꜥbw

"*Hetep-di-nsw* (offering) (to) all who enter this temple, being pure, pure, pure, pure."

RIGHT JAMB OF DOOR TO CHAPEL G

THE INSCRIPTION

Below sun disk

Bḥdt nṯr ꜥꜣ nb pt sꜣb šwty nb msn

"Behdet, great god, lord of heaven, variegated of feathers, lord of Mesen."

Above the king

ꜥnḫ nṯr nfr nb tꜣwy (*mry Ỉmn Rꜥ nb Hbt wsr hpš*)¦ *sꜣ Rꜥ nb ḫꜥwt* (*Dryš*)¦ *di ꜥnḫ ḏt mi Rꜥ*

"Live the good god, lord of the two lands, (beloved of Amun Re, lord of Hibis, powerful of strength)¦, son of Re, lord of appearances, (Darius)¦, given life like Re forever."

Behind the king

Sꜣ ꜥnḫ ḥꜣ.[*f nb*]*///*

"[All] protection and life behind [him] ///"

In front of the king

Ḥtp di nsw ʿḳ nbw r pr pn iw wʿbw wʿbw wʿbw wʿbw

"*Hetep-di-nsw* (offering) (to) all who enter this temple, being pure, pure, pure, pure."

THE PANEL BETWEEN CHAPEL F AND CHAPEL G

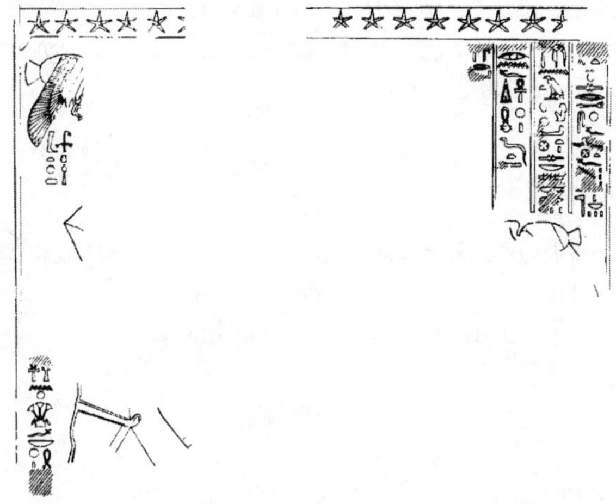

Figure 12: Panel between chapel F and chapel G
(after Davies, *The Temple of Hibis*, Part 3, detail from pl. 12)

Most of the scene in this panel is destroyed. On the left side, traces indicate that the king is wearing the blue crown and a belted kilt. Nekhbet is depicted in vulture form above the king's head. On the right are traces of Mut's head, with her iconographic vulture headdress. Traces of an inscription attest to a third figure, unfortunately now lost, at the center of the scene.

THE INSCRIPTION

Below Nekhbet

Nḫbt ḥḏ Nḫn

"Nekhbet, the White one of Hierakonpolis."

Behind the king

Sꜣ ʿnḫ ḥꜣ.f nb mi Rʿ///

"All protection and life behind him like Re///"

Above missing figure between Mut and king

/// Wsr ḫpš/// ir n.f di ʿnḫ mi Rʿ ḏt

"/// powerful, /// for he has made a giving life like Re forever."

Above Mut

Ḏd mdw in Mwt ʿḥʿ niwt.s nbt pḏwt ḥ[nt] sšr ḫsf ḫryw nṯrw nbw

"Words spoken by Mut, fighter of her city, lady of the bows, mis[tress] of the arrow, who overthrows the enemies of all the gods."

THE REVEALS OF THE DOOR TO CHAPEL G

EAST REVEAL

Sꜣ Rꜥ Dryš///m[r] ꞽImn Rꜥ nb Hbt nṯr ꜥꜣ wsr ḫpš ỉr n.k pr nfrw
"Son of Re, Darius///, b[eloved] of Amun Re, lord of Hibis, great god, mighty of power, who made for you a house of beauties."

WEST REVEAL

Sḥb nṯr ḥwt.k m ḫt///pr n.k m ḏw3// ḏi ꜥnḫ ḏt
"He who adorned your temple after/// you have gone forth from the mountains, given life forever."

Figure 13: East and west reveals of door to chapel G (after Davies, *The Temple of Hibis*, Part 3, detail from pl. 18)

EAST WALL —REGISTER I

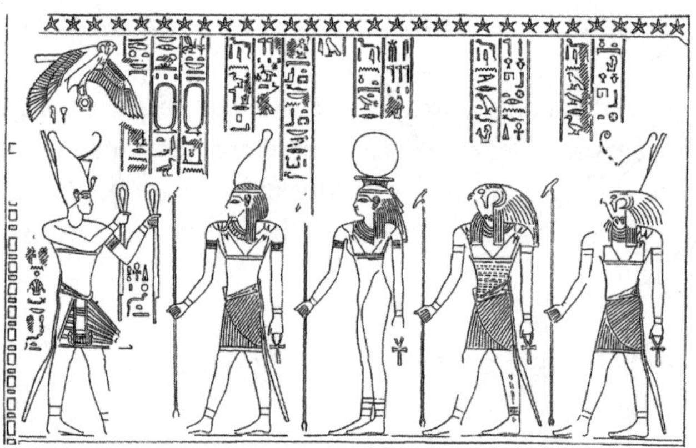

Figure 14: East wall of chapel G, Register I (after Davies, The *Temple of Hibis*, Part 3, detail from pl. 18)

In this scene the striding figure of the king faces right and wears the double crown, a uraeus, a kilt with a starched, pleated, triangular apron, an ox tail, and a decorated sash ending in two cobras with solar disks. He wears what appears to be a strapless shirt. Above the king's head is Behdet as a falcon holding the *shen* sign. The king offers linen to the human-headed Geb, who is standing in front of him wearing the white crown and holding the *was* scepter out in front of his body with his right hand and the *ankh* sign at his side with his left. Geb wears a curved beard, a broad collar, a two-strap garment with a pleated knee-length kilt, and an ox tail. Behind Geb stands his spouse, Nut, with her distinctive solar disk on top of a modius headdress. She wears a long tripartite wig,

3 The *pr* determinative for *ḏw* is unique; see discussion of *ḏw* and *nfrw* on pp. 71ff. and 81ff.

a broad collar, bracelets, armlets, anklets, and a long sheath garment with two straps. She, like Geb, holds the *was* scepter and the *ankh* sign. Next follows the falcon-headed Merymutef without any headdress. His clothing and jewelry are similar to Geb's and the following god Herwer's, except that his two-strap shirt appears to have had some kind of decoration, as suggested by the remaining black outlined rectangles. Herwer is standing at the end of the register with the double crown on his falcon head. He wears a two-strap garment with a pleated knee-length kilt and an ox tail. He holds the *was* scepter and the *ankh* sign.

THE INSCRIPTION

Behind the king

S3 ꜥnḫ ḥ3.f nb mi Rꜥ ḏt

"All protection and life (is) behind him like Re forever."

Around the falcon

Bḥdt nb pt s3b šwty

"Behdet, lord of heaven, variegated of feathers."

Above the king

Nsw biti nb t3wy (…)¦ nb irt ḫt (…)¦ di sšr n it.f gb nṯr nfr[4] *ir n.[f] di ꜥnḫ mi Rꜥ ḏt.*

"King of Upper and Lower Egypt, lord of the two lands (…)¦, lord of cult act. Presenting linen[5] to his father Geb, the good god [who] made giving life like Re forever."

Above Geb

Ḏd mdw in Gb rpꜥty nṯrw <m> bw šm3yw// ḥry st.f nb n bw nb mr k3.f i

"Words spoken by Geb, prince of the gods[6] <in> the place of wandering/wilderness,[7]

---

4 *Nṯr nfr* are partially destroyed, but one can still read the *nṯr* sign. However, the following sign could also be the seated god determinative.

5 Because the bag of linen is still visible, maybe the translation "linen" is more appropriate here than "cloth," see *Wb*. IV, p. 295, 12 and 13.

6 The title *rpꜥt nṯrw* is attested since the Old Kingdom and is most commonly associated with Geb; see Piankoff, *The Litany of Re. Texts Translated with Commentary*, IV, pp. 87 and 148; Leitz, *Lexikon* VII, p. 304; IV, p. 665.

7 This is a difficult title to translate because the inscriptions are unclear and the remaining signs are obscure. Cruz-Uribe (*Hibis Temple Project I*, p. 82) translated it as "True Ba in Mankind?;" however, such title is not attested. "True Ba" is attested only once in Seele, *The Tomb of Tjanefer at Thebes*, pl. 30, but even there "*bw šm3w*" is arguable as an alternative translation. The latter text mentions a list of gods and a wish that their name endure (*rwḏ*) in Heliopolis. This is the same pattern that occurs with the more common title "*bw šm3w*," particularly in connection with Geb, where for example at Edfu (*E* I, p. 504 [32] and [45]), a list of 24 deities with a wish for their name to endure (*rwḏ*), including Geb *m bw šm3w* is found in association with Heliopolis, also repeated in the Book of Breathing P CG 58007 III, 8 and P Louvre N 3083, IX, 6–7. For other examples see Leitz, *Lexikon*, VII, p. 307. One is inclined to think that this instance on this register in chapel G is a variation on the later more common title of Geb "*Gb m bw šm3yw*," "Geb in the place of wandering"; see Leitz, Lexikon, VII, pp. 306–307 (Gb am Ort der Herumirrenden); Wb.

lord of his every seat of every place which his Ka desires.[8]"

Above Nut

Ḏd mdw in Nwt wrt ms nṯrw

"Words spoken by Nut, the great one, who bore the gods."

Above Merymutef

Ḏd mdw in Mry-mwt.f nṯr ꜥ3 ḥr ib Hbt ir n.f di ꜥnḫ

"Words spoken by Merymutef, great god, who dwells in Hibis. He has made a giving life."

Above Herwer

Ḏd mdw in Ḥr-wr s3 Nwt ḥr ib Hbt

"Word spoken by Herwer, son of Nut, who dwells in Hibis."

EAST WALL — REGISTER II

Figure 15: East wall of chapel G, Register II
(after Davies, *The Temple of Hibis*, Part 3, detail from pl. 18)

The king stands below Behdet who is represented as a winged solar disk with two uraei. The king wears the blue crown with a uraeus on the forehead. Much of the lower part of

IV, p. 471. The word *šm3w* is very intriguing; scholars translate it as "(place of) wandering around" (related to Geb), but the root meaning designates a foreigner or a stranger. Wb. IV, p. 471, *šm3* "be wild untamed," *šm3yw* "foreigners;" see Wilson, Lexicon, pp. 1008ff who says that "*šm3w*" refers to someone who is not Egyptian. It occurs in the epithets of gods with influence over areas with foreign contacts. The word "*šm3yw*" would then explain the seated person determinative at the top of the third line of the inscription in this register in chapel G. This title of Geb occurs in connection with other tiles like "*Gb m ḏw*" and "*Gb m ḏw s3ḫ-bw*;" see Faulkner, An Ancient Egyptian Book of Hours, col. 20, 14–16. One may translate this sentence, then, as "Geb of the place of wilderness," referring to a periphery of the city, (like in Heliopolis, where it might have been referring to the outside of Heliopolis or its suburb) or the wild and the strangeness of a place.

8 A variant of *Gb m bw nb mr k3.f im*; see Leitz, *Lexikon*, VII, p. 306.

the king's figure is destroyed, but the starched triangular kilt apron and belt are still visible. According to the inscription, he is offering jars of wine to Sopdu, who is standing in front of him. Sopdu wears a headdress of two tall plumes with a small solar disk in between. His head is unfortunately almost completely destroyed, but we can surmise that he was falcon-headed based on the surviving line forming the outline of the upper back of his head and his typical appearance elsewhere. He holds the *was* scepter and probably the *ankh* sign as well. The details of the muscles on his calf have been given careful attention, which is also visible on the legs of the following god, Hedjhotep. Hedjhotep has a human head, a curved beard, and no headdress. He wears a broad collar and a two-strap garment with a pleated knee-length kilt. He holds the *was* scepter and the *ankh* sign. Hedjhotep is followed by the Two Ladies of Upper and Lower Egypt, Nekhbet and Wadjet, who are both standing, each with her appropriate headdress. Nekhbet wears the white crown of Upper Egypt; Wadjet wears the red crown of Lower Egypt. They are dressed in similar long, tight-fitting, shin-length sheath garments with two straps, although a second strap is not clearly depicted on Wadjet's garment. They each hold the *ankh* sign and the *was* scepter.

THE INSCRIPTION

Above the king

Nṯr nfr nb tȝwy (…)¦ *nb irt ḫt* (…)¦ *ḥnk*] //*irp nt*/// *Hbt ir n di ʿnḫ mi rʿ ḏt*

"Good god lord of the two lands (…)¦ lord of cult act (…)¦ [presenting] wine of/// Hibis, he has made a giving of life like Re forever."

Behind the king

Sȝ n///

"Protection of///"

Underneath Behdet

Bḥdt nṯr ʿȝ nb pt sȝb šwty

"Behdet, great god, lord of heaven, variegated of feather."

In front of Sopdu

Ḏd mdw in spd nfr sȝ wnt[9]

"Words spoken by Sopdu, the perfect, son of Wenut."

Behind Sopdu[10]

Smsm[11] *Ḥr*/ [*smȝ bḥdt?*][12] *nṯr ʿȝ ḥr ib Hbt ir n.f di ʿnḫ*

"The eldest, Horus [of Tell El Ballamun?], great god who dwells in Hibis, he has made a giving of life."

Above Hedjhotep

Ḏd mdw in Ḥḏ-ḥtp nṯr ʿȝ ḥr ib Hbt mr sȝ.f ʿnḫ nṯr ʿȝ.

---

9 The heart is a mistake for the *nw* jar; see Cruz-Uribe, *Hibis Temple Project I*, p. 83, n. 277.

10 The two tall plumes of Sopdu divide the inscriptions belonging to him.

11 This is a variant writing of *smsw* in *Wb*. VI, p. 142.

12 The signs at the beginning of the second line of inscription after Sopdu are difficult to read. The suggesstion of the reading of the name of *Smȝ Bḥdt* is followed by Davies, *The Temple of Hibis*, Part 3, p. 19, pl.18; Cruz-Uribe, *Hibis Temple Project I*, p. 83; Leitz, *Lexikon* VI, p. 354. For a detailed discussion of this title, see pp. 76ff.

"Words spoken by Hedjhotep, great god who dwells in Hibis, who loves his living son, the great god."

In front and above Nekhbet

Ḏd mdw in nḫbt ḥḏ [nḫ]n ꜣwt f [-ˁ]g di. K ///? ḥr ib Hbt ir n.s di ˁnḫ mi Rˁ

"Words spoken by Nekhbet, the white one of [Nekhe]n, long [of talon], [lady of] f[a]g, who dwells in Hibis, she made a giving of life like Re."

Above and in front of Wadjet

Ḏd mdw in Wꜣḏt nbt p dp ḫnt Pr wr ḥr [r-pr//?] ir s di ˁnḫ

"Words spoken by Wadjet, the lady of Pe and Dep, mistress of the Perwer shrine, in the [temple], as she makes a giving of life."

SOUTH WALL — REGISTER I

Figure 16: South wall of chapel G, Register I
(after Davies, *The Temple of Hibis*, Part 3, detail from pl. 18)

In this scene the king is running with the *hes* vessels in front of the triad of Amun. He wears the white crown of Upper Egypt with a uraeus and a false beard. His upper body is bare except for a broad collar. He wears a pleated *shendyet* kilt and an ox tail. Behind the king are the *Heb Sed* symbols, and Behdet as a solar disk with the two uraei holding the *ankh* signs is above him in the upper-right corner. Amun Re is seated on an intricate throne positioned atop an elaborately decorated base. He wears his tall crown of the two plumes, a curved beard, a collar, and a shrine-shaped pectoral. He also wears a knee-length kilt with a decorated belt. He holds the *was* scepter with his left hand and the *ankh* sign with his right hand, opposite the order of the figures on the east wall. The side of his throne bears the Sema-Tawey motif in the corner. Between the seat and the base is a rectangular foot rest or mat decorated with horizontal and vertical lines. The throne base is decorated with the *ankh* sign between two *was* symbols, on top of the *nb* sign. This motif is repeated eight times and framed by a border of small and large rectangles, of the same design as the vertical frames of every wall of the room. Mut is standing behind Amun Re, gently touching his left shoulder. She wears the double crown on her vulture headdress, a long, tight-fitting, shin-length garment with two straps, two armlets, a broad collar, and probably two bracelets and anklets. Behind Mut stands the falcon-headed Khonsu wearing his distinctive lunar crescent, full lunar disk, and uraeus. He is wearing a broad collar, two armlets, two bracelets, two anklets, a two-strap garment with a knee-length pleated kilt, and an ox tail. He holds the *was* scepter with his left hand and the *ankh* sign with his right.

THE INSCRIPTION

Above the king

Nsw biti nb tȝwy (…)¦ *sȝ Rꜥ nb ḫꜥwt* (…)¦ *di ꜥnḫ mi Rꜥ ḏt*

"King of Upper and Lower Egypt, lord of the two lands (…)¦ son of Re, lord of appearances (…)¦ who gives life like Re forever."

Below the sun disk

Bḥdt nṯr ꜥȝ nb pt sȝb šwty

"Behdet, great god, lord of heaven, variegated of feathers."

In front of the king

Ḫnp[13]*ḳbḥ n it.f imn* [*Rꜥ*] *nb Hbt nṯr ꜥȝ pr m ḫnt wȝst* [*r*] *pḫr ḏwt m nfrw.f*

"Bringing cool water to his father Amun [Re], lord of Hibis, great god who goes forth from Thebes [so as] to traverse the mountainous areas by means of his beauty."[14]

Above and in front of Amun Re

Ḏd mdw in ʾImn Rꜥ nṯr ꜥȝ nb Hbt pr ḫnty wȝst irt n.f di ꜥnḫ mi Rꜥ ḏt

"Words spoken by Amun Re, great god, lord of Hibis, who goes forth from Thebes, doing for him 'given life like Re forever.'"

Above Mut

Ḏd mdw in Mwt wrt nb[*t*] *išr ḫnt Hbt di.s ꜥnḫ mi Rꜥ*

"Words spoken by Mut, great one, lady of Asher, mistress of Hibis as she gives life like Re."

Above Khonsu

Ḏd mdw in Ḫnsw nṯr ꜥȝ ḥr ib Hbt di ꜥnḫ mi Rꜥ ḏt

"Words spoken by Khonsu, great god, who resides in Hibis, giving life like Re forever.

13 *Wb.* III, p. 290, 14.

14 This statement reveals the significant theme of this room, stressing the beginning of the important trip of Amun Re from Thebes, see commentary below.

SOUTH WALL — REGISTER II

Figure 17: South wall of chapel G, Register II
(after Davies, *The Temple of Hibis*, Part 3, detail from pl. 18)

The king is wearing an elaborate composite crown combining the crowns of Upper and Lower Egypt with the *atef* crown and the horizontal ram's horns. He wears a broad collar, two bracelets, anklets, and armlets. His two-strap garment is combined with a knee-length pleated kilt. The kilt bears a decorated sash ending with two cobras with solar disks and an ox tail. He holds a mace and a *was* scepter in his left hand, while his right hand is raised upward in front of him. He is accompanied by the semi-divine Iunmutef who, like the king, is represented with an upraised right hand. He wears a side-lock, two armlets, a bracelet, and a knee-length kilt with a decorated belt. Iunmutef holds a tail, which was probably intended to represent a panther tail, a typical motif associated with priests. Osiris stands before them wearing his *atef* crown, the curved beard, a two-strap garment with a knee-length kilt, a belt, and an ox tail. He faces the king and Iunmutef and holds the *was* scepter. Behind Osiris stands his consort, Isis, with her seat-sign headdress, a filet with a uraeus, a tripartite wig, and a long two-strap sheath garment. She holds the *was* scepter with her left hand and the *ankh* sign in her right hand. Behind Isis, Nephthys is represented with the same iconography as Isis, except for her distinctive crown combining the house and *nb* signs.

THE INSCRIPTION

Above the king

Nṯr nfr nb t3wy (…)¦ *nb irt ḫt* (…)¦ *di ꜥnḫ ḏt*

"Good god, lord of the two lands (…)¦ lord of cult act, (…)¦ given life forever."

Below the arm of the king

Sm3ꜥ[15] *ꜥ3bt nit.f Wsir iti*

"Presenting an offering to his father Osiris, the sovereign."

15 "To present," *Wb*. IV, pp. 125, 1; 167, 10–12 for exact phrase. This type of offering is considered to be a funerary offering, of various ingredients of bread, beer, fruit, vegetables, and meat; Wilson, *Lexicon*, p. 136. In most of the scenes of presenting the *ꜥ3bt* offering, the

Behind the king

S3 n ꜥnḫ ḥ3.f nb mi Rꜥ

"All protection of life is behind him like Re."

In front of the sun disk

Bḥdt nṯr ꜥ3 nb pt

"Behdet, the great god, lord of heaven."

Above Iunmutef

Ḥtp di nsw n Ỉwn mwt.f n it.f Wsir

"*Hetep-di-nsw* of Iunmutef to his father, Osiris."

Above Osiris

Ḏd mdw n wsir iti nṯr ꜥ3 m st.f

"Words spoken by Osiris, the sovereign, great god in his place."

Above Isis

Ḏd mdw in 3st snt [nṯr] Wsir n st nb [mr]r k3.f im[16]

"Words spoken by Isis, [divine] sister of Osiris in any place which his Ka desires."

Above Nephthys

Nbt ḥwt snt nṯr ir n.s di ꜥnḫ mi Rꜥ ḏt

"Words spoken by Nephthys, sister of the god, for she has made a giving of life like Re forever."

WEST WALL — REGISTER I

Figure 18: West wall of chapel G, Register I
(after Davies, *The Temple of Hibis*, Part 3, detail from pl. 18)

The scene begins with the king offering the Maat symbol to Shu and Tefnut. The king stands under the Nekhbet vulture that spreads her wings and holds the *shen* sign in her

king either wears the *hmhmty* crown or, as in our scene, the *atef* crown on the red crown. Similarly, the king holds the *ḥḏ* and *3ms* staff in the left hand; ibid., p. 136.

16 This title of Osiris is a combination of the titles *Wsir m bw nb* and *Wsir mr k3.f im*; Leitz, *Lexikon*, II, pp. 543–544.

talons. The king wears a close-fitting headdress bound by a filet with the uraeus at the front, reminiscent of the type of Kushite headdress common during the 25th dynasty. He wears a one- or two-strap garment with a knee-length kilt and a starched, triangular apron. The kilt is adorned with a sash and an ox tail. A sheer skirt underneath the kilt reaches to his shin. The longer skirt is only outlined, leaving his legs visible underneath, and he wears sandals. He holds in his left hand the Maat offering while his right hand is raised upward in a pose of adoration. Shu faces the king and has his distinctive feather on top of his human head. He has a curved beard and his tripartite wig is held in place by a filet knotted at the back of his head. He wears a two-strap garment with a pleated kilt and an ox tail. He holds a scepter in his left hand and an *ankh* in his right. The lioness-headed Tefnut is represented standing behind Shu wearing her headdress of two tall plumes with the sun disk in between, atop a modius. She is depicted with a tripartite wig, a broad collar, and a long two-strap close-fitting garment. She holds the *ankh* sign in her right hand and a papyrus scepter in her left. Behind Tefnut, facing left, is another figure of the king, this time presenting an offering to Sakhmet with his left hand, while his right hand is raised upward in a pose of adoration. The king is here in a similar guise to that of his first representation on the same register, except that he does not wear the long, sheer, second garment or sandals. Instead of offering the symbol of Maat, he presents an image of a squatting baboon, which is called a *wensheb* offering. Sakhmet is represented as a lioness-headed woman with a large solar disk on her head surmounted by the body of the uraeus. She wears a long tripartite wig, a broad collar, an armlet, a bracelet, and two anklets in combination with a long, tight-fitting two-strap garment. She holds the papyrus scepter with her left hand and the *ankh* sign with her right hand.

THE INSCRIPTION

Above the king

Nṯr nfr nb t3wy (…)¦ nb irt ḫt (…)¦ di ʿnḫ ḏt

"Good god, lord of the two lands (…)¦ lord of cult act (…)¦ given life forever."

Below the vulture

Nḫbt////

"Nekhbet///"

Below the hands of the king

Di m3ʿt n it.f Šw s3 Rʿ

"Presenting Maat to his father Shu, son of Re."

Above Shu

Ḏd mdw in Šw s3 Rʿ nṯr ʿ3 ḥr ib Hbt ir.f di ʿnḫ

"Words spoken by Shu, son of Re, great god who dwells in Hibis, as he makes a giving of life."

Above Tefnut

Ḏd mdw in Tfnwt s3t Rʿ ḥr ib Hbt ir n.s di ʿnḫ mi Rʿ ḏt

"Words spoken by Tefnut, daughter of Re who dwells in Hibis, she has made a giving of life like Re forever."

Above the image of the king on the left side

Nsw biti nb tꜣwy (...)¦ nb irt ḫt (...)¦ di ʿnḫ ḏt

"King of Upper and Lower Egypt, lord of the two lands (...)¦ lord of cult act (...)¦ given life forever."

Below Behdet

Bḥdt nṯr ʿꜣ nb pt sꜣb [šwty]

"Behdet, great god, lord of heaven, variegated of [feathers]."

Behind the image of the king on the left side

Sꜣ ʿnḫ ḥꜣ.f nb mi Rʿ ḏt

"All protection and life is behind him like Re forever."

In front of the king

Ḥnk w(n)šb n mwt.f Sḫmt

"Presenting the *wensheb* offering to his mother Sakhmet."

Above Sakhmet

Ỉrt Rʿ nbt pt ḥnt nṯrw nbw ir n.s di ʿnḫ mi Rʿ ḏt

"The eye of Re, lady of heaven, mistress of all the gods, she has made a giving of life like Re forever."

West Wall — Register II

Figure 19: West wall of chapel G, Register II
(after Davies, *The Temple of Hibis*, Part 3, detail from pl. 18)

This register seems to have suffered recent damage, as the crack in the upper register has extended further downward. Although absent from Davies' drawings, this crack now separates the last two figures from the rest of the register. The king offers either wine or milk to four human-headed male deities standing before him. He wears the *nemes* headdress with the uraeus, a broad collar, two bracelets, and a belt. Unfortunately, the lower half of the king has been destroyed. He presents two vessels on his upturned palms. Isdes is the first deity facing the king. He wears a tripartite wig, a curved beard, a broad collar, a two-strap garment, and no headdress. We can see traces of the *ankh* sign in his right hand and the upper half of the *was* scepter held by his left hand. Shesmu stands behind Isdes and wears his distinctive headdress representing grape vines on props in connection to his role as a god of wine and viticulture. He wears a two-strap garment with an ox tail. Although the bottom half of this figure has been destroyed, as well as the lower portions of most of the figures in the same register, we can still see the remains of his pleated knee-length kilt. Iaqs is the third deity and he wears a headdress of two feathers with a solar disk in between. His tripartite wig is held by a double filet and he wears a two-strap garment with a knee-length pleated kilt. He holds the *was* scepter with his left hand, and traces of the *ankh* sign are visible coming from his right hand. The last figure in the row is Ha, a deity of the desert. He wears the single sign of the hill lands on top of his head. His attire is similar to that of his companion deities, consisting of a tripartite wig, a curved beard, a broad collar, a two-strap garment with pleated knee-length kilt, and the ox tail. He holds the *was* scepter with his left hand and the *ankh* sign with his right hand.

THE INSCRIPTION

Above the king

Nsw bỉti nb t3wy (…)¦ *nb ỉrt ḫt* (*D*[*ry*]*š*)¦ *di ꜥnḫ ḏt*

"King of Upper and Lower Egypt, lord of the two lands (…)¦ lord of cult act (D[ariu]s)¦ given life forever."

Below Behdet

Bḥdt nṯr ꜥ3 nb pt

"Behdet, great god, lord of heaven."

Behind the king

S3 n ꜥnḫ ḥ3.f

"Protection of life is behind him."

Below the hands of the king

Di ỉrt? n ỉ[*t.f*]

"Presenting milk?[17] to [his f]ather."

Above Isdes

Ḏd mdw in ꞽIsds[18] *nṯr ꜥ3 ḥr ib Hbt di ꜥnḫ*

"Words spoken by Isdes, great god, who dwells in Hibis, giving life."

Above Shesmu

Ḏd mdw in Šsmw[19] *sḫr ḫry*[20]*/// Nfrw n Hbt*

"Words spoken by Shesmu who overthrows the enemies, ///the beauty of Hibis."

---

17 The remaining signs of the offering's name and iconography of the vessels can support either the word milk or wine; however, one inclines to regard it as a milk offering, especially because the wine offering has been represented on the opposite wall. We rarely see a repetition in the offerings represented within a single room inside the Hibis Temple.

18 The last sign is either *n* or *s*; see *Wb*. I, p. 134 for Isdn and Isds writings.

19 *Wb*. IV, p. 291 lists his name with different signs.

20 *Sḫr ḫry*, *Wb*. III, 321. This is the only example of this title of Shesmu; see Leitz, *Lexikon* VI, p. 579.

Above Iaqs[21]

Ḏd mdw in ḥḳꜣ[s] nb dnt nṯr ꜥꜣ ḥr ib Hbt di ꜥnḫ mi Rꜥ ḏt

"Words spoken by Iaq[s] lord of Thinis,[22] great god who dwells in Hibis, giving life like Re forever."

Above Ha

Ḏd mdw in Ḥꜣ nb imntt nṯr ꜥꜣ ḥr ib Hbt di ꜥnḫ mi Rꜥ ḏt

"Words spoken by Ha lord of the west, great god who dwells in Hibis, giving life like Re forever."

2. COMMENTARY

EAST WALL — REGISTER I

The first divine pair, Geb and Nut, are not only the children of Shu and Tefnut who are represented on the opposite west wall, but seem also to have parented the two male gods represented on the same register of the east wall: Merymutef and Herwer. Here, Geb is depicted in his usual attire in front of the king. Geb is usually represented anthropomorphically and generally wears the white crown.[23] He was the main chthonian god, whose duty was, among other things, to stabilize the earth and prevent droughts.[24] The series of titles given to Geb is significant to the discussion of the meaning of the scenes found in this chapel. If one takes the second title of Geb as *Gb m bw šmꜣyw*, or "Geb of the place of wilderness," as suggested earlier,[25] this would be the first reference to the nature of the trip that this chapel commemorates; a trip to places beyond the usually trodden areas. The word *ḏw* is written twice. Both examples show unique writing variants; the first is written on the west reveal as 𓈋𓅂𓅂𓉐𓏥; the second is written on the top register of the south wall as 𓈋𓅂𓅂𓏏𓏥. The word designates mountains or hills but could also refer to the oasis.[26] In both contexts *ḏw* is related to the king's "going forth." Such a trip necessitated and warranted the protection of the different gods who had power over the arid and desert areas. The third title reassures Geb's supremacy over any place his Ka desires, *nb n bw nb mr kꜣ.f im*, "Lord of his seat of every place which his Ka desires." Nut was the sky goddess whose head symbol was sometimes represented with a water pot, like this

21 For a complete discussion on the identity of this god, see pp. 88ff. See also Ismail, "A Brief Investigation of the God Iaq," pp. 233–237.

22 This is most probably a reference to the city of Thinis; see Gauthier, *Dictionnaire des noms géographiques contenus dans les textes hiéroglyphiques*, IV, pp. 77, 95–96.

23 Especially when possessing the title of *rpꜥty nṯrw*; see other example in Davies, *The Temple of Hibis*, Part 3, pl. 4, III, fig. 8.

24 Te Velde, "Geb," pp. 427–429.

25 See footnote 7, above. *šmꜣ* as a verb of motion always implied "wandering in search of food and permanent residence" since the Pyramid texts. See Fischer-Elfert, "Verben der Bewegung in altägyptischer Erklärung," in progress.

26 Kaper, "How the God Amun-Nakht came to the Oasis," p. 153, n. 21.

example in chapel G, and who was connected with rain and water offering.[27] And so the blessings of Geb and Nut were especially vital in the barren areas.

Geb and Nut are followed by Merymutef. Since the early attestation of this god on Middle Kingdom coffins found at Asyiut,[28] he was represented as the son of Geb and Nut. He was considered to be a manifestation of several gods: Osiris, Amun, Horus,[29] and even Dwamutef.[30] Merymutef assumed several forms: before Hibis he was always depicted as a ram-headed god.[31] Then, starting with the Hibis Temple, he took the falcon head. In the Ptolemaic Period, he could also be represented in a completely human form[32] or as a falcon with the double crown.[33]

This god, like other gods represented in this chapel, is more important than scholars have usually recognized. He is definitely featured more than twice,[34] and his importance merits more than a two-line entry in the *Lexikon der Ägyptologie*.[35] Although he manifested many gods and had several forms, he carried the unique title *nb ḫꜥyt*, "Lord of Khayet." He is mentioned in association with Khayet in several texts, such as in the Temple of Abu Simbel and on the Vienna statuette of a king's son, where he is named the "Lord of Khayet." His name has a determinative of a seated god with a ram's head.[36] The city of Khayet increased in importance during the New Kingdom.[37] According to Gardiner, Khayet, "*ḫꜥyt*," is located between Asyiut and el-Kusiyah: "It was situated at Mankabad, on the left bank of the Nile, at the edge of the desert near the village of Meir; i.e. between the Cerastes mountain nome (XII) and the nome of the lower Nedjfet-tree (XIV)."[38]

Not only was Merymutef represented as a falcon-headed deity for the first time inside chapel G in Hibis, but it was also his first time to be accompanied by Herwer or Haroeris. Scholars have justly proposed that Merymutef was Herwer's brother. Both relate to Geb and Nut as their father and mother,[39] but the status of Merymutef as the younger brother of Herwer is still arguable. In this scene, Merymutef is uncrowned, whereas Herwer is crowned. Merymutef also appears beside Herwer in Dendera as a youthful god with

---

27 Kurth, "Nut," pp. 536–537.

28 Zecchi, "In Search of Merymutef, 'Lord of Khayet,'" p. 10, n. 17.

29 Leitz, *Lexikon*, III, p. 338.

30 Cruz-Uribe, *Hibis Temple Project I*, p. 82, n. 275.

31 According to his examples in the Temple of Seti and Abu Simbel; Leitz, *Lexikon*, III, p. 338.

32 Ptolemaic sarcophagus of *Pꜣ-n-ꜣst*; Maspero, "Les Monuments Égyptiens du Musée de Marseille," pp. 7, 14; Cairo Coffin TR 4/12/20/5 in Buhl, *The Late Egyptian Anthropoid Stone Sarcophagi*, fig. 10 on pp. 37, 38; *D* V, p. 137, pl. CCCCXXIV; Leitz, *Lexikon*, III, p. 338.

33 *E* XV, p. 47.

34 Contra Cruz-Uribe, *Hibis Temple Project I*, p. 82, n. 275.

35 Helck, "Merimutef," p. 96.

36 Gardiner, *Ancient Egyptian Onomastica*, II, p. 76.

37 Ahmad Kamal, who was the first archaeologist to excavate the city, found evidence of Akhenaton's interest in the city; Kamal, "Rapport sur les fouilles exécutées dans la zone comprise entre Déîrout, au nord, et Déîr-el-Ganadlah, au sud," p. 3. According to the Ismailia naos, of the 30th dynasty, the city was understood to be a creation of the god Shu; Zecchi, "In Search of Merymutef, 'Lord of Khayet,'" pp. 7–8, 11.

38 Gardiner, *Ancient Egyptian Onomastica*, II, pp. 75–76.

39 Kurth, " Haroëris," col. 999; Zecchi, "In Search of Merymutef, 'Lord of Khayet,'" pp. 11ff.

a side-lock.[40] However, one must consider that in these scenes and in the Edfu Texts[41] Herwer is always represented following after Merymutef, which might mean that he attained lesser status despite being the elder.

Herwer was frequently associated with a more powerful image of Horus, especially in the fights against Seth and other enemies of the gods. [42] He was often represented with a falcon head with the double crown. The Hibis scene is no exception, for here he is depicted anthropomorphically with a falcon head. He had three main cult centers in Letopolis, Kom Ombo, and Qus.[43] The latter has remains of a Ptolemaic Temple of Herwer.[44] It was conveniently located near the entrance to the important southern route to Wadi Hamammat, used for mining expeditions and later the most important eastern trade center in Upper Egypt.[45] Merymutef seems to have had a female partner who shared his rule over Khayet. She was referred to as Ipipt/Ipwy and was represented as a lioness. She was even represented as the sole ruler of this city in the so-called "Litany of the Wasit" of the 19th Dynasty.[46] Inside the sanctuary of Ramesses III at Karnak, Ipipt appears between "Hathor, Lady of Meden" and "Hathor, Lady of Cusae."[47] Both Meden and Cusae are very close locations to Khayet. Furthermore, Herwer is also associated with the city of Cusae, where he is called "the son of the sky goddess (i.e., Nut)"[48]

The strong association of Merymutef and Herwer with the specific location of Khayet or Mankabad is interesting. This city lies directly on the northernmost road known to connect the Kharga Oasis with the Nile Valley. Mankabad is situated at the eastern end of the important Mankabad–Asyiut route that crosses the western desert and connects with the Kharga Oasis and from which one can also reach Dakhla Oasis. South of the oasis, this route, together with others, joins the main road of Darb el Arbain that dominates the desert routes between the oasis and lower Nubia, and is known to have existed since at least the 18th Dynasty.[49] Its increasing importance during the Late Period could have paralleled the importance of the river route of the Nile.[50]

40 Mariette, *Dendérah* III, pl. 369; *D* V, p. 137 and pl. ccccxxiv.

41 *E* I, p. 53, nn. 54 and 55.

42 Kurth, "Haroëris," cols. 999–1001. For a good overall treatement of the conflict between Horus and Seth, see Junge, "Mythos und Literarizität: Die Geschichte vom Streit der Götter Horus und Seth," pp. 83–101.

43 Kurth, "Haroëris," col. 1000.

44 Kamal, "Le Pylône de Qous," pp. 216–217

45 Fischer, "Qus," col. 72.

46 Zecchi, "In Search of Merymutef, 'Lord of Khayet,'" p. 9 and n. 12; Legrain, "La litanie de Ouasit," pp. 277 and 281.

47 Zecchi, "In Search of Merymutef, 'Lord of Khayet,'" p. 9.

48 Beinlich, *Studien zu den "Geographischen Inschriften" (10.–14. o. äg. Gau)*, p. 166; Zecchi, "In Search of Merymutef, 'Lord of Khayet,'" p. 14.

49 Dewachter, "Nubie — Notes diverses (III)," pp. 3ff.

50 Morkot, "The Darb el-Arbain, the Kharga Oasis and its Forts, and Other Desert routes," pp. 84ff.

EAST WALL — REGISTER II

SOPDU

The king offers wine to the four gods—Sopdu, Hedjhotep, Nekhbet, and Wadjet—who seem to have assumed control over the four principal cardinal directions (east–west–south–north) and to have exercised power over boundaries. Sopdu represented the east par excellence. In the Old Kingdom tombs that portray his aspect as the cosmic falcon, he is also described as "sharp of teeth"[51] and as an Asiatic warrior.[52] He was the god of the eastern frontier of Egypt, playing a double role in guarding the eastern border region against the Asiatics and also providing resources of the east such as turquoise and malachite.[53] His main cult center was at Pr Spdu (modern Saft el Henna) in the eastern Delta, but his popularity extended outside Pr Spdu, so that he appeared beyond his eastern desert zone. In Ptolemaic temples, he seems to take over the whole of the foreign lands. In Edfu, he is called the "Inheritor of Foreign Land."[54] He appears in environmentally harsh areas where the locals asked for his protection.[55] In the Temple of Hibis in general, and in this chapel in particular, his representation seems to emphasize his position as the god of the east and the god of the desert, as the discussion of his titles and relationship to other deities in the same chapel will reveal.

In this scene, Sopdu's head is unfortunately destroyed, but the long curve on the back of his neck extends longer than the curve of a human head, as attested by the next figure of Hedjhotep. Thus, his head is most probably that of a falcon, rather than a human. He also appears elsewhere in Hibis, usually as a falcon-headed deity. Inside the sanctuary, he is described as the Lord of the Desert *Ḥmt*.[56] Schumacher does not identify the exact meaning of *Ḥmt,* but she proposes that it might be around Hibis.[57] On the right scene of the north wall of hypostyle hall M of Hibis, the king also offers wine while Sopdu is seated and represented with a falcon head. He carries the title of *Spd Ḥr ẖꜣsty iꜣbtt,*

---

51 Schumacher, Der Gott Sopdu, Der Herr der Fremdländer, p. 42.

52 Borchardt, *Sahure* II, p. 19, pl. 5; Borchardt, *Neuserre*, p. 93, fig. 71. For Sopdu as an Asiatic in PT, see Schumacher, *Der Gott Sopdu*, pp. 40ff.

53 Giveon, "Sopdu," cols. 1107ff.

54 Kurth, *Die Dekoration der Säulen im Pronaos des Tempels von Edfu*, pp. 112–115.

55 He is attested in Sinai, Inscr. Sinai, Nr. 80; Giveon, "Sopdu," col. 1109. In Gebel el Silselah, Sopdu appears in an Osiris procession; see Thiem, *Speos von Gebel es-Silsileh: Analyse der architektonischen und ikonographischen Konzeption im Rahmen des politischen und legitimatorischen Programmes der Nachamarnazeit*, pp. 158, 169, 326 (where he carries the rather obscure title of "*ḥry nm.t nb snḏ,*" "who is chief of chaos and lord of fear"). For the other instance of Sopdu, Lord of the East in Gebel el Silselah, represented with the god Ha, Lord of the West, see idem., pp. 207–209, 219ff, 331–334, pl. 18 and pls. 94ff. Sopdu is also attested in Nubia; Schumacher, *Der Gott Sopdu*, pp. 98–100.

56 Davies, *The Temple of Hibis*, Part 3, pl. 3, north wall, register III, figure 16.

57 Schumacher, *Der Gott Sopdu*, p. 149; Cruz-Uribe, *Hibis Temple Project I*, p. 11 translates the title as "Sopdu, lord of the desert (in) Khem," connecting Khem with *ḫmḫm*, an area associated with Horus or with a canal in Heracleopolis.

"Sopdu-Horus of both the eastern deserts."[58] This title does not occur outside the Temple of Hibis.

The inscription above the figure of the god Sopdu gives him unique series of titles.

Figure 20: Titles of Sopdu, detail from figure 17.

The first title of Sopdu in chapel G of Hibis is Sopdu Nefer, which is attested very few times. In one example, the title is written with the determinative of Sopdu as the falcon sign (Gardiner G11), *Spd nb ỉ3btt Spd nfr b3 Rʿ*.[59] Kákosy had a question mark after *nfr*, and he mentioned that *nfr* could be equally *smʿ*. However, he suggested "Sopdu the Perfect, the Ba of Re" or "Sopdu the Image of the Ba of Re."[60] Sopdu bears the title of Sopdu Nefer elsewhere inside Hibis Temple. His image appears in hypostyle hall B, on the west wall, on the panel to the south of the door to chapel L. Above him, the inscription states "words spoken by Sopdu, the beautiful, son of Re Horakhty, Horus of the east, great god who dwells in Hibis." He is followed by Montet, "Mistress of Nebset, Lady of the east who dwells in Hibis."[61]

A second title of Sopdu here in this register is no less unique: "Son of Wenut." Wenut was a female deity, worshiped as the main deity of the region of Unut in the 15th Upper Egyptian nome (Hermopolis/El Ashmonin).[62] On the hypostyle hall M of the Temple of Hibis, east wall, north panel of screen and north jamb of gateway to N, register I, the king is in the presence of Geb, Nut, Thoth, and Wenut.[63] Above Wenut, the inscription reads: "words spoken by Wenut, who dwells in Hermopolis for she has made a giving life forever." The name of Wenut is written as that of the town instead of the name of the goddess; although it is probably a mistake, it confirms the link between the deity and the place. Wenut was also a designation of Isis[64] and Hathor.[65] She had a sanctuary in Saft el Henna (*Ḥwt-Nbs*), the main cult place of Sopdu as shown in the Ismailia Naos. On the upper part of the back outer wall, third line, the text mentions "/// who overthrows his enemies/// the god who is inside the shrine of Wenut," which associates Sopdu with Wenut.[66]

Both Sopdu and Wenut occur in contexts connected with the cardinal directions, even in connection with deities from the same register, especially Wadjet and Nekhbet.

58 Davies, *The Temple of Hibis*, Part 3, pl. 30; Leitz, *Lexikon*, VI, p. 291.

59 Kákosy, *Egyptian Healing Statues*, p. 137, fig. 27, pl. 41 of the statue Neapel 1065, see the inscription on the left shoulder.

60 Kákosy, *Egyptian Healing Statues*, pp. 137ff.

61 Cruz-Uribe, *Hibis Temple Project I*, p. 48; Davies, *The Temple of Hibis*, Part 3, pl. 8.

62 Bonnet, *Reallexikon der ägyptischen Religionsgeschichte*, p. 841.

63 Cruz-Uribe, *Hibis Temple Project I*, 141; Davies, *The Temple of Hibis*, Part 3, pl. 36.

64 Leitz, *Lexikon*, II, p. 391.

65 *Wb*. I, p. 317, 11–12; Schumacher, *Der Gott Sopdu*, p. 147 has a question mark next to Sopdu, son of Wenut, but does not offer an explanation for this title·

66 This naos is now in the Cairo Museum, CG 70021 § 314; Naville, *The Shrine of Saft el Henneh*, pp. 1–13, pls. 1–7; Roeder, *Naos*, pp. 58–99, pls. 17–32, 33b; Schumacher, *Der Gott Sopdu*, p. 170.

The word *ỉꜣb*, "left" or "east", can be written with the serpent sign of Wadjet.[67] Wadjet and Nekhbet were the goddesses of Lower and Upper Egypt. They became the ladies of the north and south who were either represented as cobras, vultures, or women with the symbols of the respective animals on their heads. In the Mammisis of Edfu and Dendera are many attestations of *Sopdu nb ỉꜣbt*, "Sopdu Lord of the East," together with *Wadjet nbt ỉmntt*, "Wadjet Lady of the West."[68] Sopdu of the east and Ha *nb ỉmntt*, who is represented on the opposite wall in chapel G, are also depicted after one another in the first register of the south wall of the sanctuary of Gebel el Silselah.[69] Beside Isis and Hathor, Wenut was a designation for Wadjet and Nekhbet. This is attested in the titles of *wnut mḥw*, "Wenut of the North," and *wnut šmꜥw*, "Wenut of the South."[70] *Wenut mḥw* is represented as a designation for Wadjet in the Kom Ombo and Esna Temples.[71] Also, *wnut šmꜥw* appears as a designation of both Nekhbet and Wadjet.[72]

Behind the figure of Sopdu in chapel G, scholars have read the rather unusual title of *Spdw smsm Ḥr Smꜣ-Bḥdt*, translated as "Sopdu, the eldest, Horus of Tell el Ballamun," without further comment.[73] No other examples of such a title appear elsewhere. Moreover, Sopdu does not seem to have any theological relationship with the city of Tell el Ballamun in the northeast of the Delta. One would have expected Pr Spdu, "Saft el Henna," where Sopdu was the preeminent god. The inspection of the wall clearly shows *smsm Ḥr* but does not offer support for the word *Smꜣ-Bḥdt*. In fact, the remaining inscription after *smsm Ḥr* shows only faint traces of signs. The first component of the title is the word *smsm*, a variant of *smsrw* or *smsw*, meaning "the eldest one."[74] Several examples of this title associated with Sopdu exist, both before and after the date of the example in chapel G in the Hibis Temple. The earliest and most relevant example is found in the Middle Kingdom story of Sinuhe. This example contains an expression of some epithets of Sopdu that are very similar to his titles inside chapel G. It is written .[75] This inscription includes both titles of Sopdu as "*nfr*" and "*smsrw*." The latter is written with the falcon deity at the end. In the New Kingdom, the title of *smsrw* occurs also in association with Sopdu, in the inscriptions of Sinai belonging to Thutmosis III[76] and on the Temple of Ramesses II at Abydos.[77] The example at Abydos is written with slight variation as , *Spdw smsrw sṯt*, which Kees renders as "Sopdu, der

67 Wilson, *Lexicon*, p. 32.

68 *D Mammisis*, p. 139, 13, pl. 61; *E Mammisis*, p. 169, 14, pl. 44, 2.

69 Thiem, *Speos von Gebel es-Silsileh*, pp. 207 and 334

70 Leitz, *Lexikon*, II, pp. 391-392.

71 In *Kom Ombos*, p. 819, 2= Gutbub, *Ko*, p. 217; *Esna* IV, p. 426, 8.

72 In *Kom Ombos*, p. 819, 1= Gutbub, *Ko*, p. 217; *Esna* IV, p. 426, 7.

73 Leitz, *Lexikon*, VI, p. 354; Davies, *The Temple of Hibis*, Part 3, p. 19; Cruz-Uribe, *Hibis Temple Project I*, p. 83; Schumacher, *Der Gott Sopdu*, p. 267.

74 *Wb.* IV, pp. 142-143.

75 Kees, "Ein Herrschaftsspruch aus den Pyramidentexten des A.R. und Sopdu der smsrw," p. 39, n.5; Gardiner, "The God Semseru," pp. 75–76. See also Darnell, *Theban Desert Road Survey in the Egyptian Western Desert*, I, n. j, p. 100.

76 Gardiner-Peet, *Inscriptions of Sinai*, pl. 64, no. 198; Gardiner, "The God Semseru," p. 75.

77 Kees, "Ein Herrschaftsspruch aus den Pyramidentexten," p. 39; Gardiner, "The God Semseru," p. 75; Leitz, *Lexikon*, VI, p. 291.

smsrw Asien" and mentions Sethe's comment that *smsrw* refers to "an Asian deity" that is associated with Sopdu.[78] The Khaset sign of hill country is represented at the end of the following word in both examples. The latter Ptolemaic examples of Dendera and Esna, [hieroglyphs] and [hieroglyphs][79] have the standing man leaning on a stick as determinative for *smsw*, and the Khaset sign at the end of the last two words at the end of both examples. Sopdu's title of *nfr-bꜣw* appears in a "fuller form" in the inscription of Wadi el Hôl as *nfr bꜣw n Rꜥ*.[80] Based on the comparison with the Late Period corpus of the magical texts called "*bꜣw- Rꜥ*," Darnell suggested that this epithet of Sopdu may associate him with the "manifestation of the power of the sun."[81] Note that this epithet in Wadi el Hôl is followed by *smsrw Ḥr iꜣbty*, "The eldest, Horus the Easterner." Both the titles of Sopdu as "Nefer" and "Horus the Easterner" appear together in Hibis hypostyle hall B.[82]

None of the previously mentioned examples of Sopdu's titles refer to a specific location after *smsm Ḥr*. They do, however, refer to a general location, such as the "the east," "the desert," or "the foreign land." This implicitly argues against the reconstruction of the last word in the epithets of Sopdu in chapel G as "*Smꜣ Bḥdt*," or Tell el Ballamun, a specific place. The inspection of the remaining traces of this controversial word on the wall of chapel G enables only the confirmation of a vertical sign, a hill-country sign (*ḫꜣst* sign), below one or two *t* signs: [hieroglyphs] . This might be a variation of the word *smyt*, "desert,"[83] or the word *smꜣty*, "road" or "path."[84]

On the other hand, Tell el Ballamun would not be an impossible suggestion; it is the place most commonly associated with the marshland, a geographic environment connected with the character of Sopdu. Its backland is described as "stretching to the sea not far away, was a region of swamps and lagoons abounding in jungle-like growths of papyrus and reeds."[85] Gardiner argued that Sma Behdet was the birthplace of Horus, where Isis, hiding amid a thicket of papyrus, nursed and safeguarded her infant. This event is illustrated in numerous places. Sopdu was another son of Isis, and it is not inappropriate to connect him with Sma Behdet as well. The Temple of Edfu is abundant in examples connecting Sma Behdet with the marshes and reeds; sometimes the king

78 Kees, "Ein Herrschaftsspruch aus den Pyramidentexten,"p. 39, n. 7.

79 *D* III, p. 12; The Esna example occurs in the hymn to the god Khnum; see Kees, "Ein Herrschaftsspruch aus den Pyramidentexten des A.R. und Sopdu der *smsrw*," p. 40.

80 Darnell, *Theban Desert Road Survey in the Egyptian Western Desert*, I, n. j, p. 100 (Rock inscription 5 of the 12th Dynasty).

81 Darnell, *Theban Desert Road Survey in the Egyptian Western Desert*, I, n. j, p. 100–101. See also Assmann, *Liturgische Lieder an den Sonnengott*, pp. 222–223.

82 Davies, *The Temple of Hibis*, Part 3, pl. 6, on panel to south of door to chapel L.

83 *Wb*. III, pp. 444, 8 and 445, 13.

84 *Wb*. III, p. 452, 17–19. See also Wilson, *Lexicon*, pp. 844–845. An example of *smꜣty* on a block in the Red Chapel of Hatshepsut was understood as a reference to "two meridian directions," either east and west or north and south; Lacau-Chevrier, *Une chapelle d'Hatshepsout à Karnak* 1, 148–149b; Wilson, *Lexicon*, p. 844. It is interesting that this word exists in the middle location between Sopdu of the east and Hedjhotep, who presumably might have indicated the west.

85 Gardiner, "Horus the Behdetite," pp. 53–58.

offers papyrus reeds and rushes to Amun of Sma Behdet, or the lord of Sma Behdet offers marshland to the king.[86] This city is usually referenced as the northernmost town of the land.[87] Sma Behdet is actually mentioned in Hibis as the place of the unification of the country. This is mentioned in a long "panegyric" addressed to Amun Re by the eight primeval beings of Hermopolis. The inscription states "You have united the Two Lands beneath your throne of union(?) on your seat of Sma Behdet, your pure place."[88] Other texts in Dendera and Edfu repeat this idea of the unification of Egypt occurring in Sma Behdet.[89]

Perhaps a good parallel to this scene of Sopdu in chapel G is found inside Gebel el Silselah. Sopdu is attested twice inside the rock chapel of Horemheb in Gebel el Silselah, once with the Osiris triad and once among a procession of seated gods who wish the king a good year.[90] The procession is arranged in three long registers, each with 12 seated divinities. They include the Theban triad, the Ennead of Heliopolis, Onuris, and Shu, different manifestations of Horus, and the cataract's triad: Khnum, Satis, and Anukis. In the last register are different deities closing the procession: Mafdet, Wepwawet, and then the desert gods Ha *nb imntt*, "Lord of the West," and Sopdu *nb i3btt*, "Lord of the East," Dedwen from Nubia as a representative of the south, and another unidentified god, who might have been a representative of the north.[91] Not only do Sopdu and Ha appear with their titles as "Lord of the East" and "Lord of the West," respectively, but they also appear together with other deities that represent an aspect of the environment of the region, like the triad of the cataract area and Dedwen of Nubia.

HEDJHOTEP

Hedjhotep first appears in the Coffin Texts as the originator of light or simply white things.[92] In the New Kingdom, he is less frequently attested until he becomes more popular in the Greco-Roman temples. He is associated with weaving and textiles, especially the godly ones. For example, he appears in the processions carrying the royal and divine cloth (*ḥbs-nṯrw*).[93] The connection with weaving also appears to be associated with his partner Tait,[94] with whom he appears several times especially in the Ptolemaic temples.

86 See the detailed examples of Gardiner, "Horus the Behdetite," pp. 45ff.

87 Gardiner, "Horus the Behdetite," pp. 39, 41ff.

88 Gardiner, "Horus the Behdetite," p. 45, nn. 6 and 7.

89 Gardiner, "Horus the Behdetite," p. 45.

90 *PM* V, p. 213; Champollion, *Notice descriptive des monumens égyptiens du Museé Charles X*. I, p. 264; Schumacher, *Der Gott Sopdu*, pp. 96–97.

91 *PM* V, p. 213; Champollion, *Notice descriptive des monumens égyptiens du Museé Charles X*. I, p. 264, who saw remains of the signs *i* and *n* and suggested Anubis for the identity of the last deity; however, it could also refer to Isdes/Isden who is represented in chapel G as well.

92 Hornung, "Hedjhotep," col. 1078

93 *Opet* I, p. 206; *E* IV, p. 200, 11 and pl. 98; *E* XV, p. 49. See also the recent work of Backes, *Rituelle Wirklichkeit. Über Erscheinung und Wirkungsbereich des Webergottes Hedjhotep und den gedanklichen Umgang mit einer Gottes-Konzeption im Alten Ägypten.*

94 For the goddess Tait, see El-Saady, "Reflections on the Goddess Tayet," p. 214; Backes, *Rituelle Wirklichkeit*, pp. 69–74 on Tait and her relationship to Hedjhotep.

The meaning of his name has been translated through the interpretation of his function. Although problematic, his name has been usually translated as "satisfied white one" or "light/white is satisfied"; *ḥḏ* is usually understood as a reference to white linen or textiles.[95] Another possible meaning of his name could lie in the basic meaning of *ḥtp* as "to rest" or "setting of the sun," thus referring to the west. However, it is hard to find solid evidence for such a connection, except for his involvement in many funerary contexts. Hedjhotep's relationship with the west appears to be reflected in his early association with the Coffin Texts. He is associated with the dead and, in particular, with Osiris. For example, in Edfu and Dendera, he clothes the naked one (*ḥbs ḥʿw*), referring to Osiris.[96] He wipes the dust from Horus' statue and clothes it.[97] He fashions Osiris' mummy bandage.[98] In Dendera, he is called *imi st Wsir*, "who belongs to the place of Osiris,"[99] a more likely indication of his place over the west. Another title he carries in this register is also rather intriguing: *mr s3.f ʿnḫ*, or "who loves his living son." This title is not attested outside chapel G of Hibis.[100] Even though he is often portrayed as the son of Isis and brother to Horus,[101] it is not known whether Hedjhotep had offspring of his own. Most probably, "the beloved son" is a reference to the king.

Hedjhotep was usually represented in complete anthropomorphic form. Only once was he depicted with a falcon head and a double crown. This representation of Hedjhotep in Hibis is, in fact, his earliest pictorial representation. He has no other unique attributes. In another scene, he has a cobra or Shu feathers on his head.[102] Previously, he was treated mainly as a weaving god,[103] providing or carrying fabrics or textiles to the king or the gods, but here in Hibis, no offerings are associated with him, nor is he associated with his partner Tait, the goddess of weaving.[104]

A close examination of the different attestations of Hedjhotep shows that he not only appears in connection with other deities from the same register, such as Sopdu *n dsw*, according to a Greco-Roman coffin,[105] but he also appears with the other gods from the same chapel, such as Isdes who, according to one papyrus, resides in the Upper Egyptian nome of Hermopolis, as *Ḥḏ-ḥtp*.[106] Evidently Isdes is associated with the west, as will be seen below. Hedjhotep is also attested with Wadjet and Nekhbet,[107] but his relationship

95 Backes, *Rituelle Wirklichkeit*, pp. 17–19; Gugliemi, "Personifikation," pp. 978–987.

96 *E* II, p. 163.14–15; *E* IX, pl. xliib; *D* IV, p. 124, 16–17, pl. cclxxx.

97 *E* IV, p. 200.11–12; *E* X, pl. xcviii; in Medamoud, Hedjhotep is "clothing the limbs with his own hand;" Drioton, "Rapport sur les fouilles de Médamoud," p. 60, nr. 129, 59, fig. 11; Backes, *Rituelle Wirklichkeit*, p. 46.

98 Backes, *Rituelle Wirklichkeit*, pp. 53–54.

99 Backes, *Rituelle Wirklichkeit*, p. 30; *D* X, p. 415, 13–15, pl. ccxlviii.

100 Leitz, *Lexikon*, III, p. 342.

101 Backes, *Rituelle Wirklichkeit*, pp. 57ff. He is never, though, represented as the son of Osiris. For this problem, see chapter 6 of Backes.

102 Backes, *Rituelle Wirklichkeit*, pp. 22ff.

103 Backes, *Rituelle Wirklichkeit*, pp. 42–44.

104 El-Saady, "Reflections on the Goddess Tayet," pp. 214ff.

105 Leitz, *Lexikon*, V, p. 602, coffin of *ʿnḫ-Ḥp* son of *T3y.f nḫt*: CG 29303.

106 Leitz, *Lexikon*, V, p. 602; Backes, *Rituelle Wirklichkeit*, pp. 90–92.

107 *D* IV, p. 124, 10; *D* IV, p. 141, 3–5.

with Shesmu is dominant. In all his association with these gods, he does not offer linen or textiles. In the *wabet* of Edfu (P), east wall, second register, first scene, Hedjhotep stands next to Shesmu in front of the king. Both deities have cobras on their forehead and no other attributes. They might have been represented as priests involved in the celebration of the New Year.[108]

Although Backes stated that Hedjhotep is only a protective god through his function as a textile offerer,[109] it appears that his role as a protector was more extensive than previously thought. In Dendera, Hedjhotep plays an important protective role. He is represented with a lion's head and has the title *snḏ.t-n.t-sḫm.t* (*Schrecken der Sekhmet-Stoff*) "material of the horror of Sakhmet" and he is connected with the power of the wild ones (*der Macht der Wilden*).[110] In a coffin of Harmachis, son of Anemher, he is portrayed as the protector of the dead.[111] Backes mentioned chapel G in Hibis as a precursor example to the treasury rooms, magazines, and crypts that would be called "cloth rooms" inside Edfu and Dendera.[112] None of his cited examples of "cloth rooms" show significant resemblance to chapel G in Hibis. Only one room in Dendera presents a superficial similarity; it lies on a relevant place in the temple, the south side of the offering hall, and Shesmu is on the west side of the room.[113] Moreover, the absence of any offerings of linen or textiles in connection with this god in chapel G throws much doubt on this theory.[114]

SOUTH WALL

As in most chapels in Hibis, the Theban triad takes the upper register while Osiris, followed by Isis, Horus, or Nephthys, takes the lower register of the same wall. The king is offering libation to Amun who is seated on his elaborate throne. The line of inscription between the king and Amun is significant to understanding this chapel.[115] It states that the king is bringing cool water to his father Amun Re who goes forth from Thebes to traverse the mountainous areas. The identity of those who went on this trip is confirmed by the inscriptions above Amun that repeat his departing from Thebes. However, the king, or his representative Iunmutef, might have participated, together with the divine representatives.

According to the inscriptions, Amun started from Thebes or south of Thebes.[116] This corresponds with the exact location of the closest roads to Kharga from the Theban

108 *E* I, p. 430,11–12,15–16; *E* IX, pl. XXXIIIB. See also Traunecker, "Les ouabet des temples d' el Qal'a et de Chenhour. Décoration, origine et evolution," pp. 241–281.

109 Backes, *Rituelle Wirklichkeit*, p. 47.

110 Backes, *Rituelle Wirklichkeit*, pp. 23–24, n. 21; Dendera (cloth room) (P), West Wall, South side, 3rd register (*D* IV, p. 144, 10) and *D* IV, p. 233, 8–9.

111 Backes, *Rituelle Wirklichkeit*, p. 47.

112 Backes, *Rituelle Wirklichkeit*, pp. 33ff.

113 *D* IV, p. 140, 14, pl. CCLXXXV.

114 More detailed discussion on a possible "cloth room" and or "Wabet room" will be presented in the conclusion; see pp. 214ff.

115 This line was omitted from Cruz-Uribe's translation (*Hibis Temple Project I*, p. 83.)

116 Taking "*pr m ḫnt*" in the inscription in front of the king and "*pr ḫnti*" in the inscription in front of Amun to refer to "going forth in front of or southward," see *Wb*. III, pp. 302–303

nome—the Esna–Rezeigat–Kharga that began at Armant, south of Thebes, a road known from at least the Middle Kingdom[117] (see pls. 19 and 20).

The purpose of this trip was, according to the inscriptions on the east wall, to *pẖr*, or to go about and encompass the mountains with his (Amun's) beauty. The four lines of inscriptions between the king and Amun reflect what is written on the east and west reveals of the doorway from hypostyle hall B to chapel G. Curiously enough, both key words (*ḏw* and *nfrw*) are used in both locations. The east and west reveals of the door to the chapel mention that Darius made a house of beauties to Amun Re after he went forth from the mountains. One is then inclined to understand the word *nfrw*, or *beautiful things*, in register I of the east wall as referring to either the beauty of the mountains or to Amun's beauty.[118] The first suggestion is in line with the meaning of its corresponding word, *nfrw*, on the east reveal; it is more likely to mean the *treasures of the mountains*, perhaps precious or semiprecious stones that the king brought from the mountains on his desert trip to adorn the Temple of Hibis for his god Amun, as reflected from the east and west reveals.[119]

The names of Amun of Hibis are attested among Persian Period graffiti left by desert travelers at Armant.[120] In one of the Armant graffiti (Graffiti 5), the name of Amun of Hibis is supplemented by this curious title: *Ỉmn Ḥb ti šꜣy nfr*, "Amun of Hibis who gives a good fate."[121] This title may suggest the importance of Amun of Hibis in protecting the desert travelers and guaranteeing their safe return.

Khonsu might have played a double role in this register. He is the third member of the Theban triad and follows his father Amun and his mother Mut in front of him, but he is also known for his great role in desert travel. He manifested the moon that travellers relied on for directions to avoid getting lost at night. He helped people traverse

---

and 306 in association with the city of Thebes. However, if the intended phrase is to state that the trip started at Thebes, then it may be a reference to the important Farshût Road that began at the Valley of the Kings and later joined the Esna–Rezigat Road westward into the northern end of Darb el Arbaeen into Kharga. For this important road, see Darnell, "Opening the Narrow Doors of the Desert: Discoveries of the Theban Desert Road Survey," pp. 132–139.

117 Osing, "Die beschrifteten Funde," pp. 39ff. Part of this route is called Darb el Rayayna route; see Darnell, "Opening the Narrow Doors of the Desert," p. 150.

118 Assmann interprets *nfrw* when associated with Amun as the "morning sun." Assmann, *Liturgische Lieder an den Sonnengott*, p. 74; Assmann, *Re und Amun. Die Krise des polytheistischen Weltbilds im Ägypten der 18.–20. Dynastie*, p. 107.

119 In some texts, *pẖr* is used with the implication of having access of the native wealth of the different regions, for example, in the stela, mentioned by Fisher, belonging to a minor official named *sꜣ-ḥtḥr*, who was the "Assistant Treasurer" of King Amenenhet II; Fischer, "A God and a General of the Oasis on a Stela of the Late Middle Kingdom," p. 228 (British Museum 569). The same verb, *pẖr*, is used in the same order: first, Sa-Hathor records that he traveled through the Oasis and "went about its lands "*pẖr*" and then he proceeds to say that he brought back *sš*, a vegetable product popular in the oasis area.

120 Di Cerbo and Jasnow, "Five Persian Period Demotic and Hieroglyphic Graffiti from the Site of Apa Tyrannos at Armant," pp. 33–38.

121 Di Cerbo and Jasnow, "Five Persian Period Demotic and Hieroglyphic Graffiti from the Site of Apa Tyrannos at Armant," pp. 32–33.

the desert and keep track of time by his lunar cycle, and it seems only natural that he is included in chapel G.

In the lower register, Iunmutef is depicted as a priest in his more common representation with the side-lock and the panther skin, intermediating between the king and Osiris. This might indicate that the priest substituted for the king's presence on this presumed trip. The inscription of the lower register reflects the usual wish for protection and a *Hetep-di-nsw* formula, but in the inscription of Osiris and Isis an emphasis is put once again on the *places* of Osiris and any place his Ka desired.

WEST WALL — REGISTER I

Here the king wanted to guarantee the satisfaction of the main gods representing the powers of the cosmic, and especially the desert atmosphere. The king offers to the fierce Shu, the savage Tefnut, and the ferocious Sakhmet. He offers the symbol of Maat to the divine couple Shu and Tefnut, who gave birth to Geb and Nut, who are represented on the east wall. This chapel thus reunites the second and third generations of the Heliopolitan Ennead. Shu, the god of air and sunlight, is represented in his usual anthropomorphic form as a human wearing a feather on his head, while his sister-wife Tefnut, who manifested moisture, is represented as a lioness-headed goddess. This specific representation refers to her leonine identity and is identified with Sakhmet, who stands behind her in this scene with the title of "the Eye of Re." Next, the king stands and offers the *wensheb* to Sakhmet in front of him. She is depicted as a lioness-headed woman with a long wig and a solar disk surmounted by a serpent on her head. Her main cult center was at Memphis, where she was worshipped with her spouse Ptah and their son Nefertum, but she had also many different sanctuaries all over the country, even in Nubia.[122] In this scene, she is called the Eye of Re, a title given to many important deities, usually those with feline aspects. Many versions of a myth deal with the Eye of Re who argues with her father, Re, leaves Egypt, and wanders in the desert until one or more deities persuade her to return. The Eye of Re also fights for her father Re when humans rebel against him, leading to the famous story of the destruction of mankind, in which Sakhmet as the Eye of Re takes a ferocious role in the massacre of people.[123] Although her destructive nature is also associated with other female deities, such as Bastet, Mafdet Pakhet, Hathor, Mut, Tefnut, and Wadjet, Sakhmet was the most forceful. In the Coffin Texts, she is said to be the one who is "strong enough to cut off heads, and sharp is the flame which is on her mouth against the knives which are in the hands of the gods. Sakhmet is she who wielded the

---

122 The numerous Sakhmet statues discovered in the vicinity of the Mut Temple at Karnak and built by Amenhotep III show an extensive collection of titles and place names, connecting Sakhmet with various locales. Some of these titles are still unidentified. See Hoenes, *Untersuchungen zu Wesen und Kult der Göttin Sekhmet*, pp. 100–142, where she lists evidences from at least 74 locales attesting to Sakhmet's worship there. For Nubia, see ibid., pp. 162–165.

123 For this myth, see Germond, *Sekhmet et la protection du monde*, pp. 131–148; De Cenival, *Le mythe de Œil du soleil*, pp. 1–71; Darnell, "The Apotropaic Goddess in the Eye," pp. 35–48; Otto, "Augensagen," cols. 562–567.

Cerastes-Mountain knife on the night of the great battle and on the morning dividing what was complete, like the stems of their Khasw plants."[124] Her fiery breath represented the destroying force against the enemies of Ramesses II, as well as the dangerous heat of the desert.[125] She was propitiated during the dangerous transition from the old to the new year, and she also helped the king and the kingship.[126] Yet her most obvious role in this specific scene might concern the establishing of order against the chaotic forces of the universe subsisting in the dangerous desert areas. This can be achieved through her appeasement by the *wensheb* offering, which was more commonly presented to leonine goddesses.[127]

The rite of offering the *wensheb* or *shebet* from (*šbt*)[128] started as early as the 18th dynasty, in the reign of King Amenhotep III in the Luxor Temple.[129] Later, in the Greco-Roman temples, this offering was also called *wnšb* or *wtṯ*.[130] This offering was almost exclusively offered to female deities, most predominantly Mut, Sakhmet, and Hathor.[131] Some authors have discussed the exterior appearance of the *wensheb* offering; however, the significance and meaning of its representation on temple walls remains relatively unexplained. Three elements characterize this object: the baboon, the pillar, and the base. These different elements developed from one age to another and have become useful for dating.

Some authors explain the *wensheb* offering as a symbol of a real time-measuring clepsydra based on the existence of the baboon or at least expressing a symbolic allusion to its function.[132] Others reject this idea and explain it as a cult or votive object.[133] Even if

124 Faulkner, *Coffin Texts*, I, p. 228, spell 311. The Cerastes-Mountain is the XII Upper Egyptian nome, situated not far from the localities mentioned in this chapel, especially those mentioned on the east wall.

125 Pinch, *Egyptian Mythology*, p. 188.

126 Germond, *Sekhmet et la protection du monde*, pp. 165ff.

127 Handoussa, "A propos de l'offrande *Šbt*," pp. 72–73; Handoussa, "The Goddess Mikt," pp. 101–105.

128 *Wb*. IV, p. 438. On the different terminology of this offering, see Sambin, *L'offrande de la soit-disant "clepsydre", Le symbole šbt / wnšb / wtt*, pp. 234–241.

129 Handoussa, "A propos de l'offrande *Šbt*," p. 65; Sambin, *L'offrande de la soit-disant "clepsydre,"* p. 20. An earlier example of this offering might have existed on the destroyed scene in Buhen's sanctuary, where Queen Hatshepsut offers the symbol of *wensheb* to the goddess Miket. Unfortunately, this scene is now destroyed; ibid , p. 24; *PM* V, II, p. 136(29); Caminos, *Buhen II*, pp. 82–83 and pl. 71.

130 *wnšb* (*Wb*. I, p. 325) or *wtṯ* (*Wb*. I, p. 382).

131 The only example of a male deity receiving this object from the king is Ptah in the Temple of Abu Simbel where he was labeled with the unusual title of the Lord of the Sky; Handoussa, "A propos de l'offrande *Šbt*," pp. 66–67; Sambin, *L'offrande de la soit-disant "clepsydre"*, pp. 325–328.

132 Handoussa, "A propos de l'offrande *Šbt*," pp. 71ff., where she translates the meaning of the composition of the *wensheb* sign as "putting time in order," "controlled time," "years in order," or simply "eternal years," taking the last sign (the pillar) *ḥn* to mean control or order or as *tr*, meaning years.

133 Graefe, "Das Ritualgerät *šbt/wnšb/wtṯ*," pp. 895–905; Graefe, "Die Deutung der sogenannten 'Opfergaben' der Ritualszenen ägyptischer Tempel als 'Schriftzeichen,'" pp. 147–148.

one cannot confidently say that this object reflects the clepsydra, enough resemblance remains to convey the symbolic idea behind the clepsydra, that is, the maintenance of cosmic order, especially because the baboon sometimes represents Thoth, the reckoner of time.[134]

The offering of the *wensheb* parallels the offering on the right side of the scene, where the king is offering Maat to his father Shu. Offering the *wensheb* to the female deities serves a similar purpose to the offering of Maat nearby, that is, to satisfy a god with a forceful power to guarantee some kind of balance and world order and to confirm the king's legitimacy in the meantime.[135] Offering the *wensheb* further seems to guarantee universal order and extraterrestrial control.

WEST WALL — REGISTER II

ISDES

The king is most likely offering milk to Isdes who is standing in front of him. Whether the offering is wine or milk, they both seek to appease the deity.[136] The iconography of Isdes lacks any headdress or attributes, a phenomenon that is repeated in each register of the opposite east wall. Instances where gods are represented without headgear or distinguishing attributes generally reflect different ideas. Some instances provided the needed space for longer texts or avoided repetition, especially in contexts displaying various crowns and headdresses. In other cases, these undistinguished deities were usually minor deities or younger members of a triad. They are not, however, consistently represented without head attributes.

The writing of the name of Isdes seems to have led to some confusion in identifying this god. He is sometimes known as Isdes or Isden.[137] Unfortunately, the last sign of his name in this register in chapel G is not sufficently clear to determine whether the name was written as Isden or Isdes. Apparently, Isdes is the original form of the name because the other variation occurs only later.

---

134 Handoussa, "A propos de l'offrande *Šbt*," p. 71; Graefe, "Das Ritualgerät *šbt/wnšb/wtṯ*," p. 896. Sambin, *L'offrande de la soit-disant "clepsydre,"* p. 304, argues that Thoth was not associated with epithets that characterize him as a regulator or organizer of time. However we do have sufficient evidence for the association of Thoth and time; see Wells, "Re and the Calendars," p. 17; Dunand, "Le Babouin Thot et la Palme. A propos d'une terre cuite d'Égypte," pp. 341–348. On the association of Thoth with the palm tree as a symbol of time and eternity, see Spieß, *Der Aufstieg eines Gottes. Untersuchungen zum Gott Thot bis zum Beginn des Neuen Reiches*, chapter 5.

135 Cf., Teeter, *The Presentation of Maat. Ritual and Legitimacy in Ancient Egypt*, pp. 83ff.

136 Schott, *Das schöne Fest vom Wüstentale*, pp. 842–843; Leclant, "Le rôle du lait et de l'allaitement, d'après les Textes des Pyramides" pp. 123–127.

137 The main confusion in his name came about as a result of the writing of the two vessels 𓏁 (*ds*) and 𓏌 (*nw*), that were incorporated in the standard writing of the name of the god, or simply between the signs *n* 𓈖 and *s* 𓋴; Boylan, *Thoth, the Hermes of Egypt: A Study of Some Aspects of Theological Thought in Ancient Egypt*, p. 201, Appendix c. Note that some scholars gave two separate entries for this god, like Leitz, *Lexikon*, I, pp. 558 and 560.

Iconographically, Isdes is usually represented as a baboon or a jackal-headed deity, or, less frequently, in a completely human form. Many scholars have pointed out the relationship of this god with Thoth, especially during the New Kingdom,[138] which appears to have reached its climax in the Ptolemaic texts.[139] In fact, the name of Isdes frequently incorporated a baboon sign or ended with a determinative of ibis-headed Thoth.[140] Isdes acted as the messenger of Thoth[141] and was the one who seized enemies with his magic spells.[142] He helped Thoth as an advocate in the judgment of the dead.[143] They also shared titles such as *nb ẖmnw*, "Lord of the Ashmonein," and *nb hdn*, "Lord of the Hdn-plant."[144] Thoth and Isdes seem to also be connected with a locale in Upper Egypt called *ḥsr.t*, in the village of Hermopolis Magna, the capital of the 15th Upper Egyptian nome.[145] However they both seem to have shared an important title that is most relevant to this scene: "Lord of the West" or "Lord of the Westerners."[146]

In the Late Period, Isdes became more frequently associated with the designations of the kings. In the majority of the Ptolemaic temples, Isdes is represented aiding the king in rituals. The king is also said to be his heir, his son, his likeness, his equal, or his brother: *s3 'Isdn, snn n 'Isdn, mi 'Isdn*.[147] In many of these representations, Isdes and the king engage in a ritual with the *wensheb* symbol. Isden is represented as the artisan of the symbol.[148] Furthermore, Isdes acts as the mediator who lets the *wensheb* symbol arise from the king to the recipient goddess. For example, in the Kom Ombo Temple, the king offers *wensheb* to Sakhmet and claims that "he is the first born to god Isdes, in trying to ascend the symbol to the face of her majesty."[149] The existence of Isdes in our scene might be linked to the offering of the *wensheb* in the first register.

It is because of the work of Isdes, the representative of Thoth, that the goddesses receive this offering. In many examples, Isdes facilitates the passing of the *wensheb* offering to various goddesses. The relationship of Isdes with *wensheb* also points to the association of *wensheb* with the calculation and flow of time. In fact, Derchain argued:

> cette clepsydre qui, dans l'écrasante majorité des cas, est offerte à Hathor de Dendera, correspond trés précisément aux variations auxquelles la pléntitue

138 Bleeker, *Hathor and Thoth. Two Key Figures of the Ancient Egyptian Religion*, p. 107.

139 Boylan, *Thoth, the Hermes of Egypt*, p. 203.

140 See the variant writing of his name in *Wb.* I, p. 134; Leitz, *Lexikon*, VI, p. 558.

141 Grieshammer, "Isden," cols. 184–185; idem, "Isdes," col. 185.

142 Sternberg, *Mythische Motive und Mythenbildung in den ägyptischen Tempeln und Papyri der griechisch-römischen Zeit*, p. 149.

143 Bonnet, *Reallexikon der ägyptischen Religionsgeschichte*, p. 325.

144 Derchain-Urtel, *Thoth à travers ses épithètes dans les scènes d'offrandes des temples d'époque gréco-romaine*, pp. 119ff.

145 Derchain-Urtel, *Thoth à travers ses épithètes*, pp. 69, 79.

146 Boylan, *Thoth, the Hermes of Egypt*, p. 203; Bleeker, *Hathor and Thoth*, p. 107.

147 *E* I, p. 60,15; *Kom Ombos*, pp. 521, 955; *D* I, p. 107, 15; *D* II, p. 65, 14; *E* V, p. 98,6; *D* III, p. 81, 8; *E* IV, p. 82,13; *Esna* II, p. 24,7.

148 Sambin, *L'offrande de la soit-disant "clepsydre,"* Document 15 (9), pp. 69, 292.

149 Sambin, *L'offrande de la soit-disant "clepsydre,"* pp. 184–185; *PM* VI, p. 197(230–231), pl. xii, fig.1; *D* II, p. 65, 14.

> de l'œil est soumise réguliérement, c'est-à-dire que cette correspondence, à la façon d'un veritable parallélisme, s'explique par la function même de cet instrument dont le but est de rendre visible l'écoulement du temps, par des moyens matériellement perceptibles.[150]

Not only is Isdes connected with the *wensheb* symbol but also with the *udjat* eye, as both seem to represent symbols of controlling time and the cosmos. In the Dendera sanctuary, the scene of the king offering the *wensheb* to Sakhmet is paralleled by a scene of the king offering the *udjat* eye to Bastet.[151] In Dendera, an inscription declares "Take for yourself the *wensheb*; it is the Ka of the eye of *udjat*."[152] Derchain-Urtel notes that at Dendera, in Hathor's sanctuary, the text says "offering the eye *udjat*. Words spoken: take for yourself the *udjat* eye, under the divine control (sometimes Isdes is mentioned here); it is splendid like the work (*k3t*) of *ḥsb-inw* (because) his white and his black are good in place and his pupil is safe without default."[153] The scene in Dendera of the offering of *wensheb* to Sakhmet evokes the same theme.[154] In the Mammisi of Philae, the king offers *wensheb* to Isis and mentions that he is "the son of Mehy who completes the *udjat* eye at your place." Thus, there seems to be a stress on the general connection between *wensheb*, *udjat* eye, and the eye of Re.[155]

SHESMU

The wine press on Shesmu's head was also used to write the deity's name. This sign is sometimes misinterpreted as Gardiner's Hieroglyphic sign Aa 23 (𓌞), which has led some authors to give the same god two names: Shesmu and Medjed.[156] Shesmu was depicted completely anthropomorphically or as falcon-, lion-, or ram-headed deity. He was a productive god whose primary job was to press wine, provide oil and perfume, and bring provisions to the dead king. However, the funerary books (Pyramid Texts, Coffin Texts, and Book of the Dead) portray him as a cruel god who can injure the gods themselves.[157] He is portrayed in many barbaric images. His position as squeezer is sometimes brutal, as when he presses the heads of the people instead of grapes in his wine presses.[158] In the temple reliefs of the Greco-Roman temples, he is represented as

150 Derchain-Urtel, *Thot à travers ses épithètes*, p. 31.

151 *D* I, p. 46.

152 Derchain-Urtel, *Thot à travers ses épithètes*, p. 31; Germond, *Sekhmet et la protection du monde*, pp. 315–318.

153 Derchain-Urtel, *Thot à travers ses épithètes*, pp. 37–39.

154 Derchain-Urtel, *Thot à travers ses épithètes*, pp. 37–39.

155 Sambin, *L'offrande de la soit-disant "clepsydre,"* pp. 145, 147.

156 Peterson, "Der Gott Schesemu und das Wort *mḏd*," pp. 86–87; Ciccarello, "Shesmu the Letopolite," p. 48.

157 See for example, Pyramid Texts § 403; De Buck, *Coffin Texts*, I, p. 123;VI, 8, 32, 179, 349; Allen, *The Book of the Dead*, p. 30, Spell 17b s1.

158 Schott "Das Blutrünstige Keltergerät," pp. 88–93 and pl. VI.

lord of special rooms, translated as "laboratories" (*nb ỉswty*), reserved for the production and storage of ointment, oils, and unguents.[159]

Ciccarello suggested that the representations of Shesmu with a wild or calming nature can be reflected in either a human or a lion's head, respectively.[160] Some attestations of Shesmu defy this categorization; for example, in the mortuary Temple of Ramesses III at Medinet Habu, he is represented completely anthropomorphically in his helpful nature as the guardian of the Sokar sanctuary.[161] However, his two sides appear on an important scene on the western side of the east staircase inside the Temple of Hathor at Dendera.[162] The scene is among a series that depict a long procession of the king, followed by a number of priests and deities. One of these priests is followed by a lion-headed god called "Shesmu Lord of the Laboratory" (see pl. 21). After nine representations of deities and priests is another representation of Shesmu as a human figure (see pl. 22). He carries pieces of meat, and the inscription gives him a rather chilling character, wild and destructive. It reads "Shesmu, Lord of the slaughter house of Horus, chief of the slaughter block, who hacks up the oryx, wild of countenance, who overthrows enemies, who slays all the beasts of the desert, mighty in his arm, who strikes down the rebels, who propitiates the heart of Hathor with what she likes."[163] This representation of Shesmu in Dendera seems to be a good parallel for his representation in the Hibis Temple.

As in the Hibis scene, in this Dendera scene Shesmu is represented anthropomorphically and is entrusted with overthrowing the enemies, as the remaining inscription behind Shesmu indicates. In fact, comparison of the two scenes of Dendera and Hibis might help in the translation of some of the missing signs from the chapel G scene, suggesting that the last sign before the plural strokes in the third line of the inscription above Shesmu is most probably , which is Gardiner's sign A 14A (blood interpreted as an axe), as a determinative of *ḫry* (enemies) or *rkyw* (adversaries).[164] The following title in Dendera relates an important character of Shesmu that is most relevant to the Hibis scene: "the slayer of the beasts of the desert."

The incorporation of Shesmu in this scene in Hibis implies his protective power against the foes of the desert and might also reflect his basic connection with Kharga as a famous center of wine production.[165] In Papyrus Harris, Ramesses III states that he made

---

159 These laboratories are room "Z" in Edfu, *E* II, pl. XLIIIA–D, and "A" in Dendera, *D* I, pls. XLVII–LIII; also in Kom Ombo, *PM* VI, p. 182 (22–23); Ciccarello, "Shesmu the Letopolite," pp. 47–50.

160 Ciccarello, "Shesmu the Letopolite," p. 43.

161 Gaballa and Kitchen, "The Festival of Sokar," pp. 3, 49–50.

162 Mariette, *Dénderah* IV, pls. XIV and XVI.

163 Translation after Ciccarello, "Shesmu the Letopolite," p. 51; Mariette, *Dénderah* IV, pl. XVI; This scene is repeated on the opposite wall of the staircase, with the direction of the procession going the other way. The two figures are also separated by nine figures; however, Shesmu's name is not mentioned over the first figure with the lion head. See *D* IV, pl. V–VII.

164 Wilson, *Lexicon*, p. 529.

165 Poo, *Wine and Wine Offering in the Religion of Ancient Egypt*, p. 19.

numerous wine gardens for Amun in Kharga and Bahariya.[166] The Green Horus-Eye was used to refer to wine offerings since the Ptolemaic Period and was often mentioned as coming from the Kharga Oasis.[167]

IAQS

Figure 21: Inscription above Iaqs, detail from figure 19

Investigating the identity of the third figure on the second register of the west wall invites discussion of some of the so-called "minor deities" inside and outside chapel G. According to the inscription, the name of this god reads *Ḥḳy*.

In their preliminary publications about the temple, Winlock and Davies did not recognize this god.[168] Cruz-Uribe commented in his footnote: "it is uncertain whether to identify this god with the Heka/ Magician."[169] The dictionaries have no separate entries for a god named *Ḥḳy* or *Ḥḳ3*, and it is hard to establish the connection, if it exists, between him and the magician god *Ḥk3*, or to establish whether the two are assimilation, coexistence, or totally different beings. Could this be simply Late Period practice of the sign *ḳ* replacing *k*?[170]

The iconography of the headdress does not clarify the matter, because the magician god Heka was never represented wearing such a crown. His epithet, *nb dnit*, however, is very significant. It is necessary to briefly set aside the identity of the god and consider his accompanying title first. The title reveals a unique connection to the city of Denet. It has been established that Denet refers to the Thinis nome, which was the 8th Upper Egyptian nome [hieroglyph].[171] Brugsch proposed the village of El-Tineh, near Bardis, not far from the Nile, as the location of Thinis.[172] Although the exact location of Thinis is still obscure, it is certain that the city was located on the west bank of the Nile, like the majority of locales mentioned in the discussion of this chapel.

The location of Thinis is also associated with the main south road connecting the oasis to the Nile. It is known as the Girga/Thinis–Kharga road and is considered to be the best and shortest route between Kharga and the Nile.[173] The importance of this southernmost

166 Poo, *Wine and Wine Offering*, p. 11; Erichsen, *Papyrus Harris* I, pp. 7, 10–12.

167 Dils, "Wine for Pouring and Purification in Ancient Egypt," pp. 118–119; Poo, *Wine and Wine Offering*, pp. 24–25, such as in *Philae* II, p. 219,12: "Take for yourself the good wine of Khargeh and Baharia, namely the Green Horus Eye."

168 Davies, *The Temple of Hibis*, Part 3, p. 19.

169 Cruz-Uribe, *Hibis Temple Project I*, p. 85, n. 291.

170 For the conflation of *ḳ* and *k* in the Late Period, see Vittmann, "Zum Gebrauch des *k3*-Zeichens im Demotischen," pp. 1–12.

171 Gauthier, *Dictionnaire des noms géographiques*, VI, pp. 77, 95–96.

172 Brugsch, *Dictionnaire géographique de l'ancienne Égypte*, pp. 950–952; Gauthier, *Dictionnaire des noms géographiques*, VI, p. 77.

173 Morkot, "The Darb el-Arbain, the Kharga Oasis and its Forts, and Other Desert Routes," pp. 86–87. For reference to this road, see Darnell, *Theban Desert Road Survey in the Egyptian Western Desert*, I, pp. 6, 29, 43ff; Darnell, "The Deserts," p. 36. See also Valloggia, "This sur la route des Oasis," pp. 185–190.

direct road from Thinis goes back as far as the Old Kingdom. In Herkhuf's biography, he writes of several trips to the land of Yam, "*Ỉ3m*," most probably some parts of Nubia, during the 6th dynasty. Here one encounters for the first time the general name of the oasis, "*Wḥ3t*." Herkhuf sets out to visit the oasis and, consequently, Nubia from a region identified with the Thinite nome.[174] Many authors appropriately understand the oasis mentioned in the biography as the Kharga Oasis.[175]

Looking carefully at the inscription of this god in chapel G, one sees an unexplainable bolt *s* sign attached to the name of the deity. The location of this sign is obscure, as it comes after the deity's determinative. This may suggest another exciting possibility for identifying this god. A few sources from ancient Egypt refer to a god called Heqas or Iaqs. The name of this god is written in different forms: [hieroglyphs], [hieroglyphs], [hieroglyphs], [hieroglyphs] and [hieroglyphs]. Kees suggested reading his name as *Ỉ3ḳs*, based on the word play with the verb *ỉ3ḳ* in Pyramid Text 452.[176] Like the other deities in chapel G, scholars have also characterized Iaqs as "a minor deity," making him a good match to the other characters in this scene. More importantly, this god occurs outside the Hibis Temple with some of the gods represented in this chapel—notably Ha, Lord of the West and Desert,[177] represented in his following on the second register of the west wall of the chapel G; Hedjhotep,[178] represented on the opposite east wall; and Igai,[179] Lord of the Oases, who was highly regarded in the Kharga Oasis.[180]

Unfortunately, the identity of Iaqs is unclear, partly because of a lack of information about him and because scholars have failed to treat him as a unique entity. Instead, they have tended to pair Iaqs with Hepwy, [hieroglyphs], "who belongs to the two fans." Hepwy was perhaps a personification of the two fans behind the king, and scholars dubbed him as the "partner" of Iaqs.[181] The functions and attributions of Hepwy flowed and were easily extended to Iaqs, even though they are not always represented together. Iaqs was overshadowed by his partner Hepwy and to some extent by another god called "Dwa Wr," or "the Great Morning," who personified the royal beard as well as toilet items, face-washing, and shaving.[182] Sethe was the first to render the meaning of Iaqs as "Herrscherbinde" or "royal handkerchief;" he also cites the incidents of writing the determinative at the end

174 Edel, *Inschriften des Alten Reiches. V. Die Reiseberichte des (Herchuf)*, pp. 62–63, 73.

175 Fischer, "A God and a General of the Oasis on a Stela of the Late Middle Kingdom," p. 227; Yoyotte, *Pour une localisation du pays de Iam*, p. 174. For reconstruction of Harkuf's route, see Giddy, *Egyptian Oases. Bahariya, Dakhla, Farafra and Kharga During Pharaonic Times*, pp. 51–52.

176 Kees, "Kulttopographische und Mythologische Beiträge. 7. *Ỉ3ḳs* und *ḥpi*, zwei Königsinsignien als Gottheiten," p. 25.

177 Naville, *The Festival-hall of Osorkon II*, pl.12.

178 *Opet* I, p. 206.

179 Naville, *The Festival-hall of Osorkon II*, pl.12.

180 His name is attested among the graffiti of Gebel el Teir; Fischer, "A God and a General of the Oasis," p. 232. See pp. 94ff., below.

181 Gutbub, "Remarques sur les dieux du nome tanitique à la Basse Époque," p. 58; Kees, "Kulttopographische und Mythologische Beiträge," pp. 24ff.

182 For example, the royal barber appears to have been called "priest of 'Dwa-Wr.'" Gardiner, "Horus the Behdetite," p. 29, nn. 2 and 3.

of [hieroglyphs] with the cloth determinative.[183] This could represent a variant for the writing of the more common determinative of the cattle hobble [hieroglyph] (V 19 from the Gardiner list). In the only mention of this god in the *Lexikon der Ägyptologie*, Meyer grouped the three gods Hepwy, Dwa Wr, and Iaqs as personifications of the royal garb, "Gewande."[184] Leitz added a few different examples of the writings of this god's name only because they occur in connection with Hepwy.[185] Such divinization and personification of royal insignia is certainly possible, but the only evidence for such association comes from the ideogram of the two fans in the name of Hepwy and the two occurrences of the cloth determinative of the name of Iaqs.[186] No single text testifies to that association.

Since the early attestations of Iaqs, he was represented as a protector; he fills the *udjat* eyes and wards off enemies in Philae.[187] In the Mammisis of Dendera and Edfu, Iaqs defends against evil spirits holding two knives and is represented as a ram-headed figure.[188] In the Coffin Texts, he is responsible for defending against the enemies that come from the north.[189] He is identified as the protector of fishermen at the mouth of the Nile.[190] He is also associated with the lotus and papyrus,[191] sometimes accompanied by fish[192] or birds.[193] In a long geographical list at Edfu is a more detailed representation of him carrying both fish and birds in a big net, and he is given the important title [hieroglyphs], *Ꜣḳs ḥkꜣ rꜣw ḥꜣwt*, "Iaqs, Ruler of the Mouth of the Nile."[194] The mouth of the Nile is related to the swamps and backwater. Amun (of Sma Behdet) is said to be "Lord of the Marshes and Papyrus Swamps roaming the backwaters at the mouth of the Nile."[195] It is equally interesting that Hepwy carries a similar title as "Lord of the Marshes." Among the scat-

183 Gardiner "Horus the Behdetite," p. 29, n. 2; *CT* I, 184 (spell 44) and *PT* 452.

184 Meyer, "Toilettengeräte," col. 625; Gardiner "Horus the Behdetite," pp. 29ff.

185 Leitz, *Lexikon*, I, pp. 112–113; Leitz does not list this example of the god in chapel G of Hibis under the entiry for Iaqs nor for Heka the magician.

186 Aufrère, *L'univers minéral dans la pensée égyptienne*, I, p. 265 comments that the usual determinative of the cattle hobble is a corrupt version, "leçon corrompue," of the cloth determinative.

187 Gardiner "Horus the Behdetite," p. 30, n. 2; Kees, "Kulttopographische und mythologische Beiträge," p. 24

188 *D Mammisis*, p. 119, 2, pl. 61; *E Mammisis*, p. 166, 18 and pl. 43,1.

189 *CT* IV, 90a; Faulkner, *Coffin Texts*, I, p. 234.

190 Brugsch, *Dictionnaire géographique de l'ancienne Égypte*, p. 479; Naville, *The Festival-hall of Osorkon II*, p. 21, n. 8; Grdseloff, "Notice sur un monument inédit appartenant à Nebwa', premier prophète d'Amon à Sambe(det)," pp. 180–182.

191 *Kom Ombos*, p.790; *Gutbub Ko*, p. 197, 5; Lepsius, *Denkmäler aus Aegypten und Aethiopien*, II, p. 231.

192 *Kom Ombos*, p. 790; *Gutbub Ko*, p. 197.

193 *D* VIII, p. 104, 15; *D* IV, p. 205, 13.

194 Brugsch, *Dictionnaire géographique de l'ancienne Égypte*, p. 479; *E* IV, p. 199, 13, also "*nb rꜣ-ḥꜣwt*" in *Opet* I, p. 206; De Wit, *Les inscriptions du temple d' Opet, à Karnak*, I, p. 206; Legrain, "Le temple et les chapelles d'Osiris à Karnak," p. 170; Kees, "Kulttopographische und mythologische Beiträge," in *ZÄS* 64 (1929) pp. 99–112; 65 (1930) pp. 83–84; 71 (1935) pp. 150–155; 77 (1942) p. 25.

195 Gardiner "Horus the Behdetite," pp. 39–40; *E* IV, pp. 21, 35ff.

tered limestone blocks of Amenhotep I at Karnak, to the north of the 8th pylon, Hepwy is called Lord of the Marshes of the Delta.[196] This early example is repeated much later in the Temple of Edfu in several places.[197]

Iaqs' connection with a geographical or environmental nature is also confirmed from his attestation in the *Heb Sed* celebratory scenes inside the Temple of Osorkon II at Bubastis and Old Kingdom temples at Saqqara. The scene inside the Festival Hall of the Great Temple of Bubastis of Osorkon II shows an assembly of divinities.[198] Osorkon is offering to the gods of the north and south who came to witness his *Heb Sed* festival. The gods of Upper and Lower Egypt are represented inside their distinctive *pr wr* and *pr nw* shrines, respectively. Among the gods of Upper and Lower Egypt comes a group of familiar deities that are related to very specific regions or, rather, an aspect of the environmental characteristic of an area. These gods are Igai, followed by "Ha Lord of the West" who appears in chapel G, "The God of the South Wind" (*rsy ṯꜣw*), and, most importantly, "*Ꞽꜣḳs*" who is represented among the gods of the *pr nw* shrines. These are repeated in similar order in *Heb Sed* scenes on the funerary Temple of Pepi II[199] and most probably Sahure.[200] Thus, it is evident that the existence of these deities is to witness the celebration of the *Heb Sed* and to affirm the king's supremacy over not only an artificially defined nome-list but also over all of Egypt's geographical environments. This is further confirmed by an important excerpt from the Coffin Text Spell 313, titled "Being Transformed into a Falcon."[201]

> *Ꞽwty f(y) r.k m pt n ꜣt wrrt.k Ꞽwty f(y) r.k m tꜣ ꞽw.f n ꜣt šfšt.k Ꞽwty f(y) r.k n rsw? [Rꜥ] ḫsf (w) f sn Ꞽn sṯṯ nbt ꜣbw sṯt (w) s r sn m šsrw.s pw mrw spdw r.sn Ꞽwty f(y) r.k n mḥty ꞽ(w).f n ꞽꜣḳs///ḥpwy Ꞽwty f(y) r.k n ꞽꜣbty ꞽw f n(y) spdw nb ꞽꜣbty ḫsf.f sn ḏsw.k ꞽm.sn Ꞽwty f(y) r.k n ꞽmty ꞽw.f n(y) ḥꜣ nb ꞽmnty ḫsf.f sn (ꞽ)n ꜣt tm m pryw.f nw ꜣḫt*

> Who shall come against you in the sky shall belong to the striking power of your crown. Who shall come against you in land shall belong to the striking power of your respect. Who shall come against you from the south, [Re] will drive them away through Satis lady of Elephantine; She will shoot at them with her arrows, they are painful and sharp against them. Who shall come against you from the north he belongs to Iaqs and Hepwy. Who shall come against you from the east he belongs to Sopdu, lord of the east, he will drive them away, your knives being in them. Who shall come against

196 Grdseloff, "Notice sur un monument inédit appartenant à Nebwa"', pp. 180–181.

197 *E* IV, p. 47, 5–6; *E Mammisis*, p. 189, 13; *E* IV, p. 199, 13–14; E III, p. 94, 8-9; Grdseloff, "Notice sur un monument inédit appartenant à Nebwa,"' pp. 181–183.

198 Fischer, "A God and a General of the Oasis," p. 233; Naville, *Festival-hall of Osorkon II*, pp. 20–22, pl. 12 (7) and pl. 37.

199 Jéquier, *Le monument funéraire de Pepi II*, pl. 50ff.

200 Borchardt, *Sahure*, II, pl.19; in the partly destroyed version of Sahure *Heb Sed* scenes, the section where Iaqs is expected is missing, but we can assume that he existed there, especially since Horus Sma-Behdet and Dwa Wr are represented nearby; Gardiner "Horus the Behdetite," p. 29 and n. 2.3; Kees, "Kulttopographische und mythologische Beiträge," p. 25.

201 De Buck, *Coffin Texts*, IV, pp. 87–93. The excerpt comes from pls. 89–90.

> you from the west, he belongs to Ha, lord of the west; he will drive them away by the striking power of Atum in his ascending of the horizon.[202]

Although Iaqs is never associated with a specific location in the Delta, with Hepwy he became associated with the north in general. Such relation with the north is evident in astronomical representations as well. Ha, Shesmu, and Hepwy are related to the north as they are present in a scene of "What is in the Northern Sky."[203] Hepwy and Dwa Wr are present among the divinities of the constellation of the north sky in the tomb of Seti I and the funerary Temple of Ramesses II.[204]

In the Temple of Edfu, an important list of the different nomes is depicted; each nome is listed with its [hieroglyph] *mr*, representing its "canal" or "stretch of water," its [hieroglyphs] *ww*, "arable land" or "territory," and its [hieroglyph] *Pḥ*. The latter is translated as "marshland" or "hinterland."[205] Gauthier describes it as "bas-pays inondé en temps de crue."[206] *Pḥ* was used to describe the back limits of Egypt, but in later periods it became generalized as the "swamps" of every nome.[207] A list of the Pehou of Upper and Lower Egyptian nomes appears on several documents from ancient Egypt. Barguet gathered several documents of the lists of nomes with their subdivisions and in particular their Pehou. The documents start from the time of Hatshepsut's red chapel and end with the Medamoud Temple of the Roman emperor Trajan.[208] It is significant that the name Iaqs (same spelling as the name of the god Iaqs but without the seated god determinative [hieroglyphs], [hieroglyphs], [hieroglyphs]) appears as the name of the Pehou of the 8th Upper Egyptian nome (Thinis)—twice inside the Temple of Edfu, twice inside the Temple of Dendera, and once at Medamoud.[209]

---

202 Translation after Faulkner, *Coffin Texts*, I, pp. 233–235. One notes the use of gods who not only represent cardinal links but also some kind of geographical references.

203 Piankoff, "Le livre du jour et de la nuit," p. 27; *E* I, p. 52; Neugebauer and Parker, *Egyptian Astronomical Texts*, III, pp. 195 and 199.

204 Kees, "Kulttopographische und mythologische Beiträge," pp. 26–27.

205 Gardiner "Horus the Behdetite," p. 39; *E* IV, p. 21; *E* IV, p. 35; Gardiner, *Ancient Egyptian Onomastica* II, pp. 154–155, where he says that the meaning of that term "*pḥw*" is still only "vaguely defined"; Barguet "Une liste des Pehou d'Égypte sur un sarcophage du Musée du Louvre," p. 10, n. 2; also see Beinlich, *Studien zu den "Geographischen Inschriften" (10.–14. o. äg. Gau)*, especially pp. 31ff, where he translates *ww* as an arable land and *Pḥw* as "Marshland."

206 Gauthier, *Dictionnaire des noms géographiques contenus dans les textes hiéroglyphiques*, IV, p. 43.

207 Baines, *Fecundity Figures. Egyptian Personification and the Iconology of a Genre*, p. 201. *pḥ* as "hinterland," *Wb.* I, pp. 537 (5ff), 538 (1–4), while *pḥ* as swampy area of the Delta is in *Wb.* I, p. 538 (5ff).

208 Barguet "Une liste des Pehou d'Égypte," pp. 11–12. There is a Pehou list inside the Temple of Hibis, north wall of chapel K2 to the west side of the sanctuary; Davies, *The Temple of Hibis*, Part 3, pl. 25; Baines, *Fecundity Figures*, pp. 270ff. Beside the brief list in the chapel of Hatshepsut, the pre-Hibis Pehou documents come from the two temples of Abydos, that of the Temple of Seti and Ramesses II.

209 *E* IV, pp. 21–40, 172–193; *E* V, pp. 13–28, 106–124; Drioton, "Rapport sur les fouilles de Médamoud," n. 157; *D* I, pls. 61, 66; note that in this reference Heqas appears as the Pehou

The actual environment that once surrounded the Kharga Oasis conforms to the marshland character that is reflected from the representations of the gods and their epithets in chapel G. Beadnell, who visited the oasis at the turn of the 18th century, discovered lacustrine deposits and suggested that marshland was still in existence during the Roman Period, but by then it was only a thin "marshy swamp."[210] In addition to his association with the environments of the oasis, Iaqs could also be related to the notion of acquiring the riches of the desert, which is also reflected in the inscription of the doorway of this chapel. During the ritual of "replenishing the *udjat* eye," he offers silver, chamomile, and an unidentified *Seshemt* mineral.[211]

HA

The last deity in this register is Ha (*Ḥ3*) who appears as far back as the 3rd dynasty.[212] His earliest anthropomorphic representation dates to the 18th dynasty, during the time of Hatshepsut.[213] Brugsch associated him with the Upper Egyptian nome of Oxyrhynchus, current Behnessa,[214] west of Bahr Jusuf and closely connected with the Bahariya Oasis.[215] Its standard of the three hillsides became the god's distinguished head attribute. His association with the arid regions increased with time. Like Isdes, the first deity on the same register, Ha was also Lord of the West. In the Coffin Texts and the temple scenes of later periods, he was called "Lord of the West," "Lord of the Desert," and "Lord of the Western Desert" in particular, where he provided protection from the dangerous animals and such foreign enemies as the Libyans or the nomadic tribes of the desert.[216] Even the

---

of both the 8th and the 7th Upper Egyptian nome; Barguet "Une liste des Pehou d'Égypte," pp. 11–18.

210 Beadnell, *An Egyptian Oasis: An Account of the Oasis of Kharga in the Libyan Desert*, p. 118. The author thanks Professor Darnell for this reference.

211 Aufrère, *L'univers minéral dans la pensée égyptienne*, I, pp. 264ff,

212 Wildung, "Ha," col. 923; ibid., nn. 1–2; He was only represented once with a falcon head in *D Mammisis*, p. 141, 24, on the east wall where he was also called *nb imntt*. A new study of the god Ha is currently being conducted by Kata Jasper, University of Budapest, Ph.D. thesis in progress.

213 He is represented on the middle colonnade at the northern wall and associated with the purification of queen Hatshepsut; Naville, *Deir el-Bahari* III, 8, pl.63; Wildung, "Two Representations of Gods from the Early Old Kingdom," pp. 146, 157.

214 Brugsch, *Dictionnaire géographique de l'ancienne Égypte*, pp. 35–36, 719, 1291–1321; *E* I, p. 331, 16, where *ḥ3* is represented with the emblem of the nome and the title *nb imntt*.

215 Graefe, "Oxyrhynchos," pp. 638–639.

216 Wildung, "Two Representations of Gods from the Early Old Kingdom," pp. 157–159; Wildung, "Ha," col. 923; Leitz, *Lexikon*, V, pp. 10–11. See also *CT* IV, 90e; *E* III, p. 342,7; *E* II, p. 31, 15; Yoyotte, "Recherches de géographie historique et religieuse: sources et méthodes," pp. 625–645; Jasper, "Will the Hunger Be Repelled in the End? Notes on Scribal Solutions and Textual Transmission — The Case of PT 204, § 119b," pp. 47–70; Jasper, "Did the Ancient Egyptian Traveller Consider Ha, God of the Western Desert, while Traversing his Domain?" pp. 62–73.

king is identified with Ha in his position as Lord of the Western Mountains.[217] In Edfu, Ha provides sand in the ritual of the foundation of the temple.[218] He has a strong connection with the Oasis of Bahariya as well.[219] Not only did he reside on the main road to the oasis, but he was also regarded as the main deity of the western desert. Kamose sent his troops to devastate the Bahariya Oasis while he was in Keis (*s3ḳ3*), a short distance from the Oxyrhynchite nome.[220] An important road crosses the middle of the western desert from the Oxyrhynchite nome westward, leading to the Bahariya Oasis; then, the road turns southward, connecting to the Dakhla Oasis and finally joining the Kharga Oasis.

Despite his ancient origin, nothing more is documented about this god. However, his relationship with another god, Igai (*Ig3i*), who might have been his partner, reveals important answers to the reasons behind the particular representation of Ha in this scene. The relationship with this even lesser-known deity called Igai or Ga reinforces the importance of Ha in the desert areas surrounding the oasis. Ga also appears since the 3rd dynasty and is often labeled as "Lord of the Southern Oasis," most probably referring to Dakhla and Kharga.[221] Ha and Igai are mentioned together in the Coffin Texts (spells 755–756)[222] in a punning relationship. The spells are titled "A man is not to putrefy in the realm of the dead." These spells wish for the protection of the members of Osiris "by avoiding decay or putrefaction (*ḥw3*)[223] like Ha and avoiding being compact (*gw3*)[224] like Ga." The resemblance between the emblem of the Oxyrhynchite nome and the writing of the name of Igai suggests that he might have been the god of this nome, a predecessor of Seth.[225]

Many gods are associated with the desert in general, but they may have been associated with one or two geographic aspects of the location. For example, Seth was called Lord of the Desert and could have represented its chaotic atmosphere; Sopdu was not just associated with the eastern desert but also the marshy desert, Dedwen with the southern rocky desert, Ha with the sandy desert, and Igai with the more compact escarpment of the desert.[226] In other words, most of those gods probably do not belong to a single place alone but collectively to various places of the same geographical and environmental character.

217 Morgan, *Kom Ombos: Catalogue des monuments et inscriptions de l'Égypte antique*, p. 282, E.

218 The ritual of "*ḏb3 snṯ m šʿy ḫ3st*," *E* II, p. 31, 15.

219 Fakhry, *Bahria Oasis*, I, p. 88, pl. 34B, tomb of *B3-n-ntyw*; ibid., p. 158, pl. 51A (Ain el muftella).

220 Habachi, "Preliminary Report on Kamose Stela and Other Inscribed Blocks Found Reused in Foundations of Two Statues at Karnak," p. 202; Fischer, "A God and a General of the Oasis," p. 233, n.56.

221 Fischer, "A God and a General of the Oasis," pp. 230–235. See also the study of this god in Arafa, "Le Dieu Igay," pp. 11–22.

222 Faulkner, *Coffin Texts*, II, pp. 288–289; De Buck, *Coffin Texts*, VI, pp. 384, 386.

223 *Wb*. III, pp. 50–51, "to decay." The same word is used in connection with Ha in *E* III, p. 342, 7, where he *ḥw3* the peg of Baba in the west.

224 *Wb*. V, pp. 159–60, *gw3*, "to draw together;" Faulkner, *Coffin Texts*, II, p. 288 translates it as "choke." Since the rest of these spells choose words that rhyme but have opposite meanings, one can translate *gw3* as opposite of putrefying, which is being solid or compact.

225 Fischer, "A God and a General of the Oasis," pp. 233–235, n. 57.

226 Note the use of the name of the god in a pun with *gw3*, "to be compact," in the previously mentioned *CT* 755–756. One can also recall the previously discussed scene from the Gebel

Thus, Ha and Igai might have formed two facets of the environment of the oasis. Although Igai is absent from the inscriptions and decoration of Hibis Temple, the rock inscription of Gebel el Tarif nearby provides his name and title, *Ig3i nb w3ḥ3t*, "Igai, Lord of the Oasis."[227] The representation of Ha instead of Igai in chapel G goes well with the main theme that commemorates the trip to the oasis, thus requiring the protection of the road gods. Ha also appears on the north reveal of the entrance doorway to the sanctuary, on register IV.[228] He is labeled as "Horus Ha of the Desert" and is represented in anthropomorphic form with the three hillside signs. He is holding a bow with his left hand and a knife with his right and has captured two bound men, perhaps foreign prisoners or nomads. There, as well as in this scene in chapel G, he fulfills his function as another guardian against the desert foe.

This review has stressed a *theology of places*, a theme that is quite common in the texts throughout the chapel. Among the titles of Geb is a specific attachment to the place of wilderness and general emphasis on his lordship in every place that his Ka desires. The same idea is expressed by means of Osiris' titles. On the first register of the south wall, we see the specific mention of Amun's trip in the mountainous areas; on the second register is the rather uncommon use of Osiris' title "Great God in his Place." Isis repeats the title of Osiris, adding a more generalizing auxiliary "Osiris of any Place in which his Ka desires." Almost every word, title, or iconographic detail seems to correspond closely to a general theological plan that the ancient Egyptians formed for this chapel, revealing the unique Egyptian thought of space and how they categorized, analyzed, and interacted with their surroundings. The temple walls provided a convenient milieu to express their views, geographical associations, and sense of environment that gave rise to specific aspects of gods and characters of local cults. The great works of Hibis, Doush, Qasr el Ghuita, Manawir, and Deir el Haggar are evidence of the great importance that the ancient Egyptians gave to the desert regions, their roads, and their ecology.

The theologians of this chapel listed the main cities *au depart* of these paths, thus enabling us to trace their actual or fictional foot steps. The analysis of this chapel suggests a reference to the two primarily well-attested routes: the northern Mankabad–Asyiut route and the southern Girga–Thinis route. The northern road from Asyiut measures about 201 km and is protected by two small forts, Someira and el Gib. The forts are Roman–Byzantine, 4th to 5th century, but surely earlier precedents must have existed. The road from Girga represents the shortest route to Kharga, measuring about 193 km long and protected by a large fort, el Deir.[229] Indirect routes are also alluded to by mention of Ha

el Silselah, where these three gods of the desert appear following each other; see pp. 78ff., above. *PM* V, p. 213; Champollion, *Notice descriptive des monuments égyptiens du Museé Charles X*. I, p. 264; Schumacher, *Der Gott Sopdu*, pp. 96–97.

227 The inscription was first discovered by Fakhry, *The Rock Inscriptions of Gabal el-Teir at Kharga Oasis*, pp. 413 (5) and 415 (fig.25), but Fischer was able to correctly identify and read the name of Igai; Fischer, "A God and a General of the Oasis," p. 232, and he dated it between the 26th dynasty and the Ptolemaic Period.

228 Davies, *The Temple of Hibis*, Part 3, pl. 5.

229 For information about these roads, see Morkot, "The Darb el-Arbain, the Kharga Oasis and its Forts, and Other Desert Routes," pp. 84–86, also see figs. 1, 3 and 4.

who, in addition to his attributes to the desert in general also functions as the deity of the Upper Egyptian nome, the Oxyrhynchite, currently Behnessa. This city is located at the edge of the desert, bordering the route to the Bahariya Oasis that extends southward until it leads to the Kharga Oasis. The south wall perfectly reflects the trip from Luxor, where one can also use either the Farshût Road or the Esna–Rezeigat Road to Kharga. Both roads showed archaeological evidence of dating to the Persian Period. The name of Amun of Hibis is attested among Persian Period graffiti left by desert travelers at Armant,[230] at the head of the Esna–Rezeigat Road. A concentration of Persian pottery is also found on the Farshût Road.[231] At the midpoint of the main northern route between the Nile and Kharga is found a desert outpost called Tundaba, which had an important cistern.[232] The site shows continuous use from at least the New Kingdom to the Roman Period. Persian pottery is also attested in this area.[233] The chapel seems to memorialize a ritual or mythological theme that involved the king or his representative, the high priest or Iunmutef, who visited the Temple of Hibis during a circuit of the desert region. They may have diverted to visit peripheral places in the desert regions that were rich in mineral resources and ultimately brought their precious products to adorn the Temple of Hibis.

230 Di Cerbo and Jasnow, "Five Persian Period Demotic and Hieroglyphic Graffiti from the Site of Apa Tyrannos at Armant," pp. 33–38.

231 Particularly in the southwestern portion of the Gebel Roma caravansaray (on the plateau over the Wadi el-Hôl); personal communication with Professor Darnell.

232 Darnell, "The Deserts," p. 41, fig. 3.6; Darnell, "Opening the Narrow Doors of the Desert," pp. 147–149. See also http://www.yale.edu/egyptology/ae_tundaba_cistern.htm.

233 Personal communication with Professor Darnell.

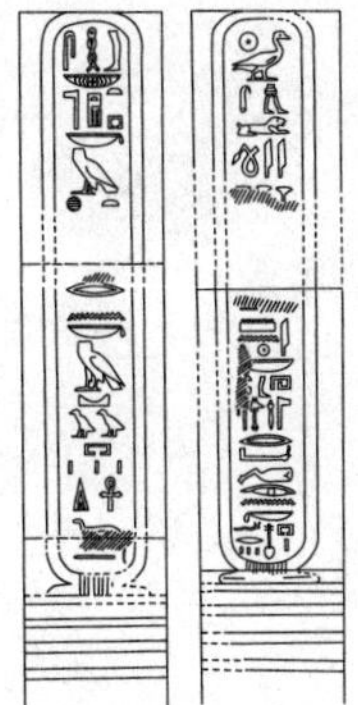

4
Chapel Complex H

1. DESCRIPTION

Chapels H1 and H2 are located in the south of the roof of Hibis Temple. These two decorated chapels are reached by the undecorated stairway H. Chapel H1 leads westward into an undecorated space, H3. Only the south wall of chapel H1 and the north and east walls of chapel H2 still exist (see pls. 23ff.).[1]

THE DOORWAY — LINTEL OF DOOR TO CHAPEL COMPLEX H

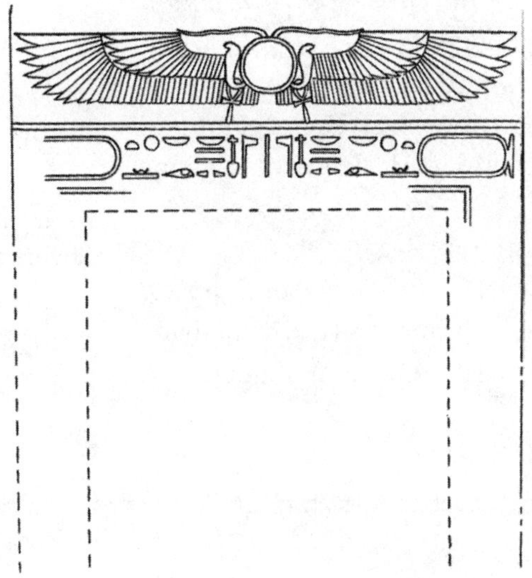

Figure 22: Doorway to stairway H
(after Davies, *The Temple of Hibis*, Part 3, detail from pl. 11).

The winged solar disk with the two cobras is at the top of the main panel of the lintel of the door to H. Two *ankh* signs dangle from the bodies of the cobras. Below is one horizontal line of inscription surrounded by two blank cartouches.

1 For the publication of these two chapels and their doorway, see Winlock, *The Temple of Hibis*, Part 1, p. 12, pls. XXII, XXXIV; Davies, *The Temple of Hibis*, Part 3, pp. 19–20, pls. 11, 19–20; Cruz-Uribe, *Hibis Temple Project I*, pp. 61, 85–90.

THE INSCRIPTION

Nṯr nfr nb tꜣwy nb ỉrt ḫt (…)¦
"Good god, lord of the two lands, lord of cult act (…)¦!"

Nṯr nfr nb tꜣwy nb ỉrt ḫt (…)¦
"Good god, lord of the two lands, lord of cult act (…)¦!"

WEST JAMB AND WEST REVEAL TO DOOR TO H

The east jamb and the east reveal are unfortunately destroyed. Davies did not record the west jamb. Cruz-Uribe recorded an outline of the west jamb and the west reveal.

THE INSCRIPTION

West Jamb of Door to H
Sꜣ Rꜥ nb ḫꜥwt (…)¦ [*mry*] *ỉmn* [*nb*] *Hbt nṯr ꜥꜣ*[2] *wsr* [*ḫpš*] *dỉ n.f dỉ ꜥnḫ ḏt.*
"The son of Re, lord of appearances (…)¦ [beloved] of Amun [lord] of Hibis, great god, powerful of [strength], for he has made a giving life forever."
West Reveal of Door to H
Sꜣ Rꜥ nb ḫꜥwt (Dryš)T ꜥnḫ ḏt mry Ỉmn Rꜥ nb hbt.
"Son of Re, lord of appearances (Darius)¦, living forever, beloved of Amun Re, lord of Hibis."

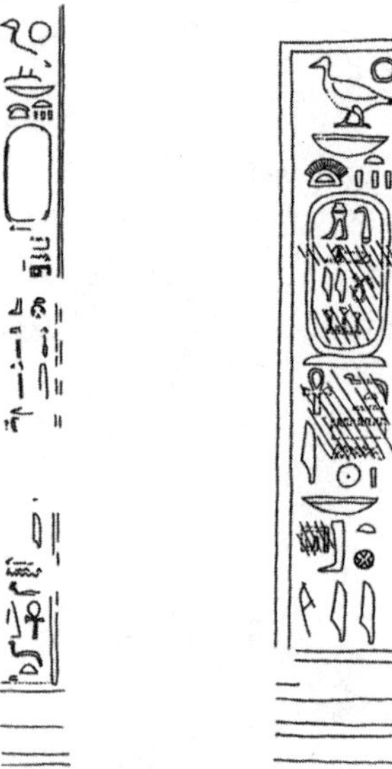

Figure 23: West and east reveals of door to stairway H (after Cruz-Uribe, *Hibis Temple Project I*, pl. 11A)

CHAPEL H1 — SOUTH WALL

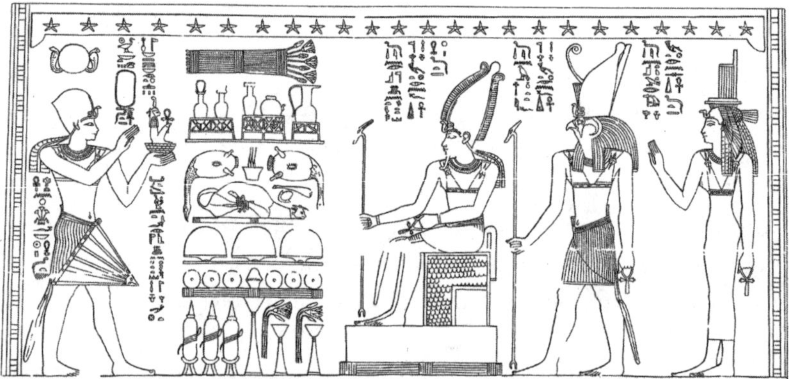

Figure 24: South wall of chapel H1 (after Davies, *The Temple of Hibis*, Part 3, detail from pl. 19)

2 Cruz-Uribe, *Hibis Temple Project I*, p. 61, n. 140 corrects the *nfr* sign in the drawing to the ꜥꜣ sign.

In this scene, the image of the king is on the left. He wears the *khepresh* crown with a uraeus at the front and the two streamers on his shoulders. He is barefoot, wearing a two-strap garment with a pleated kilt and a starched apron. Above the king's head is the image of the solar disk with two uraei. Between the king and the deities are various offerings laid on top and beneath an offering table; the offerings are a complex arrangement, including jars containing liquids, flower bouquets, bread, incense, two ducks, and a slaughtered cow. The first deity facing the king is Osiris seated on a throne. He wears the *atef* crown with a uraeus on his brow and a false beard. He holds the *ankh* sign in his left hand resting on his thigh and the *was* scepter in his right with the end propped on the front edge of the throne base. His garment is a two-strap shirt with a short kilt. His throne is decorated with a feather or *rishi* motif and is elevated on top of a rectangular base and a mat. The falcon-headed Horus is standing behind Osiris and wearing the crown of Upper and Lower Egypt and a uraeus on his brow. He wears a broad collar, a two-strap shirt with a short kilt, and an ox tail. He holds the *ankh* sign in his left hand at his side and the *was* scepter out in front of his body with his right. Isis is standing at the end of the row of divinities, wearing her distinctive throne sign on top of her head, combined with the vulture headdress. She wears a broad collar with a two-strap long, fitted garment that leaves her breasts exposed; she holds the *anḫh* sign with her left hand at her side, while her right hand is raised in front of her in a gesture of protection.

THE INSCRIPTION

Behind the king

S3 ꜥnḫ nb ḥ3.f mi Rꜥ dt

"All protection and life behind him like Re forever."

Above the arms of the king

Nṯr nfr nb t3wy nb irt ḫt s3 Rꜥ nb ḫꜥwt (…)¦ ꜥnḫ ḏt

"Good god, lord of the two lands, lord of cult act, son of Re, lord of appearances (…)¦ living forever."

Below the hands of the king

Ḥnk m3ꜥt n it.f Wsir ḫnty imntt nṯr ꜥ3 ḥr ib Hbt

"Presenting Maat to his father Osiris, foremost of the west, great god who dwells in Hibis."

Above Osiris

Ḏd mdw in Wsir ḫnty imntt nṯr ꜥ3 ḥr ib Hbt ir n. f di ꜥnḫ mi Rꜥ ḏt

"Words spoken by Osiris, foremost one of the westerners, great god who dwells in Hibis. He made a giving life like Re forever."

Above Horus

Ḏd mdw in Ḥr nḏ {t} it.f nṯr ꜥ3 ḥr ib bt ir n.f di ꜥnḫ

"Words spoken by Horus, avenger of his father, great god, who dwells in Hibis for he has made a giving life."

Above Isis

Ḏd mdw in 3st wrt mwt nṯr ḥr ib Hbt ir n.s di ꜥnḫ ḏt

"Words spoken by Isis, the great, the divine mother who dwells in Hibis for she has made a giving life forever."

CHAPEL H1 — NORTH WALL

Figure 25: North wall of chapel H1
(after Davies, *The Temple of Hibis*, Part 3, detail from pl. 19)

This wall no longer exists; therefore the description is based on the outline published by Davies.[3] According to Davies' reconstruction, the north wall of H1 had six images of the guardian deities on both jambs of the doorway to H2. These deities were kneeling on top of a dais with a cavetto cornice. Above each figure was a *pt* or a sky sign with decorated stars, reflecting the idea of the stellar bodies floating inside the body of the sky goddess Nut. One large standing figure of a god was depicted behind the three guardian deities on each side of the door jamb.

THE EAST JAMB

The uppermost knife-carrying genie or guardian deity on the east section or jamb of the north wall of H1 has the head of a baboon. There are remains of two hieroglyphic signs, *r* and perhaps *w*. The middle guardian deity has a front-facing human head. Traces of perhaps a seated determinative sign making up part of the god's name remain in front of him. The head of the lower figure is unfortunately not preserved. However, a seated god determinative, preceded by an arm sign, remains in front of him.

An inscribed block bears the formula *Ḏd mdw in Ḥr*, "words spoken by Horus." Another smaller block preserves the word *ḏt*, "forever." The inscriptions on these blocks, together with the comparison of the west jamb of this wall, confirm Davies' reconstruction of the figure of Horus on the east jamb of the north wall of chapel H1.

THE WEST JAMB

The only attested iconography of the guardian deities on the west jamb is part of the two long ears of the missing top figure, indicating that this figure may have had a jackal's

3 Davies, *The Temple of Hibis*, Part 3, pl. 19.

head.[4] Fortunately, a block with a representation of part of the middle figure together with a key inscription bearing part of the name *nb ḫmnw*, or "lord of Hermopolis," provide a clear reference to Thoth, whose image must have been on the west jamb of this wall. Another block preserved the middle part of Thoth's body, containing his striped kilt and remains of one or two land signs, *tȝ*, and *n* sign of water.

CHAPEL H2 — NORTH WALL

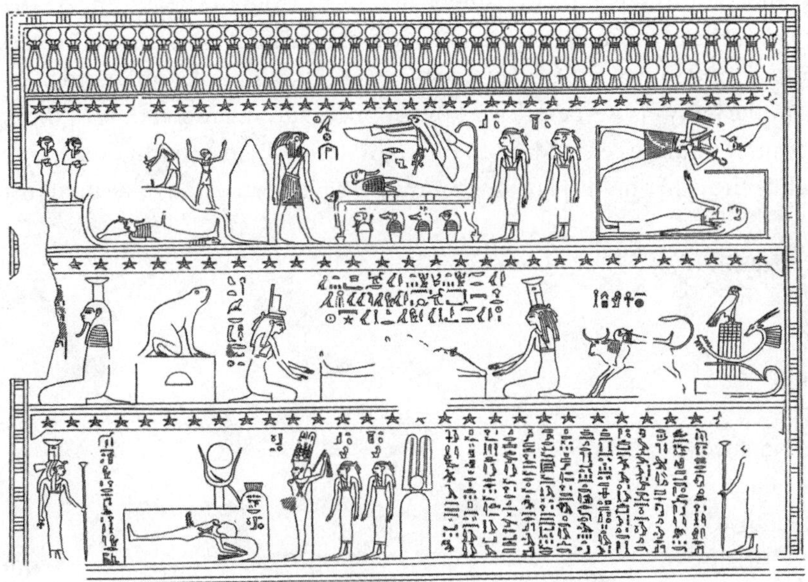

Figure 26: North wall of chapel H2
(after Davies, *The Temple of Hibis*, Part 3, detail from pl. 20)

The wall is decorated at the top with a *kheker* frieze. Each register is separated by a double band and framed on the top by the star-filled *pt* sign representing heaven. The depictions on this wall seem to express various events, reflected by the different vignettes on each register. The vignettes are separated from each other by means of several iconographic features, including the different directions the figures face, the different scales of the figures, and, as in the case of the first scene of the first register, a totally different ground-line orientation. The separation of these scenes may reflect different moments in time or place.

REGISTER I

On the right is a scene of the king or Osiris entering into a shrine of a goddess. The scene is rotated about 90 degrees clockwise from the normal horizontal level of the other scenes in the same register. The male figure is facing downward while the goddess is facing upward. The male figure wears the white crown and a short kilt. He also holds

4 For these guardian deities, see Guilhou, "Génies funéraires, croque-mitaines ou anges gardiens," pp. 365–417; Goyon, *Les dieux-gardiens et la genèse des temples: d'après les textes égyptiens de l'époque gréco-romaine.*

the crook and the flail with his crossed hands. The female goddess wears a long garment and no crown. One of her arms is raised in a welcoming gesture toward the other figure.

The focus of the center vignette is the funeral bier on which lies the body of Osiris. Isis, followed by Nephthys, stands to the right at the foot of the bier. With one leg advanced, the falcon-headed Horus stands to the left at the head of the bier. Four canopic jars with figural lids depicting the Four Sons of Horus are beneath the funeral bier. A kite holding the *ankh* sign, probably referring to Isis, flutters over Osiris' body. The pyramid-topped mound behind Horus separates the funeral bier scene from the next scene on the register.

In the last scene of the upper register, the ithyphallic body of Osiris is enclosed within an irregular rounded space that may represent a heap of grain or a mound of earth. It is enclosed by the body of a serpent. Two swathed male figures are standing to the left, while two other male figures are standing to the right. One of the latter figures has his hands raised, while the other holds part of what might have been a hoe or a ritual instrument.

THE INSCRIPTION

Above Isis
ꜣst
"Isis"
Above Nephthys
Nbt-ḥwt
"Nephthys"
Above Osiris
Wsir
"Osiris"
In front of Horus
Ḥr Rꜥ n?[5] *sḥ nṯr*
"Horus Re[6] [of] the divine booth."

REGISTER II

The first element is the emblem of a falcon on top of a rectangular facade or *serekh*, with a bow decorated at one end with an oryx head and at the other end with a *djed* pillar. These emblems rest on a sledge with a curved side. The following image represents the body of Osiris on the back of a running bull. This image of Osiris is at a smaller scale relative to the other figures in the register. The following vignette incorporates the ithyphallic image of Osiris lying on a rectangular bed and flanked on both sides by Isis and Nephthys. On the left side, behind Isis, is a large frog seated on top of a square base with

5 For the *niwt* city sign as *n* or *ḫnt*, see Cruz-Uribe, *Hibis Temple Project I*, p. 86, n. 296. A similar representation of this scene, with the *niwt* sign giving the phonetic rendering of *n* or *nt*, exists inside the sanctuary; see Davies, *The Temple of Hibis*, Part 3, pl. IV, reg. IV, fig. 5; Cruz-Uribe, *Hibis Temple Project I*, p. 29.

6 Horus Re occurs once more in Hibis, on the exterior wall, north wall, register I, right center (1st scene); Davies, *The Temple of Hibis*, Part 3, pl. 45.

the *t* sign of half a bread. According to the inscription, the image is to be understood as Heqat. This image seems to belong to the middle vignette of Osiris, Isis, and Nephthys, rather than the next vignette, based on the direction that Heqat faces. The last figure to the left on the second register represents a kneeling, mummiform, male equivalent to Nephthys. He has similar emblems on top of his head and a curved false beard. In front of him is a partly destroyed vertical line of inscription.

THE INSCRIPTION

Above the running bull

Ḥʿpy ʿnḫw

"The living Apis."

Above ithyphallic Osiris

Ἰw.k r ḥḥwt in ḥḥwt[7] *iw b3.k ḫʿwt m ḥr ḥnʿ b3 n Rʿ Ἰw.i m šw m hrw iw.k m iʿḥ m krḥw*

"You will (live) millions of millions (of years). Your Ba is appearing in heaven with the Ba of Re. I am as the sunlight by day, you are as the moon by night."

In front of Heqat

Ḥḳ3t nb<t> 3bḏw

"Heqat lady of Abydos."

In front of the kneeling figure

/////nwb

"///nwb"

REGISTER III

The third register (the lower register) on each of the four walls of room H2 includes the detailed passages of a spell involving a ritual to protect and awaken the body of Osiris. A physical representation of the latter most probably resided within this room.[8] Few parallels exist for these passages, and most come from papyri of the Greco-Roman Period, including Papyrus Berlin 3037, recto, columns 1–3; Papyrus 47.218.138 of the Brooklyn Museum; Papyri 3237 and 3239 of the Louvre Museum; and, most importantly, Papyrus 35.9.21 of the Metropolitan Museum of Art, recto, columns 26–32.[9] The latter was an important resource for deciphering the meaning of some atypical words in this chapel. Another important parallel comes from the lintel of the gateway of Hall IV of the Edifice of Taharqa at Karnak.[10]

7 *ḥḥwt in ḥḥwt*; *Wb*. III, p. 153.

8 This theory will be thoroughly discussed in the following commentary section.

9 These papyri are mentioned by Goyon, "Textes mythologiques. II: Les Révélations du Mystère des Quatre Boules," pp. 349–352.

10 *PM* II, p. 73(5–7); Leclant, *Recherches sur les monuments thébains de la XXVe dynastie dite éthiopienne*, pl. 47; Leclant, "Quelques données nouvelles sur l'édifice dit de Taharqa," pp. 181–192; Goyon, "Les cultes d'Abydos à la Basse Époque d'après une stèle du musée de Lyon," p. 43.

The third register on the north wall focuses on an important speech of Nephthys and Bastet who are at the left and right ends of the register, respectively. The text of their speech takes almost all the right half of the register. The image of Bastet is unfortunately mostly destroyed, but the lioness head can be restored with certainty along with her *wadj* scepter. Nephthys has her emblem on top of the vulture headdress. She holds the *ankh* sign in her right hand at her side and the *wadj* scepter in front of her body with her left hand. Arranged to the right of the text column in front of Nephthys are an ithyphallic reclining figure and a procession of Nephthys, Isis, and Min, separated from the lines of inscriptions of the speech by a round-topped stela with two feathers and a sun disk on top. The reclining Osirid figure is identified with Min of Coptos, according to the inscription above him. He is inside a sarcophagus or a tomb, on top of which is an emblem combining the solar disk between the cow horns with a third single intersecting ram-horn. Similar emblems also appear beside the figure of Min inside the Temple of Hibis.[11]

THE INSCRIPTION

In front of Bastet

Ḏd mdw i͗n Bȝstt ḥr rsy[12] *ḥr sni͗.s wsi͗r*

"Words spoken by Bastet watching over her brother Osiris."

The long speech in front of Bastet

(1) *Sw*[13] *mi͗ sṯ pȝ nšnyw*[14] *ẖfty* (2) *pfy ḥnmmt ḥm.wt rȝ p<ȝ>nty n i͗wi͗w* (3) *ḥr.f ḥsȝ*[15] *i͗w i͗rty.f i͗nḥw m* (4) *ḳrg*[16] *i͗w.f ḥr ḳni ꜥȝ m* (5)*wḥm ḥr-i͗r n.f r ẖftyw n Wsi͗r tȝ ḥȝt* (6) *m-ḏr di͗.f mḥi͗.f n ḏȝt*[17] *ḥr mw ḥꜥtw.f nb* (7) *pštw ḥm*

11 See, for example, plate 4, register V, figure 8; plate 22, east wall top and plate 51, south wall, left center; Davies, *The Temple of Hibis*, Part 3, p. 20.

12 This could equally be *ḥr srs*; however, both seem to imply the same meaning, "to awaken" as well as "to watch over;" *Wb*. IV, pp. 200–201; *Wb*. II, p. 450, 10.

13 It is better to take *sw* as a bare initial subject; see Cruz-Uribe, *Hibis Temple Project I*, p. 87, n. 306.

14 *Wb*. II, p. 342, 1. This could also be *Pȝ n šnyw*; *Wb*. V, p. 20, 5.

15 *ḥsȝ*, "fierce;" Lesko, *A Dictionary of Late Egyptian*, I, p. 331; *Wb*. III, p. 161. Note that the *s* is facing the wrong direction.

16 *ḳrg* for *grg*, "falsehood, wrongdoing." This could be implying the word *ḳri*, "storm," sometimes with the Seth animal determinative, which can in turn be a word play with *ḳni* in the same line.

17 This is an important phrase. The word *mḥi* appears several times in connection with Osiris' murder, esp. in the Memphite Theology; Breasted, "The Philosophy of a Memphite Priest," pls. I–II, lines 8, 19 and 62. See also Einaudi, "The 'Tomb of Osiris:' An Ideal Burial Model?," p. 475, n. 2. The word *ḏȝt* has multiple meanings, all of which can be applied here: *ḏȝt ḥr*, "to proceed," *Wb*. I, 403, *ḏȝt*, "amulet," "spell," *Wb*. I, p. 401, or "transgress, oppose," Lesko, *A Dictionary of Late Egyptian*, II, p. 261; *ḏȝt* with a house determinative can also mean "chest," *Wb*. V, p. 515. The latter meaning could refer to the beautifully decorated chest that was used by Seth to entrap Osiris, as reflected in the story by Plutarch (Griffiths, *Plutarch's De Iside et Osiride*, § 13, 138ff.). It is not improbable that the Egyptian theologians were aware of all these meanings and thus the word was chosen intentionally to reflect all the inherent

ir.k[18] *ḥr.k n ḥ3.k im.k* (8) *tkn r nṯr ḥ῾wt ntk ir ḏd t3 fdw.t tbt*[19] (9) *n tḥnt nty m ḥwt ῾3t*[20] *m iwnw sn.t imy* (10) *st*[21] *n p3 hrw ḥwiw tp.k sḥtmw* (11) *b3.k n nwnw.k* (12) *r m3 nṯr ῾3 mi ṯs tw Wsir* (13) *wn-nfr mk sẖrw sbiw.k*

"(1) He is like Seth, the raging one, (2) that enemy of the sun folk, and so forth, the one who is in coming. (3) His face is fierce. His eyes are rimmed with (4) falsehood. He has committed great offense (5) repeatedly, because he had acted towards the enemy of Osiris,[22] (6) after he caused that he be drowned by proceeding on water (and that) all his limbs were (7) divided. Turn back, your face behind you. You should not (8) draw near the divine flesh. You are the one who said: the four blocks of (9) faience, which are in the great temple of Heliopolis. Two therein (10) are broken up today. Those have struck your head (and) (11) annihilated your Ba.[23] You will not come back/be assembled[24] (12) to see the great god. Come, rise up Osiris Wennefer. Your enemies are being overthrown."

Above Nephthys

Nbt ḥwt

"Nephthys"

Above Isis

3st

"Isis"

In front of the standing figure of Min

Gbtyw

"The Coptite"

---

meanings. The comparable papyri in Goyon, "Textes mythologiques. II. Les Révélations du Mystère des Quatre Boules," pp. 356ff, list this phrase in variable ways; Papyrus New York 35.9.21 has a barque determinative for *d3y*, while Papyrus Brooklyn 47.218.138 has the man with the stick determinative. The rarity of the mention of the death of Osiris could be explained by Spell 1335–1336 of the Pyramid Texts, where Horus is making sure that the death of his father is never stated; Vernus, "Le mythe d'un mythe: la pretendue noyade d'Osiris; de la derive d'un corps à la derive du sens," pp. 19–34.

18 *ḥm ir.k*; *Wb.* III, p. 79.

19 *tbt* for *ḏbt*; *Wb.* V, p. 553.

20 *ḥwt ῾3t* also occur in association with the temple of Heliopolis in Papyrus Harris; see Grandet, "Le Papyrus Harris I," p. 282; Lesko, *A Dictionary of Late Egyptian*, I, p. 304.

21 *st* is perhaps a stative here; for *st*, "to break up, smash," see Lesko, *A Dictionary of Late Egyptian*, II, p. 97; *Wb.* IV, p. 373, 4, 8 for parallel spelling.

22 The construction of this sentence is problematic, see Cruz-Uribe, *Hibis Temple Project I*, p. 87, n. 316. For the euphemistic term "enemies of Osiris," see Posener, "Sur l'emploi euphémique de *ḫftj*(*w*) 'ennemi(s),'" pp. 30–35; Quack, "Sur l'emploi euphémique de *ḫft* 'ennemi' en démotique," pp. 197–198.

23 See Cruz-Uribe, *Hibis Temple Project I*, p. 88, nn. 319–320.

24 *N nwnw.k* future negation; *nwnw*, "to return, come back" (*Wb.* II, pp. 220, 16, 221, 2) can also be a word play with *nwi*, "to gather, assemble" (Lesko, *A Dictionary of Late Egyptian*, I, p. 230). The latter meaning would be an interesting comparison between what Seth has inflected on Osiris by dividing his limbs, *ḥ῾tw.f pštw*, and what has become of Seth himself.

Above the reclining figure

Mn, nb Gbtyw

"Min lord of Coptos."

In front of Nephthys

Ḏd mdw in nbt ḥwt ḥr rsy ḥr sni.s Wsir

"Words spoken by Nephthys watching over her brother Osiris."

CHAPEL H2 — SOUTH WALL AND WEST WALL

Unfortunately, both the south wall and the west wall no longer exist. Davies outlined their reconstruction based on his eye-witness account of the individual blocks that had been reused in the foundation of an ancient mosque in Kharga City. He gave no details or photographs of their exact whereabouts or condition.[25] Davies' outline confirms the architectural plan of the chapel complex H and is a dependable reconstruction. However, Cruz-Uribe challenged the order and the positioning of some blocks.[26] The following description is based on Davies' drawing.[27] A description of Cruz-Uribe's reexamination and comments will be provided below.

SOUTH WALL

As mentioned above, this wall is no more than 20 cm in thickness. It divides chapel H1 from chapel H2 and forms an entrance between the two. Its southern face is the northern wall of H1 and its northern face is the southern wall of H2. It is divided into two jambs and each jamb is divided into two registers bordered by the stars-filled *pt* sign of heaven.

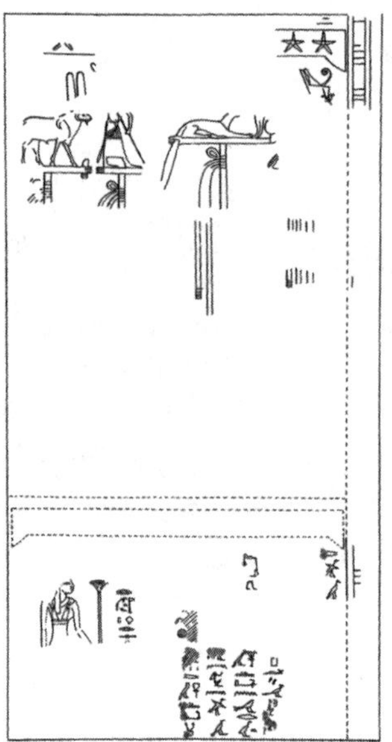
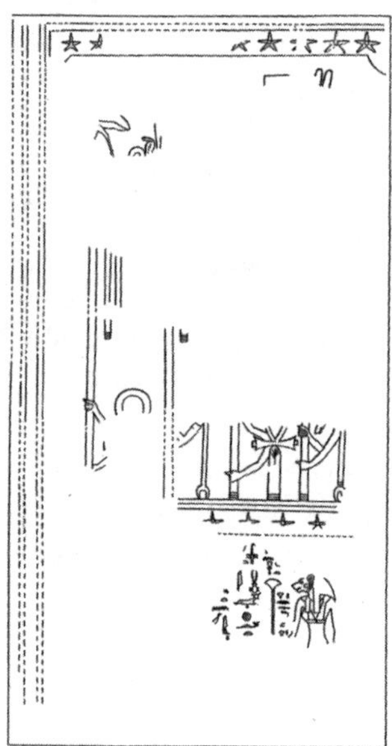

Figure 27: South wall of chapel H2
(after Davies, *The Temple of Hibis*, Part 3, detail from pl. 19)

25 According to a quick survey of the construction history of the ancient mosques of the current city of Kharga, the mosque mentioned by Davies seems to be the one called el Gamee el Kabir. Unfortunately, it was rebuilt several times during the past era and it is hard to presume these blocks still exist. A local inspector suggested the mosque of Een el Dar as an alternative choice.

26 Cruz-Uribe, *Hibis Temple Project I*, pp. 86 and 90.

27 Davies, *The Temple of Hibis*, Part 3, pls.19 and 20.

REGISTER I

The upper registers on both jambs have many different standards with no labels. On the hypostyle hall B, south wall, the king is performing rituals in front of a large number of similar standards that most probably represented different images of local gods.[28] On the right jamb are the remains of four standards carried alternatively by the *ankh* and the *was* signs with arms. On the left jamb is another set of four standards. Much of their top emblems have been preserved, so that it is possible to identify them: the first is a falcon with the crown of Upper and Lower Egypt and a uraeus, representing Horus. The second is a recumbent jackal, either Wepwawet or Anubis, and the third is Onuris, who is similar to his previous representation on the first register of the east wall, with a harpoon, two kilts, and an ox tail. The south standard has a ram with two tall plumes.

REGISTER II

Davies originally assigned a block with the name and image of Sakhmet and a few lines of inscriptions to the right jamb. On the left jamb he placed few blocks of inscriptions in front of a block with an unnamed goddess. Cruz-Uribe, however, suggested that this order is incorrect and that the biggest block with four lines of inscriptions should be placed on the opposite right jamb. The reading of the inscriptions then would start from the right side of the right jamb, in front of Sakhmet, and continue to the right side of the left jamb and then to the left in front of the unnamed deity.[29]

THE INSCRIPTION[30]

In front of Sakhmet

[*Ḏd mdw in*] *Sḫmt ḥr rsy ḥr* [*sni.s wsir*]

"[Words spoken] by Sakhmet watching over [her brother Osiris]"

The main inscription

(1) *Sw mi Stẖ ḫft pfy* [*ḥnmmt*] (2)// [*ḥmt-rw*][31] /[*p3*]*nty n iwiw* [*r*] *sḫm n wrd*[32] (3)[*ib*]//*n.i n p3* (*S*)//*ẖ*//*r sḫm in?*

"He is like Seth, that enemy of [the sun folk] (2)// [and so forth] /[the one] who is in coming [in order to] prevail over the weary (3) [of heart]//I have/// to the/// (4)//// to prevail//"

28 Davies, *The Temple of Hibis*, Part 3, pl. 33, as well as pls. 13 and 22.

29 Contra to Cruz-Uribe's suggestion that the hymn began on the left and continued from the right side of the door to the left; see Cruz-Uribe, *Hibis Temple Project I*, pp. 85–86.

30 See alternative reconstruction of this wall on p. 111, figure 29.

31 The reconstruction of lines 1 and 2 is based on the similar lines 1 and 2 on the opposite north wall, see above.

32 *Wrd-ib* as in the first stanza of Papyrus New-York 35.9.21, col. 26, line 3; Goyon, "Textes mythologiques. II. Les Révélations du Mystère des Quatre Boules," p. 355.

Register II of the left jamb has one block that can be confidently reconstructed, as Davies pointed out, based on its one worked edge. It contains only two hieroglyphic words: *pꜣ* and *ṯs*. Thus, the left jamb appears to be continuing the inscriptions that contained the refrain "*ṯs tw Wsir wn-nfr mk sẖr sbiw.k*," "raise yourself Osiris Wennefer. Behold your enemies are overthrown." The other block on the left jamb has the representation of the unnamed goddess and the remains of the important titles "[*w*]*r*[*t*] *Mwt nṯr*," "[the great], divine mother." The inscription continues with the usual phrase, *ḥr rsy* [*ḥr sni.s Wsir*], "watching over her brother Osiris." The title of "divine mother" was attributed to many goddesses but most importantly to Isis and Neith, who are both to be expected here.

WEST WALL

This wall conforms to the norm of the other walls of the chapel that are divided into three registers, each being decorated on top by a *pt* sign of heaven filled with stars.

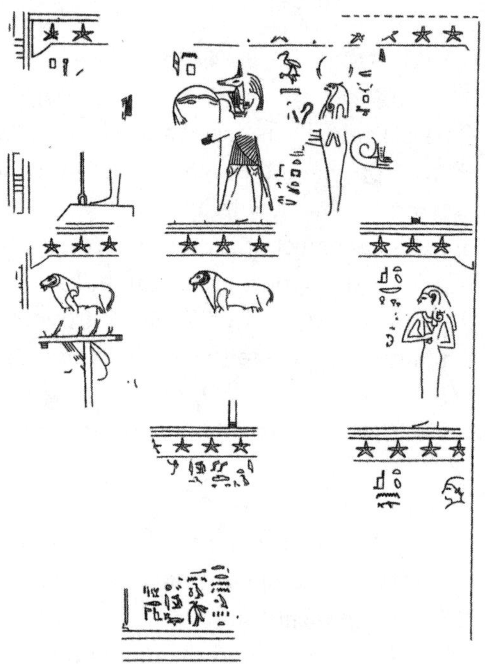

Figure 28: West wall of chapel H2 (after Davies, *The Temple of Hibis*, Part 3, detail from pl. 20)

REGISTER I

The top register contains three deities. The first deity from the left side is the mummified Ptah. He is standing on a pedestal and may have been holding the composite insignia. The following figure is that of the jackal-headed Anubis holding a stela with two eyes. The third figure is the mummiform, ibis-headed Thoth who has the lunar disk on top of his head. He holds the *heka*-scepter and the flail. At the right side of this register is a partly destroyed emblem, perhaps of Wepwawet, that was also found before in the nearby chapel E1.

THE INSCRIPTION

In front of Ptah
Ptḥ
"Ptah"
In front of Anubis
ꞽInpw
"Anubis"

In front of Thoth
Ḏḥwty ḥry st wrt
"Thoth over the great place"[33]
Behind Thoth
Wp-wȝwt
"Wepwawet"

REGISTER II

According to Davies' reconstruction, only three figures were in the second register of the west wall: two ram standards and the figure of Isis at the right end. Cruz-Uribe suggested that the block of the name of Isis on the third register on the west wall be transferred to the second register, thus making up a fourth figure on the second register.[34] By his explanation, the second ram standard would be moved to the left and so the left foot of Anubis would be his right foot. Consequently, the block below would move a little to the left to allow the shaft of the standard to match the new position of the second ram. The inscription of Isis, *ȝst n Hb*[*t*], "Isis of Hibis," on the debated block argues in favor of this alteration since she has a specific attribution. On the lower registers of all the walls of chapel H2 the female deities are depicted in their general form only, local variations or attributions are not indicated. The inscription in front of the goddess is even slightly larger than the other inscription on the lower register. The only troubling issue with this reconstruction is that the head of Isis of Hibis appears to be in a higher position than in the preceding figure of Isis.[35]

THE INSCRIPTION

In front of the first Isis
ȝst n Hb[*t*]
"Isis of Hibis"
In front of the second Isis
ȝst nbt ḫ//
"Isis lady of ///"

---

33 This title is more commonly associated with Ptah and Horus, but it does appear with connection to Thoth in six examples, four of which are in the Hibis temple. Note that Leitz, *Lexikon*, V, pp. 375–376 only mentions the three examples of the title *ḥry st wrt* connected with Thoth inside the sanctuary and does not mention the example on the west wall; see Davies, *The Temple of Hibis*, Part 3, pl. 2, VIII, 4, V and 5, VI. In the temple, the title occurs in several other instances inside the sanctuary, in connection with many other deities like Amun Re, Onuris-Shu, Osiris-Naref, nmty, Horus, Hr-Behdet, and Harmerti; see Leitz, *Lexikon*, V, pp. 375–376; Davies, *The Temple of Hibis*, Part 3, pls. 3, II, IV, V; 4, II, IV; 5, III–V and VIII.

34 Cruz-Uribe, *Hibis Temple Project I*, p. 90.

35 See alternative reconstruction of this wall on p. 111, figure 30.

REGISTER III

Only two blocks exist after the relocation of the right block of Isis to the second register. They contain parts of the hymn, narrated by the different goddesses. According to the *aide mémoire* of the inscription on the east wall, four goddesses are supposed to recite the hymn: Sakhmet, Bastet, Wadjet, and Shesemtet. There is valid reason to believe that they correspond to the south, north, west, and east walls of chapel H2. Two of the other four goddesses are Nephthys and Selkit. The latter group of deities represents the group of the guardian goddesses often shown on the corners of sarcophagi or canopic chests. It is only natural to expect that the missing goddesses on the west and south wall are Isis and Neith. The fragment of the block in the third register of the south wall with the title *Mwt nṯrt* supports that presumption. Despite the missing name of the goddesses on the third register, it is evident that one is Wadjet. She was probably on the right side facing the same direction as the hieroglyphs. The other is either Isis or Neith. The fragment of *Mwt nṯrt* on the south wall could be relocated to this register especially because its inscription matches well with the first line of inscription of the lower block; however, there is no evidence to argue against its position on the south wall.

THE INSCRIPTION

In front of the goddess on the left side

[Ḏd mdw ỉn//[w]r[t]/ mwt nṯr ḥr rsy ḥr] sni.s Wsỉr

"Word spoken by/// the great, divine mother watching over /awakening] her brother Osiris."

The main inscription[36]

(1) *Ỉ [b] sp sn Sṯẖ* (2) *i hꜣ[y*[37] *sp sn ỉw k r d]nw*[38] (3) *rd/// [nꜣ nḏb.i ḏ]d rn n tꜣ fdw.t* (4) *tỉwt*[39] *[nty m ḥwt bnbnt m ỉwnw]*

"O, [Be[40]] O Be, O, Seth, O the fa[llen] [41](one)] O the Fa[llen] (one), [You are] restrained, turn back[42]///[it is my wish]. (I) will speak the names of the four images [that are in the house of the pyramidion at Heliopolis]."

---

36 The inscription is reconstructed based on the comparison with Papyrus New York 35.9.21, col. 26, lines 12–14; see Goyon, "Textes mythologiques. II," p. 49.

37 Traces of the signs *ꜣ* and *h* still exist of the word , "to fall;" *Wb.* II, p. 473, 17ff.

38 The same word *dnw* occurs in line 1 of the main inscription on the east wall.

39 In Papyrus New York, 35.9.21. col. 26, line 14 it is written , see Goyon, "Textes mythologiques. II," p. 363.

40 On Be, see Massart, "The Egyptian Geneva Papyrus MAH 15274," pp. 172–185; Leitz, "Auseinandersetzungen zwischen Baba und Thoth," pp. 103–117; Derchain, "Bébon, le dieu et les mythes," p. 25, n. 6; *E* VI, pp. 121, 146; Sander-Hansen, *Die religiösen Texte auf dem Sarg der Anchnesneferibre*, p. 121 (383); Goyon, "Textes mythologiques. II," p. 362, n. 1.

41 Goyon, "Textes mythologiques. II," p. 362 gives also the meaning "The Hey-monster," referring to the Seth animal. See also Goyon, *Les dieux-gardiens*, p. 180; *Wb.* II, p. 483, 15–17.

42 The parallel example has *int*, "turn back;" Goyon, "Textes mythologiques. II," p. 363. Perhaps the scribe intended here *ini rd*, "remove your feet."

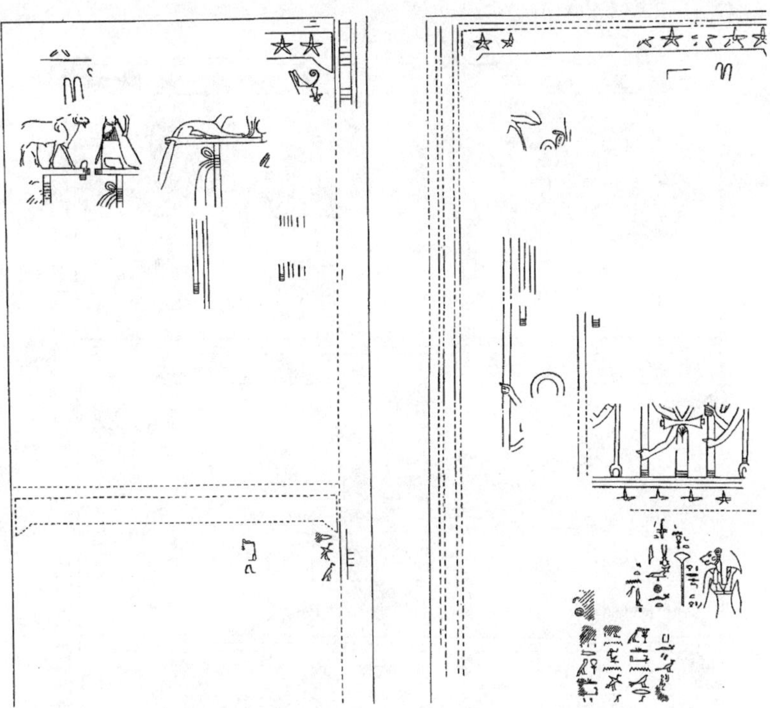

Figure 29: An alternative reconstruction of the south wall of chapel H2

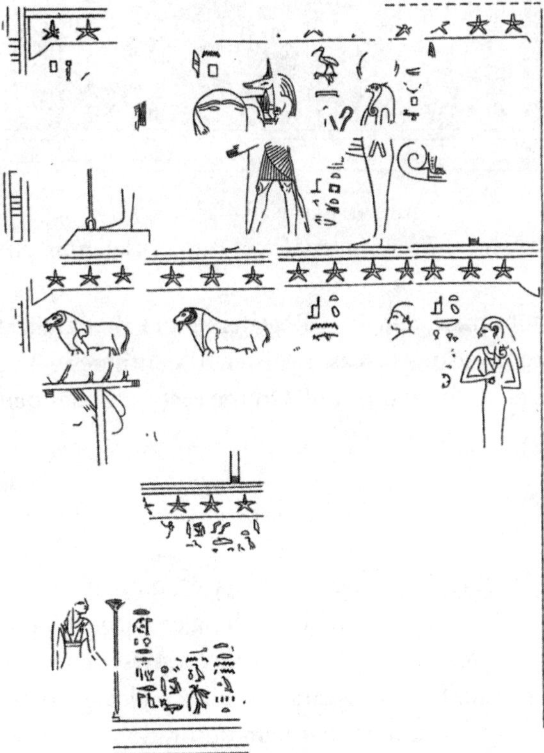

Figure 30: An alternative reconstruction of the west wall of chapel H2.

CHAPEL H2 — EAST WALL

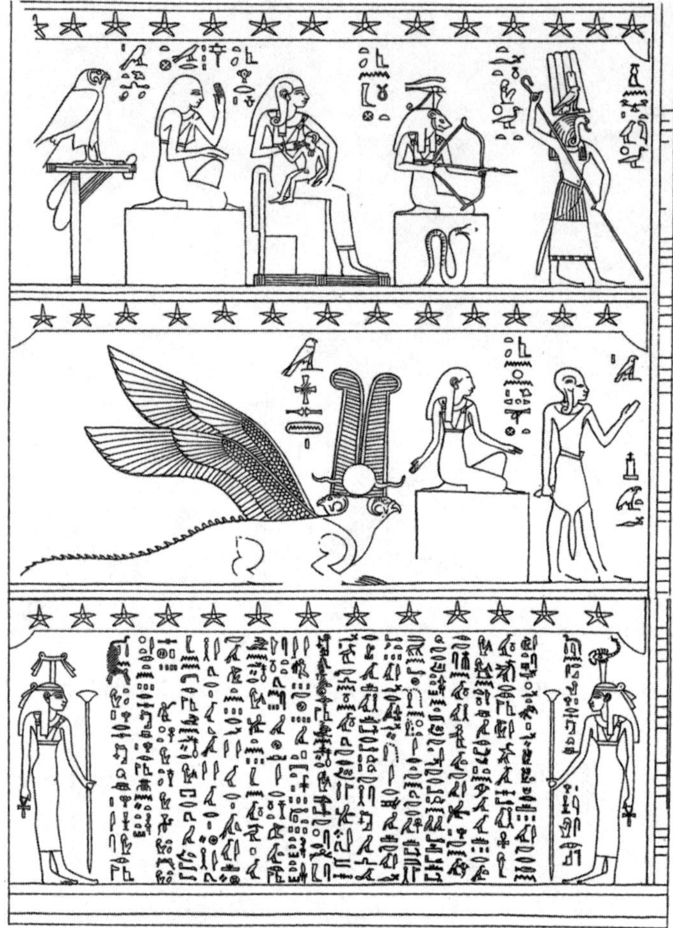

Figure 31: East wall of chapel H2
(after Davies, *The Temple of Hibis*, Part 3, detail from pl. 20)

This wall is divided into three registers. Registers I and II contain different representations of local gods from various places. Register III continues with a similar version of the same spell or ritual on the south wall. On the east wall, the spell is recited by Selkit and Shesemtet.[43]

REGISTER I

Five figures are in the first register, and they all face right. The first figure is Onuris Shu, with a snake head and a beard, and wielding a long crook as if harpooning. He wears a composite crown of four feathers and a miniature representation of a falcon with two feathers on top of his head. He also wears two kilts: a pleated knee-length kilt layered over a longer plain kilt with a rectangular hem decoration. An ox tail is attached to his

43 On the identification of this goddess as Shesemtet and not Satis or Neith, see detailed discussion in the commentary below, pp. 140ff.

belt. The second figure is a lioness-headed female deity described in the text as Tefnut, daughter of Re. She kneels on a pedestal that is decorated with a cobra. She holds a bow and pulls back the string with her right hand while steadying the notched arrow with her left. She wears a two-strap gown, a broad collar, and a tripartite wig. The *udjat* eye sign rests atop her head. The third figure is a female deity on a throne, nursing a child seated on her lap. She wears a tripartite wig with a Hathoric side lock; according to the inscription, she is Isis of Coptos. The fourth figure is a goddess kneeling with one raised knee on top of a rectangular platform. Her right hand rests on her raised left knee, while her left elbow rests on her right hand. Her left palm is open and held in front of her face. In the inscription she is named Isis of Thinis. The last figure in the register is a falcon on a standard. In the inscription he is named Horus of Khenty-enirty. The inscriptions are brief and include only the names and titles of the deities.

THE INSCRIPTION

Above the first figure
ꞽn Ḥrt Šw sꜣ Rꜥ
"Onuris Shu, son of Re"
Above the second figure
Tfnwt sꜣt Re
"Tefnut, daughter of Re"
Above the third figure
ꜣst n Gbtyw
"Isis of Coptos."
Above the fourth figure
ꜣst ḥr ib tꜣw-Wrt[44]
"Isis who dwells in Thinis"
Above the fifth figure
Ḥr ḫnty n irty[45]
"Horus Khenty -enirty"

REGISTER II

This register is similar to the register above in that it continues the depictions of the different local deities who perhaps came to witness the Osirid rituals. As in the register above, the figures all face right. The first figure is the divine priest Iunmutef who is standing and raising his left arm in a gesture of protection. He wears the panther skin

44 According to Hannig, *Grosses Handwörterbuch Ägyptisch–Deutsch*, p. 1400, it is the name of the 8th Upper Egyptian nome (Thinis).

45 *ḥr ḫnty n irty* is listed as a variant of *ḥr mḫnty (n) irty* in Leitz, *Lexikon*, V, p. 279, who says that the reading of his name is unclear. His name has been translated by Grapow, *Religiöse Urkunden*, pp. 19, 47, as "Horus der beiden Augen," while Faulkner, *The Egyptian Book of the Dead: The Book of Going Forth by Day: Being the Papyrus of Ani*, pls. 9 and 13, gives him the contrasting name of "Horus the eyeless."

mantle and holds its paw with the right hand. He is also shown with a side lock on his otherwise bald head. The second figure is Isis of Achmim. She is kneeling; her arms are held out to the sides, and her left raised knee is on a rectangular platform. Her left hand rests on her left knee. The third and last figure in the scene is the double falcon-headed and winged crocodile of Horus of Sumenu. He is represented with two tall feathers and a sun disk with two horns.

THE INSCRIPTION

Above the first figure
Ḥr ꞽIwn mwt.f
"Horus Iunmutef"
Above Isis
ꜣst n[t] ḫnty Mnw[46]
"Isis of Achmim"
Above the third figure
Ḥr ỉmy smnw
"Horus who is in Sumenu"

REGISTER III

The inscription on the third register recounts a version of the protection and awakening spell represented on all the walls of chapel H2. On the east wall, it is narrated by Selkit, who is represented with her usual scorpion headdress, and Shesemtet with a tie or knot on her head. The two goddesses stand on both sides of the text; Selkit on the right facing left and Shesemtet on the left facing right.

THE INSCRIPTION

In front of Selkit
Ḏd mdw ỉn srḳt ḥr rsy ḥr sni.s Wsir
"Words spoken by Selkit watching over her brother Osiris."
In front of Shesemtet
Ḏd mdw ỉn šsmt ḥr rsy ḥr sni.s Wsir
"Words spoken by Shesemtet watching over her brother Osiris."

---

46 *ꜣst- nt- ḫnty- mnw*, "Isis of Achmim," and *ꜣst-nt-ḫnty-mnw*, "Isis in Achmim," are only attested in Hibis; Davies, *The Temple of Hibis*, Part 3, pl. 4, V; Leitz, *Lexikon*, I, p. 76. (The more common title was *ꜣst nbt ỉpw*.)

The Long inscription between the two goddesses

(1) *Ỉ St<ẖ>*[47] *ḫft pfy ḥnmmt ḥm wt-rꜣ ỉw.k r dnw*[48] (2) *r wsỉr ỉ pꜣ sꜥḥ* (3) *šps*[49] *n ḳdỉ*[50] *m*[51] *ỉr ỉn ỉwt n ḥꜣw r tꜣ* (4) *ỉr.k msnḥw*[52] *tw.k ỉmỉ ḥr.k n* (5) *ḥꜣ.k r mꜣꜣ ỉꜣbtt nt pt*[53] *mꜣꜣ.k ỉt.k Rꜥ nmꜥ*[54] (6) *m ẖnw ꜥḫ n ḫt ỉr tkn.k r sḫm m nṯr* (7) *ḥꜥtw ỉw.f r ḏꜣfy ỉr tm.k ỉw.f* (8) *r wḏꜣ ḥwỉ Rꜥ ḥꜣ.k sḥtm.* (9) *f bꜣ.k nn nwnw.k r mꜣꜣ nṯr ꜥꜣ mỉ* (10) *ṯs<tw> wsỉr wn-nfr mk sḫr* (11) *sbỉw.k*[55] *sp fdw m pt rsyw mḥtyw ỉmntt ỉꜣbtt* (12) *sḳttw*[56] *sn m sp*

---

47 The *h* on the wall must be a mistake for *ẖ* or the stone slab determinative.

48 This word is problematic. Cruz-Uribe, *Hibis Temple Project I*, p. 89, n. 330, translated the sentence as "you will be raised over Osiris." This rendering is in disagreement with the general meaning of the spell. Goyon, "Textes mythologiques. II," pp. 364, 387, and 389 seems to have had problems with this sentence. He translated the parallel passage in the New York Papyrus 35.9.21, col. 27,1–3, "*ỉw.k r tnw ỉw wsỉr*" as "où que tu sois par rapport à Osiris." They both seem to have taken *dnw* as *ṯnw*; *Wb.* V, p. 374.11. However, it may be taken as a variation on *dni*, "to hold back, restrain;" *Wb.* V, p. 464, 10–17.

49 *sꜥḥ šps* is a reference to the mummy of Osiris; *Wb.* IV, p. 52 , 11. *sꜥḥ* is often used in mortuary contexts, see Reymond, "The *sꜥḥ* 'Eternal Image,'" pp. 132–140; Fox, "A Study of Antef," p. 408, n. 9; Hornung, *Buch der Anbetung des Re im Westen (Sonnenlitanei)*, p. 120, n. 189.

50 *ḳdi*, "to sleep" (*Wb.* V, p. 78, 11–14) can imply a word play with *ḳd*, "form" (*Wb.* V, p. 75, 3–77.11) that is often associated with the two previous words, *sꜥḥ* and *šps*. *n ḳdi* can form one word, "to sleep" (*Wb.* II, p. 345,1), so the translation could also be "Oh the mummy, the noble one and the sleeping one."

51 This perhaps should be taken as negative command and not as a proposition as done by Cruz-Uribe (*Hibis Temple Project I*, p. 89), who translated it as "in performing a bringing and a coming."

52 *msnḥw*, "to rotate, turn backward, turn away;" *Wb.* II, p. 146.

53 The *pt* sign is not clear here but it is confirmed, based on the parallels mentioned by Goyon, "Textes mythologiques. II," pp. 364ff.

54 *Nmꜥ*, "lie down, sleep;" *Wb.* II, p. 266, 7–10. It can also imply the sleep of death: a room with this name is related to Osiris in Dendera and Philae; *Wb.* II, p. 266, 3–5. *nmꜥ* and the derived noun *nmit*, "bed, bier," are usually used in mortuary contexts together with *sꜥḥ šps*, see *E* VI, p. 312, 2; Wilson, *Lexicon*, pp. 516–517; in *E* I, p. 167, 1, the protective gods around Osiris "abhor sleep (*ḳdi*) and hate rest (*nmꜥ*)" (Wilson, *Lexicon*, p. 517). Here *nmꜥ* is clearly referring to the god Re, could it be referring to Re as Osiris? The parallel passages of almost all the comparable papyri mentioned by Goyon, "Textes mythologiques. II," give the name of Re Horakhty instead of Re.

55 This seems to be the start of an *aide mémoire* or an instruction manual on reciting the spell by the eight goddesses.

56 From *sḳd*, "to convey, to circle, to go around;" *Wb.* IV, p. 308, 7, 309, 8; Lesko, *A Dictionary of Late Egyptian*, II, pp. 85, 161–162; Kitchen, *Ramesside Inscriptions* 1, p. 48, 1. This can be a reference to the recitation of the spell by the eight goddesses represented on each side of the wall of the chapel, as if the goddesses are here playing the role of a synchronous chorus.

wꜥ[57] *ir nḏt*[58] *tw* (13)*Wsir Wn-nfr m-ꜥ tn bnw pw* (14) *kꜣ tn r.f ii w-r ḳꜣiw sp sn* (15) *iḥ-rw ḳꜣ iiꜣ-r sp sn iḥ* (16) *bnn Wsir Wn-nfr pr m mꜣꜥ*[59] (17) *sp fdw i Sḫmt Bꜣstt Wꜣḏt Šsmtt* (18) *iḫ(t)*[60] *ir. tn rsy ḥr Wsir ḫnty imntt*

"(1) Oh Seth, that enemy of the Sun folk, and so forth, where are you heading? (2) towards Osiris. Oh the mummy (of Osiris), (3) the noble one (who is) in sleep, do not make a bringing and a coming in addition to that (4) which you do. May you be turned backward. Place your head to your (5) back in order to see the eastern sky. May you see your father Re laid down (6) inside a brazier of fire. If you approach in order to prevail over the divine body, he will burn. If you do not,[61] he will be safe.[62] May Re strike your head so that he annihilates your Ba. You will not come back to see the great god. Come, (10) rise up Osiris Wennefer.[63] Behold, your (11) enemies are overthrown. Four times.[64] In the southern, northern, western, and eastern sky. (12) They shall be conveyed simultaneously. When

57 It is more convincing to translate *m sp wꜥ*, "simultaneously" or "with one accord," rather than "once;" Lesko, *A Dictionary of Late Egyptian*, II, p. 30 takes *n sp* as "simultaneously." Notice that the space of these *aide mémoire* is stretched out; the artist may have designed the two goddesses first and their two *ḏd mdw* lines, then the speech and might have ended up with more space than expected, so he added more unusual details in the following lines. Notice also the space left blank before the vocative in line 17.

58 The orthography of the word suggests the word *ḥsi*, "praise." However, all the other examples in the comparative papyri in Goyon, "Textes mythologiques. II," give the word *nḏ*, "to ask, take counsel, inquire;" *Wb.* II, p. 371, 5. The determinative of the man with hand in mouth can also appear, though in very few examples, in the word *nḏ* with the traditional meaning of "to protect;" Lesko, *A Dictionary of Late Egyptian*, I, p. 256; Wilson, *Lexicon*, p. 563, ex. 6. The latter meaning might be a better choice in the Hibis case. The translation can be given as the following: "If Osiris is protected from you" (referring back to *stẖ*) or "if Osiris is protected by you" (referring back to the goddesses) "then you (referring back to the goddesses) shall say the *bnw* spell about it." In any case, the exact meaning in this sentence is unclear.

59 *Wb.* II, p. 22, 15.

60 *iḫ* is a non-enclitic particle, then. Therefore, it evidently points out the usage of the last phrases as instructions for the four goddesses on how to perform the ritual of protection and awakening of Osiris.

61 We can supply here "if you do not approach the divine body," based on the parallel passage from Papyrus New York 35.9.21., col 27, 1–3, "*ir tm.k tkn r nṯr ḥꜥwt.*" Papyrus Brooklyn 47.218.138 records here "*ir tm.k ir ḳnw*; if you do not perform the offense;" Goyon, "Textes mythologiques. II," p. 366, n. 2.

62 The sentence from *ḥwi Rꜥ* until the refrain "*ṯs tw wsir…sbiw.k*" is repeated on the previous north wall.

63 All of the parallel papyri mention *wsir ḫnty imnty* in the refrain, except the Brooklyn papyrus 47.218.138; it has *wsir wnnfr*; Goyon, "Un parallèle tardif d'une formule des inscriptions de la statue prophylactique de Ramsès III au Musée du Caire," pp. 154–159.

64 The beginning part of this sentence is missing in the Hibis version. The New York Papyrus 35.9.21, col.27, 7–8 (Goyon, "Textes mythologiques. II," pp. 368–369) gives the phrase "perform the protection of Osiris, perform the protection of Osiris N as well."

Osiris is called upon/ praised by you, (then) it is the Bnw (Phoenix)[65] that you (14) shall say about it. *Ỉiw-r-ḳꜣ-iw* Twice. (15) *Ỉḥ-rw-ḳꜣ-iiꜣ-r* twice. *Ỉḥ* (16) *bnn*[66] Osiris Wennefer has come with outstretched arms (17) four times. O Sakhmet, Bastet, Wadjet, and Shesemtet. This is how you may perform an awakening / watching over Osiris, foremost of the west."

2. COMMENTARY

CHAPEL H1 — SOUTH WALL

This wall has one main scene and it is similar in its formation to the scene on the west wall of E1 on the roof of Hibis. Both scenes have a single register. The king is the predominant figure and he is offering Maat to a row of deities. In the middle, between the king and the divinities, is a pile of different kinds of offerings. Some differences appear between the two scenes. On the south wall of H1, the offering, placed on top of an offering table, has slightly fewer components than the offering table on the west wall of E1. The king is presenting an image of Maat, whereas on the west wall, the offering of Maat is indicated only by the text in front of the king. More importantly, the king is offering to the Osiris triad only, while on the west wall the king is offering to the triad of Amun together with the Osiris triad. The inscriptions clearly identify the scene as an offering of Maat by the king to Osiris, foremost of the west. Osiris is elevated, seated, and labeled as Osiris, foremost of the West. Behind Osiris is Horus, the avenger of his father, followed by Isis, the great and divine mother. This is a rather traditional scene, but the absence of any mention of Amun of Hibis, together with the analysis of the scenes of the neighboring chapel H2 suggest that this is perhaps an antechamber to the chapel H2, and that both formed an important complex for the Osirian rituals.

CHAPEL H1 — NORTH WALL

This once-thin wall that divided chapel H1 from chapel H2 is missing. Davies outlined the reconstruction of this wall and noted that he made his reconstructions from various blocks he saw being reused in the foundation of a local mosque in the city of Kharga.[67] The southern side of this thin wall formed the north wall of H1 and the northern side formed the south wall of H2. The wall consisted of two sections or jambs flanking the entrance between the two chapels.

65 The mention of the *Bnw* or phoenix is perhaps because of its symbolism for resurrection after death, as reflected later in the Greek myths; see Van den Broek, *The Myth of the Phoenix*, pp. 14ff.

66 These meaningless phrases are taken by Goyon ("Textes mythologiques. II.," p. 368, n. 5) and followed by Cruz-Uribe (*Hibis Temple Project I*, p. 89) as magical words of the Abracadabra type. Different versions exist in the comparative papyri and they have a common stress on *ii-r/iw-r/ ꜣ-r* and *iḥ-r* plus *ḳꜣ / ḳꜣiw* syllables. *ḳꜣiw/ ḳꜣiiꜣ* (lines 14 and 15) could be a strange variation of the verb *ḳꜣr/ ḳꜣi*; *Wb*. V, p. 59, 1–7.

67 See footnote 25, above.

The north wall of chapel H1 consists of two jambs flanking the doorway to chapel H2. Each jamb depicts three kneeling "genii" or protective deities carrying knives. Behind these deities are a large figure of Horus on the east jamb and Thoth on the west jamb. Different so-called "genii" existed among the ancient Egyptian deities. In Hibis, they seem to be reduced to only the type represented on the north wall, the so-called "génies protecteurs."[68] These gods functioned primarily as guardians of the doorways of important chambers, warding off evil spirits and in particular those who threaten the body of Osiris. The close relationship between these guardian deities and Osiris is defined more closely in association with the embalming ritual and Anubis.[69] They also appear in connection with the germination of Osiris[70] and the *Stundenwache* of Osiris.[71] Their representations inside chapel H1 protecting the doorway to chapel H2 provide further evidence that chapel H1 functioned perhaps as an antechamber to H2.

CHAPEL H2 — NORTH WALL

REGISTER I

The middle vignette designates the general function of the chapel, that is, a *Sḥ-nṯr*, a divine booth, a place where funerary and especially the main embalming rituals took place. Horus as the son of Osiris is taking the place of Anubis as the chief liturgist during the embalming ceremonies. The inscription in front of him labels him as Horus-Re of the divine booth (*Sḥ-nṯr*). The term *Sḥ-nṯr* was used to refer to special rooms around the sanctuary in Edfu.[72] Some Ptolemaic documents refer to Horus as Anubis performing the embalming of Osiris in the *Sḥ-nṯr*.[73] As is common in representations of Osiris on his funerary bed, he is accompanied by Isis and Nephthys. Isis, as a kite, is hovering over his body and the four canopic jars of the Four Sons of Horus are under the bed. The bed takes the form of a lion: the head of a lion is at one end, the feet are lion claws, and the tail is stylistically curled upward.

The angled images of the male and female figures on the right side of the register imitate the floating figures[74] that are usually depicted in the astronomical friezes known

68 Cauville, *Le temple de Dendara: les chapelles, osiriennes [2] Commentaire*, p. 264. She discuses this kind together with other kinds like "génies de Pharbaïtos"and "Agathodemons" in ibid., pp. 45–50, also see pp. 90–96. See also Goyon, *Les dieux-gardiens et la genèse des temples.*

69 Guilhou, *Génies funéraires, Croque-mitanies ou anges gardiens?*, p. 388 (according to the Book of the Two Ways, Chapter 1084, *CT* VII, 355d–356c).

70 Guilhou, *Génies funéraires*, p. 389.

71 Guilhou, *Génies funéraires*, p. 410.

72 Wilson, *Lexicon*, pp. 889–890.

73 Vandier, "Quelques remarques sur le XVIII nome," p. 211; *E* I, p. 342; *Papyrus Jumilhac* X, 17; XIV, 6; XXII, 5.

74 To avoid representing the figures completely unattached or "floating" in the scene, a depiction usually reserved for inert or inactive figures; for example, in a *sẖr*, "enemy," the two figures are given their own ground level.

since at least the New Kingdom.[75] They are generally attributed to be representations of the different decades or, more specifically, to Orion and Sothis referring to Osiris and Isis, respectively.[76] Davies described this scene as "the living Osiris entering the chamber of Isis."[77] The iconography of Osiris emphasizes that this is in fact the "living" Osiris. He is striding and wears the white crown of Upper Egypt and the short kilt, rather than an enveloping mummiform garment. This "living" aspect may be a reference to his "living Ba" that is "surrounded by the goddess Nut," according to Coffin Text 60.[78] The squared frame surrounding the upper half of the female figure may designate a chamber of darkness or a coffin. In Coffin Text 49, the spell mentions the place of embalming and calls on the wardens of the chambers who are in the darkness to light a torch and protect the lord of the "white crown."[79] The word for darkness, *snkt,* has a determinative of [80] which is similar to the enclosure between the female goddess and Osiris in the scene on the top register. Similar signs are represented in the hieroglyphs, relating to a "hall" or "shrine" (Gardiner O13–15) or corner of wall (Gardiner O38), as in the word *ḳnbt*, "corner, angle," and also *ʿrrt*, "gate" (*Wb.* I, 211, 8–12). Equally interesting and perhaps fitting in our case is the word *ḳrrt*, "cavern" or "cave," (*Wb.* V, 62, 1–3) , , later *ḳrrty*, , .[81] This term is closely associated with the rituals of Osiris, the concealment of his body, and the protection of his tomb.[82] In this case, the goddess is inside a "chamber" that might represent a tomb or a coffin, welcoming the living Ba of Osiris.

Two important and unique images confirm the association of the two angled figures as Osiris and Nut (see pls. 30 and 31). The first representation comes from the Temple

75 For example in Dorman, *The Tombs of Senenmut*, pls. 84–86; Parker, *Calendars*, pl. IV, register 4; *EAT* III, pls. 9, 15, 19, 25, 29, 30.

76 Cruz-Uribe, *Hibis Temple Project I*, p. 86, n. 298; *EAT* I, pp. 97ff; Parker, *Calendars*, pl. IV. On the astronomical ceiling of west chapel 2 of Dendera's roof chapels, two representations resemble the angled scene (Cauville, *Le temple de Dendara. Vol. X/2 Les Chapelles osiriennes [Plates]*, pl. 204). One representation occurs on the body of Nut.The female goddess is holding hands with the male figure and between them is a large solar disk. The male figure has a headdress, and there is no inscription around him, but he is represented with his left leg forward while her legs are joined together just as in the chapel H2 scene. The other representation occurs in the space between the two celestial deities, on the east side. The unidentified figures are represented similar to the representation of the figures in H2, except for the absence of headdresses and the angle or building sign.

77 Davies, *The Temple of Hibis*, Part 3, p. 20.

78 Faulkner, *Coffin Texts*, I, pp. 54–55. In the vignette of this top register, the goddess is surrounding the god from one side while her extended star-filled *pt* sign is surrounding Osiris from the other side.

79 Faulkner, *Coffin Texts*, I, pp. 45–47. Osiris is called the Prince of the White Crown several times, especially in the context of the Osiris mysteries, for example in Dendera; Cauville, *Le temple de Dendara. Vol. X/2 (Plates)*, pl. 413; Cauville, *Le temple de Dendara: les chapelles, osiriennes [1] Transcription et traduction*, p. 225.)

80 Faulkner, *Coffin Texts*, I, p. 46, n.9.

81 Wilson, *Lexicon*, p. 1066.

82 Egberts, *In Quest of Meaning: A Study of the Ancient Egyptian Rites of Consecrating the Meret-Chests and Driving the Calves*, pp. 346ff and 349.

of Dendera. It depicts Nut on the left, on her side facing upward, just as in chapel H2.[83] She is inside a building decorated with the *kheker* motif. She has dwarfed legs, carries no emblems, and her arms rest straight at her sides. The inscription clearly gives her the name "Nut." The second representation, from the vignette of Papyrus Rhind I, depicts Nut and a smaller figure, probably Osiris.[84] Both figures are looking to the side and are inside an angled D-shaped structure or mound. One *nw* jar is on top of her head, her arms are raised slightly up toward the nearby figure, and her hands carry no emblems.

The inscription surrounding this representation is significant:

> *N3 šsw n t3 Nwt nty n t3 ḏb3t ii.tw m ḥtp r-ḫnt ḏb3t.k st ib.k pw n ḏt ꜥwy.i pg3 r ḥpt ḥꜥw.k nṯr ḫw.ḏt.k mkt sꜥḥ.k sꜥnḫ.i b3.k r nḥḥ*
> "The texts of the Nut who is in the coffin: Welcome in peace in your coffin; it is the place of your heart forever. My arms are spread to embrace your divine limbs. I shall protect your body, a protection of your mummy. I shall make your Ba live forever."[85]

This "mother coffin" is addressed in the second Book of Breathing to go to Osiris NN and allow him to enter her body and the *dwat*.[86] Billing adds that "this integration shall enable him (Osiris NN), to enter and come forth following the pattern of the sun."[87] By welcoming Osiris into the intimate and heavily protected funerary realm of Nut, she guarantees his integration into his own domain of the Underworld, the living forever of his Ba and enables his initiation into the eternal resurrection cycle. Both this "union with the mother" and the concept of the Ba-corpse are typical representations for the nocturnal journey of the sun god.[88]

The third and last scene of the first register depicts another mummified form of Osiris. It is a very important scene and iconography plays a great role in its decipherment.

The scene begins with the pyramid-topped mound behind Horus. The ithyphallic body of Osiris is enclosed inside an irregular rounded space that might represent a heap or rather a pit of grain, sand, or earth. It is outlined by the body of a serpent. Two swathed male figures are standing to the left while two other male figures are standing to the right. One of the latter figures has his hands raised up while the other is holding part of what most probably would have been a hoe. These two latter figures hold the clue to understanding this multilayered scene. The priest who carries the hoe is a clear indi-

83 Drioton, "Un Oudja à représentation Hermopolitaine," p. 82, fig. 3.

84 Rusch, *Die Entwicklung der Himmelsgöttin Nut zu einer Totengottheit*, p. 37, fig. 4.

85 Translation after Billing, *Nut, the Goddess of Life: In Text and Iconography*, p. 156, fig. 8; Rusch, *Die Entwicklung der Himmelsgöttin Nut zu einer Totengottheit*, p. 42.

86 Billing, *Nut, the Goddess of Life*, p. 156. See also Schott, "Nut spricht als Mutter und Sarg," pp. 81–87; Assmann, *Tod und Jenseits im Alten Ägypten*, pp. 225–230.

87 Billing, *Nut, the Goddess of Life*, p. 156.

88 Assmann, *Egyptian Solar Religion in the New Kingdom: Re, Amun and the Crisis of Polytheis*, p. 61; Assmann, *Liturgische Lieder an den Sonnengott*, pp. 56ff. This "Ba-corpse" concept is expressed in the Amduat, Book of Caverns, and Coffin Texts; see Assmann, *Egyptian Solar Religion in the New Kingdom*, pp. 61–62 with references.

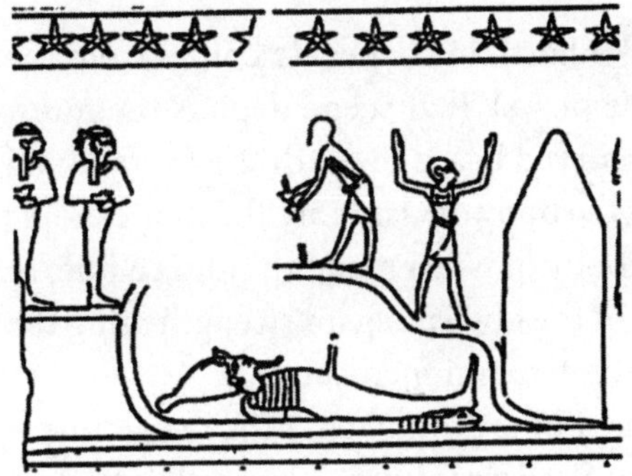

Figure 32: Left vignette of the north wall of chapel H2, Register I, detail from figure 26

cation of the *ḫbs tꜣ*, or "Hacking the Earth," which was an important feast among the ancient Egyptian festivals.[89] This feast was also most importantly connected with the Khoiak festivities, usually celebrated around the 22nd of the month of Khoiak.[90] The ritual is generally performed at night.[91]

Even though the identification of this ritual does not immediately help in identifying the surrounding figures of the priest with the upraised arms or the two swathed figures, it helps in understanding the pyramidion-topped mound behind Horus as an obelisk. Graindorge reported that the Theban tombs of Rekhmire and Sennefer associate the celebration of the Hacking of the Earth with the erection of two obelisks that in turn recall the two trees of the tomb of Osiris, denoting his resurrection.[92] The Henu Barque that is depicted in the following scene at the beginning of the second register of the north wall of chapel H2 is also mentioned in association with the Hacking of the Earth. The inscription on the left wing of the door of Shrine I from the tomb of Tut-ankh-amun records a speech by Thoth revealing his role in the Osiris ritual. Thoth declares:

> I have seen the Mysteries in Ro-Setau. I am the one who recites the ritual for the soul of Mendes. I am the Sem Priest in all his functions. I am the Great Leader of Works on the day when the Henu-Barque is being placed on its stand. I am the one who hoes (?) on the day of Hacking the Earth.[93]

It should be noted that Thoth claims to be a Sem Priest. The role of the Sem Priest associated with the Hacking of the Earth will prove significant in the identification of this representation, as indicated below.

89 See Bleeker, *Egyptian Festivals*, pp. 72–75; Montet, "Le rituel de fondation des temples égyptiens," pp. 85–87; Sternberg-el-Hotabi, "Die 'Götterliste' des Sanktuars im Hibis-Tempel von El-Chargeh. Überlegungen zur Tradierung und Kodifizierung religiösen und kulttopographischen Gedankengutes," pp. 240–243.

90 Graindorge-Héreil, *Le dieu Sokar à Thèbes au Nouvel Empire 1*, pp. 196–210, esp. pp. 196–197. This could be referring to "Osiris in the place of the earth-hoeing" that is mentioned in the British Museum Papyrus 10569; Faulkner, *An Ancient Egyptian Book of Hours*, col. 16,14. This form of Osiris occurs directly after the mention of "Osiris in his form of Re;" Faulkner, *An Ancient Egyptian Book of Hours*, col. 16,13.

91 Graindorge-Héreil, *Le dieu Sokar à Thèbes au Nouvel Empire 1*, pp. 200–203; Assmann, *Death and Salvation*, pp. 283ff.

92 Graindorge-Héreil, *Le dieu Sokar à Thèbes au Nouvel Empire 1*, p. 203; Davies, *The Tomb of Rekh-Mi-Re*, II, pl. LXXXIII.

93 Piankoff, *The Shrines of Tut-Ankh-Amun*, p. 137.

A very close parallel to the scene of Hacking the Earth in chapel H2 comes from the tomb of Amenhotep in the Bahariya Oasis[94] (see pl. 32) That scene depicts the mummified body of Osiris with the white crown and curved beard beneath the overarching body of a female deity, most probably Nut. Below the body of Osiris are the four canopic jars of the Four Sons of Horus. Over the arching body of Nut a man is holding a hoe. In front of the entire scene a stylized tree is in place of the obelisk, again strengthening the association of the obelisk and the tree of Osiris' tomb mentioned above.[95]

The Hacking of the Earth might refer to the state of the ground after the reenactment of the battle between Osiris and Seth.[96] Coffin Text Spell 7 recounts: "the earth is hacked up after the two companions have battled, after their two feet have dug up the divine pond in Heliopolis."[97] Assmann prefers to interpret the ritual as primarily a slaughtering ritual.[98] In any case, its violent character is evident. In the Dramatic Ramesseum Papyrus, the beating of the barley by the ass of Seth is naturally paralleled to the hacking of the body of Osiris.[99]

The other priestly figures nearby in the vignette at the left corner of register I appear in a similar guise to the ones participating in another rite titled "The Sleeping Sem." The ritual occurs in the ceremony of the Opening of the Mouth (episodes 9–11).[100] The main components of the ritual involve a night of sleeping by the Sem priest "in order to see the august one." After the night of sleeping, the Sem priest was awakened by other priests and then declared: "I was lying down and one roused me. I was asleep and one touched me. I have seen my father in his every form."[101] The Sem priest appears during the sleeping ritual wearing a garment similar to the two figures on the far right of the scene in Hibis chapel H2. He is wrapped in a long close-fitting garment or a cloak, probably the skin of a bull. His hands are clasped together on his breast, his elbows projecting from his sides. The other figure with the upraised hands might represent the same or another priest in jubilation after the declaration of the seeing or, more accurately, the "finding of the god." Episode 11 depicts a transition: "The Sem priest changes costume. He has removed the cloak and appears wearing a sash."[102] An allusion to this moment is described on a private stela where the owner desires to hear the rejoicing at the appearance of the Sem priest.[103]

---

94 Fakhry, *Baharia Oasis*, 1, p. 142, fig. 112; Billing, *Nut, the Goddess of Life*, fig. C55.

95 Sometimes both the trees and the obelisks are depicted together surrounding Osiris, for example on the sarcophagus of Lisbon and the sarcophagi Cairo 1868/1899; Koemoth, *Osiris et les Arbres*, figs. 12 and 13.

96 Assmann, *Death and Salvation*, pp. 283–284.

97 Faulkner, *Coffin Texts*, I, pp. 3–4.

98 Assmann, *Death and Salvation*, p. 283.

99 Sethe, *Dramatische Texte zu altägyptischen Mysterienspielen*, pp. 103–138 (scenes 9–18).

100 Otto, *Das ägyptische Mundöffnungsritual I*, pp. 53–60; Fischer-Elfert, *Die Vision von der Statue im Stein: Studien zum altägyptischen Mundöffnungsritual*, p. 8ff; Altenmüller, "Die Wandlungen des Sem-Priesters im Mundöffnungsritual," pp. 1–32.

101 Budge, *The Book of the Opening of the Mouth*, pp. 26–31; Otto, *Das ägyptische Mundöffnungsritual I*, pp. 53–60.

102 Gillam, *Performance and Drama in Ancient Egypt*, p. 71.

103 Otto, *Egyptian Art and the Cults of Osiris and Amon*, p. 42.

The association of the feast of Hacking the Earth and the "Seeing" of Osiris is indicated in a hymn recited by Thoth. Inside chapel K1 on the first floor of Hibis, on the south wall, Thoth declares that the Hacking of the Earth festival is celebrated for Osiris.[104] Line 16 begins: "[…] your […] hacked up horns of the bulls and the hoofs of the asses. The Hacking of the Earth festival is celebrated today. His beauty is before (17) Re. His voice is heard, but there is not that he has been seen."[105] The last sentence is problematic, but it may be better to translate it as "He has not been seen yet," referring back to the "seeing" of the god by the Sem priest.

Just as the ritual of the Hacking of the Earth represents a violent action, the following episodes of the Opening of the Mouth (episodes 12–18) deal with the smiting of the god. In these episodes the Sem Priest says: "Stamp for me my father…make for me a likeness of my father… Who is he who will hit my father? Who is it who will seize his head?"[106]

The fact that this ritual is incorporated into the Opening of the Mouth ritual indicates that it is a magical action aimed at the reanimation of the god's statue that was perhaps buried in the ground. As will be discussed below, an important aspect of the Osiris ceremonies in general was the yearly manufacturing of a pseudo-mummy of Osiris, usually made of grain. This image was supposed to replace the one of the previous year. The new image received the different purification, embalming, mummification, and Opening of the Mouth rituals that were performed on the mummy of the deceased, and it was kept in a temporary tomb, or an Upper *Dwat*, while the previous year's image was buried in the necropolis, or Lower *Dwat*.[107] It is possible that at the beginning of the ritual of the following year, the ritual of the Sleeping Sem and the Hacking of the Earth played a part in the search and the finding/destruction of the previous images in the Lower *Dwat*. The text and vignettes of Papyrus Jumilhac (Louvre no. E 17110)[108] are very revealing in this regard. One vignette of the papyrus[109] depicts the mummified ithyphallic Osiris wearing the white crown, the broad collar, the curved beard, and the uraeus. These features match the iconography of Osiris inside the mound on the chapel H2 north wall, except that in Papyrus Jumilhac twenty-four ears of corn sprout from his body. Furthermore, the inscriptions surrounding this vignette recount different aspects of the *ḫbs tꜣ* ritual. The first part of the inscription (lines 1–10) explains how to guarantee the germination of

---

104 Davies, *The Temple of Hibis*, Part 3, pl. 23.

105 Cruz-Uribe, *Hibis Temple Project I*, p. 99. For the translation of this speech of Thoth, see Barucq and Daumas, *Hymnes et prières de l'Égypte ancienne*, pp. 301–306, no. 86.

106 Otto, *Das ägyptische Mundöffnungsritual I*, pp. 60–71; Gillam, *Performance and Drama in Ancient Egypt*, pp. 71–72. The certain kind of "beating" that is mentioned in connection with this episode of the OM is usually understood as a reference to the sculptor's work on the statue. However, one may suggest an allusion to the beating of the barley or the grain representing Osiris. In this episode, the Sem Priest repeatedly says "Do not strike my father," a phrase that is found in the Ramesseum Dramatic Papyrus at the threshing of the barley; Sethe, *Dramatische Texte zu altägyptischen Mysterienspielen*, pp. 1031–138 (scenes 9–18).

107 These locations will be discussed further in details below; see discussion of the text of the third register of the north wall of chapel H2.

108 Vandier, *Le Papyrus Jumilhac*.

109 Vandier, *Le Papyrus Jumilhac*, pl. III.

the Osiris grain mummy at the beginning of the *ḫbs tꜣ* feast. At the end of this first part, the inscription emphasizes that all aspects of the ritual *ḫbs tꜣ* should be fully followed.[110] The second part of the inscription surrounding the vignette of the germinating Osiris (lines 11–18) associates the "Hacking of the Earth" with the Opening of the Mouth of Osiris,[111] while the last two lines (19–20) associate the "Hacking of the Earth" ritual with the gathering of the limbs of Osiris.[112]

The Sleeping Sem ritual seems to develop independently of the Opening of the Mouth ritual under the title of the Haker festival, sometimes even called the Night of Sleeping, *Sḏr.t* or *Sḏri.t*.[113] Just like the Hacking of the Earth ritual, the Haker festival was a nocturnal ritual.[114] In the autobiography of the Middle Kingdom official Mery, the Abydos Formula includes a wish from the deceased to hear "Jubilation from the mouth of Tawer at the Haker feast of the Night of Sleeping, the sleeping of Horus-the-fighter."[115] Otto suggests a scenario for the ritual as follows: "the sparse allusions to the Haker Festival probably involve this: the fighter Horus sleeps in the temple of Osiris. He calls on the soul of Osiris, which is hovering in the night air: 'Descend to me!'[116] and he 'animates' the statue. In the morning he is able to announce to a jubilant crowd that the buried god has been resuscitated."[117]

One may add two pieces of evidence to the important relationship between the Hacking of the Earth and the Haker Feast, or the Night of Sleeping. Textual evidence comes from the Ptolemaic Period Papyrus of Imouthes, and iconographical evidence comes from a scene inside the Tomb of Rekhmere.

110 Vandier does not translate the feast as "Hacking of the Earth;" rather, he uses the unexplained form "La fête du labour;" Vandier, *Le Papyrus Jumilhac*, pp. 135, 225, n. 847.

111 Vandier, *Le Papyrus Jumilhac*, p. 136.

112 Vandier, *Le Papyrus Jumilhac*, p. 136. One should note that the same vignette in Papyrus Jumilhac represents Aker as a two-headed lion next to the germinating body of Osiris. It is interesting to see that among the representations of the nightly journey of the sun god in the third section of the Book of Caverns of the tomb of Ramsesis VI, Aker is represented above a similar image of the ithyphallic corpse of Osiris. Osiris is depicted inside a mound that is formed by the encircling body of a snake. A sun disk is represented in between the two gods, which could emphasize the Osiris–Solar resurrection cycle; see Piankoff, *Le Livre des Quererts*, pl. XXVII.

113 Helck, *Untersuchungen zur Thinitenzeit*, pp. 27–28; Otto, *Egyptian Art and the Cults of Osiris and Amon*, pp. 42–43. See also Kamal, "The Stela of Shtpibre in the Egyptian Museum," pp. 278–280; Griffith, "Hakerfest," cols. 929–931; Lavier, "Les mysteres d' Osiris," pp. 289–295.

114 Assmann, *Death and Salvation*, pp. 226ff.

115 Lichtheim, *Ancient Egyptian Autobiographies*, pp. 86–88. On p. 88, n. 9, she understands *sḏrt* to mean "vigil" and not "sleep."

116 Translating "*Hꜣ.k r.i*." This is alternatively interpreted as an appeal by Osiris to Re; see Kamal, "The Stela of Shtpibre in the Egyptian Museum," p. 279; Clark, *Myth and Symbol in Ancient Egypt*, p. 130.

117 Otto, *Egyptian Art and the Cults of Osiris and Amon*, p. 43.

In the recently published Ptolemaic Period Papyrus of Imouthes in New York[118] the relationship between the Hacking of the Earth Festival and the Night of Sleeping is evident, strengthening the analysis of the scene of chapel H2. The manuscript begins with addressing Osiris with his lunar epithet and that his Ba will appear in glory in the full moon.[119] The text starts:

> The great decree that is issued to the nome of the netherworld/Silent Land (*igr.t*), fixed in the night of the diadem in order to cause that Osiris be installed as ruler in the nome of the netherworld…While his Ba appears in the Hale Eye and is transformed atop his corpse so that he lives and is complete. To be recited/ carried out during the *nṯri.t*-night, in the dreadful night, that night of going away and becoming distant, that night of the going forth of the voice, that night of lonely sleep, that night of great defensive magic, that night of Hacking the Earth and weeping, that night of loneliness, that night of mourning, that night of Hacking the Earth, when the whole land sees Sokar.

Later in the text the same papyrus provides the date of this ritual as being set toward the end of the month of Khoiak. The following section concerns the performing of the Opening of the Mouth Ceremony.[120] The text continues:

> The great Hacking of the Earth was carried out for you, and on day 25 of the fourth month of the inundation season, you were conveyed when you went out in the night, borne by the Sons of Horus, and Horus before you, the rope in his hand. Your ways were prepared. The god's servants have been purified at the opening of the mouth with the Opening of the Mouth Ritual.[121]

The iconographical evidence comes from the tomb of Rekhmere,[122] on the south wall of the passage, as part of rites before Osiris.[123] The scene begins on the right side with one priest erecting two obelisks. Another priest behind him is holding the hoe, clearly reflecting the feast of Hacking the Earth.[124] This scene is followed by two priests purifying two shrines of Upper and Lower Egypt. One of these priests is labeled as the Sem priest, whose image in this jubilating mode follows his earlier prostrating guise on a couch as

118 Goyon, *Le Papyrus d'Imouthes fils de Psintaes au Metropolitan Museum of Art de New-York (Papyrus MMA 35.9.21)*, p. 27, pl. 1, cols.1–5; Smith, "The Great Decree Issued to the Nome of the Silent Land," pp. 217–232.

119 Smith, "The Great Decree Issued to the Nome of the Silent Land," p. 217.

120 Smith, "The Great Decree Issued to the Nome of the Silent Land," p. 218.

121 Translation after Assmann, *Death and Salvation*, pp. 267, 281; Smith, *Traversing Eternity: Texts for the Afterlife from Ptolemaic and Roman Egypt*, p. 76; Goyon, *Le Papyrus d'Imouthes*, cols. 18.14–19.7, p. 52, and pls. 17–18.

122 Davies, *The Tomb of Rekh-Mi-Re*, II, pl. LXXXIII.

123 Davies, *The Tomb of Rekh-Mi-Re*, I, pp. 70–78.

124 This was misunderstood as a "digging a foundation episode;" Davies, *The Tomb of Rekh-Mi-Re*, I, p. 72.

the *Teknu*. This *Teknu* is most probably an indication of his "Sleeping Night."[125] Coffin Text Spell 557 links the *ḫbs tꜣ* with "seeing Osiris" and six Osirian festivals:

> Ho N! Come, that you may see Osiris; the Earth is hacked up for you, the offering is presented to you, reverence is paid to you; it means that the king will come down. O N, live and be a spirit for ever in these your six festivals of eternity, that is (to say) the fourth-day and the eighth-day festivals, the Msyt and the *wꜣg*, the shouting festival and the festival of Sokar.[126]

Coffin Text Spell 62 also mentions "the earth is Hacked Up will be recited for you, the rebel will be repulsed, the one who comes in the night and the robber in the early morning."[127] An account follows of what is in store for Osiris after his resurrection. Perhaps in the realm of the dead, "you will cross the steppes with Re; he will show you the places of enjoyment, you will find the wadis full of water and wash yourself to your refreshment."[128] The text continues with the different kinds of offerings that will be brought to Osiris together with Re and then ends with this statement:

> A ladder to the sky will be knotted together for you, and Nut will stretch her arms out to you. You will fare on the winding Lake and set sail in the eighth boat. Those two crews will navigate you, the imperishable ones and the unwearying ones. They will punt you and tow you to the bank with their ropes of bronze.[129]

The last scene in the first register of the north wall of chapel H2 deals with two nocturnal rituals, relating to the finding of the body Osiris as part of the main Osiris ceremonies in general and the earlier part of the embalming and mummification ceremonies in particular. The meaning of this scene is also reflected in Plutarch's account of the ceremonies that most probably formed parts of the Khoiak celebration, when

> On the night of the nineteenth day, they go down to the water, and the stolist and priests take out the sacred box which housed a golden casket. Into this they pour some drinking water which they have brought with them, and the people shout 'Osiris has been found' then they mingle fertile earth with water and having mixed precious spices and incenses with them, they fashion a

125 For the identification of the Tekenou with the sleeping Sem see, Moret, *Mystères égyptiens*, pp. 42–102; Baly, "Notes on the Ritual of Opening the Mouth," pp. 173, 178ff rejects Moret's argument. However, the inscription above the crouching figure in this tomb is reassuring as to the identification. See also Davies, *The Tomb of Rekh-Mi-Re*, I, p. 76, n. 17. This episode was later followed by the arrival of the barque at Abydos; see Davies, *The Tomb of Rekh-Mi-Re*, I, p. 72, pls. LXXIX–LXXX, row 3.

126 Faulkner, *Coffin Texts*, II, p. 167.

127 Assmann, *Death and Salvation*, p. 271.

128 Assmann, *Death and Salvation*, pp. 271ff.

129 Assmann, *Death and Salvation*, pp. 271–272.

> crescent-shaped image, and this they clothe and adorn, indicating that they regarded these gods (Isis and Osiris) as the principles of earth and water.[130]

Later, Plutarch confirmed the relationship between the Hacking of the Earth and the mourning ceremonies: "When they (the Egyptians) hack up the earth with their hands and cover it up again after having scattered the seeds, wondering whether these will grow and ripen, then they behave like those who bury and mourn."[131]

REGISTER II

Just as the middle scene in the first register is the most important scene of the register, the middle register of the Osiris bed surrounded by Isis and Nephthys is the main scene in the second register. The position of the two goddesses on either side of the funerary bed of Osiris is a reflection of the lamentation of the two goddesses as an important rite of the vigil.[132] The text of papyrus Berlin 3008, "Lamentation of Isis and Nephthys," dating to the Ptolemaic Period, begins with the statement that such praises are performed by the two sisters (naturally referring to Isis and Nephthys), "in the temple of Osiris, first of the westerners, on the 25th day of the fourth month of Inundation."[133]

The inscription written between the two goddesses does not represent a dialogue between the two of them, but rather a talk between the two major players in the roof chapels in general, that is, Osiris and (Amun)Re. Above ithyphallic Osiris, the inscription recounts: "You will (live) millions of millions (of years). Your Ba is appearing in heaven with the Ba of Re. I am as sunlight by day; you are as the moon by night." Some of the glosses left by later theologians on certain Coffin Texts reveal important information. For example, Spell 335 of the Coffin Texts, titled "the going out into the day from the realm of the dead," describes the rise of the sun as Re, but the commentators add the name of Osiris to many of those description of Re, as in the gloss "As for yesterday, it is Osiris; as for tomorrow, it is Re,"[134] over the phrase "yesterday is mine, I know tomorrow." This is also reflected in the famous Chapter 17 of the Book of the Dead.[135]

Osiris and Re seem to share such a balanced relationship that they complement each other. The phrase "I am as sunlight by day and you are as the moon by night" is a direct

---

130 Griffiths, *Plutarch's De Iside et Osiride*, pp. 178–180. See Beinlich, *Die "Osirisreliquien:" Zum Motiv der Körperzergliederung in der altägyptischen Religion*, pp. 285ff.

131 Griffiths, *Plutarch's De Iside et Osiride*, pp. 227ff.

132 Assmann, "Egyptian Mortuary Liturgies," p. 17.

133 Faulkner, "The Lamentations of Isis and Nephthys," pp. 338–340 and pls. II–III; For a new study on the Lamentation of Isis and Nephthys, see Kucharek, *Altägyptische Totenliturgien 4: Die Klagelieder von Isis und Nephthys in Texten der Griechisch-Römischen Zeit*; Kucharek, "Frauen im Tempel: Zur Frage der Ritualakteure in den 'Klageliedern von Isis und Nephthys,'" pp. 185–199.

134 Faulkner, *Coffin Texts*, I, pp. 262–263.

135 Naville, *Das ägyptische Todtenbuch* I, pl. XXXIII, 8–9.

speech by Re to Osiris, because the sun and the moon were regarded as manifestations of Re and Osiris, respectively.[136]

The only barque represented in the roof chapels of Hibis is depicted on the right side of the second register of chapel H2. It carries the main characteristic features of the Henu barque of Sokar: the crescent-shaped hull with a series of horizontal projections, a *djed* pillar at its prow, and a backward-facing antelope at the other end.[137] This Osiris-Sokar barque in chapel H2 is similarly represented on the roof of the Temple of Dendera, for example, in East chapel 1.[138] Cauville understood the scene of the barque in Hibis as a reference to the city of Memphis.[139] However, it could also be a reference to a specific episode in the Khoiak ceremonies, in particular the rituals that occur around the 26th of Khoiak. At this time, the Henu barque played an important part in the rituals. At Medinet Habu, in a version of the Sokar feast that occurred on the 26th of Khoiak, the divine barque of Sokar was accompanied by five ships belonging to Hathor, Wadjet, Shesemtet, Bastet, and Sakhmet.[140] The latter four goddesses are on the bottom registers of the four walls of chapel H2.[141] This barque also aids in the accession of the dead god king to the sky during the Khoiak ceremonies.[142]

The following scene of the Apis bull running while carrying the body of Osiris is rarely attested in the decoration of Egyptian temples; however, it is not uncommon in the decoration of stelae, where the bull is often depicted carrying the mummy[143] of the deceased in front of an obelisk-shaped tomb,[144] indicating the occurrence of this episode directly before the final interment. One similar representation occurs on the west side of the south gallery inside the catacombs of Osiris of Ptolemy IV at Karnak.[145] The remaining inscription reveals *pḥrr ḥnꜥ Ḥp ꜥnḫ in ḥꜥw-nṯr m spꜣwt tꜣ šmꜥw*, translated as "Running with the Apis who brings the divine body (parts) from the nomes of Upper Egypt."[146] This is

136 Willems, *Chests of Life*, p. 153.

137 Brovarski, "Sokar," cols. 1066–1067. For the elaborate version of the Henu barque descriptions, see Eaton, "The Festival of Osiris and Sokar in the Month of Khoiak," pp. 80–81.

138 Cauville, *Le temple de Dendara. Vol. X/2 Les Chapelles osiriennes (Plates)*, pls. 6, 11, photo 21. This image of the Sokar-Osiris barque is located on the right side of the north wall of east chapel 1, quite distinguished from the barque of Osiris located on the opposite left side of the north wall; see ibid., pls. 6, 14, and photo 24.

139 Cauville, *Le temple de Dendara: les chapelles, Osiriennes [2] Commentaire*, pp. 261, 263.

140 Graindorge, "La quête de la lumière au mois de Khoiak," pp. 83–105.

141 See pp. 140ff. for further discussion of these goddesses.

142 Graindorge-Héreil, *Le dieu Sokar à Thèbes au Nouvel Empire 1*, pp. 29ff, also see table on page 434.

143 In almost all scenes of the bull carrying Osiris on its back, Osiris is clearly depicted as a coffin, identified with the large head and shorter body; for scenes of the manufacture of similar coffins, see David, *Religion and Magic in Ancient Egypt*, p. 299.

144 For example Meeks, *Daily Life of the Egyptian Gods*, fig. 17.

145 Cauville, *Le temple de Dendara: les chapelles, osiriennes [2] Commentaire*, p. 263, n. 480; Marchand, *Karnak X*, p. 216.

146 Marchand, *Karnak X*, p. 216; Cauville, *Le temple de Dendara: les chapelles, osiriennes [2] Commentaire*, p. 263, n. 480. See also Vandier, "Memphis et le taureau Apis dans le Papyrus Jumilhac," pp. 116–118.

an important reference to the gathering of the limbs of Osiris, but it does not explain how this is achieved by the carrying of the mummy on the back of the bull, unless the bull is carrying the mummy while eating the grain or corn symbol of Osiris and therefore gathering the limbs inside his body. This idea finds support from an explicit scene illustrated inside the sanctuary of Hibis,[147] where the bull is running and the mummy of Osiris is inside his belly.

In the following scene, the goddess Heqat in full frog form is seated on a square pedestal that bears an unexplainable sign *t*, ⌓. In front of the goddess, the line of inscription gives her the title "Heqat, lady of Abydos." Because of the multitude of frog births following the annual inundation of the Nile, the frog became a symbol of fertility and renewal. The goddess was thus closely associated with Osiris and his resurrection. In the Temple of Abydos, the goddess seems to have received a dedicated cult. One scene depicts King Seti I offering *nw* jars to the goddess, who is represented as a frog seated inside a shrine that is placed on top of a sledge.[148] Heqat appeared as one of the followers of Osiris in the Temple of Seti I, inside the hall of Osiris as well as in the central hall of the Osireion.[149]

In particular, she figures in scenes where the sexuality of Osiris is emphasized. In Dendera, the goddess is represented in a similar manner to that in Hibis chapel H2: completely as a frog seated on a pedestal at the foot of the bier of Osiris, who is holding his erect phallus underneath Isis, who is hovering over him as a kite. In another scene in Dendera, the goddess is a frog-headed woman standing next to the bed of Osiris, aiding Anubis in the reconstitution of the body of Osiris.[150]

The figure of Heqat is followed by a rather unique representation of a deity who is wearing the crown of Nephthys, yet has a curved beard. The inscription in front of this figure is unfortunately destroyed. Perhaps one should understand the figure as a male representation of Nephthys; the curved beard is intentionally given to indicate the male gender. In the eleventh hour of the Book of the Amduat, four figures of Neith have female bodies and curved beards. The inscription gives definite evidence to the identity of the figure as *Nyt Ṯꜣyt*, "Male Neith."[151] Similarly, Isis is shown with the male divine beard among the vignette of the Book of Caverns where she casts a magical spell.[152] The function of such a deity in this scene might reflect her important role in Osiris' resurrection in general,[153] but could also personify the idea of the help of a male nurse during his rebirth.

147 Davies, *The Temple of Hibis*, Part 3, p. 7, pl. III, reg. IV, fig. 13. *CT* 15 records "O you (Osiris) whom the Bull begot;" Faulkner, *Coffin Texts*, I, p. 9.

148 Calverley and Gardiner, *Abydos* III, pl. 14. See also pp. 136ff., below.

149 Eaton, "Memorial Temples in the Sacred Landscape of Nineteenth Dynasty Abydos," p. 240; Frankfort, *The Cenotaph of Seti I at Abydos*, pl. LXXIII.

150 Budge, *Osiris and the Egyptian Resurrection*, I, p. 280; Mariette, *Denderah*, IV, pls. 78–80.

151 Hornung, *The Egyptian Amduat: The Book of the Hidden Chamber*, p. 343.

152 Leitz, *Lexikon*, I, p. 63.

153 For the role of Nephthys and Isis in the Osiris ritual, see the explicit details of Papyrus Imouthes; Goyon, *Le Papyrus d'Imouthès*, pp. 21ff; Smith, "The Great Decree Issued to the Nome of the Silent Land," pp. 223ff.

For example, Heh is assisting in the rebirth of the sun god.[154] The Book of the Earth, Part D, in the tomb of Ramesses VI includes a scene of Isis and Nephthys helping Osiris, who is shown with a stretched curved body, while he is giving birth to Horus.[155] In another similar scene in the same register, Isis and Nephthys are substituted by a male god with a curved beard who is helping Osiris give birth to Horus.[156] This is in agreement with Heqat beside him, stressing his fertility and cycle of rebirth. The discussion of the third register of the north wall of chapel H2 will continue after the discussion of the east wall of chapel H2 below.

CHAPEL H2 — SOUTH WALL

As mentioned above, the wall that once stood between chapels H1 and H2 is now completely missing. An alternative reconstruction to that of Davies and Cruz-Uribe has been suggested above.[157] The upper registers in each jamb of this wall represent four different standards carried by alternating *ankh* and *was* signs. Both signs have been provided with human arms to hold the standards. The identification of the four standards on the right is difficult to assess based on the outlined blocks. However, the standards on the left can be identified as that of a falcon god, perhaps Horus, a jackal representing Wepwawet or Anubis, Onuris, and a ram with two tall plumes perhaps representing Amun. Entering from chapel H1, this wall would have been considered the first wall of the chapel.[158] The depiction of the different standards can be a reference to a previous "public" part of the Osiris ceremonies depicted in hypostyle hall M, in which the carrying of the different standards played a major role.[159] The depiction of the different standards could also mean that the rituals that followed on the roof on Hibis began with the procession of the different standards of the gods—similar to the elaborate procession of priests carrying the different standards of the gods climbing up the staircase of the Dendera Temple, where they were connected with the destruction of the enemies of Osiris.[160]

In the second register are two goddesses: Sakhmet and either Neith or Isis. The remaining sections of the inscription are parts of the longer text for the protection of the body of Osiris that continues over the bottom of the other three walls of this chapel. For

154 For example, on the beautiful coffin lid of the sacred ram CGC 29792, the Ogdoad represented by Hehet and Hehw are attending to the birth of the sun god represented as a child; Bomhard, *The Naos of the Decades*, fig. 53. See also Leitz, *Lexikon*, V, p. 468.

155 From the Book of Earth, part D, from the tomb of Ramesses VI; Hornung, *The Ancient Egyptian Books of the Afterlife*, pp. 98–99, fig. 57. A similar scene is represented in section 4 of the Book of Caverns, where they also lift Osiris and the sun disk in order to "initiate his resurrection;" Hornung, *The Ancient Egyptian Books of the Afterlife*, p. 87, fig. 50.

156 Hornung, *The Ancient Egyptian Books of the Afterlife*, fig. 57.

157 See figures 29 and 30.

158 This is in agreement with its mention at the beginning of the list of walls recorded in the text of the east wall; see discussion of the text and the eight goddesses below, pp. 138ff.

159 Davies, *The Temple of Hibis*, Part 3, pls. 32, 33.

160 Corthals, "The Procession of the New Year in the Staircases at Edfu and Dendera," pp. 119ff.

the discussion of these goddesses and the texts, see the discussion of the third register of the north wall below.[161]

CHAPEL H2 — WEST WALL

According to Davies' outline, this wall was divided into three registers. The first shows the outline of four figures whose identity is fortunately confirmed by the inscriptions in front of them. First is Ptah standing on a pedestal, followed by Anubis holding a stela with two eyes. The third is Thoth with an ibis head and lunar disk. The fourth is a figure, or rather an emblem, of Wepwawet. In the second register are two standards of the ram followed by either one or two figures of Isis. The third register continues the text of the protection spell of Osiris that was most probably recited by Wadjet and either Isis or Neith.

This wall represents different gods and goddesses depicted in a similar manner to the other deities on the opposite east wall. They are in a static pose, not presenting or receiving any offerings, and they are usually designated by specific titles that attribute each of them to a specific region. Almost all of these gods have a direct relationship with the protection of Osiris during his revival ceremonies or belong to a specific location that was known to have an important Osiris cult. In the first register of the west wall, Ptah, Anubis, Thoth, and Wepwawet play an important role in the Osiris mysteries in general and in the protection of his body, or rather his pseudo-mummy.[162] In addition to his major role in the Osiris mysteries, Anubis with the stela bearing the two eyes might suggest the specific attribution of his city, Cynopolis (nome 17 of Upper Egypt).[163] The analysis of the meaning and function of these divinities and their standards should be continued in relationship to the other figures on the east wall, while the discussion of the remaining text and representation of the third register will be presented together with the third register of the north wall of chapel H2.[164]

CHAPEL H2 — EAST WALL

The east and the north walls are the only two walls still standing in chapel H2. The east wall is divided into three registers. Registers I and II include different gods and goddesses of various locales, while register III perhaps contains the last part of the protection spell of Osiris mentioned on the bottom registers of the other four walls. An important source for comparison of a similar combination of the deities represented on the east and west wall on the first and second registers comes from the Temple of Dendera. As the main wife and savior of Osiris, Isis and many of her manifestations are in both chapel H2 and in the chapel East 3 of the Osiris chapels on top of the roof of the Dendera Temple. In the latter,

161 See pp. 138ff.

162 For example, Ptah is among the most important gods who played a role in the manufacture of the figures of Osiris in Dendera; Cauville, *Le temple de Dendara: les chapelles, osiriennes [2] Commentaire*, pp. 33–34.

163 Vandier, "Quelques remarques sur le XVIII nome," p. 208; Kees, "Der Gau von Kynopolis und seine Gottheit," pp. 157–175

164 See pp. 138–145.

one finds Isis in the forms of Isis of Abydos, Isis of Coptos, as well as Isis of Achmim/Panopolis—all of which are in the first and second registers of chapel H2.[165] Among the other forms of Isis in the Dendera Osiris roof chapels is that of Behbeit el-Hagar, which is written as *nbt ḥbyt*, .[166] One might suggest that the unidentified title of Isis on the second register of the west wall in chapel H2 may have been this manifestation of the goddess, especially since some of the remaining signs may suggest a variation of the spelling of the title. The specific iconography of some of the deities on the east and west walls similarly occur in the Dendera roof chapels. One example is the reclining figure of the mourning goddess with upraised knee, seated on a socle, on the first register of the east wall of chapel H2. In Dendera she is depicted closest to the Osiris mummy, like the four depictions of Isis surrounding the main tableau in Dendera chapel East 3.[167] The second figure of Isis in the second register of the east wall with one knee raised and two hands down is, however, unattested.[168] The standing figure of Isis with her hands clasped under her breast on the west wall, second register, of chapel H2 is common among the representations of the protectress figures of Isis in Dendera, as in chapel East 3.[169] The wig with a side lock of the figure of Isis of Coptos on the first register of the east wall and of Isis of the unidentified region on the second register of the west wall of chapel H2 in Hibis are not found on any female goddesses in Dendera.[170]

Onuris seems to have played an important part inside chapel H2, as evident from his two representations, once at the head of the first register on the east wall and once among the standard symbols of the left jamb of the south wall. In the Abydos region, Onuris

165 The goddess Isis of *T3-wr* refers to the important cult of Isis in the vicinity of Abydos, particularly during the New Kingdom; Münster, *Untersuchungen zur Göttin Isis: Vom Alten Reich bis zum Ende des Neuen Reiches*, p. 165.

166 Cauville, *Le temple de Dendara. Vol. X/1 Les chapelles osiriennes (Inscriptions)*, p. 202, 2.

167 Cauville, *Le temple de Dendara. Vol. X/2 Les chapelles osiriennes (Plates)*, north wall (pl. 87, register 2 from the bottom), detailed in X 96; east wall (pl. 88, register four from the bottom); and west wall (pl. 90, register 4 from the bottom). Also in West chapel 3, north wall, pls. 236, 239, 243, 247. In the majority of the representations of the goddess with one knee raised, she is raising her left hand in front of her, while in Hibis she is holding her right hand up. See also Cauville, *Le temple de Dendara: les chapelles osiriennes [2] Commentaire*, pp. 230–231.

168 There is one scene with a slight variation in Cauville, *Le temple de Dendara. Vol. X/2, Les chapelles osiriennes.(Plates)*, pl. 102, where the goddess holds her left forearm with her elbow-up angled right hand. There she is identified as Shentayt. The gesture of her hands is similar to that of the four goddesses on the East 3 chapel of Dendera, northeast side, pl. 94. They are called the *fdw*, the four goddesses, most probably referring to the four guardian goddesses Isis, Nephthys, Neith, and Selkit.

169 Cauville, *Le temple de Dendara. Vol. X/2 Les chapelles osiriennes (Plates)*, south wall, pl. 89, west side, register four from bottom, pl. 102.

170 It is only found on Iunmutef. For example, West 3 chapel, northwest wall: Cauville, *Le temple de Dendara. Vol. X/2 Les chapelles osiriennes (Plates)*, pl. 247. However, that figure of Iunmutef has a uraeus on the forehead. Except for the uraeus, his iconography matches that of Iunmutef on the second register of the east wall of chapel H2 of Hibis.

played an important role for the protection of Osiris.[171] A whole room in the Temple of Ramesses II at Abydos (room I/IV) seems to be dedicated to his worship.[172] Onuris Shu appears in the Osiris chapels in Dendera in a very similar guise, standing with the harpoon and wearing the long garment and the ox tail with a serpent face.[173] However, in the Hibis representation, he has a few extra icons, including the falcon inside his crown, the uraeus, and the extra kilt over the long garment.

Horus *ḫnty n irty*, who is on the first register of the east wall of chapel H2, is alternatively called the blind and the seeing Horus.[174] This is the only representation of this god as a complete falcon. Above all, he is associated with the protection of the deceased and, more specifically, with the Osiris burial. In chapters 17 and 18 of the Book of The Dead, he is connected with the *ḳrst nt wsir*.[175] He is also associated with the city of Letopolis, which was an important Osirian cult center.[176] Beside his fundamental role in the protection of the burial of Osiris, he is sometimes manifested as two sacred animals of the sun god.[177]

The falcon-crocodile Horus of Sumenu is associated with Sobek, who is also given the title the lord of Sumenu.[178] The city of Sumenu is associated with the modern city of El-Rezeigat.[179] In the Book of the Dead, chapters 17 and 18, Horus *Mḫnty* and Sobek are combined in a spell to protect the body of Osiris: "Horus *mḫnty* and Sobek and those in the waters protecting Osiris' burial."[180] Sobek, whose name was possibly derived from *s3ḳ/sbḳ*, "he who unites (Osiris limbs),"[181] was similar to Horus *ḫnty n irty*—connected with both Osiris and Re, especially in the hymns of the Late Period.[182]

CHAPEL H2 — NORTH WALL

REGISTER III — THE VIGNETTE

Nephthys and Bastet appear at the end of the corners of this register and belong together with the text that continues across the four walls of the chapel. The third register

171 Cauville, *Le temple de Dendara: les chapelles, osiriennes [2] Commentaire*, p. 228.

172 Eaton, "Memorial Temples in the Sacred Landscape of Nineteenth Dynasty Abydos," p. 239, fig. 5, and 243.

173 Cauville, *Le temple de Dendara. Vol. X/2 Les chapelles osiriennes (Plates)*, pl. 101.

174 See footnote 45.

175 See Grapow, *Religiöse Urkunden*, pp. 19 (43, 1) and 47 (119, 7); Faulkner, *The Egyptian Book of the Dead*, pls. 9 and 13; Leitz, *Lexikon*, V, p. 263.

176 Weill, "Notes sur l'histoire primitive des grandes religions égyptiennes," pp. 101ff.

177 Brunner-Traut, "Spitzmaus und Ichneumon als Tiere des Sonnengottes," pp. 131–140, 153–157.

178 Cruz-Uribe, *Hibis Temple Project I*, p. 88, n. 327 with references; Yoyotte, "Études géographiques I. La «Cité des Acacias» (Kafr Ammar)," pp. 80–87.

179 Sauneron, "Quelques monuments de Soumenou au Musée de Brooklyn," pp. 57ff; Yoyotte, "Le Soukhos de la Maréotide et d'autres cultes régionaux du dieu-crocodile d'après les cylindres du Moyen Empire," p. 95.

180 Faulkner, *The Egyptian Book of the Dead*, pls. 9 and 13.

181 Bresciani, "Sobek, Lord of the Land of the Lake," p. 200.

182 Bresciani, "Sobek, Lord of the Land of the Lake," pp. 200–201.

depicts an interesting vignette inserted between the one line of inscription in front of Nephthys on the left and the fourteen lines of the inscriptions on the right.

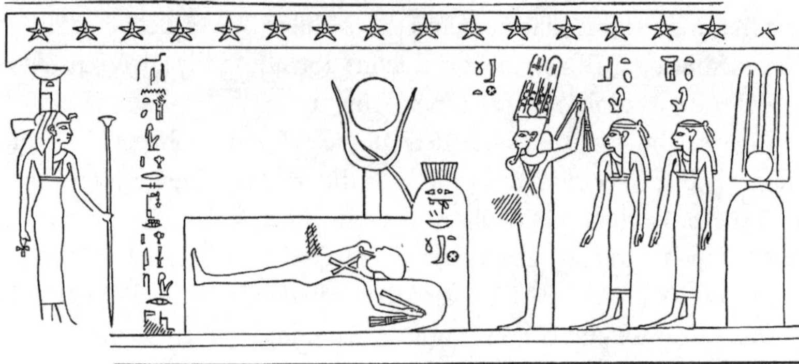

Figure 33: Vignette on the north wall of chapel H2, register III, detail from figure 26.

Similar to the above registers, the vignette focuses on the buried body of divine Osiris. In this case, the body is associated with Min of Coptos, according to the inscriptions above him. This figure is followed by a procession of three deities standing in front of a stela with a round top crowned with two feathers and a sun disk, a variation of the Abydene symbol of Osiris.[183] The deities are Nephthys, Isis, and another representation of Min. The reclining god is buried inside what appears to be a sarcophagus or a mound, the right side of which resembles the sign of the mound *i3t* (Gardiner N30) 𓈋.[184] The following sign is an emblem combining the sun disk between the cow horns with a third, single ram horn intersecting the two horns. Such an emblem appears on top of a papyrus column beside the figure of Min inside the Temple of Hibis in connection with his *sḥnt* shrine.[185] Scholars have briefly commented on this scene as a reference to the tomb of Osiris at Coptos.[186] However, one wonders about the purpose for exchanging the characters of Osiris and Min in this particular representation in the Khoiak celebration.

Min, as the principal deity of fertility and male sexual potency, was readily assimilated into the representations of both Amun and Osiris. Since at least the Middle Kingdom,

183 Davies, *The Temple of Hibis*, Part 3, p. 20.

184 Traunecker, *Coptos. Hommes et dieux sur le parvis de Geb*, p. 361.

185 For example Davies, *The Temple of Hibis*, Part 3, pl. 4, register V, figure 8; pl. 22, east wall top, and pl. 51, south wall, left center. For the *sḥnt* shrine of Min, see *Wb*. IV, p. 218, 10–12; Munro, *Das Zelt-Heiligtum des Min*, pp. 48, 52. In Davies, *The Temple of Hibis*, Part 3, pl. 22, east wall of chapel K and on the south exterior wall, a similar emblem occurs in connection with the Sehenet chapel of Min. It is interesting also to read on the west wall of hypostyle hall M, register I, left scene, that the god Min is associated with the god Amun in his role as the lord of the Sehenet-shrine; Davies, *The Temple of Hibis*, Part 3, pl. 32; Cruz-Uribe, *Hibis Temple Project I*, p. 87, n. 305; Feder, "Das Ritual *sʿḥʿ k3 sḥn.t* als Tempelfest des Gottes Min," pp. 31–54. For the relation of Min and Horus, see Münster, *Untersuchungen zur Göttin Isis*, pp. 130ff.

186 Traunecker, *Coptos. Hommes et dieux sur le parvis de Geb*, p. 361; Ballet, *Coptos. l'Égypte antique aux portes du désert*, p. 125.

Min had been synchronized with Amun, in the form of Amun/Min Kamutef.[187] The earliest incorporation of Min and Osiris seems to have developed toward the middle of the New Kingdom.[188] This blending with Osiris takes several forms. Min sometimes replaces Osiris completely, taking his role among the Osirian triad,[189] sometimes both deities are side-by-side,[190] or, as in this case in Hibis, Min is simply assimilated into the representation of Osiris: "Osiris und Min in einer Gestalt," perhaps intermingling the agrarian and chthonian aspects of the two gods in one.[191] In the Temple of Opet, a text says "his double (Osiris) is on earth like Min."[192] Inside the Temple of Hibis, Min seems to have occupied a particular role. Together with his *sḥnt* shrine, he is frequently depicted on the interior and exterior of the temple. In one case, these scenes show the influence of the Theban feast of Min that is similarly depicted in Medinet Habu, and sometimes also connected with the Sed feast of Osiris.[193] The scene on the top register (register I) of the east wall of chapel K on the ground floor of Hibis depicts Min standing in front of his *sḥnt* shrine. The inscription identifies him as "the Coptite, lord of Akhmim, lord of the two shrines," while the inscription above the female goddess facing him reads "the one who binds."[194] The two shrines might indicate the shrines in Coptos and Akhmim, but also could refer to Coptos and a shrine of Min at Hibis that could be equated with the Osiris-Min representation inside the mound on the north wall of chapel H2. The association of Min with the binding most probably refers to the binding of the mummy of Osiris during the Khoiak ceremony.

It is thus compelling to try to understand the vignette of Osiris-Min in light of this ceremony. In Dendera, many representations of Min occur, but this specific scene of Min as the mummiform Osiris inside a shrine or tomb is not paralleled in the roof chapels of Osiris at Dendera. However, inside chapel East 3 of Dendera, whose function is similar to that of chapel H2, as will be shown below, two interesting figures of Min occur on the

187 Roberts, *Hathor Rising. The Serpent Power of Ancient Egypt*, pp. 82–86.

188 Gabolde, "La statue de Merymaât gouverneur de Djâroukha (Bologne K.S. 1813)," p. 273. He identifies an early example, belonging to the 18th dynasty, of a statue of a governor called Merymaat that attests to this particular divine form of the personality of the god Min with the Osiris character. "L'hymne de la statue de Merymaât atteste maintenant l'ancienneté de cette forme divine particulière alliant la personnalitè de Min aux caractère propres d'Osiris;" ibid., p. 273. This is reflected in Hibis chapel H2, north wall.

189 George, "Eine Stockholmer Statuette des Gottes Osiris-Min," p. 16. For example, a stela dating back to the Ramesside Period represents the king offering to Min who is at the head of the Osirian triad of Isis and Horus without Osiris; Petrie, *Koptos*, pl. 18.

190 As in a steatite figure (George, "Eine Stockholmer Statuette des Gottes Osiris-Min," pp. 16–17) or a relief from Coptos (Perrin, "Néron et l'Egypte: une stèle de Coptos montrant Néron devant Min et Osiris [Musée de Lyon]," pp. 117–131). One also notes that on the Stela of Sobek-iry, Louvre C 30, the verso is inscribed with a hymn to Min, while the recto is inscribed with a hymn to Osiris. On the verso hymn to Min, he is equated with Horus; Lichtheim, *Ancient Egyptian Literature*, I, pp. 202–204.

191 George, "Eine Stockholmer Statuette des Gottes Osiris-Min," p. 16.

192 *Opet* I, p. 41.

193 Feder, "Das Ritual *sʿḥʿ kꜣ sḥn.t* als Tempelfest des Gottes Min," pp. 40–43.

194 Davies, *The Temple of Hibis*, Part 3, pl. 22; Cruz-Uribe, *Hibis Temple Project I*, pp. 93–94.

second register. One represents a standing Min, his phallus erect and his upheld right arm holding a flail. He is wearing a curved divine beard and has no crown or headgear. The inscription identifies him as *Mnw Ḥr s3 3st nṯr ꜥ3 ḥry-ib Nṯrwy*, "Min-Horus son of Isis, the great god, who resides in Coptos."[195] The other representation occurs in the same register but on the opposite side of the wall. Here Min stands in his classical iconography, but the inscription adds an important title to the scene, *Ḏd mdw in Mnw nb ḥsp nṯr ꜥ3 ḥry-ib iwnt sḫm šps nb Ipw*, "Words spoken by the god Min, lord of *ḥsp* (Cuve-gardin), the great god who resides in Iounet, the noble controller of Panopolis."[196] An important point may be noted from the iconography and text of these representations. The iconography of the first figure of Min is the same as the figure of Min lying down inside the tomb on the third register of the north wall of chapel H2 of Hibis. This provides an interesting argument that perhaps this reclining figure could be the equivalent of Min-Horus, son of Isis, or, according to the inscription of the second figure, is the "*nb ḥsp*." This title, which is usually translated as "lord of the basin/gardin," refers to the place where the manufacture of the Osiris figurines takes place during the celebration of the Khoiak rituals.[197] This important title seems very suitable to the pertinent composition of the third register of chapel H2. Both the representation of the eight goddesses and the long text of the "four balls" concern the sole protection of Osiris, most probably represented by a pseudo-mummy, as will be discussed below.

The evidence from the Temple of Seti I confirms the above argument. Min appears as Min-Horus, son of Isis, three times in the Osiris complex. One of these instances seems very relevant. It is located inside the Osirian hall, east wall, second section from the south.[198] Min appears here not only below a representation of the frog goddess Heqat inside her naos on top of a sledge[199] and next to Shentyt as a cow also inside a naos on a sledge, but he is also associated with Osiris. In this scene, he has the iconography of Osiris, rather than Min.[200] He is standing inside a shrine in front of the king, who is unlocking its door. The god has a mummiform body, wears the white crown, and holds the flail and crook in his crossed hands. The inscription in front of him says *Min [Ḥ]r s3 3st*, "Min-[Ho]rus son of Isis." The long inscription repeats the same name: "Min-Horus son of Isis who gives the king years of Tatennen." This scene occurs among other episodes of the Osiris celebrations.[201] The wall preserves many scenes that, as have been shown,

---

195 Cauville, *Le temple de Dendara: les chapelles, osiriennes [1] Transcription et traduction*, p. 111; Cauville, *Le temple de Dendara. Vol. X/2 Les chapelles osiriennes (Plates)*, pls. 101, 130.

196 Cauville, *Le temple de Dendara: les chapelles, osiriennes [1] Transcription et traduction*, p. 115; Cauville, *Le temple de Dendara. Vol. X/2 Les chapelles osiriennes (Plates)*, pls. 103, 132.

197 See discussion on pp. 214ff.

198 Calverley and Gardiner, *Abydos III*, pl. 14.

199 See p. XXX, above.

200 A similar depiction of Osiris associated with the "Coptite" was recovered by Gabolde in Karnak. In front of Osiris is a representaion of his *I3t*; see Marchand, *Karnak X*, pl. XII.

201 David, *Religious Ritual at Abydos*, pp. 220–224; David, *A Guide to Religious Ritual at Abydos*, p. 127, where she calls these episodes on the east wall "preparatory stages" of the ritual. However, one can possibly understand the scenes as detailed episodes of the actual ritual, vis-à-vis the summarized narrative of the relatively small Hibis Osiris chapels on

greatly resemble scenes of the north wall of chapel H2 of the Temple of Hibis, but bear even more resemblance to chapels K and K2 on the ground floor of Hibis.[202]

In this guise on the north wall of chapel H2, the reclining god is still pre-resurrected, before he is arisen and allied with the complete form of the fully crowned Min nearby. Spell 371 of the Coffin Texts associates Neper, god of the grain identified as Osiris, with the hope to rise up as Wepwawet with plumes on his head like Min of Coptos.[203] The existence of the "living" form of Min standing at the head of the accompanying procession simulates the rising of the god, with full fertility and procreation capabilities. In essence, the feast of Osiris implies a harvest feast where Osiris as the grain is called to arise and germinate. Min not only resides over the month of Tybi,[204] which follows the month of Khoiak, also his *sḥnt* shrine is correlated with a granary.[205]

Min, associated with foreign lands and the desert in general, protected expeditions in Wadi Hammamt and the mountains of the eastern desert.[206] Even within the Khoiak celebration in the Temple of Dendera, this aspect of Min is recalled: "He is the foreign youth from Coptos."[207] The association between Min and Horus, son of Isis or Haroeris, is inscribed on the walls of the main temples at Coptos and Qus.[208] Aufrère argued that both deities were involved together in the mining tradition of the desert during the Greco-Roman Period.[209] The fact that Min was chosen to be associated with Osiris in such a prominent figuration inside the roof chapels and the chapel complex K seems to also reflect the importance of his different locales, such as Coptos and Akhmim, to theology at Hibis.

---

the roof or the lower chapels K–K2. The opposite west wall represents the culminating scenes of the ritual, such as the raising of the *djed* pillar and the representation of the Abydene symbol. Some of the culminating ceremonies of the Khoiak celebration are represented in chapels E1, K2, and L. For more details on this see Chapter 6, below.

202 The scenes of chapel K and K2 (Davies, *The Temple of Hibis*, Part 3, pls. 22, 24–25) and the east wall of the inner Osiris Hall in Abydos (Calverley and Gardiner, *Abydos III*, pls. 13–18) include the deities Isis, Nephthys, Heqat, Shentyt, Min, Andjeti, Wepwawet, Horus-upon-the-papyrus-plant, and an unidentified god with two heads of a crested bird on a human body whose name is unfortunately lost in both scenes. These gods are all closely associated with the Khoiak celebration. In the Hibis scenes, they are represented standing in a procession with other deities headed by the image of the king offering to them collectively, while in Abydos the king is individually offering to each one of them.

203 *CT* V, pp. 33–34; Faulkner, *Coffin Texts*, II, p. 9.

204 Wiedemann, "Bronze Circles and Purification Vessels in Egyptian Temples," pp. 272, 274; *E* XV, p. 55; *D Mammisis*, p. 141, 18.

205 Egberts, *In Quest of Meaning. A Study of the Ancient Egyptian Rites of Consecrating the Meret-chests and Driving the Calves I*, p. 344.

206 Feder, "Das Ritual *sʿḥʿ k3 sḥn.t* als Tempelfest des Gottes Min," pp. 38–40.

207 Chassinat, *Le mystère d'Osiris au mois de Khoiak* II, pp. 676–677.

208 Aufrère, "Religious Perceptions of the Mine in the Eastern Desert in Ptolemaic and Roman Times," pp. 6–7; *PM* V, pp. 135–36; Bleeker, *Die Geburt eines Gottes*, pp. 15–18.

209 Aufrère, "Religious Perceptions of the Mine in The Eastern Desert in Ptolemaic and Roman Times," pp. 7ff.

REGISTER III — THE TEXT

The text continuing around the four walls of the chapel belongs to the genre of protection spells usually called "the revealing of the four balls."[210] The ritual of the four balls dates as far back as the Old Kingdom.[211] This ritual is primarily an execration act. Papyrus 47.218.138 of the Brooklyn Museum and Papyri 3237 and 3239 of the Louvre mention the spell of the "four balls" as a magical spell for the protection of the king against serpents and reptiles, inherently referring to the evil spirits of Seth that may come from every cardinal point.[212] In Papyrus New York 35.9.21, col. 26, 1–4, the four balls (*bnn.t*) are supposed to be *ḫꜣꜥ*, "cast," toward the four cardinal points.[213] The revealing of the four balls has resemblance to the ritual of *sḳr ḥmꜣ*, or "striking the ball," that appeared since the New Kingdom.[214] It denoted primarily a magical spell against the evil forces of Apophis.[215] Similarly, these balls were made of clay.[216] The technique of striking the balls or other apotropaic vessels occurs in exchange with throwing the objects to the ground or dashing them against each other.[217]

According to the terminology used in the text in chapel H2, the spell here should perhaps be called "striking of the four bricks." The only tools mentioned are the *tbt* or *ḏbt* of faience, and the technical term is *ḥwi*, "to strike." Several points can be made from this text. On each wall the text begins with an offense aimed at demeaning the reprehensible Seth. On the north wall, his great transgression is mentioned: "He had committed great offense (5) repeatedly, because he had acted as the enemy of Osiris, (6) after he caused that he be drowned by proceeding on water (and that) all his limbs were (7) divided." The spell then continues with commanding Seth to stop and turn back and not draw near the noble body of Osiris during such a critical stage. The following part deals with Seth's physical rebellion. According to the north wall, by striking the two blocks of faience to his head, "Two (of the four blocks) therein are (10) broken up today. Those have struck your head (11) annihilating your Ba. You will not come back (12) to see the great god." A menacing threat is issued on the east wall, that the great god Re would be burned if Seth approached, "May you see your father Re laid down inside a brazier of fire. If you approach in order to prevail over the divine body, he will burn. If you do not, he will be safe. May Re strike your head so that he destroys your Ba. You will not come back to see the great god." Then the spell ends with a call on Osiris to rise up and

---

210 Goyon, "Textes mythologiques. II," pp. 349-399

211 Goyon, "Textes mythologiques. II," pp. 349ff; Ziegler, "A propos du rite des quatre boules," p. 439, n. 4.

212 Goyon, "Textes mythologiques. II," pp. 350-351.

213 Further discussion of the ritual of the four balls in Quack, "Philologische Miszellen 1," pp. 151–153, and Kákosy, "Solar Disk or Solar Globe?," pp. 1057–1067.

214 Kousoulis, "Some Remarks on the Ritual of 'Striking The Ball' in the Liturgical Environment of the Ptolemaic Temples," pp. 153–154.

215 Kousoulis, "Some Remarks on the Ritual of 'Striking The Ball,'" p. 154.

216 Kousoulis, "Some Remarks on the Ritual of 'Striking The Ball,'" pp. 155–156.

217 Kousoulis, "Some Remarks on the Ritual of 'Striking The Ball,'" p. 157; Ritner, *The Mechanics of Ancient Egyptian Magical Practice*, pp. 144–145, n. 655.

be elevated while his enemies are being toppled: "Come, rise up Osiris Wennefer. Your enemies are overthrown."

The east wall further elaborates on the actual way the spells are to be recited in an explicit stage direction on how to perform the ritual:

> [Perform the protection of Osiris] in the southern, northern, western, and eastern sky. (12) They shall be conveyed simultaneously. When Osiris is called upon by you, (then) it is the Bnw (Phoenix) that you (14) shall say about it. *Ἰiw-r-ḳ3-iw* twice. (15) *Ἰḥ-rw-ḳ3-ii3-r* twice. *Ἰḥ* (16) *bnn* Osiris Wennefer has come with outstretched arms (17) four times. O Sakhmet, Bastet, Wadjet, and Shesemtet. This is how you may perform an awakening over Osiris, foremost of the west.

The southern, northern, western, and eastern heavens correspond to each wall of the chapel. Lines four and five of the inscription on the east wall confirm that the eastern heaven is the actual eastern wall when they mention, "May you be turned backward. Place your head to your (5) back in order to see the eastern heaven." The *aide mémoire* continues that the spell on each wall shall be recited *m sp wʿ*, "simultaneously," clearly referring to a chorus performance.[218] "If Osiris is called upon by you" most probably refers to the moment the goddesses call on Osiris to rise up, found in the last part of the spell. So on reaching this part of the spell, they shall say the "Bnw Spell" that consists of the recitations of the following enigmatic phrases; the first phrase (*Ἰiw-r-ḳ3-iw*) twice, the second one (*Ἰḥ-rw-ḳ3-ii3-r*) twice, and the last phrase (*Ἰḥ bnn*, "Osiris Wennefer has come with outstretched arms") four times. The Phoenix is attested in reference to the Khoiak ceremony.[219] This Bnw spell might indicate that this is the strongest kind of spell, combining the forces of Re with those of Osiris.[220]

---

218 Some texts surrounding the Opening of the Mouth ceremony were intended to be read concurrently; Ayad, "Towards a Better Understanding of the Opening of the Mouth Ritual," pp. 109–116.

219 As, for example, the texts of the sarcophagus of the divine Adoratrice Ankhnesneferibre, which also refer to the manufacture of a corn-mummy as part of the funerary ceremonies; Sander-Hansen, *Die religiösen Texte auf dem Sarg der Anchnesneferibrê*, pp. 99–109, 113–14; Tooley, "Osiris Bricks," p. 178, n. 44; Tolmatcheva, "Ancient Egyptian Roots of the Phoenix Myth: On the History of the Problem," p. 97. Reference to Osiris as the "Phoenix" occurs in the ritual of smiting of the four balls; Goyon, *Le papyrus d'Imouthès*, col.27, 110; idem., "Le cérémonial pour faire sortir Sokaris," p. 90, n. 11.

220 The reference to the Benben, the main solar symbol of Heliopolis, closely associates Osiris and Re. The Phoenix was both the Ba of Re and the Ba of Osiris; Žabkar, *A Study of the Ba Concept in Ancient Egyptian Texts*, pp. 13–14. The head of Osiris depicted on an obelisk in a relief further emphasizes this association; Stricker, "Osiris en de obelisk," pp. 41ff, pl. 5. For the relation of the Benben to both Osiris and Re, see Lecoco, "Les Sources Égyptiennes du Mythe Du Phénix," pp. 217–220; Kákosy, "Phoenix," col. 1032. On the detailed history of the literature on the Bnw, see Tolmatcheva, "Ancient Egyptian Roots of the Phoenix Myth: On the History of the Problem," pp. 93–98; Tolmatcheva, "A Reconsideration of the Benu-bird in Egyptian Cosmogony," pp. 522–526.

The main actresses of this ritual of the four balls in chapel H2 of Hibis are clearly labeled as Sakhmet, Bastet, Wadjet, and Shesemtet, corresponding to the same order of the southern, northern, western, and eastern walls where their images are represented, respectively. Scholars have debated the identity of the latter goddess.[221] The writing of her name included many determinatives as [hieroglyph], [hieroglyph], or [hieroglyph], but was mostly abbreviated into the sign that she carries here (the shoulder-knot; Gardiner S22, [hieroglyph]),[222] which led to her being confused with Neith or Satis.[223] The identity of this goddess as Shesemtet is also supported on theological grounds, as she is associated with the protection of the deceased and the concept of rebirth.[224] In the Temple of Seti I at Abydos, she bears a title that makes her more suitable to be assiciated with chapel H2 than Satis or Neith: "destroyer of the enemies against Osiris."[225] She appears with the other goddesses in chapel H2 of Hibis in other instances relating to the protection of the deceased.[226]

The analysis of the previous vignettes of the different registers of chapel H2 identifies them clearly as episodes of the Khoiak celebration that occurred during the fourth month of the inundation season. Beside the roof chapels, the lower chapels K, K1, and K2 provide further evidence. To understand the extent of the meaning of the decorations of the different episodes of the rituals on top of the Hibis roof, especially inside the H1–2 complex, one should refer to the decorations inside the complex chapels K–K2.

On the east wall of chapel K, in the second register, the inscription reads: "Fourth month of inundation, day ten [227]/// the goddess Djedit, ///speaking about it: being satisfied because of the entering of the musicians to the *pr ʿnḫ ỉrw*, in order to place seed grain upon water. D[jedit] places Lower Egyptian grain upon water/// in the garden (*ḥspt*), 12 cubits wide."[228] This leaves little doubt as to the association of the Khoiak celebration

---

221 Davies, *The Temple of Hibis*, Part 3, p. 20 identified her as Satis. Valbelle, *Satis et Anoukis*, p. 128 suggested Neith. Cruz-Uribe, *Hibis Temple Project I*, p. 88, n. 329 favors the latter suggestion as Neith but labels her as Shesemtet.

222 Lacau, "La déesse *šsmtt* [hieroglyph]," pp. 198–200; Newberry, "Šsm.t," pp. 316–323.

223 Cruz-Uribe, *Hibis Temple Project I*, p. 88, n. 329.

224 *CT* V 24d–25; *BD* 174 ; *PT* § 262–266; Kitchen and Gaballa, "The Festival of Sokar," pp. 10, n.3, 63–66.

225 Calverley and Gardiner, *Abydos III*, pl. 29a.

226 Habachi, *Tell Basta*, pp. 96, 113, 120, pl. 29B, 113 and n. 1. See also Kitchen and Gaballa, "The Festival of Sokar," pp. 10, n. 3, 63–66; Habachi, "Divinities Adored in the Area of Kalabsha, with a Special Reference to the Goddess Miket," pp. 175–176.

227 For the restoration of this number see p. 144.

228 Davies, *The Temple of Hibis*, Part 3, pl. 22; Cruz-Uribe, *Hibis Temple Project I*, p. 95.Yoyotte is the first scholar to point out this important inscription and associate the scenes and texts of the lower chapel K with the Khoiak mysteries; Yoyotte, "Religion de l'Égypte ancienne," pp. 189, 192ff; idem, "La cuve osirienne de Coptos. Tanis: problèmes, bilans et perspectives," pp. 163ff; idem, "Textes relatifs au culte d'Osiris et de Sokaris," pp. 194ff. In the brief article of Osing, "Zu den Osiris-Räumen im Tempel von Hibis," pp. 511–516, he discussed the association of the chapel complex K with the Khoiak feast and pointed out a possible relationship to the upper roof chapels H1 and H2, but concluded his article saying "Dieser Dachtempel des Osiris in Hibis (H1–3) war vielleicht ebenso wie der in Dendera für die Durchführung wesentlicher Teile der Osiris-Mysterien bestimmt, und in disesem

with these chapels as well. The following inscription, found above the scene in register II on the east wall of chapel K, is equally important: "[presentation] of the king when he offered incense and cool water to his par[ents, Osiris, Nu]t, Heqat, and Shentyt. Hail to you, eldest one, august mummy (*sꜥḥ šps*), for your father Geb has created you and your mother Nut has borne you///."[229] Beside the representation of Isis, Nephthys, and Min the Coptite, chapels H2 and K share the reference to the august mummy (*sꜥḥ šps*) of Osiris. This may allude to the pseudo-mummy of Osiris that most probably was the focus of the rituals in both chapels.

From the first glimpses known of the Osiris mysteries or celebration in the Ikhernofret account in the Middle Kingdom to the later Greco-Roman versions, the focus of such rituals was predominantly a figure of Osiris over which some burial, embalming, and resurrecting rites were carried out. Such figurines are called "corn Osirises" but are also known as "Kornmumien," "Pseudo-momies d'Osiris," or "Osiris Végétant."[230] The texts from the Dendera roof chapels provide the single most important document on the actual manufacture of these figurines.[231] They were made of a combination of grain and earth or sand that had been watered for several days.[232] Some of these figurines have been recovered from different sites, but unfortunately they were not attached to constructions of any kind; rather, they were buried in the sand of the necropolis.[233] Based on the few examples that have been attributed to a specific locale, they seem to be usually connected with the places of the Osiris Cult.[234] Scholars have debated whether these recovered figurines are the actual figurines discussed in the literary data relating to the Osiris mysteries.[235] However, the many Osirian representations and objects found on or near the wrappings

---

Fall hat wohl auch ein funktioneller Zusammenhang mit dem unteren Osiris-Heiligtum des Hibis-Tempels (Raum K–K2) bestanden. Genaueres läßt sich hierzu jedoch derzeit nicht ermitteln." For more on the lower chapels (K–K2), see Chapter 6, below.

229 Davies, *The Temple of Hibis*, Part 3, pl. 22; Cruz-Uribe, *Hibis Temple Project I*, p. 95.

230 Quack, "Die Rituelle Erneuerung der Osirisfigurinen," p. 5; Centrone, "Corn mummies, Amulets of Life," p. 33; Centrone, "Corn-Mummies: A case of 'Figuring it out,'" pp. 293–301; Raven, "Corn Mummies," pp. 7ff.

231 Chassinat, *Le mystère d'Osiris au mois de Khoiak* I, pp. 40–49. Other important evidence comes from the Papyrus Jumilhac (Vandier, *Le Papyrus Jumilhac*, p. 135, pl. III.8) and the south wall of the Osiris Room in Philae (Bénédite, *Le temple de Philæ*, p. 124, pl. XL).

232 *Dendera* X, p. 29, 2–4; Chassinat, *Le mystère d'Osiris au mois de Khoiak* I, pp. 40–49. See also Quack, "Die Rituelle Erneuerung der Osirisfigurinen," pp.7ff.

233 Raven, "Corn Mummies," p. 9 ; Raven, "Four Corn Mummies in the Archaeological Museum at Cracow," pp. 5–11. The total number collected so far is 92 figurines, which, considering the relatively easy process of the manufacture of such figurines, is remarkably few. They seem to have been a monopoly of priestly activity only handled during specific sacred rituals.

234 Centrone, "Corn-Mummies: A case of 'Figuring it out,'" pp. 298ff.

235 See the recent discussion by Centrone, "Corn mummies, Amulets of Life," pp. 37ff; "This is the form of […] Osiris of the mysteries, who springs from the returning waters," ibid., p. 360. However, the apparent crude shape of the figurines might be because they were associated with local versions of the feast or as a result of the difference between "the literary theory and the actual praxis," as noted by Raven ("Corn-Mummies," p. 28).

of these figurines confirm that they belong to an Osiris ritual.[236] The underlying symbolic meaning of the corn Osiris is similarly rejuvenation and resurrection, especially because some corn Osirises had artificial erect phalluses attached to the wrappings.[237] This not only reflects the obvious notion of the procreation power of the god, but also presents an image of the many transformations and representations of Osiris depicted among the decorations of chapel H2. When the theologians fashioned the chest related to the Osiris burial, they were supposed to make the image crescent-shaped, because the moon, whenever it comes near the sun, appears crescent-shaped.[238] The allusion to the moon and the sun in this particular instance certainly refers to the Osirian ceremonies in relation to the solar cycle, which were closely connected. It is not surprising, then, to find spell 15b of the Book of the Dead inscribed on some of the Osiris figurines.[239]

The detailed analysis of the different vignettes of chapels H1 and particularly H2 strongly supports the association of chapel H2 with an actual pseudo-mummy of Osiris. Architecturally, the narrow room is too small to be used as anything other than a depository; it measures about 120 by 230 centimeters.

Good archaeological evidence to support the idea that chapel H2 housed a coffin containing the pseudo-mummy of Osiris comes perhaps from the necropolis of Tihna, the place of the Pharaonic town of Dehenet and the Greek town of Acoris. Many corn mummies were recovered there,[240] but, more importantly, four balls of clay were found, each inscribed with the names of the four protectress goddesses—Bastet, Sakhmet, Shesemtet, and Wadjet—who are represented on the decoration of the north wall of chapel H2.[241] The four guardian goddesses—Neith, Nephthys, Selkit, and Isis—represented in the

236 Raven, "Corn Mummies," pp. 21–22, examples 11–14, Note that some of these figurines bear references to Osiris *ḫnti-imnti*, the name *par excellence* of these figurines, according to Dendera texts. For example, Raven, "Corn Mummies," p. 22, catalogue number 9, 11; Chassinat, *Le mystère d'Osiris au mois de Khoiak* I, pp. 40–49, II, pls. xv–xvi.

237 Centrone, "Corn-Mummies: A case of 'Figuring it out,'" p. 294; see Raven, "Corn Mummies," p. 35, pl. i.

238 Griffiths, *Plutarch's De Iside et Osiride*, pp. 181, 185.

239 Raven, "Corn Mummies," p. 25, example 4. The spell 15b deals with the praising of Re when he illuminates the Netherworld "who shines by day (and is also) lord of the night, making festive the twin cavern;" Allen, "Some Egyptian Sun Hymns," p. 353. This part of the spell bears resemblance to the text between Isis and Nephthys on the second register of the north wall of chapel H2. Other solar symbolism represented on these corn mummies includes texts praising Horakhty and other sun hymns (Raven, "Corn Mummies," p. 25); texts of the Pyramid Text utterance 368 (Raven, "Corn Mummies," p. 26), whose beginning mentions Osiris's name as "Horizon from which Re goes" (Faulkner, *Pyramid Texts*, p. 121).

240 Raven, "Corn Mummies," pp. 21–24.

241 Louvre nos. E 12196–12199, 12202–12203, and 12205; Ziegler, "A propos du rite des quatre boules," pp. 437–439, pl. 1; Osing, "Zu den Osiris-Räumen im Tempel von Hibis," pp. 514–515; Lefebvre, "Sarcophages égyptiens trouvès dans une Nécropole gréco-romaine à Tehneh," pp. 227–231. For parallels in the Übersee-Museum at Bremen, see Karl, "Einige magische Kleindenkmäler griechisch-römischer Zeit," pp. 411–421.

same text, play a major role in the Sokar/Osiris rituals in general,[242] but are frequently found in connection with the more intimate rituals immediately surrounding the coffin or sarcophagus of the deceased.[243] Thus, by the writing and representation of these guardian goddesses, together with the other four protectress goddesses in chapel H2, they formed an enveloping, encircling belt of protection surrounding the mummy of Osiris. Furthermore, according to Graindorge, the four balls inscribed with the names of Sakhmet, Shesemtet, Wadjet, and Bastet are probably "l'écho tardif de la protection de Sokar dans la Chapelle-*štyt* de la barque-*ḥnw* au Nouvel Empire du 18 au 25 Khoiak."[244] This association with the "*štyt* Chapel" will provide significant information regarding the exact use and function of chapel H2.

According to the Dendera text on the roof, the yearly Khoiak ceremonies took place between the 12th and the 30th of the fourth month of the inundation season.[245] According to the Medinet Habu calendar, the celebrations began on the 21st of the month. In most of the New Kingdom evidence, the Khoiak ceremonies began on the 18th.[246] The corn Osiris was manufactured during the early part of the mysteries (day 12 to 21) in the *ḥwt-ḥsp*, or "Cuve-gardin."[247] On day 21, the corn mummy of the figure of Osiris was wrapped and placed in a coffin and brought to the "*štyt ḥrt*" where an elaborate ritual of embalming and mummification took place before the final interment.[248] As the discussion of the vignette of the north wall of chapel H2 points out, inside the chapel the ceremonies were

242 Goyon, "Le cérémonial pour faire sortir Sokaris," p. 68; Kitchen and Gaballa, "The Festival of Sokar," pp. 63–66.

243 They frequently appear decorating each corner of the sarcophagi or coffins, for example on the sarcophagi of Tut-ankh-amun and Ay. Evidence can also be provided from the existence of the "four magical bricks" located at the ends of the sarcophagus inside the burial chamber; see Roth, "Magical Bricks and the Bricks of Birth," pp. 121–139, esp. 124ff and table 1. See also Wilkinson, *Symbols and Magic*, pp. 78–80.

244 Graindorge, "La quête de la lumière au mois de Khoiak," p. 92.

245 Chassinat, *Le mystère d'Osiris au mois de Khoiak* I , pp. 69–73.

246 Graindorge-Héreil, *Le dieu Sokar à Thèbes au Nouvel Empire 1*, pp. 189–191

247 Chassinat, *Le mystère d'Osiris au mois de Khoiak* I, pp. 53–54, 69–73; Griffiths, *Plutarch's De Iside et Osiride*, pp. 181ff. The text of Papyrus Jumilhac states that the preparation of the figure of Osiris took place inside the *ḥsp*; Vandier, *Papyrus Jumilhac*, pp. 135, 224. See also Cauville, "Les mystères d'Osiris à Dendera. Interprétation des chapelles osiriennes," p. 25; Tooley, "Osiris Bricks," p. 175.

248 Egberts, *In Quest of Meaning*, I, pp. 352–353, n. 198 and p. 382, n. i. All in all, one can designate three main places connected to these figurines: (1) the *ḥwt-ḥsp*, where its manufacture took place. In Hibis, chapels K1–K3 seem to have been the most appropriate place for this stage, see discussion for chapels K1–K3 below; (2) the "Upper Dwat," "*dw3t ḥrt*," or "*štyt ḥrt*" that designates the temporary tomb that housed the image for one year. The most appropriate place in Hibis for such a place is certainly chapel H2, similar to Chapel West 3 in Dendera, see Cauville, *Le temple de Dendara: les chapelles, osiriennes [2] Commentaire*, p. 212; (3) finally one designates the "Lower Dwat," or "*dw3t ẖrt*," with the desert necropolis where the corn mummies of the previous year/s were permanently kept and later discovered by archaeologists. See Chassinat, *Le mystère d'Osiris au mois de Khoiak*, pp. 37ff, 227–233, 277–97; also Osing, "Zu den Osiris-Räumen im Tempel von Hibis," p. 512.

engaged with the embalming, resurrection, and, above all, the protection rituals that were performed over the mummy of Osiris from at least the 21st of the month of Khoiak. This consequently suggests that chapel H2 functioned most probably as the *dwꜣt ḥrt*, "Upper Dwat," or *štyt ḥrt*, "Upper Tomb."

When the corn mummy was transferred to this temporary tomb, it was accompanied by a procession of 34 barques and 365 lamps.[249] The procession reminds one of the number of astronomical figures on chapel E1, which represented the days of the year and which might, among other things, be a symbolic reflection of that solemn procession of the coffin of Osiris. Some comparable places were identified with the Upper *Dwat* and the Lower *Dwat*.[250] For example, inside the Osireion, the sarcophagus room with the texts of the Book of Nut[251] and the Osirian Island in the central hall were identified as the Upper *Dwat* and the Lower *Dwat*, respectively.[252] Cauville identified chapel West 3 on top of the Dendera roof as a "*štyt ḥrt*," or "Upper Tomb."[253]

Cauville suggested that the partly destroyed number from the above-mentioned inscription dating the Khoiak celebration on the east wall of chapel K could be restored as day 20,[254] but later proposed day 12.[255] This latter suggestion is also confirmed by collation of the wall itself.[256] The text on chapel K thus refers to the preparatory episode of the feast, that is, as is clear from the text itself, the manufacture of the Osiris figurine. An earlier segment of the celebration of the Khoiak festival usually involved a public celebration that is alluded to in hypostyle hall M.[257] However, in this intimate part of the temple, as well as on the roof, the private episodes of the celebration took place. Thus, one can propose that the number 12 refers to the manufacture of the figure of Osiris. Then, starting from day 21 or 24,[258] the different embalming episodes of the celebration usually occurred on top of the roof chapels.

The analysis of the different vignettes of the walls of chapel H2 in particular reflected many nocturnal rituals, such as the embalming and protection rituals of Osiris' corpse, the Hourly Vigil, and the "union with the mother."[259] The importance of the ritual of

249 Raven, "Corn Mummies," p. 28; Leitz, "Die obere und die untere Dat," pp. 47ff.

250 Eigner, *Die monumentalen Grabbauten der Spätzeit in der thebanischen Nekropole*, pp. 163ff; Leitz, "Die obere und die untere Dat," pp. 41–43. Chassinat, *Le mystère d'Osiris au mois de Khoiak* I, pp. 8, 618, 621

251 Von Lieven, *Grundriss des Laufes der Sterne: Das sogenannte Nutbuch.*

252 Frankfort, *The Cenotaph of Seti I at Abydos*, p. 31 discusses the two places identified by Eigner as an Upper and Lower Dwat; Leitz, "Die obere und die untere Dat," p. 49.

253 Cauville, *Le temple de Dendara: les chapelles osiriennes [2] Commentaire*, p. 212; Beinlich, *Die "Osirisreliquien:" Zum Motiv der Körperzergliederung in der altägyptischen Religion*, pp. 276–283; Leitz, "Die obere und die untere Dat," pp. 53ff, n. 106. For the use of the catacombs at Karnak as "*štyt n Wsir*," see Marchand, *Karnak X*, pp. 221ff.

254 Cauville, "Une offrande spécifique d'Osiris: le récipient de dattes (*mꜥdꜣ n bnr*)," p. 57, n.71.

255 Cauville, *Le temple de Dendara: les chapelles osiriennes [2] Commentaire*, p. 262, n. 475.

256 See also Cruz-Uribe, *Hibis Temple Project I*, p. 94, n. 383.

257 See also p. 224.

258 Egberts, *In Quest of Meaning*, I, n. 198 on pp. 352–353; Gillam, *Performance and Drama in Ancient Egypt*, pp. 100–108.

259 As reflected through the icon of the angled figure of Osiris and Nut, see pp. 118ff.

Hacking of the Earth, the Night of Sleeping, the Lamentation of Isis and Nephthys, reflected from the north wall of chapel H2, is made clear in the Papyrus of Imouthes, which specifically sets the recitation of the text during the "divine night."[260] Goyon suggested that this "divine night" took place between the 24th and the 25th of Khoiak,[261] while Smith argued for a time between the 25th and the 26th.[262] Moreover, the starting location of the rituals of Osiris according to the Papyrus of Imouthes is the House of Shentyt,[263] whose reference is found in the lower chapel complex K of Hibis, suggesting that the beginning of the ceremonies of Osiris took place there and then proceeded to chapel complex H on the roof. The following section of the Papyrus of Imouthes (4/6) concerns the performance of the Opening of the Mouth ritual.[264] An explicit reference to that ceremony is depicted later on the walls of the adjoining chapel complex E of the Hibis roof, as will be discussed below.

260 Smith, "The Great Decree Issued to the Nome of the Silent Land," p. 218. For this important night, see Assmann, *Death and Salvation*, pp. 260ff; Herbin, *Le livre de parcourir l'éternité*, pp. 223–224.

261 Goyon, *Le Papyrus d'Imouthès*, p. 21.

262 Smith, *Papyrus Harkness (MMA 31.9.7)*, p. 174; Smith, "The Great Decree Issued to the Nome of the Silent Land," p. 218.

263 Smith, "The Great Decree Issued to the Nome of the Silent Land," p. 218.

264 Smith, "The Great Decree Issued to the Nome of the Silent Land," p. 218.

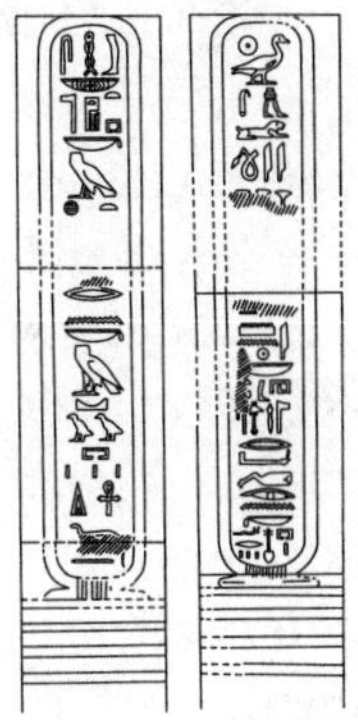

5
Chapel Complex E

1. DESCRIPTION

Directly south of the main sanctuary of the Hibis Temple, a door opens to the undecorated stairway E. This doorway leads to a series of narrow undecorated crypts through two trap doors cut into its lower end (see pl. 17). At the top of the stairway are the decorated chapels E1 and E2, as well as the rest of the undecorated roof of the temple. A mark in the floor of chapel E1 and a fragment of a drum suggest that this chapel had a column at the center of its facade. Two pilasters are constructed at both ends of the chapel (see pl. 34). The decoration of chapels E1 and E2 is in shallow sunken relief, except for the figures of the king and deities on the west, north, and south walls of chapel E1, which are decorated in raised relief. Some colors remain, especially on the west wall of chapel E1 (see pls. 33ff).[1]

THE DOORWAY — LINTEL OF DOOR TO E

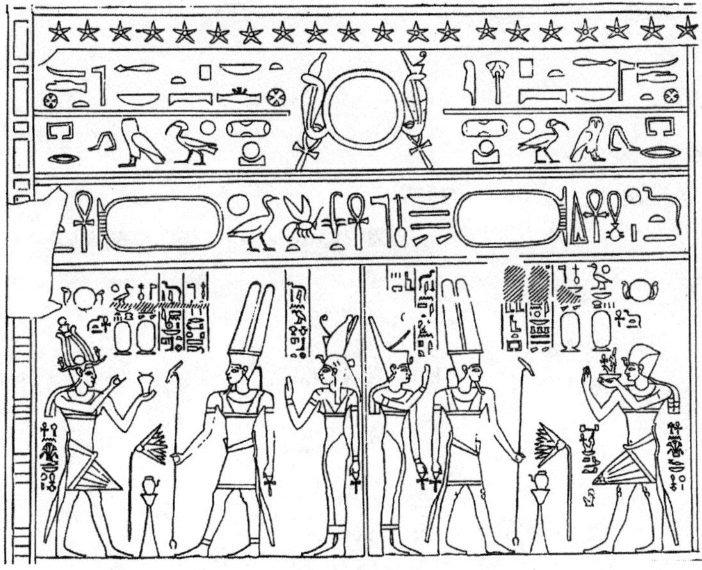

Figure 34: The doorway lintel to stairway E
(after Davies, *The Temple of Hibis*, Part 3, detail from pl. 7)

1 For the publication of these two chapels and their doorway see Winlock, *The Temple of Hibis*, Part 1, pp. 10–11, pls. XXII, XXXIII, XXXIV, XXXVII; Davies, *The Temple of Hibis*, Part 3, pp. 18–19, pls. 7, 15–16; Cruz-Uribe, *Hibis Temple Project I*, pp. 45–46, 75–79, and 185–191.

The solar disk of Behdet is represented in the middle of the top register, dividing two double rows of inscriptions. The solar disk has two uraei and each has an *ankh* sign hanging from its body. The uraeus on the right wears the red crown of Lower Egypt and the one on the left wears the white crown of Upper Egypt. Like other lintel decorations, the distribution of the types of royal crown follows the cardinal points of the temple direction: the red crown of Lower Egypt is to the north, while the white crown of Upper Egypt is facing south. Note that the whole scene of the lintel decoration is framed from the top by the star-filled extended *pt* sign of the sky. The cosmographic image is continued through the solar disk below and the king's names and epithets, reflecting the earthly embodiment of the sun god, on the following register. The main panel of the lintel has two mirrored representations of the king offering to Amun Re and a female goddess. A solar disk with the two uraei is above each image of the king. A tall standing lotus flower and an offering table with a *nemset* jar on top separate the king's image from the divine images. On the right, the king is wearing the *khepresh* crown and a two-strap garment with a knee-length kilt with a starched apron. He offers the Maat sign to Amun Re with his left hand and holds his right hand up in a gesture of adoration. Amun Re is wearing his feathered crown on top of a modius and is followed by Amunet, who wears the crown of Lower Egypt. She holds an *ankh* sign in her left hand, while her right hand is raised in a gesture of protection behind Amun. On the left side, the king is in similar attire to that on the right scene, but he wears the *atef* crown with uraei on the outspread horns. The king offers an ointment jar to Amun Re. Behind Amun Re is Mut, wearing her double crown on top of the vulture headdress. She holds an *ankh* sign with one hand while the other is raised in protection toward Amun Re.

THE INSCRIPTION

REGISTER I

Right of Behdet

Bḥdt nṯr ꜥꜣ nb pt sꜣb šwty pr m ꜣḫt[2]

"Behdet, great god, lord of the sky, variegated of feathers, who goes forth from the horizon."

Left of Behdet

Bḥdt nṯr ꜥꜣ nb pt nb msn pr m ꜣḫt

"Behdet, great god, lord of the sky and Mesen, who goes forth from the horizon."

REGISTER II

The *ankh* sign divides the line of inscription.

Nṯr nfr nb tꜣwy (…)¦ *di ꜥnḫ mi Rꜥ ḏt nsw biti sꜣ Rꜥ* (…)¦ *ꜥnḫ* [*ḏt*]

"Good god, lord of the two lands (…)¦ given life like Re forever.

2 Note that the bread loaf determinative in the word *ꜣḫt* also occurs in the north reveal of the entrance to E, but with the addition of the house determinative. This is a variation of the land sign; *Wb*. I, p. 7, 13, 14.

The king of Upper and Lower Egypt, the son of Re(…)¦ living [forever.]"

REGISTER III, RIGHT SIDE

Above the King

Nṯr nfr nb tȝwy (…)¦ *sȝ Rʿ nb ḫʿwt* (…)¦ *ʿnḫ ḏd*

"Good god, lord of the two lands (…)¦ son of Re, lord of appearances (…)¦, living forever."

Behind the King

Nb sȝ ʿnḫ n ḥȝ.f mi Rʿ

"All protection and life behind him like Re forever."

Below the hands of the king

Ḥnk Mȝʿt //

"Presenting Maat"

Above Amun Re

// //Imn Rʿ nb nswt tȝwy

////[Ἰpt] swt

"///Amun Re lord of the thrones of the two lands.

/// [Karnak]"

Above Amunet

Ḏd mdw in Ἰmnt n Ἰpt swt.

"Words spoken by Amunet of Karnak."[3]

REGISTER III, LEFT SIDE

Above the king

Nṯr nfr [*nb*] *tȝwy* (…)¦ *sȝ Rʿ nb ḫʿw* (…)¦ *ʿnḫ ḏd.*

"Good god, [lord] of the two lands (…)¦, son of Re, lord of appearances (…)¦, living forever."

Behind the king

Sȝ ʿnḫ n ḥȝ.f nb mi Rʿ

"All life and protection behind him like Re."

3 This title of Amunet is rarely attested outside the Hibis Temple; Leitz, *Lexikon*, I, p. 358. Amunet seems to have enjoyed great status in the Hibis Temple. In hypostyle hall M are several scenes of Amunet standing behind Amun of Hibis, in the place where Mut is usually represented. On the east wall of hypostyle hall M, for example, Amunet appears in the northernmost bay in registers I and III on the north panel of the screen. On the west wall of hypostyle hall M, she is represented north of the doorway in registers II and III, and south of the doorway in register I. In most of these scenes, she wears the red crown of Lower Egypt.

SOUTH AND NORTH JAMB OF DOOR TO E

Figure 35: The jambs of the door to stairway E
(after Davies, *The Temple of Hibis*, Part 3, detail from pl. 7)

THE INSCRIPTION

South Jamb of Door to E

Nsw biti (Imn Rᶜ Wn(n) nfr)| pt t3wy dw3t[4] *mnty ḫr*[5] *wḏy*[6]*.k*

"The king of Upper and Lower Egypt, Amun Re Wennefer,[7] the heaven, earth and the netherworld are established under your command."

---

4 *dw3t/d3t* is in *Wb*. V, p. 415, 4–10, but the exact writing here is unique.

5 Note that the word *mnty* has the dual determinatives of the pestle and mortar, surrounding the first sign of the word *ḫr*.

6 Note the pun between this word and the word *w3ḏyt* on the opposite north jamb.

7 This exact formation of the combined names of Amun Re and Wennefer in a single cartouche is not attested elsewhere; however, the designation of the king as Wennefer or Onouphis is not unusual (Leitz, *Lexikon*, II, pp. 375–376). The combined name of *Imn Rᶜ* (outside the cartouche) with *Wnn Nfr* (inside the cartouche) = *Imn Rᶜ (Wnn Nfr)|* occurs in *Opet* I, p. 90; Leitz, *Lexikon*, I, p. 324. In the Hibis example, the king is paralleled to *Imn Rᶜ Wnn Nfr* who is, in turn, parallel to Amun Re and Osiris, with both solar and funerary aspects. Since the king is Horus, this Amun Re Wennefer amalgam inside a cartouche could be a detailed expression of the king as Horus. In fact, in *E* I, p. 81, 6, Horus is called "lord of heaven, earth and the underworlds," a title that Amun Re Wennefer carries here on the south jamb of the door to E chapel. See below, pp. 176ff., for additional discussion of these epithets.

North Jamb of Door to E

Ii.ṯ m pr.k [ḏ3/wḏ3][8]*.k ḥr m Rʿ w3ḏyt mḥty m šfytw.k.*

"Welcome to your temple. As you cross the heaven as Re, the columned hall[9] is filled with your respect."

SOUTH AND NORTH REVEALS OF DOOR TO E

THE INSCRIPTION

The inscriptions on the door reveals are enclosed in a long rectangle with double borders.

South Reveal of Door to E

Ḏd mdw in Imn [Rʿ ḫnm][10] *msḳt*[11] *ʿḏʿḏ*[12] *n.k imy sn wḏ3.k ḥry m nb ʿnḫ ḏd w3s*

"Words spoken by Amun [Re] [who joins] the *msḳt*, those in them rejoice for you, when you cross through heaven[13]/ above, in all life stability and dominion."

North Reveal of Door to E

Ḏd{t} mdw in Imn w[nn].k[14] *m ḥrt ḥrwt m 3ḫt m3w.k tkn ḥrw*[15]

"Word spoken by Amun. As long as you are in the sky, being far in the horizon, your rays approach the faces."

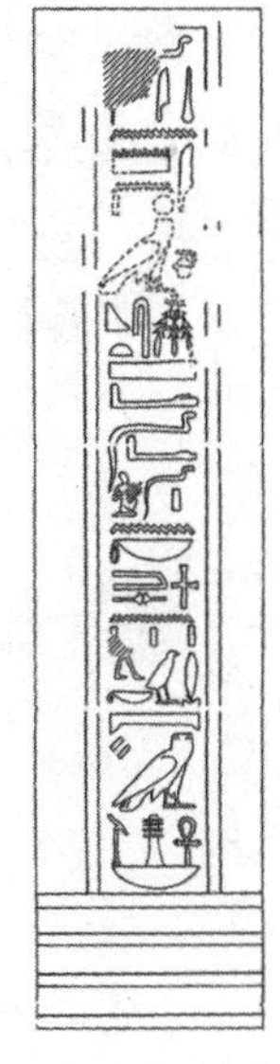

Figure 36: South and north reveals of doorway to stairway E (after Davies, *The Temple of Hibis*, Part 3, detail from pl. 16)

8 Cruz-Uribe, *Hibis Temple Project I*, p. 45, reads the particle *mk*, before heaven; however, reading it as *wḏ3* or *ḏ3i* yields better sense, especially since *wḏ3* is repeated again nearby on the south reveal at the entrance to E, "*wḏ3.k ḥry*." The remaining bottom half of the bird hieroglyph suggests *3* rather than *m*. *Wḏ3* also makes a pun with the following word *w3ḏyt*, as well as complementing the pun on the opposite jamb that also has *w3ḏ*. The outline in Brugsch (*Reise nach der grossen Oase El Khargeh in der libyschen Wüste*, p. 55, pl. XVII, n. 5a) restores *m[r]*, "wo du weilest."

9 *W3ḏyt* is used generally as a term for parts of the temple with columns; Spencer, *The Egyptian Temple: A Lexicographical Study*, p. 70.

10 In the outline of Brugsch, *Reise nach der grossen Oase El Khargeh*, pl. XVII, n. 6b, the suffix *k* is indicated after *ḫnm*; however, Davies later ignored it.

11 *Msḳt* with a barque determinative refers to the night barque; *Wb.* II, p. 150, 10. However, in this specific example, with the rectangular determinative, it most probably refers to a part of the heaven or the netherworld; *Wb.* II, p. 149, 15, 16. Its earliest use in the Pyramid and Coffin texts was to indicate parts of the sky or a celestial region. A more detailed discussion of *msḳt* will follow in the commentary below, see pp. 179ff.

12 *ʿḏʿḏ* means " to rejoice," "be prosperous," "flourish;" *Wb.* I, p. 241.

13 This phrase is repeated earlier on the north jamb of the door to E.

14 Restoring *wnn* thus creates a "Wechselsatz" with the later phrase.

15 Note the strange order of writing at the bottom half of the inscriptions.

CHAPEL E1 — NORTH PILASTER

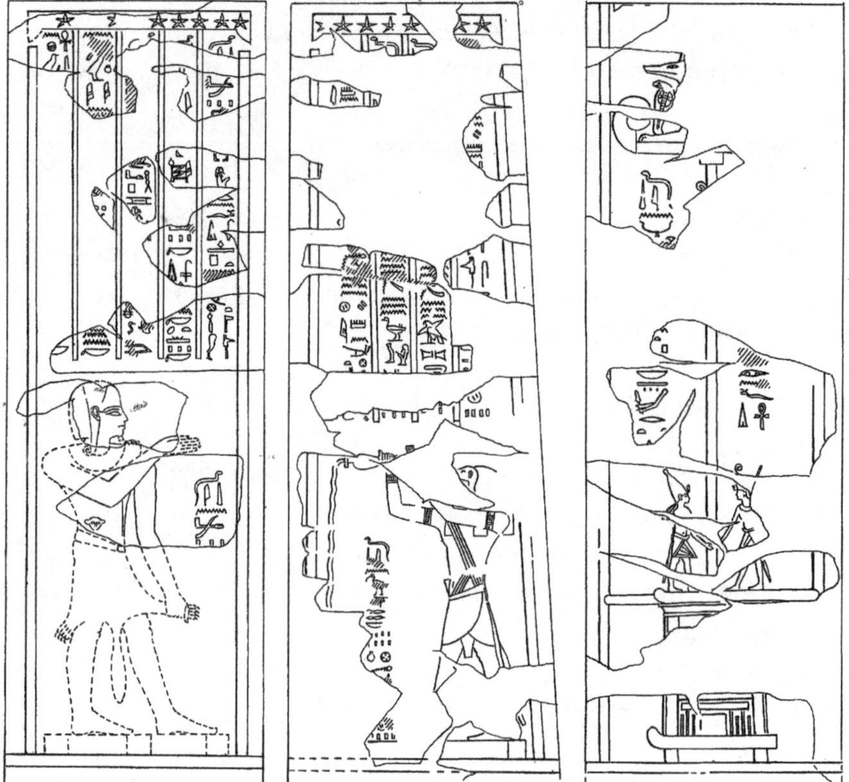

Figure 37: North Pilaster of chapel E1
(after Davies, *The Temple of Hibis*, Part 3, detail from pl. 15)

Like the north wall, the north pilaster suffered the most damage in chapel E1. Among the remaining fragments of the north pilaster, several belong to the top portions of the scenes. This enabled the partial reconstruction of the south pilaster of E1, as noted below. Both pilasters have three sides with similar decorations. Furthermore, their adjoining walls—the south and north walls—bear almost identical decorations, making both sides of this room mirror images. All sides of the pilasters are framed by the star-filled extended *pt* sign of the sky on top and by rectangular bands on the other sides. On the outer sides of the pilasters—the left side of the south pilaster and the right side of the north pilaster—is the standard of Wepwawet with the double image of the king. Two images of deities occupy the center of both pilasters—Horus on the south pilaster and Thoth on the north pilaster. The inner sides of the pilasters—the right side of the south pilaster and the left side of the north pilaster—are decorated with the images of Iunmutef and the purification priests. This order allows the viewer who enters room E 1 to see the standards of Wepwawet first, then the images of Horus and Thoth, and finally the images of the priests inside the chapel.

On the right side of the north pilaster—the most northern—are two almost identical images of the king supporting the long standard of Wepwawet and wearing a short kilt with a starched apron and an ox tail. As in the south pilaster, the iconography of the king's crowns follows the direction of the cardinal points; the northern image has the red crown of Lower Egypt, while the southern image has the white crown of Upper Egypt. The standard at the top is decorated with Wepwawet as a recumbent jackal and an erect cobra over a curved sledge. The king and the staff are being carried over a shrine with decorated facade.[16] On the center of the north pilaster, the ibis-headed Thoth, wearing a short kilt with one strap over his shoulder, performs a purification ritual with a libation vessel. The purification priest is located on the right side of the north pilaster. Unfortunately, much of his body is destroyed, but based on the comparison with the decoration of the southern pilaster, he may have been wearing the distinctive side lock of hair, a short beard, and the panther skin.

THE INSCRIPTION

Right Side[17]

Above the image of the king with the Lower Egyptian crown

Ḏd mdw in ꞽImn Rꜥ [nṯr ꜥ3 nb Hbt] ir n.f di ꜥnḫ

"words spoken by Amun Re, [great god, lord of Hibis], as he has made a giving life."

Above the image of the king with the Upper Egyptian crown

Ḏd mdw in Wp[w3w3t šmꜥw][18]*/// nb t3 ḏsr.t //*

"Words spoken by Wep[Wawet of the south],/// lord of the sacred land//"

Center Side

Above Thoth

(1)*///Imn////ꜥbw sp sn ꞽImn Hbt* (2) *Ḏd [mdw]///[ꜥbw.k] ꜥbw Gb ///*(3) *Ḏd mdw// [ꜥbw.k] ꜥbw Dwn ꜥnwy ṯs pẖr* (4)*///wsr///sp fdw*

"(1) ///Amun/// be pure twice, Amun of Hibis (2)Words[spoken]///[your purification is the] purification of Geb/// (3)Words spoken///[your purification is the] purification of Duenanwey vice versa (4)///be powerful///four times."

Below the hands of Thoth

Ḏd mdw in Ḏḥwty ꜥ3 ꜥ3 nb ḫmnw wꜥb sp fdw

"Words spoken by Thoth, the twice great, lord of Hermopolis, be pure four times."

---

16 This elaborate image of "the staff with a sledge" appears to be borrowed directly from the iconography in the Ramesside period. Inside the tomb of Ramesses IX is a similar motive in a purification ritual by an Iunmutef priest, reciting similar passages of the purification of Duenanwey; Guilmant, *Le tombeau de Ramsès IX*, pl. LXXXV.

17 Two inscribed fragments on the wall are missing from Davies' outlines.

18 Although this word is not written, based on the parallel with the south pilaster and the fact that the inscriptions are written on the side where the king wears the Upper Egyptian crown, it is reasonable to reconstruct it as *šmꜥw*. For *Wp-W3wt Mḥw* and *Wp-W3wt šmꜥw*, see Otto, "Die Lehre von den beiden Ländern Ägyptens in der ägyptischen Religionsgeschichte," pp. 10–16; In *D* II, p. 142, 3, Wepwawet of the north performs the Opening of the Mouth on Wennefer.

Left Side

Above the priest

(1) *Ḏd mdw i͗[n]ꜥb/// i͗r n.f ḥtp di͗ nsw//[nb] Hbt nṯr ꜥ3 wsr ẖpš* (2) *Ḏd* [*mdw*] *i͗*[*n*]/// *ꜥ3bt///.k ḥ*[*tp*] *di͗ nsw nkt*[19]*.k* (3) *///r ḥꜥpy//*[*ḥnkt*] *k3w 3bḏw m///* (4)*Nny*[20]*///mw.k* (5) *ꜥnḫw ///*

"(1)Words spoken b[y] the purification priest/// he made a *Hetep-di-nsw* offering ///[lord] of Hibis, great god, powerful of strength. (2) Words[spoken b]y /// of yours, *Hetep-di-nsw* (offering)//of your things. (3) //to the Inundation/// beer, oxen and fowl in///(4) The Flood waters/// your water. (5) living ones ///"

Below the hand of the priest

Ḏd mdw i͗n ꜥb///

"Word spoken by the purification priest."

CHAPEL E1 — SOUTH PILASTER

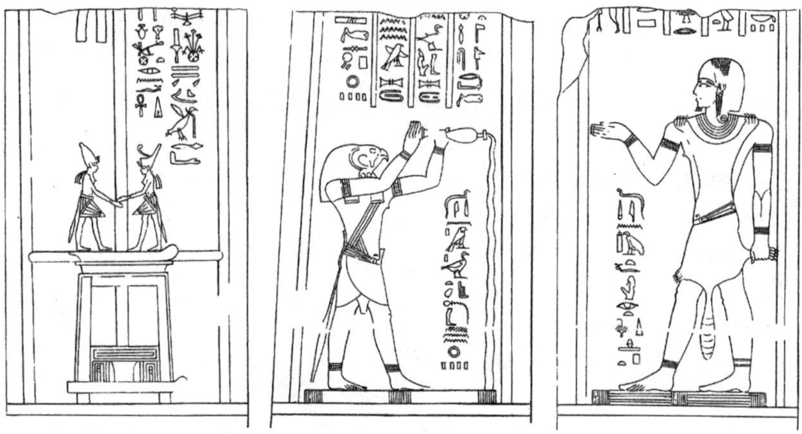

Figure 38: South pilaster of chapel E1
(after Davies, *The Temple of Hibis*, Part 3, detail from pl. 15)

The top part of this pilaster is destroyed. However, it was partly reconstructed based on a comparison to the opposite north pilaster. On the left side of the south pilaster are two almost identical images of the king. He wears a short starched kilt in each but the northern image has the red crown of Lower Egypt, while the southern image has the white crown of Upper Egypt. The images are facing each other and holding the long standard of Wepwawet atop a shrine with a decorated facade. In comparison with the more preserved side of the north pilaster, this staff was topped with the representation of the jackal Wepwawet recumbent on a curved sledge. He was perhaps flanked by one or two cobras. In the center of the south pilaster, the falcon-headed Horus purifies with a libation vessel. He wears a short *shendyet* kilt with one strap over his shoulder and an ox tail. On the right side of the south pilaster is the Iunmutef priest. He wears the distinc-

19 "Things" or "pieces," *Wb.* II, p. 347. However, it does not have the egg determinative that is represented here.

20 *Wb.* II, p. 221, 3–13.

tive side lock of hair, a short beard, and a panther skin. He holds one paw of the animal skin with his left hand, in a typical priestly gesture. Both Horus and the Iunmutef priest are standing on rectangular mats. Horus faces right and the Iunmutef priest faces left.

THE INSCRIPTION

Left Side

Above the image of the king with the Lower Egyptian crown

[Ḏd mdw in Wp]wꜣwꜣt mḥw ḫrp tꜣwy ḳmꜣ ꜥꜣ[21] *[ḏd mdw in Wsir nṯr ꜥꜣ] ḥr ib Hbt ir n.f di ꜥnḫ*

"[Words spoken by Wep]wawet of the north, controller of the two lands, the great creator

[words spoken by Osiris,[22] great god], who dwells in Hibis, for he has made a giving life."

Center Side

Above Horus

////nṯr ꜥꜣ wsr ḫpš//[ꜥbw.k ꜥbw]/Gb[23] *ṯs pẖr/[ꜥbw.k ꜥbw] Dwn ꜥnwy ṯs pẖr*[24] *[ḫp]š sp fdw*

"/// great god, powerful of strength///[your purification is the purification[25]] <of> Geb vice versa, [your purification is the purification] <of> Duenanwey[26] vice versa, powerful four times."

---

21 *ḳmꜣ ꜥꜣ* is a designation for Wepwawet only in Hibis (Leitz, *Lexikon*, VII, p. 189). The other example of this title for Wepwawet is in Room L, south wall, register I, where Wepwawet is seated on a throne while the king, wearing the Lower Egyptian crown, presents *nw* jars to him. In the latter example, Wepwawet has the title of "Wepwawet of the South," rather than the north as in room E.

22 This restoration of the name of Osiris here is suggested by Cruz-Uribe, *Hibis Temple Project I*, p. 74, n. 202, based on the existence of the name of Amun Re on the corresponding side on the north pilaster. This parallelism between Amun Re and Osiris, almost consistent throughout the scheme of the temple decoration, fits nicely with the rituals on the roofs, as will be described in details below.

23 While examining the wall, the author discovered an egg sign over the bird below the traces of the *n* water sign.

24 *Wb.* V, p. 404. "wiederholen;" this expression may refer to the repetition of an actual ritual action by recitation or by physical repetition of the purification ritual.

25 The reconstruction of *ꜥbw.k ꜥbw* before both Geb and Duenanwey is based on comparison with other parallels, see footnote below on Duenanwey.

26 Since his earliest attestation, this god, Duenanwey, whose name probably means "spreader of wings/arms," (*Wb.* V, p. 432, 16), is represented as the guardian of Osiris (Wilson, *Lexicon*, p. 1188). He was the god of the 18th Upper Egyptian nome and, more importantly, lord of the east; Kees, "Anubis, Herr von Sepa und der 18. Oberägyptische Gau," pp. 79–101; Westendorff, "Duananui," cols. 1152–1153. He is also represented in many solar contexts; Egberts, *In Quest of Meaning*, I, p. 294, n.10. He plays an important rule in the purification rituals together with Horus, Seth, and Thoth, and this is also the case in the present chapel; Gardiner, "The Baptism of Pharaoh," pp. 9ff. The formula *(w)ꜥbw.k (w)ꜥbw dwn ꜥnwy ṯs pẖr* has an almost exact parallel in some texts—for example, the tomb of Ramesses VII (Hornung,

Below the hands of Horus

Ḏd mdw in Ḥr sꜣ ꜣst wꜥbw sp fdw

"Words spoken by Horus, son of Isis, purified four times."

Right Side

Above Iunmutef

The bottom part of the inscription is unintelligible, except for the words *wsr ḫpš*, "powerful of strength," in the first vertical line.

Below the hand of Iunmutef

Ḏd mdw in ꞽIunmwt.f irt ḥtp di nsw

"Words spoken by Iunmutef, making a *Hetep-di-nsw* offering."

CHAPEL E1 — THE NORTH WALL

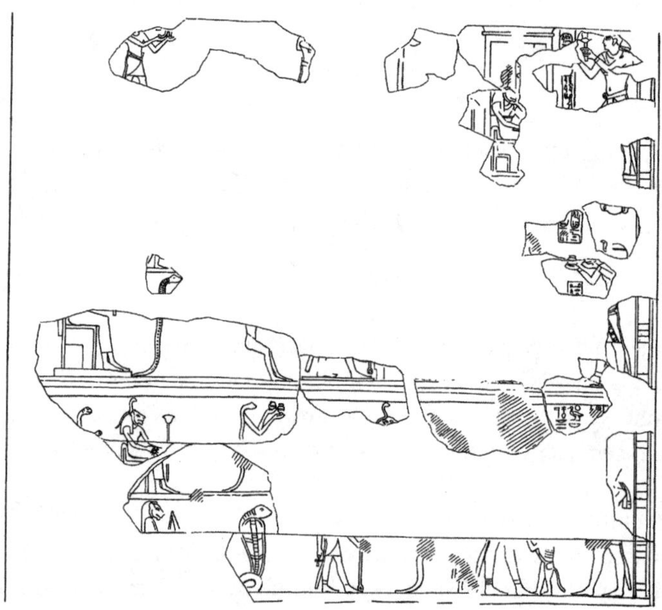

Figure 39: North wall of chapel E1
(after Davies, *The Temple of Hibis*, Part 3, detail from pl. 15)

This wall and the southern wall of E1 are similar in content to the main sanctuary A. They are divided into small registers with multiple small figures in procession, some of which are enigmatic. This wall is very badly damaged; however, some features are evident. It is divided into five horizontal registers with no space dividers or vertical separating lines such as on the opposite south wall. Double bands separate the third register form the fourth register.

Zwei Ramessidische Königsgräber: Ramses IV. und Ramses VII, pp. 59–60, pl. 104) and Ramesses IX (Guilmant, *Le tombeau de Ramsès IX*, p. 20, 9, pl. 85); *CT* IV, 402b; VI, 120c. This is considered part of the second scene of the Opening of the Mouth ritual in the House of Gold; see Otto, Das Ägyptische Mundöffnungsritual, I, p. 5, 2b. For the significance of this finding, see commentary below, pp. 185ff.

The identification of the figures of these registers on the south and the north walls of E1 essentially follows that of Cruz-Uribe,[27] who based his identification on the comparison with the Seti I B list, catalogued by Neugebauer and Parker, *Egyptian Astronomical Texts, Volume III* (*EAT III*), pp. 133–140. However, comparing this list with the Seti I B list and other lists in *EAT III* one can offer alternative identifications for some of the figures, as noted below.[28]

Numbers are given to the figures from left to right, without counting the representations of the king.

Figure 40: Cruz-Uribe's reconstruction of the north wall (Cruz-Uribe, *Hibis Temple Project I*, pl. 15A).

REGISTER I

The king stands holding a sistrum in front of a shrine of a female deity. A vertical line of inscriptions in front of the king reads:

> *///Imn ///iḥy*
> "///Amun///making music"

27 Cruz-Uribe, *Hibis Temple Project I*, pp. 185–191, esp. pp. 187–188; Kákosy, "Decans in Late Egyptian Religion," pp. 163ff. It should be noted that Davies was first to associate these deities with the deities of the dual year; Davies, *The Temple of Hibis*, Part 3, p. 18.

28 See pp. 160ff.

1) The first figure is a lioness-headed goddess. She has a uraeus on top of her head and is seated on a throne inside a shrine. She is identified with the first decan, Sopdet. 2) The second is a lion-headed god, seated, holding the *ankh* sign and the *was* scepter. He is identified with *ʾIn-ḥr-m3t-t3y*, decan 1a. 3) The third is a seated lioness-headed goddess who holds the *ankh* sign and a sistrum. She is identified with *3ry-ḫpd-knmt*, decan 4. 4) The fourth is an erect snake with three small snakes crossing his body. He is identified with *Knm*, decan 3. 5) Fifth is a standing ibis-headed god, offering the two *nw* jars. He is identified with *St*, decan 2. 6) The sixth and last figure on this register is a standing god with either a human or a falcon head. He offers the *udjat* eyes and is identified with *Ḫnty-ḥry*, decan 4a.

REGISTER II

The remaining fragment supports the existence of one representation of the king occupying the space at the beginning of registers II and III, similar to the representation on the first and second registers of the south wall. The king holds the *nw* jars and wears a short kilt, a uraeus, and an ox tail. Above his head are a winged disk and a few hieroglyphs that comprise the remains of a cartouche of Darius and the words:

> *Di* [*ʿnḫ*] *ḏt*
> "Given [life] forever."

Below the hand of the king.

> *Ḥnk ir*[*p*]
> "Presenting w[ine]"

1) The first figure in the second register is a snake on a low pedestal in the form of a *mr* sign and is identified with *Ḥ3t-ḏ3t*, decan 5. 2) The second is an erect serpent with his tail curved behind him and is identified with *Pḥwy-ḏ3t*, decan 6. 3) The third is a lioness-headed goddess, with a snake on top of her head. She is seated on a low throne, holding the *ankh* sign on her knee with her right hand and the *wadj* scepter with her left. She is identified with *Tm3t*, decan 7. 4) The fourth is a standing lion-headed god with the crook and flail. The crook is held in an unusual position, facing in front of him, while the flail is against his right shoulder. He is identified with *Stwt-rhn-pt*, decan 7a. 5) The fifth is an erect snake holding the two *nw* jars. He has human arms and legs and his tail is curved behind him. He is identified with *Wš3t-bk3t*, decan 8.[29]

29 Many similarities appear between this reconstruction and the Dendera list D on the ceiling of the outer Hypostyle Hall, second middle strip to the west and second middle strip to the east from center; *PM* VI, pp. 44, 49; *EAT* III, pp.78, 130–140. For full discussion of those similarities, see below. According to the Dendera D list, figures 4 and 5, who are identified with decans 7a and 8, respectively, could have different representations: decan 7a could have a cat-headed deity and decan 8 could be a serpent-headed baboon.

REGISTER III

1) The first figure is an erect snake, his tail curved behind him. He is identified with *Ỉpsd*, decan 9. 2) Second is a lioness-headed goddess seated on a low-backed throne. She holds the flail over her right shoulder and the *was* scepter in front of her with her left hand. She is identified with *Sbššn* (*mr ꜣḫw*), decan 10. 3) Third is a standing male deity with a human head and beard. Wearing a short kilt and an ox tail, he holds the *was* scepter in his left hand and the flail in his right. He is identified with *ꜥꜣ-pḥty-rhn-pꜣ-tꜣ*, decan 10a. 4) Fourth is a feather-headed deity with upward-raised arms. He freely defies gravity as if he is seated in the air or simply flying, a position appropriate for a figure with feather iconography. He is identified with *Tpy-ꜥ-ẖnt*, decan 11. 5) Fifth is an erect snake with his tail curved backward. He is identified with *Ḫnt-ḥrt*, decan 12. 6) The sixth and final figure is a seated lioness-headed goddess. She holds the flail with her right hand against her shoulder and the *ankh* sign out in front of her body with her left hand. She is identified with *Ḫnt-ẖrt*, decan 13.

REGISTER IV

Another representation of the king stretched between two registers occupies the beginning of the fourth and fifth registers. Unfortunately, the top half of the king cannot be reconstructed, making it difficult to identify the offering he presents to the following deities. The only remaining inscription reads:

> *Nṯr nfr nb tꜣwy sꜣ* [*Rꜥ*] *nb* [*ḥbt*]
> "Good god, lord of the two lands, son of [Re], lord of [Hibis]"

1) First is a large standing figure, almost the same scale as the king. Even though he is standing on the line of the fifth register, schematically he belongs to the fourth register. He has a lion head and is flanked by two baboons with arms upraised to touch his hands. He is identified with *Ỉmsti-m-ibw*, decan 13a. 2) Second is a lioness-headed goddess seated on a low throne and wearing a uraeus on top of her head. She holds the *wadj* scepter out in front with her left hand and the *ankh* sign with her right hand against her right knee. She is identified with *Ḥry-ib-wiꜣ*, decan 16. 3) Third is an erect serpent, with human arms, offering the two *nw* jars. He is identified with *Tms-ẖnt*, decan 14.[30] 4) Fourth is a seated lioness-headed goddess with a uraeus on top of her head. She holds the *wadj* scepter out in front with her left hand and the *ankh* sign with her right hand against her right knee. She is identified with *Ṯpy-ꜥꜣ-smd*, decan 19. 5) The final figure is another erect serpent. He has human arms held out in front, and his tail is curved behind him. He is identified with *Spt-ẖnwy*, decan 15.

30 This reconstruction is not attested anywhere for decan 14, *tms-ẖnt*. This decan is either represented as a lion-headed or ram-headed god; *EAT* III, pp. 136ff.

REGISTER V

1) Behind the large figure of the deity with the two baboons is an erect serpent with human arms. He offers two *nw* jars and is identified with *Šmw*, decan 17. 2) The second figure is standing, but the head cannot be identified. He holds the *was* scepter in his left hand and the a*nkh* sign at his side with his right hand. He is identified with *ꜣḫ-nḫḫ*, decan 16a. 3) The third figure is an erect cobra with a coiled lower body, identified with *Knm*, decan 18. 4) Fourth is a mummiform lion-headed god, holding the flail in front. He is identified with *Smd*, decan 20. 5) The final figures on the north wall are one or two erect serpents with their tails behind them, identified with *Srt*, decan 21.

Figure 41: An alternative reconstruction of the north wall of chapel E1

Based on comparison with similar decan lists, an alternate identification of the figures on this wall can be reconstructed as follows:[31] Register IV, figure 1: the two baboons should be looking away from the middle figure, instead of looking toward him as attested in the only preserved copy with a similar representation of decan 13a in the Dendera D list. Register IV, figure 2 could be a standing figure of a lion-headed god, *Tms (n) ḫnt*, who is identified with decan 14;[32] figure 3 could be the erect serpent *Spty ḫnwy*, who is identified as decan 15; figure 4 could be the lion-headed goddess *Ḥry-ib wiꜣ*, decan 16; figure 5 (the last figure) is not decan 15 but rather decan 20. The remaining fragment of this last figure has the head of the snake and a tiny representation of a rounded shape near his top half. Cruz-Uribe reconstructed him as decan 15, with two rather dwarfish arms. Usually

31 See EAT III, esp. pp. 130-140.

32 Even though decan 14 appears as a male deity, it seems that there is gender confusion in this list. In register II on the south wall, decan 26, who is usually represented as a male deity, appears as a female deity; see south wall, figure 2.

in such lists the serpents are either erect with no hands at all or with hands carrying two *nw* jars. No representation remains, nor does space allow for the reconstruction of two arms carrying two *nw* jars. Furthermore, the human hands of the serpents seem to attach to the body of the serpent almost directly below the head on a much higher level than in the case of figure 5. This round shape could be very puzzling, unless it was, as suggested, the god *Smd* who is identified as decan 20. This god is represented as an erect serpent with another serpent crossing its body, thus explaining the rounded shape on our figure. This reconstruction accommodates two very legitimate alternations in the identification of Register V of the north wall and Register I of the south wall; the two last figures on register V would be reduced to only one, that is, the erect serpent god *Srt*, decan 21, and the first figure of the opposite south wall would naturally be understood as the lioness-headed seated goddess *tpy-ʿ-smd*, decan 19. The identification of this goddess as decan 19 is more probable than her identification with Sakhmet, suggested by Cruz-Uribe[33] (see figure 41).

CHAPEL E1 — THE SOUTH WALL

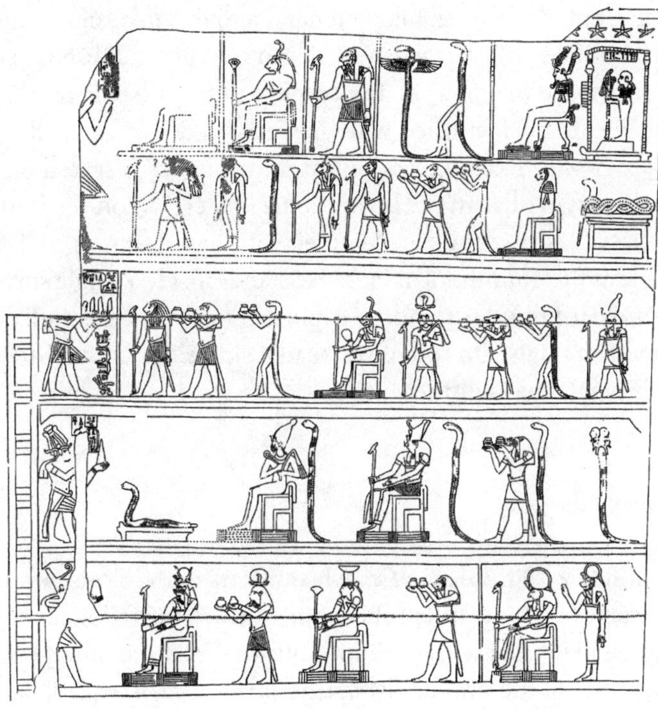

Figure 42: South wall of chapel E1
(after Davies, *The Temple of Hibis*, Part 3, detail from pl. 15)

The south wall of chapel E is divided into five horizontal registers. At the top, it is bordered by a frieze of stars within the extended *pt* sign of the sky. The three lower registers are framed from the top by an extended *pt* sign of the sky. Some figures in the first and fifth registers are separated by vertical space dividers. Few inscriptions appear on this wall.

33 Cruz-Uribe, *Hibis Temple Project I*, p. 187. The identification of the last figure on the last register of the south wall of chapel E1 as Sakhmet is more probable, see below.

However, one important inscription contains one of the smallest examples of the cartouche of Darius from the Temple of Hibis, roughly depicted on the third and fourth registers. The identity of some figures, especially the last figure on each register, is problematic.

REGISTER I

A relatively large figure of the king, facing right, occupies the left side of the two top registers. The remaining depiction shows the king's hands raised in a gesture of adoration to the deities. A short line of inscription might have existed, but, if so, it is now unintelligible. 1) From left to right, the first figure is a seated deity, but the upper half is missing. Cruz-Uribe reconstructed this figure as a lioness-headed goddess, identified with Sakhmet.[34] However, according to the reconstruction offered above, this figure could be the decan number 19. 2) Another seated lioness-headed female figure follows after the vertical space divider. She holds the *was* scepter in her right hand and the *ankh* sign in her left and has the uraeus on top of her head. She is identified with *Sȝ-srt*, decan 22. 3) The following figure, separated by a space divider, is a standing lion-headed god, holding the *was* scepter in front of him with his right hand and the *ankh* sign at his side with his left hand. He is identified with *Wtt ỉmy-wš.f*, decan 22a. Behind him two erect serpents stand between two space dividers. 4) The serpent in front is winged; the one behind has human legs. The first is identified with *3ry-ẖpd-srt*, decan 23, while the latter, 5) is identified with *Ṯpy-ʿ-ȝẖw*, decan 24. 6) A mummified figure is seated on a low-backed throne on top of a rectangular mat. He wears the *atef* crown on his human head. His iconography is that of Osiris, yet he is identified with *ȝẖw*, decan 25. 7) The last figure is easily recognizable as the mummiform Ptah. He stands inside a single shrine with a door that opens outward. He holds his standard triple scepter, wears the skull cap, and stands on top of a sledge-front dais. On top of his head a single horizontal line of inscription with very small hieroglyphs identifies him as:

> *Ptḥ it nṯrw*
> "Ptah, father of the gods"

Here Ptah is identified with the decan *Qd*, who appears in the Tanis family of decans as a variation on decan 28.[35] This is still problematic, since in the following register another figure could also be identified with decan number 28. A discussion about his identity, as well as the identities of the similar last figures on each register, will be offered below.

REGISTER II

1) The head of the first figure is probably that of a lion. The figure is standing and holds the *was* scepter in his right hand and the flail in his left. He is identified with *Wp-wȝt*, decan 25a. He is followed by a standing female figure, whose head is missing. 2) The second figure holds the *ankh* sign with her left hand, while the other one rests flat against

34 Cruz-Uribe, *Hibis Temple Project I*, p. 187.
35 Cruz-Uribe, *Hibis Temple Project I*, p. 187.

her thigh. She is identified with hesitation with *Ṯpy-ˁ-b3wy*, decan 26. 3) An erect snake, with his tail in front of him, is next. He is identified with *B3w*, decan 27. 4) The fourth figure is a standing lioness-headed goddess wearing a long close-fitting dress and holding the *wadj* scepter in her right hand and the *ankh* sign in her left. She is identified with *H̱nt-ḫr*, decan 28.5) She is followed by a lion-headed god wearing a short kilt and an ox tail and holding the *was* scepter in front of him.[36] He is identified with *Ḥr-tp-nfr*, decan 28a. This god is followed by two figures holding the *nw* jars. 6) The first is a lion-headed human wearing a short kilt and an ox tail. 7) The second is an erect snake with human arms and legs, his tail curved behind him. They are both identified with *H̱nt-ḫr*, decan 29, and *S3-ḳd*, decan 30, respectively. 8) These figures are followed by a seated mummified deity. He is identified with *H̱3w*, decan 31. 9) The last figure in the second register is a coiled snake with a raised head. He lies on top of a pedestal with a shrine facade and is identified with *Pẖr-ḥr*, who represented the constellation Leo.[37]

REGISTER III

The king offers the field sign *sḫt* to a row of deities. Unfortunately, his head is destroyed, but it can still be seen that he is wearing the starched kilt with an ox tail. The inscription above the king reads:

> *S3 Rˁ (Dryš)¦///ˁnḫ dt*
> "Son of Re (Darius)¦ living forever."

The inscription below the king's hands reads:

> *Ḥnk sḫt n it.f imn Hbt*
> "Presenting the field to his father Amun of Hibis."

A space divider is located after the figure of the king, separating him from the deities he faces. 1) The first lion-headed male deity holds the *was* scepter in his right hand and the *ankh* sign in his left. 2) The second figure holds two *nw* jars. Both deities wear a pleated short kilt with an ox tail. They are identified with *Sm3-nb-3ḫw*, decan 31a, and *ˁrt*, decan 32, respectively. 3) An erect serpent is next. His tail is curved backward, while his human legs are striding. He holds two *nw* jars and is identified with *Rmn-ḥry*, decan 33. A slightly bigger space appears between the snake deity and the following figures. This gap is even more noticeable in the last two registers. 4) The next figure is a lioness-headed goddess seated on a low-backed throne. She holds the *wadj* scepter with her right hand and a mirror or a sistrum with her left. She has a uraeus on top of her head and is identified with *Ṯs-ˁrḳ*, decan 34. 5) A standing male deity is behind her. He holds the *was* scepter with his right hand and the flail with his left. He has a solar disk with a cobra and two horizontal horns placed on top of his head. He is identified with *Rˁ-m-ḥtp*, decan 34a. 6)

---

36 Davies, *The Temple of Hibis*, Part 3, p. 18 identified them both as Tefnut and Shu.

37 Cruz-Uribe, *Hibis Temple Project I*, p. 187, citing Kákosy, "The Astral Snakes of the Nile," pp. 255–260, n. 25; *EAT* III, p. 202, n. Aa and pl. 42.

Next is the standing figure of a crocodile-headed deity. He offers the two *nw* jars and is identified with *Wꜥrt*, decan 35. 7) Next is another erect snake with both human legs and arms, identical to the previous snake from the same register. He offers the two *nw* jars and is identified with *Tpy-ꜥ-spdt*, decan 36. 8) The final figure is a male deity wearing the white crown of Upper Egypt. He holds the *was* scepter with his right hand and the *ankh* sign with his left. He is identified with the southern constellation Orion.[38]

REGISTER IV

King Darius offers a conical bread to the row of deities, for the most part identified with the Epacts who represent 11 extra days that make up for the difference between the lunar year of 354 days and the solar year of 365 days. The king wears the composite crown and the starched kilt. Above the king, the present inscription reads:

> *Sꜣ Rꜥ (Dryš)¦ di ꜥnḫ ḏt*
> "Son of Re (Darius)¦ given life forever."

1) The first figure in front of the king is a partially erect snake on a low pedestal, identified with *Wšꜣt-bkt*, Epact 1. 2) The second figure is seated on a throne with two arms crossed over his chest. He holds the crook and the flail and wears the white crown. He is identified with Osiris, Epact 2. 3) Directly following Osiris is an erect serpent with his tail toward the back, identified as *Wšꜣti*, Epact 3. 4) Next is a falcon-headed god seated on a throne. He wears a short pleated kilt, the double crown, and holds the *was* scepter with his right hand and the *ankh* sign with his left on top of his left knee. He is identified with Horus, Epact 4. 5) Horus is followed by an erect snake with his tail behind him, identified with *Wšꜣti*, Epact 5. 6) The sixth is a standing male presenting two *nw* jars. He is identified with *Bꜣ-ḳd*, Epact 7. Based on this identification, his now-destroyed head might have been a jackal or a crocodile. 7) The seventh figure is another erect serpent with his tail behind him, and he is positioned directly behind Horus. He has no equivalent representation on similar lists and may be a substitute for Seth as Epact 6.[39] 8) The last figure in this register is a four-headed snake with his tail behind him. He is difficult to identify, as such a deity never occurs in any similar decan list.

REGISTER V

The king wears the red crown of Lower Egypt and the kilt with a starched, triangular apron. He presents a conical loaf of white bread to the row of deities in front of him. 1) The first is a goddess seated on a throne. She wears the Hathoric crown with the vulture headdress

38 Cruz-Uribe, *Hibis Temple Project I*, p. 188; *EAT* III, p. 201, n. P.

39 Some lists ignore the representation of Epact 6, perhaps because of his association with Seth. For example, Dendera A and D lists do not list him, while on the bracelet of Hornekht and the Cairo Menat fragment, Seth is replaced by Thoth; *EAT* III, p. 140. If the identification of figure 7 on register VI with Epact 6 is true, then this list contains the greatest number of Epacts represented on a single document, more than the Dendera D list suggested by *EAT* III, p. 139.

and holds the *ankh* and *was* scepters. She is identified with Isis, Epact 8. 2) She is followed by a standing male deity offering the two *nw* jars. He has a sun disk with two horns and a uraeus on top of his head and is identified with *ʿnḫ-m-ḫry*, Epact 9. 3) Third is a female deity seated on a throne, holding the *wadj* scepter and the *ankh* sign. She has a Nephthys emblem on top of her head and is thus identified with Nephthys, Epact 10. 4) Fourth is a standing lion-headed deity offering the two *nw* jars. He wears a short kilt and an ox tail. He is identified with *Snn*, Epact 11. A space divider separates the following two figures from others in this register. 5) Fifth is a seated god with a solar disk and a uraeus at the forehead. He has a falcon head, is holding the *was* scepter in his left hand, and probably held an *ankh* sign in his right. He is simply identified as Re Horakhty and is not associated with any decan list. 6) Last is a standing lioness-headed goddess. She wears a solar disk with a uraeus on her head and holds the *ankh* sign in her left hand, while the other is raised in gesture of protection. She is identified with Sakhmet and is not associated with a decan list.[40]

The reconstruction offered above leaves the last figure on registers I–IV and the last two figures in register V partly unidentified. In total, 65 figures appear on both the south and the north walls. They represent 36 decans, 12 pseudo-decans, 11 Epacts, and 6 unidentified figures. The first of those unidentified figures is the last figure on register I. He has the iconography of Ptah; however, he does not appear among the similar lists of deities in the Seti I B family of decans. He does however, occur in other families of decans including the Tanis group, as Qd, decan 28.[41] Since he is attested in relation to decan 28 elsewhere, his representation in the Hibis scene could be a new pseudo-decan 27a. [42] The last two figures on register V could be Re Horakhty and Sakhmet, based on their iconography and the fact that Re Horakhty is actually mentioned without a corresponding image on the west wall. Sakhmet might be represented here to invoke her protective abilities throughout the year.[43] The other unidentified figures might also be intended as representations for certain planets or constellations. The last figures on registers II and III are identified as the constellations Leo and Orion.[44] A detailed discussion of these unidentified figures will be continued in the commentary.[45]

Many similarities exist between the figures on the north and south walls on the one hand and the list of the Dendera Temple, called list D by Parker and Neugebauer in *EAT III*, on the other.[46] Because the north wall is mostly a reconstruction, examples from the south

40 While the identification of the first figure of the south wall with Sakhmet by Cruz-Uribe has been refuted earlier, the identification of Sakhmet as the last figure of the south wall is more probable; see Cruz-Uribe, *Hibis Temple Project I*, p. 188.

41 *EAT* III, pp. 146, n. 28; 163, n. 48.

42 *EAT* III, p. 146

43 This connection was discussed by Cruz-Uribe, *Hibis Temple Project I*, p. 189; Germond, *Sekhmet et la protection du monde*, pp. 10, 194ff and 329ff; Yoyoytte, "Une monumentale litanie de granit: les Sekhmet d'Aménophis III et la conjuration permanente de la déesse dangereuse," pp. 63ff; Bryan, "The Statue Program for the Mortuary Temple of Amenhotep III," pp. 60ff.

44 Cruz-Uribe, *Hibis Temple Project I*, pp. 178ff.

45 See pp. 193ff.

46 Dendera list D is on the ceiling of the Outer Hypostyle Hall, second middle strip to the west and second middle strip to the east from center = *PM* VI, pp. 44, 49; *EAT* III, pp. 78, 130–140.

wall only are given: Register I, figures 3, 4, 5; register II, figures 1, 3, 4, 5, 6, 7; register III, figures 1, 3, 4, 6; register IV, figures 1, 2, 3, 4, 5; register V, figures 1, 4. Figures 2 and 3 on register V are similar to those of Dendera D, except that their crown iconography is exchanged. In Hibis, figure 2 wears a horned disk with a cobra, and figure 4 wears only the Nephthys crown. In the Dendera D list, figure 2 is bareheaded, while Nephthys wears the horned disk and the Nephthys crown.

CHAPEL E1 — THE WEST WALL[47]

The west wall contains one large scene of the king offering to the procession of gods facing him. According to the inscription below the king's hands, he offers incense to Re Horakhty; however, the scene is more complicated. The king offers not only incense but a pile of ritual offerings heaped on four horizontal levels. The offerings include meat of oxen, birds, and gazelles, bread, fruits, vegetables, and liquids. The king also offers Maat to Amun Re. More significantly, Re Horakhty is totally absent. It is very rare that the main deity named in the text as the receiver of the offering is absent. An explanation of this peculiarity will be offered below.[48]

THE WEST WALL — NORTH SECTION

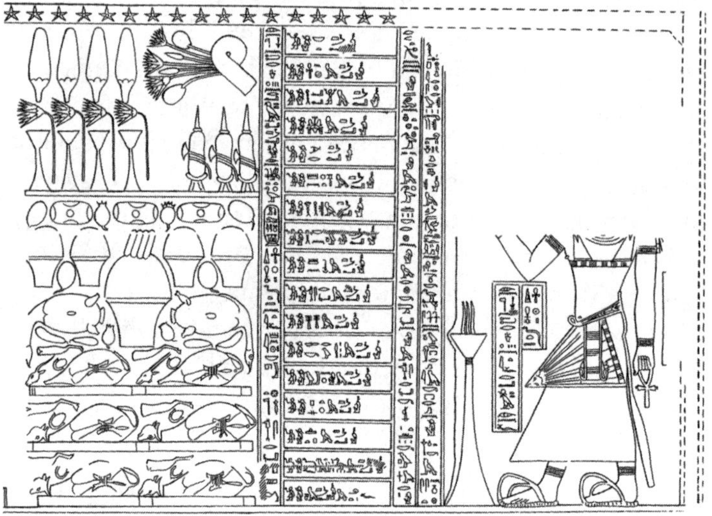

Figure 43: West wall of chapel E1- north section
(after Davies, *The Temple of Hibis*, Part 3, detail from pl. 16)

The king is represented at the northern end of the wall. Unfortunately, the whole upper block that once bore his head is missing. In what remains, he is wearing a two-strap gar-

47 This wall seems to be a favorite place of memoranda for the ancient and modern travelers who left their graffiti on its surface. It might have attracted such pillagers because it was the most beautifully preserved scene with much pigment left, as evident from the blue, red, and white all over the surface.

48 See pp. 181ff.

ment with a long skirt, topped by a starched kilt with a long sash ending with two cobras and a long ox tail, and sandals with high arching bands. He is the only figure on this wall wearing sandals; the others are barefooted. He holds the *ankh* sign in his left hand. The exact gesture of the right arm can never be known for sure because of the missing block, but it might have been an adoration or offering gesture with an open palm, as is usually represented near the dedication of offerings. In front of him is a tall standing brazier.

THE INSCRIPTION

Before the offering pile between the king and the procession of the six gods on the south side are columns of inscriptions to be read from south to north or right to left. They comprise one vertical line at the beginning and seventeen horizontal lines and then end with two vertical lines.

Below the hands of the king

Ỉr sntr n ỉt.f Rꜥ ḥr ꜣḫty ir n.f di ꜥnḫ mi Rꜥ ḏt

"Censing his father Re Horakhty for he has made a giving life like Re forever."

The first vertical line

Ỉr sntr n Rꜥ ḥr ꜣḫty di mꜣꜥt ir n. nswt biti sꜣ Rꜥ (Dryš)¦ di ꜥnḫ mi Rꜥ ḏt n ỉt.f Ỉmn Rꜥ nb Hbt nṯr ꜥꜣ wsr ḫpš

"Censing Re Horakhty and giving Maat is what the king of Upper and Lower Egypt, son of Re, (Darius)¦, given life like Re forever has made for his father Amun Re, lord of Hibis, great god, Powerful of strength."

The horizontal lines

1) *Ỉ Rꜥ nb{t} Mꜣꜥt*
   "Oh Re, lord of Maat."
2) *Ỉ Rꜥ ꜥnḫ m Mꜣꜥt*
   "Oh Re, who lives in Maat."
3) *Ỉ Rꜥ ḥꜥi m Mꜣꜥt*[49]
   "Oh Re, who rejoices at Maat."
4) *Ỉ Rꜥ smꜣ tꜣwy m Mꜣꜥt*
   "Oh Re, who unites the two lands in Maat."
5) *Ỉ Rꜥ mr Mꜣꜥt*
   "Oh Re, who loves Maat."
6) *Ỉ Rꜥ mnḫt m Mꜣꜥt*
   "Oh Re, who becomes splendid/ effective in Maat."
7) *Ỉ Rꜥ wꜣḥ m Mꜣꜥt*
   "Oh Re, who endures in Maat."
8) *Ỉ Rꜥ ḥknw m Mꜣꜥt*[50]
   "Oh Re, who praises Maat/acclaims Maat."
9) *Ỉ Rꜥ mn m Mꜣꜥt*
   "Oh Re, who is established in Maat."

---

49 *Wb.* III, p. 40, 2–6, 14.

50 *Wb.* III, p. 178, 12.

10) *Ỉ Re wsr m M3ʿt*
"Oh Re, who is powerful in Maat."
11) *Ỉ Rʿ ḏd m M3ʿt*
"Oh Re, who is enduring in Maat."
12) *Ỉ Rʿ ẖkrw m M3ʿt*
"Oh Re, who is adorned with Maat."
13) *Ỉ Rʿ wbn m M3ʿt*
"Oh Re, who shines/ rises in Maat."
14) *Ỉ Rʿ pst*[51] *m M3ʿt*
"Oh Re, who shines in Maat."
15) *Ỉ Rʿ ḥtp m M3ʿt*
"Oh Re, who is satisfied in Maat."
16) *Ỉ Rʿ ḏf3w m M3ʿt*
"Oh Re, who is nourished/abounds in Maat."
17) *Ỉ Rʿ ẖnm M3ʿt m ḥ3t.f*
"Oh Re, who joins Maat in his front."

The last two vertical lines

1) *Ỉrt ʿbw m wnwt 3ḫ n.i m 3ḫw.k rḫ.n.i m rḫ.k iṯi n.i m wsr.k ḥmt.k pw imy r.i*
"The making of purification (is what is) in Hermopolis. It is through your power that I have become effective. It is through your knowledge that I know. It is through your strength that I have seized. What is in my mouth is your skill."[52]

2) *[Ỉ Rʿ w3]ḥ sp sn ikr sẖr mty ḥ3ty grg m M3ʿt km3 n.f ii n.i r.k ink ḏḥwty snnwy*[53]*.k pr im.k pr n.i nḏt.k m ssnwt.*
"Oh Re, enduring enduring, who is excellent of counsels, exact of heart, who establishes order after he created it. I have come to you. I am Thoth, your likeness which goes forth as you. I have come to protect you in Hermopolis."

THE WEST WALL — SOUTH SECTION

Figure 44: West wall of chapel E1, south section
(after Davies, *The Temple of Hibis*, Part 3, detail from pl. 16)

51 *Pst* for *psḏ*; *Wb.* I, p. 556, 16.

52 *ḥmwt*, "skill;" *Wb.* III, p. 85.1–2, Cruz-Uribe, *Hibis Temple Project I*, p. 76, n. 212.

53 *snn*(*wy*), "images;" *Wb.* III, p. 460, 6–17.

Amun Re leads the procession of the gods. He is seated on a throne, elevated by two rectangular bases; one is decorated with horizontal and vertical lines, the other with the repeated hieroglyphic formula of an *ankh* sign flanked by two *was* scepters atop a *nb* basket sign. The first base is probably a mat placed underneath the base of the statue of Amun Re. Amun Re might have been carrying the symbols of the *ankh* and *was* in both hands, but unfortunately this is not clear because of another missing block from the wall. The top part of the *was* scepter is still visible. Amun Re wears his distinctive crown of the two tall feathers. He is followed by the standing figure of his consort, Mut. She wears her double crown, the vulture headdress, and a long, tight-fitting dress. She holds the *ankh* sign with her right hand and the *wadj* scepter with her left. The couple is followed by Khonsu, the third member of the Theban triad. He has his unique iconography of the lunar disk and the side lock. He wears a broad collar with the counterpoise on his back. He is mummiform and holds the combined insignia of the *was* scepter and the flail. Traces are seen of the crook and the *djed* pillar, similar to the insignia held by Osiris, the next figure. Khonsu stands on top of a rectangular base, with a triangle of steps attached to one side. The other side is unfortunately destroyed. The triad of Thebes is followed by the second most important triad in Hibis: Osiris, Horus, and Isis. Osiris stands on a rectangular base. He is mummiform and holds the flail, the crook, and the combined *ankh-djed-was* scepter in both hands. He wears a false beard and the white crown of Upper Egypt, with a row of nine cobras at its base and one cobra, with its body coiled and its tail extended, along the middle part of the crown.[54] He also stands on a rectangular base that contains seven peculiar signs. The first two signs can be recognized as *s3b šwty*, "variegated of feathers." The last two signs on the base look like two bows.[55] Osiris is followed by the standing figure of his son Horus who is falcon-headed and wears the double crown. He wears a two-strap shirt, a kilt, and an ox tail. In his right hand he holds the *ankh* sign and in his left he holds the *was* scepter. He is followed by his mother Isis, who has the two cow horns surrounding a solar disk, with a cobra attached to her horns. She also wears the vulture headdress, a broad collar, two bracelets, an armlet, and two anklets. She holds the *ankh* sign with her right hand and the *wadj* scepter with her left. A substantial amount of pigment, mostly red and blue, still remains on most of these deities on the west wall, especially on the garments of Mut, Osiris, and Isis.

THE INSCRIPTION

Above Amun Re

Ḏd mdw in ꞽImn Rꜥ nb Hbt nṯr ꜥ3 wsr ḫpš ir n.f di ꜥnḫ mi Rꜥ ḏt

"Words spoken by Amun Re, lord of Hibis, great god, powerful of strength, for he has made a giving life like Re forever."

---

54 The number of uraei on the crown of Osiris varies from 7 to 11; Derchain, *Le papyrus Salt 825*, p. 184, n. 178 . Another instance with exactly ten serpents occurs in the Abydos temple: Calverley and Gardiner, *The Temple of King Sethos I at Abydos*, III, pl. 43. In Edfu Temple, Osiris Wennefer is said to "illuminate the Shetat, who shines with the White Crown, surrounded by serpents (*mḥnt*);" Derchain, *Le papyrus Salt 825*, p. 184, n. 178.

55 For complete discussion of these symbols, see pp. 184ff.

Above Mut

Ḏd mdw in Mwt wrt nb<t> išrw nb<t> Hbt ir n.s [di] ꜥnḫ mi Rꜥ ḏt

"Words spoken by Mut, the great, lady of Isheru, lady of Hibis, for she has made a giving life."

Above Khonsu

Ḏd mdw in Ḫnsw nṯr ꜥ3 ḥr ib Hbt ir n.f di ꜥnḫ [mi Rꜥ ḏt]

"Words spoken by Khonsu, great god who dwells in Hibis, for he has made a giving life [like Re forever]"

Above Osiris

Ḏd [mdw i]n Wsir nṯr ꜥ3 ḥr ib Hbt Ir n [.f ꜥnḫ] mi Rꜥ dt

"Words [spoken] by Osiris, great god who dwells in Hibis, for [he] has made a giving [life] like Re forever."

Above Horus

[Ḏd mdw in] Ḥr nḏt it.f nṯr ꜥ3 ḥr ib [hb]t ir n.f di ꜥnḫ mi Rꜥ dt

"Words spoken by Horus, protector of his father, great god, who dwells in Hibis, for he has made a giving life like Re forever."

Above Isis

[Ḏd mdw in] 3st wrt mwt nṯr [hr ib] Hbt ir n.s di ꜥnḫ mi Rꜥ ḏt

"[Words spoken by] Isis, the great, divine mother [who dwells] in Hibis, for she has made a giving life like Re forever."

CHAPEL E2 — THE EAST WALL

Unfortunately, only the east wall of this chapel survives.

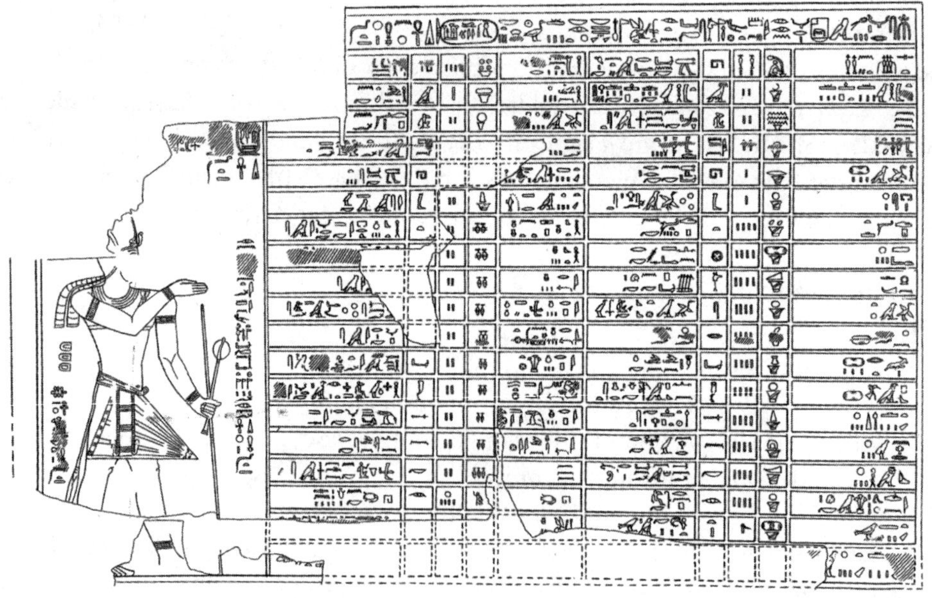

Figure 45: East wall of chapel E2
(after Davies, *The Temple of Hibis*, Part 3, detail from pl. 16)

This wall has a rather unusual offering list preceded by the king, who stands in front of it in a striding, dedicatory stance. The list is composed of a detailed multi-sectioned offering formula. Beneath the first horizontal register, the list is divided vertically into two main sections (A and B). Each has five vertical columns including the type of offering, the offering determinative, the quantity, a hieroglyphic sign that is part of a repeated verse read vertically across the whole section as "Oh Amun of Hibis, powerful of strength, take for yourself the eye of Horus," and finally a reprise or a phrase that has a word play with the name of the corresponding offering of the same horizontal row. Many novel word plays with the corresponding phrase in the fifth column appear in the vertical verse of the fourth column, as will be discussed below. Originally, nineteen horizontal rows were in each section, but the last two rows are badly damaged in both sections.

The upper north side of this wall is destroyed, but it can be assumed that the king wears the blue crown with two streamers behind his head and the cobra on his brow. He wears a two-strap shirt and a short starched kilt with an ox tail. The kilt has a long sash ending with two cobras. He holds a long staff and a short scepter in his left hand, while his right hand is palm-open to the side. Behind the king are three land markers around which he is supposed to perform a ritual circuit for dominance over the universe.[56]

THE INSCRIPTION

Behind the king

S3 ꜥnḫ nb ḥ3[.f] mi Rꜥ ḏt

"All protection and life behind [him] like Re forever."

Above the king

(/// nṯr ꜥ3 wsr ḫpš mr)¦ di ꜥnḫ ḏt///Nḫbt///[57]

"(///great god, powerful of strength, beloved of///)¦ given life forever///Nekhbet///"

In front of the king

Ir n/// n. it.f Imn Hbt nṯr ꜥ3 wsr ḫpš hnꜥ psḏt.f ir n.f di ꜥnḫ mi Rꜥ ḏt

"Making of/// to his father Amun of Hibis, great god, powerful of strength, together with his Ennead,[58] for he has made a giving life like Re forever."

---

56 Spencer, "Two Enigmatic Hieroglyphs and their Relation to the Sed-Festival," pp. 52–55; Egberts, *In Quest of Meaning*, I, p. 64.

57 The wall is destroyed here, but the remaining traces suggest the writing of *nḫbt*, which indicates that an image of the vulture goddess Nekhbet might have been represented at the top of this corner of the wall. Note that the epithet of Amun of Hibis is placed in a cartouche above the king, in the place reserved for the royal cartouche. The importance of this cartouche inscription will be discussed below.

58 Is this a reference to an Ennead of Hibis? Are they the group of the six gods and goddesses represented on the west wall? On the south wall of chapel K 1, the other occurrence of the term *Psḏ* in Hibis comes after a "*ḏd mdw in ḏḥwty*" and refers to Hermopolis; Davies, *The Temple of Hibis*, Part 3, pl. 23. The word can refer to any number of gods forming a group in a particular place and is not necessarily limited to a group of nine. For the development of the word, see Barta, *Untersuchungen zum Götterkreis der Neunheit*, pp. 19–26. See also Sethe, "Untersuchungen über die ägyptischen Zahlwörter," pp. 8ff; Brunner, "Neunheit," cols. 473–479.

The top horizontal line

Ms wp-r snn[59] *m ḥwt nwb wp-r irty n ꞽImn Hbt ntr ꜥ3 wsr ẖpš irt n nsw biti ntr nfr nb t3wy nb ꞽIrt ẖt s3 Rꜥ nb ḫꜥw (D3ryš)¦ ḏi ꜥnḫ mi Rꜥ ḏt.*

"Fashioning /creating the opening of the mouth of the image in the house of gold. Opening the mouth and eyes of Amun of Hibis, great god, powerful of strength, which the king of Upper and Lower Egypt, the good god, lord of the two lands, lord of cult act, son of Re, lord of appearances, (Darius)¦, given life like Re forever, performed."

Section A

1) *S3ṯ*[60]*<ḥr> ḫnt sbty/ḥstw 2 iṯi n.k rdit m ḫnty.k*[61]
   "Libation <upon> the libration stone, 2 jars; take for yourself that which is placed in front of you."
2) *Tbḥw <ḥr> ḥtpw sn tbḥw.k ḥtpw.k ḥr.s*
   "Offering meal <upon> the offering tables, 2; May you request what satisfies you upon it."
3) *Mw sn ꜥb n.k mw imy st*
   "Water, 2; the water in it cleans for you."
4) *Bt sn bd bt*
   "Natron, 2; purify (yourself with) Natron."
5) *Ḥt3 wꜥ iṯi n.k r r.k*
   "*Hta*-bread, 1; take to your mouth for yourself."
6) *Ps<n> wꜥ ḫw psf*[62]*ḥr. st*
   "*Ps<n>*-bread, 1; avoid that he suffers because of it."
7) *Dpty fdw dptw n.k*
   "*Dpty*-bread, 4; taste (it) for yourself."
8) *Šꜥ<t> fdw nn šꜥ.s r.k*[63]
   "*Shat*-bread, 4; it will not cut against you."
9) *Šns fdw šsp n.k tp.k*[64]

59 *snn*, *Wb*. III, pp. 460ff.

60 *s3ṯ*, *Wb*. III, p. 423, 2.

61 For *s3ṯ ḥr ḫnt* see *Wb*. III, p. 301. Notice the word play between *ḫnt*, the "Libation stone," and *ḫnty*, the adverb "in front."

62 Here is an evident link between the hieroglyph in the 4th column, that is, a part of the vertical repeated verse of Amun and the following phrase in the 5th column. The intended word play is made between *ps*[*n*] bread and *p3s/b3s* in the phrase that is made up of the *b/p* in the 4th column and the *3* and *s* in the 5th column. There are three possibilities for the rendering of *P3s*: , *Wb*. I, p. 499, 2, "to suffer," sometimes also written as *B3s* , "das Wassernäpfchen des Schreibers," "water pot," *Wb*. I, p. 499, 5; or, finally, , "to cook, roast, bake," Lesko, *A Dictionary of Late Egyptian*, I, p. 155.

63 *Nn šꜥ.s* is the future negation *nn sḏm .f*.

64 The *wsr* sign in the 4th column could also mean *wsrt* = neck, which is similar to the meaning of *tp.k*, "your head," in the 5th column. In the Temple of Edfu (*E* IV, p. 47, 12), the bull of Punt brings an offering *šps ḥr Wsrt*; Wilson, *Lexicon*, 258; *Wb*. I, p. 360, 1-2.

"Shenes -bread, 4; receive for yourself (what is on) top of you."[65]

10) *Pꜣt fdw spꜣt*[66] *ḳꜣḳꜣ*[67]*.k sw*
"*Pat*-bread, 4; *Spat*-bread that you eat it."

11) *Ḫnf fdw ḫ[n]fỉ n.f*
"*Khenef*-cake, 4; that he baked."[68]

12) *Ỉwrt fdw rd*[69] *wnwn*[70]*.k*
"*Iwrt*-bread, 4; may your travel flourish."

13) *Pꜣḳ*[71] *fdw nn pꜣḳ*[72] *ỉb.k ḥr*[73] *st*
"Flat cake, 4; your heart will not long for it."

14) *T-ḥḏ fdw ḥḏ ḥtp.k ḥr st*
"White bread, 4; your offering is illuminated by it."

15) *Nḥr fdw nḥrw r.k*
"*Nhrw*-bread, 4; may (they) resemble you."

16) *Ḳmḥ fdw (k)m(ḥ)*[74] *n.f nḥm n.f r-pw*
"*Kmh*-bread, 4; 'which he saw' or 'which he seized.'"

17) *Ỉdn*[75] *ḥꜣ.k fdw rnp.k*[76]
"*Iden*-bread behind you, 4; may you be young."

---

65 *šns* refers to the shape of the bread, most probably a triangle, as indicated by its determinative. This kind of bread is associated with the eye of Horus. The king is usually represented lifting his arm with this kind of bread so that his hands are on the same level as his head and so it goes well with the expression that is used here "*šsp n.k tp.k*;" Wilson, *Lexicon*, pp. 1022–1023.

66 This could be read as *Pꜣt* or *spꜣt*, if one associates the *s* in the 4th column with the phrase in the 5th column. Both *Pꜣt* and *spꜣt* are kinds of bread, see *Wb*. I, p. 495, 6–8 and *Wb*. IV, p. 101, 7. The determinative ⊗ is unsuitable in both cases; however, it could be an influence from the word *spꜣ.t*, "nome."

67 The spelling of the word suggests *ḳꜣḳꜣ* (Lesko, *A Dictionary of Late Egyptian*, II, p. 145), instead of *wnm*.

68 *ḫnfỉ*, "baked," *Wb*. III, p. 291, 15–16. Taking the *r* of the 4th column together with *ḫnfỉ* can lead to the word [hieroglyphs] = "divine statue;" Lesko, *A Dictionary of Late Egyptian*, I, p. 276. Another possibility is *ḫnr (tw).f n.f*, "may it be scattered for him;" *Wb*. III, p. 298, 8.

69 The forearm with hand holding the stick in the 4th column could be the determinative for *rd*, "flourish" or "restore" (Lesko, *A Dictionary of Late Egyptian*, I, p. 280); however, the *nw*-jars at the end of *wnwn* are inexplicable.

70 *Wb*. I, p. 318.

71 *Wb*. I, p. 499, 9.

72 *Wb*. I, p. 499, 7.

73 Notice the unusual writing of the *ḥr* sign here.

74 This translation was constructed based on associating the hieroglyphic sign *k* in the 4th column with the first sign in the 5th column and, more importantly, based on the intended word play with *ḳmḥ*. The resulting word would be *gmḥ/kmḥ*; *Wb*. IV, p. 170, 8, [hieroglyphs].

75 *ỉdn* is a kind of bread for the Sokar feast, attested in Medinet Habu offering lists; Helck, *Materialien zur Wirtschaftsgeschichte des Neuen Reiches*, pp. 660–667. Notice the inexplicable walking legs determinative.

76 *Wb*. II, p. 434, 15.

18) *T-wr*[77] *wꜥ im3ẖ*[78]*.k ḥr wr*
"*Twr*-bread, 1; may you be justified, Horus the great."

19) *T-w*[*t*]*///////*
"*Twt*- bread"

Section B

1) *Ḥb*[*n*]*nt*[79] *//r fdw ḥbnn*[80]
"*Hbnnt*-bread//, 4; spring up."

2) *Ḥwn wꜥ ḥwnt*[81] *n.k*
"*Hwn*-bread, 1; rejuvenation belongs to you."

3) *P3t//*[82] *sn dp*[83] *n.f*
"*Pat*-bread///2; which he tasted."

4) *Šnf*[84]*/// m it.i šni.f<s>t*
"*Shenf*-cake///; with my father, he encircles it?"

5) *T imy t3*[85]*/// iṯi n.k st*
"*Imy-ta*-bread///; take it for yourself."

6) *T 3šr*[86] *sn 3sb*[87] *šmw.k*
"Toasted bread, 2; may your harvest be baked."

---

77 According to Helck, this type of bread usually has a round shape; Helck, *Materialien zur Wirtschaftsgeschichte des Neuen Reiches*, p. 677; *Wb.* V, p. 209, 12; Hannig, *Grosses Handwörterbuch Ägyptisch-Deutsch*, p. 522.

78 *Wb.* I, p. 82, 18.

79 *Wb.* III, p. 63, 15. This type of bread also appears in Medinet Habu; Helck, *Materialien zur Wirtschaftsgeschichte des Neuen Reiches*, pp. 677ff.

80 *ḥbnn*, "to spring up," see Faulkner, *The Ancient Egyptian Pyramid Texts*, PT 25, 30. In *Wb.* III, p. 63, 1–5, this word is associated with water in general. In the beginning of the 5th column, there is a trace of a sign that looks like *s*; if this is the case, then this word could be read as *ḥbs* , in *Wb.* III, p. 67, 4, also relating to water.

81 This *ḥwn* offering could also be a kind of meat offering (*Wb.* III, p. 55, 3), especially since there is a flesh determinative in the 5th column. However, it is also attested in Barta, *Die altägyptische Opferliste von der Frühzeit bis zur griechisch-römischen Epoche*, p. 124, n. 50 as referring to a kind of bread. *ḥwn*, "to rejuvenate," is in *Wb.* III, p. 52, 3–4.

82 According to Janssen, "The Daily Bread. A Contribution to the Study of the Ancient Egyptian Diet," p. 30, the *Pat* were small loaves, probably rolls; *Wb.* I, p. 495, 6.

83 The hieroglyphic sign of the seated man with finger in his mouth in the 4th column could function as the determinative for the relative form of the verb *dp*, "to taste".

84 *šnf* cake is *Wb.* IV, p. 514, 13.

85 *Wb.* V, p. 209, 8 as a kind of bread for the dead.

86 *t 3šr* = "roasted bread/toast," similar to PT, 78; *3šr* in *Wb.* I, p. 21. See also Helck, *Materialien zur Wirtschaftsgeschichte des Neuen Reiches*, p. 679, where this kind of bread appears in the offering lists N.19 and Medinet Habu. However, it is doubtful that they are the same kind of bread as the *sšr* bread referred to by Janssen, "The Daily Bread. A Contribution to the Study of the Ancient Egyptian Diet," pp. 22–23.

87 Using the ideogram in the 4th column, one is able to translate this phrase as rendered above. Other scholars designated this phrase as unintelligible, as in Faulkner, *The Ancient Egyptian Pyramid Texts*, p. 27 and Cruz-Uribe, *Hibis Temple Project I*, p. 78, n. 238. The

7) *Inḳt špnt sn ḥnḳt prỉ m.k wp r.k ỉm.s*
"Beer (in) jars, 2; beer that come forth from you, open your mouth with it."

8) *Ḥnḳt sn////*
"Beer, 2///"

9) *ỉrp sn///.k ỉm. s*
"Wine, 2///you with it."

10) *ỉrp ʿbšty sn [bš]ỉ n.f s ḫw ʿmꜣ.f s*
"Wine (in) jars, 2; he spat it out, without swallowing it."

11) *ỉrp n wꜣḥꜣt sn wp r.k ỉm.s*
"Wine from the oasis, 2; open your mouth with it."

12) *ỉrp mḥyt sn mḥ*[88] *{m} ỉt.k [r.k] m.s*
"Wine of Lower Egypt, 2; may your father fill [your mouth] with it."

13) *ỉrp wꜣḏt*[89] *sn ḥwn ỉmy ỉrt ḥr wp r.k ỉ[m.s]*
"Wine of Buto, 2; rejuvenate what is in the eye of Horus, open your mouth with [it]."

14) *ỉrp ḥꜣmyt sn ḥꜣm*[90] *n.f wp r.k ỉm.s*
"*Hamyt*-wine, 2; which he caught, open your mouth with it."

15) *ỉrp swny sn nn swn*[91]*.s r.k*
"*Swny*-wine, 2; it will not perish/diminish with regard to you."

16) *Mw sn ʿb n.k mw ỉmy.s*
"Water, 2; purify for yourself the water that is in it."

17) *Hꜣ*[92] *4 hꜣ n.k ỉbw.sn*
"Jubilations, 4; would that you had their hearts."

---

first word in the 5th column could also be *bs* (*Wb.* I, p. 476, 1); however *ꜣsb/ỉꜣsb* in *Wb.* I, p. 20 rhymes better with *ꜣšr*.

88 This is one instance of the many words discussed here that conjure up several meanings; *Mḥ* with the ideogram of the forearm with hand holding a stick as a determinative, in the 4th column, means "to grasp" or "to carry" (*Wb.* II, p. 119, 5–8), which, according to Wilson (*Lexicon*, p. 451) is semantically linked with *mḥ*, "to fill" (*Wb.* II, p. 116, 6; 118, 9). This last meaning, "to fill," is perhaps what is intended for its meaning in the reprise; however, it is written with the water determinative, which recalls the word *mḥ*, "to be immersed in water," "to drown" (*Wb.* II, pp. 121–122, 11).This word appears on the third register of the north wall of chapel H2, line 6. It is often associated with Osiris: in the Memphite Theology, it occurs several times in connection to his murder, see Breasted, "The Philosophy of a Memphite Priest," pls. I–II, lines 8, 19, and 62. In the Book of Gates, ninth hour, Osiris is called *mḥi*, "the drowned one,; Hornung, *Altägyptische Jenseitsbücher*, pp. 62ff; Wilson, *Lexicon*, p. 450.

89 The ox leg in the 4th column could be taken as an adverb *wḥm*, "repeatedly," after *ḥwn*.

90 *ḥꜣm*, "catch" or "fish," Wb. III, p. 31, 12–13. For *ḥꜣmyt* as the name of a wine, see *Wb.* III, p. 32, 5,8. There is an unexplainable determinative of the forearm with hand holding stick between *ḥꜣm n* and the suffix pronoun *f*.

91 *šwny* refers most probably to wine from Aswan (*Wb.* IV, p. 69, 4) or Pelusium (*Wb.* IV, p. 155, 8). In Greco-Roman texts *ḥꜣmt* is listed as a wine producing region together with *swnt*; see Wilson, *Lexicon*, p. 616.

92 *hꜣ* from *ḥi*, "jubilate," *Wb.* II, p. 471, 10.

18) *Bity////*
"Honey///"
19) *////*
/////

2. COMMENTARY

Both the jambs and the reveals of the door to chapel complex E provide significant information regarding the intended theology of the surrounding architectural space. The south jamb introduces a unique combination of Amun Re and Osiris as one entity being encircled by the royal cartouche, preceded by the usual royal coronation epithet of *nsw biti*, "King of Upper and Lower Egypt." Symbolically, this cartouche refers to the main rulers of the divine dynasty that governed Egypt "in the beginning of time" when the sun god Re—later Amun Re—and Osiris ruled over Egypt as "King of Upper and Lower Egypt."[93] But perhaps it correlates with the background of divine kingship and the assimilation of the god's power and attributes with that of the king. According to the inscription of the doorway E, this divine kingship is associated with both solar and Osirian characteristics. This combination corresponds with the meanings of the decoration of that part of the temple, accessed by staircase E. By coming out of this door, the king becomes the embodiment of both Amun Re and Osiris; the features of both are dominant in the roof chapels of complexes E and H, respectively.

The ancient Egyptian texts have abundant examples of the title *Wsir Wnn-nfr*. These make it unreasonable to try to reconstruct a specific attribution or designation of such an epithet.[94] However, the number of examples declines significantly when found written in a cartouche, especially in earlier times.[95] It is even more rare when associated with Amun's name.[96] Only one example exists for the combination name of Amun Re Wennefer inside a single cartouche.

The context of this combined name, Amun Re Wennefer, is important to the overall discussion of this chapel and should be discussed in relative detail. The Temple of Opet in Karnak provides a comparable context of the combination title Amun Re Wennefer. In the central hall of the Opet Temple, (VII) north side, 3rd register,[97] the king is standing offering Maat to the Theban triad Amun, Mut, and Khonsu, who are represent-

93 Žabkar, *A Study of the Ba Concept in Ancient Egyptian Texts*, pp. 5–6, notes 1, 5–7. Evidence comes from the PT for example §886a, 2120a, *CT* I 189 f–g, 197, *CT* III 334 c–d, *BD* 175.

94 Generally, the title may indicate an Abydene origin, especially during the Ramesside period, when Abydos was the land of Wennefer; Otto, *Ancient Egyptian Art. The Cult of Osiris and Amon*, pp. 28, 54. The title means quite literally "he who remains matured," an epithet that indicated the eternal immortality of the god; see Assmann, *The Search for God in Ancient Egypt*, p. 78.

95 Gardiner, "Onnouphris," cols. 50–51. For divine names inside cartouches, see Assmann, *Solar Religion in the New Kingdom*, pp. 148–149.

96 *Opet* I, p. 90; Leitz, *Lexikon*, I, p. 324.

97 *Opet* I, p. 90; II, pl. 2e; III, pp. 45ff.

ed, according to De Wit, "affublés d'épithètes qui les identifient en fait à Osiris, Isis et Harsiesis"[98] The inscriptions begin below the king's hands: "may you be satisfied, O Amun Re Wennefer,[99] justified, may you jubilate on land, may you be happy in heaven. (Maat) is your nourishment. It is your ///."

Above Amun, the inscription reads:

> Words spoken by Amun Re Wennefer, foremost of Thebes, who is called Amun Re, who is complete with horns, the first of the five epagomenal days, the day of the birth of Osiris on his beautiful feast in the whole land, the day when heaven was created, his mother encircling (her) beautiful city in *nnt*. Words spoken, I give you Maat, equipped in your time/ around you (*ʿpr m h3w.k*), there being no wrongdoing in you.

Above Mut, the inscription reads:

> Words spoken by Mut, the great, lady of Isheru, the lady of the rekhyt, who protects her brother, the day his body is entered (*hrw i3b.tw ẖ3t.f*) in the land where she is born. Words spoken by Mut, I gave you the diadem of Horus (*di i n.k ẖʿw n Ḥr*) together with his uraeus (*ḥryt-tp.f*) upon the earth, at the head of the living ones (*tp t3 ḫnty ʿnḫw*).

Above Khonsu the text reads:

> Words spoken by Khonsu-shw in Thebes, the divine image, the beautiful face who navigates (*d3i*) daily[100] west of Thebes in order to make offerings to the great Ba of the serpent Kematef who is there as Amun in the mound of Igret together with the souls of Khemenu. Words spoken by Khonsu, I cause Maat to be abundant (*w3ḫi*) on the land in your time.[101]

Several elements in that scene in the Opet Temple are relevant to the composition of the doorway to staircase E and chapel E1 on the roof of Hibis. Beside the similarity of the combined title of Amun Re Wennefer, the offering of Maat is significant; not only do the gods receive it from the king as nourishment, but they also give Maat to the king, equipped and abundant on earth and in his time. Amun, Mut, and Khonsu are in this scene, but, as De Wit suggested, their titles associate them with the Osiris triad, making them an abbreviated version of the row of the gods on the west wall of chapel E1 of Hibis (where the king is offering Maat to the Theban and Osirian Triads). The north and south walls of chapel E1 have a representation of the gods of the dual year, expressing both lunar and civil weeks of the year, as discussed below. Similarly, near to that scene of the Opet, the king and queen are raising their arms in adoration before the gods, representing the thirty days of the moon.[102] Opposite that list of days, the king offers incense and libation

---

98 *Opet* I, p. 90.

99 Only Wennefer is written inside the cartouche in this case.

100 *m ẖrt hrw* is left untranslated by De Wit.

101 *Opet* I, pp. 90 ff; II, pl. 2e; III, pp. 45ff.

102 *Opet* III, p. 46.

to the eight primordial deities of the Ogdoad in addition to the four Kas. Each god of the Ogdoad and the Kas gives the king an important element of rulership, such as *ꜥnḫ*, *wꜣs snb*, *ꜣwt ib*, *ḥtp*, abundance, praises, *ḫꜥw m Re* (appearance as Re), his name remaining on earth, vigorous youth (*ḥwn ꜥnḫ*), nourishment and long life/reign (*ꜥḥꜥ*) of happiness. As will be seen below, the emphasis on the many aspects of rulership was an important element in the theology of the roof of Hibis as well as the association of that power with the prosperity of the land and its people. In the previously-cited inscription of Mut/Isis in the Opet scene, she confirms the crowning of Horus at the head of the living ones.

In another instance in the Opet Temple, the title of Amun Re Wennefer is represented as the title for a standing Osiris wearing the *atef* crown.[103] The inscriptions express strong solar association with Osiris: "May you be content, may your Ba be content, the Ka of your Ba is content, your name is content. Your face is satisfied... O Amun Re Wennefer, come toward what satisfies you, (toward) Re himself...." Above Osiris, the inscription continues: "Words spoken by Osiris Wennefer, justified, the king of the gods, the god of the gods, who is at the head of the gods, the father of the gods, ruler of the Ennead, the beautiful disk, who shines in the horizon (*psḏ m ꜣḫt*), the moon in the sky, daily, made in the [*ipt*] *wrt*."[104] Note that in the Opet Temple (chapel VIII) is an important tableau of scenes of Osiris awakening on the funeral bed that are similar to scenes of chapel H2 on the roof of Hibis.

On the south jamb of the door to stairway E in Hibis, it follows that this fused entity has control over the heaven, the two lands, and the *dwat*, or the netherworld. In Egyptian texts, this three-tier worldview of the heaven, earth, and the underworld is generally used to express complete dominance over every part of the world.[105] This jamb lies at an architectural intersection of three levels of the temple (see pl. 17). It is located on the main floor level of the temple, directly south of the main sanctuary. The doorway leads to the second level of the Hibis Temple on top of the roof. The first step of staircase E leads to two concealed entrances to the only series of crypts in Hibis—C1 and C2 are below the floor level and D1, D2, and D3 are directly above the first two. These crypts were a common feature of ancient Egyptian temples in the Late and Greco-Roman Periods.[106] They functioned as the treasuries of the temples, where precious materials and portable statuettes were hidden, only to be used during the designated ceremonies.[107] In the Edfu temple, similar crypts were called the *dwat*.[108] Thus, the inscription can inherently associate the heaven with the roof of the temple, the two lands with the main or ground

103 But with no cartouche; *Opet* III, p. 56; II, pl.4 (north side, 1st register, second tableau; *Opet* I, 110.)

104 *Opet* III, p. 56.

105 Allen, "The Celestial Realm," p. 114. See also Assmann, *Egyptian Solar Religion in the New Kingdom*, pp. 174–178.

106 Traunecker, "Cryptes connues et inconnues des temples tardifs," pp. 21–46.

107 Traunecker, "Cryptes décorées, cryptes anépigraphes," pp. 571–577.

108 Wilson, *Lexicon*, p. 1181; *Wb*. V, p. 416, 44–45; cf. Waitkus, "Zum funktionalen Zusammenhang von Krypta, Wabet und Goldhaus," pp. 286ff.

level of the temple, and the *dwat* with the crypts of the temple.[109] The text of the opposite north jamb confirms some of these points; it welcomes the divine king to his temple, or rather this specific part of the temple, where he will proceed above or to the heaven as Re. An important phrase is added to the inscription: "The *wadjet* hall is being filled with your respect."[110] *Wadjet* not only made a pun with *w3ḏ* on the opposite jamb but indicated a certain type of hall, one that has columns. This can apply to hypostyle hall B on the ground floor, but also—more likely—to chapel E1 on the roof.[111]

The south reveal repeats the emphasis on the solar aspect of Amun, rather than the main god of Hibis, Amun of Hibis, and associates him with an intriguing cosmographic location called *msqt*, where everything in it rejoices for Amun Re when he, repeating the same phrase from the north jamb, "proceeds above" or "through heaven." The north reveal indicates the importance of the solar aspect of the divine king to humans, as expressed by the *Wechselsatz:* "As long as you are in the sky, being far in the horizon, your rays approach the faces."[112] The inscription on the jamb and the reveal thus connects the importance of the association of the god's power with that of the king and his subjects.

Msqt, like the other terms *akhet*, *dwat*, and *nnw* that are mentioned in this part of the temple connected with chapel complex E in particular, developed different meanings in different periods of Egyptian history. The general scheme of their location points to a cosmographic realm either under or above the earth.[113] The determinative of *msqt* varied from a desert sign, a staircase sign, a boat, or a bowl.[114] The composition in Hibis favors the association of *msqt* with a specific celestial point in the middle of the Osirian solar circuit. *Msqt* can even be closely identified with an intermediate location in the transformation, a late point in the Osirian cycle and an early point in the solar cycle. In the comparable images from the The Book of Nut, *msqt* is a place in the east where the sun god passes between the night and day, the heaven and the underworld, when the god exits the *dwat* in the east in the region of *msqt*.[115] This intermediate position explains the apparent confusion in its usage. No contradiction exists in its functioning as both a region of sunset and sunrise—sometimes in a single text[116]—as it is a two-way entrance to both the realm of Osiris, *p3 r n t3 dw3*, "the entrance to the underworld,"[117] and an

109 For the cosmological meaning of the Ancient Egyptian temples, see Assmann, *Ägypten. Theologie und Frömmigkeit einer frühen Hochkultur*, pp. 43–50.

110 North jamb of door to E, see p. 151.

111 The indication of a column has been proposed by Davies, *The Temple of Hibis*, Part 3, p. 18.

112 North reveal of door to E, see p. 151.

113 Egberts, *In Quest of Meaning*, pp. 292–293.

114 Allen, "The Cosmology of the Pyramid Texts," p. 7, n. 43, 44. Allen generally identifies *msqt* as the "beaten path of stars," that is, the Milky Way. See also Allen, "The Celestial Realm," p. 117.

115 Von Lieven, *Grundriss des Laufes der Sterne*, pp. 55ff; Assmann, *Das Grab des Basa (Nr. 389) in der thebanischen Nekropole*, p. 61b, where he translates the passage where *msqt* appears as "Die Majestät dieses Gottes steigt auf aus der *Msqt*. Er ist aufgezogen worden in der *Msqt*. Er war verklärt in den Armen seines Vaters Osiris in *T3-wr*;" Bomhard, "Le Livre du Ciel, De l'observation astronomique à la mythologie," p. 200, n. 15.

116 For example *EAT* I, p. 50 = P. Carlsberg I, II, 4–6.

117 Egberts, *In Quest of Meaning*, p. 292, n. 5; *EAT* I, 50 = P. Carlsberg I, II, 4–6; *CT* VII, 2j.

entrance to the realm of Re "where the sun rises."[118] It is mentioned as the first location to receive Osiris/Re after the victory over Seth, "grasping that evil one" when the stars are in joy and triumph.[119]

Msqt is parallel to the *akhet* in that both terms represent the early stage of the solar cycle when the sun is just being (re)born; *akhet* with the oval bread determinative appears several times on the same doorway to stairway E, twice on the lintel of the doorway, and once on the north reveal of the doorway. The oval bread determinative of the word *akhet,* written several times on the doorway to E, alludes back to its standard spelling in the Pyramid Texts,[120] where the *akhet*, usually translated as "horizon," designates the birthplace of the sun as well as the king.[121] Allen specifies the location of the *akhet* on the periphery of the heaven.[122] In the final hour of the Book of Night, the newly-born sun is described as emerging from the *dwat*, that is, the realm of Osiris. The first hour of the day begins when the sun passes through the doorway of the *akhet*:

> Emerging from the *dwat*, coming to rest in the day-barque, and sailing the Abyss at the hour of the Sun (called) "Seeing the perfection of Her Lord." Becoming Khepri, climbing to the *akhet*, having entered the mouth and emerged from the crotch. Rising from the doorway of the *akhet* at the hour (called) "Causing the Sun's Perfection to Appear."[123]

Both the *akhet* and *msqt* seem to be connected with this cosmological parameter. It is most probable that *msqt* is associated with the final hour of the night, as the last stage of the nocturnal journey of the sun as Osiris or in his realm. It is the gateway from which the sun makes the initial exit, while the *akhet* represents the final transformation before day break. The association of *msqt* with the Milky Way does not oppose this designation, as the Milky Way appears as a line of stars and constellations across the universe in the form of a band of light in the night sky.[124]

118 Assmann, *Das Grab des Basa (Nr. 389) in der thebanischen Nekropole*, p. 61; Egberts, *In Quest of Meaning*, p. 292; *CT* III 376a; *CT* VI 231q. Von Lieven, *Grundriss des Laufes der Sterne*, p. 55, n. 227, 136–137 (§ 21), similarly discusses this intermediate position of *msqt* as a transition between the realm of the dead and the sky.

119 Assmann, *Magic and Theology in Ancient Egypt*, p. 12, n. 15.

120 Allen, "The Cosmology of the Pyramid Texts," p. 17.

121 Allen, "The Cosmology of the Pyramid Texts," esp. pp. 14ff and 17; DuQuesne, "Effective in Heaven and on Earth," p. 38.

122 Allen, "The Cosmology of the Pyramid Texts," pp. 18ff.

123 Translation after Allen, "The Cosmology of the Pyramid Texts," p. 20 and n. 133, where he describes the two labels of the hours as the last hour of night and the first hour of day; Piankoff, *Le Livre du Jour et de la Nuit*, p. 80; Piankoff, *The Tomb of Ramesses VI*, I, p. 428; II, pls. 149 and 196.

124 Likewise, the *akhet* is assimilated to the light that appears before the actual rising of the sun; Allen, "The Cosmology of the Pyramid Texts," p. 21. The *ꜣḫt*-eye is notably associated with the unification of Osiris and Re; see Darnell, *Enigmatic Netherworld Books of the Solar-Osirian Unity*, pp. 87–88, n. 240–243; Graindorge, "La quête de la lumière au mois de Khoiak," p. 99.

CHAPEL E1 — WEST WALL

The northern section of the west wall of chapel E1 on top of the roof of Hibis is occupied by the figure of the king; according to the inscriptions, he is offering incense to Re Horakhty. In front of the king are several horizontal and vertical rows of hieroglyphs, including an elaborate hymn of Maat dedicated to Re Horakhty. The south section depicts a row of deities of the Theban and Osirian triads. It may seem puzzling that there is no image of Re Horakhty on this wall, even though he is named as the primary recipient of the offerings. As will be shown below, the Maat hymn proves to be part of a standard solar hymn, especially in the New Kingdom.[125] In many comparable instances of this hymn Re Horakhty is associated with other solar deities such as Re, Atum, and Amun Re. Thus the ancient theologians may not have found it awkward to represent Amun Re as a variant instead of Re Horakhty.

In chapel complex E is an equal manifestation of both physical and abstract nourishment for the gods. Beside the elaborate menu of bread, cakes, and different kinds of drinks in E2, the west wall of E1 depicts other material offerings piled over an offering table. More important is the hymn on the west wall that declares Maat, the concept of truth and justice, as a symbolic food for the god. Maat is the substance that feeds the spirituality of the gods; just like the material offerings, it enables them to function. As the food and sustenance of Re, Maat functions as the balanced energy of the solar order. It had been part of Re's diet since the Middle Kingdom.[126] The importance of this association was stressed in the tombs of the 18th dynasty, but increased in particular during the Ramesside period.[127] Sometimes the king simultaneously offers and receives Maat. The significant text in the Osireion expresses Maat's association with the divine as well as the ruler's power. Merenptah states *ẖnm kwi m M3ʿt rʿ nb ḥnḳ.i n.k st*, "I am united with Maat everyday (and) I present it to you."[128]

A very similar text of the elaborate offering of Maat appears on Berlin Papyrus 3055.[129] Chapter XLII deals with *R n ḥnḳ M3ʿt*, "utterance of offering Maat." In this papyrus, as well as in Hibis chapel E1, west wall, the recipient of Maat is Amun Re, who is similarly said to *ʿnḫ m M3ʿt, ẖnm m M3ʿt, ḥtp m M3ʿt, wnm m M3ʿt*, "live in Maat, join Maat, be

125 Assmann, *Re und Amun. Die Krise des polytheistischen Weltbilds im Ägypten der 18.–20. Dynastie*, p. 51.

126 *CT* III, 6–7 (Spell 165) " O you who are content with what you have done-Four times- and who send Maat to Re daily, the liver of Re is flourishing daily because of Maat and he partakes of the meal of the Great Goddess;" Faulkner, *Coffin Texts*, I, p. 143.

127 Teeter, *The Presentation of Maat: Ritual and Legitimacy in Ancient Egypt*, p. 15, n. 70; Westendorf, "Ursprung und Wesen der Maat, der altägyptischen Göttin des Rechts, der Gerechtigkeit und der Weltordnung," pp. 201–225; Assmann, *Sonnenhymnen in thebanischen Gräbern*, pp. 62ff.

128 Teeter, *The Presentation of Maat: Ritual and Legitimacy in Ancient Egypt*, p. 78; *PM* VI, p. 29 (1)–(2); Frankfort, *The Cenotaph of Seti I at Abydos*, pl. 22.

129 Moret, *Le rituel du culte divin journalier en Égypte d'après les papyrus de Berlin et les textes du temple de Séti Ier, à Abydos*, pp. 138–165.

satisfied with Maat, nourish in Maat…."[130] The rest of this chapter elaborates on the association of Maat with Amun Re's celestial journey, supporting him while he traverses "the east and west of heaven" and "joining him everyday, when he rests in the *dwat*,"[131] thus linking his solar cycle to the Osirian cycle in the *dwat*. Other solar manifestations of Amun Re appear throughout chapter XLII, such as Re, Horakhty, and Re Horakhty.[132] The decan-stars that appear nearby in chapel E1 are also attested in the same chapter of the Berlin Papyrus, praying to Amun Re.[133]

The preceding chapters (XXXVII–XLI) associate Amun Re with the deities Khepri, Re Atum, and Atum.[134] The context of these chapters seems to revolve around the rising[135] of the solar gods throughout the celestial realm and, most significantly, the *ḫꜥ m nsw biti*, "the appearance as the king of Upper and Lower Egypt."[136] The pharaoh is similarly said to "come toward Amun Re so that he makes him at the head of the living (by) uniting/resting (*ḥtp*) with him."[137] The Maat concept of energizing the god with the solar power on his initial rising, gained from Papyrus Berlin 3055, is found in the Great Amun Hymn in hypostyle hall M in Hibis.[138] In this hymn, Maat is connected with the birth of Amun-Re.[139] The text states:

> *nis-ḥknw r k ẖt n Nwt smꜣꜥtw mswt.k nṯrw ẖnm tw Mꜣꜥt r ꜥḥ.k štꜣ sꜣḫ tw sꜣty.k Mrty.k nhp n k stwt.k m nhp šn.k tꜣwy m psḏ.k rmn.k ḥr ḏw pwy n ꞽIgrt dwꜣtyw ḥr sšp m stwt.k.*
>
> Hymns are made for you at the womb of Nut. Your divine children raise you. Maat unites with you at your secret chamber, as your daughters, your Merti, transfigure you. It is at dawn that your rays rise early for you so that you may encircle the two lands with your radiance. When you set upon this mountain of Igaret, the Dwatyw glow in your rays.[140]

---

130 Moret, *Le rituel du culte divin journalier en Égypte d'après les papyrus de Berlin et les textes du temple de Séti Ier, à Abydos*, pp. 140–143.

131 Moret, *Le rituel du culte divin journalier en Égypte*, pp. 144-145.

132 Moret, *Le rituel du culte divin journalier en Égypte*, pp. 140–143.

133 Moret, *Le rituel du culte divin journalier en Égypte*, p. 136.

134 Moret, *Le rituel du culte divin journalier en Égypte*, pp. 125ff, 135.

135 "*ṯs m ḥtp*" is repeatedly (more than 20 times) written at the beginning of the chapters; see Moret, *Le rituel du culte divin journalier en Égypte*, pp. 121-125.

136 Moret, *Le rituel du culte divin journalier en Égypte*, p. 122.

137 Moret, *Le rituel du culte divin journalier en Égypte*, p. 128. This passage is repeated in ibid., p. 133 with slight variation.

138 Davies, *The Temple of Hibis*, Part 3, pls. 32–33.

139 Klotz, *Adoration of the Ram*, pp. 83–84, pl. 6, 38–39 (cols.8–9).

140 This section is very important because it makes a connection with the scene of the Temple of Opet (*Opet* I, p. 90), where many similarities exist, such as the combined name of Amun Re Wennefer, offering Maat to the Theban triad as Osirian triad, and the astronomical reference to the gods of the lunar months.

This part of the hymn clearly refers to an early transfiguration stage in the solar cycle, when the god was still in the "belly of Nut" making his "early rising…at dawn." His unification with Maat pushes him up, makes him rise,[141] and enables him to complete his transfiguration (*sꜣḫw*).[142] This stage seems to indicate an earlier Osirian cycle and a succeeding solar transfiguration.[143] Similarly, the association with Maat transforms the god from dusk, *iḫḫw*, to light, *iꜣḫw*.[144]

The hymn in Hibis continues to indicate another important feature, or rather a result, of this transformation. Maat enables his rays to "encircle the two lands," thus giving life to the world of the living. The same link to humans is indicated in the important inscription on the north reveals of the door to E that stresses: "your rays shall approach the faces." This unification of the god with Maat not only marks the stage of the transfiguration from Osiris to the solar gods Re or Amun Re, but also constitutes his wish to *ḫꜥ m nsw biti*, "to appear as the king of Upper and Lower Egypt," and emphasizes his cosmic duty of enlivening humans through his rays.[145] In the Coffin Texts, the direct relation between feeding on Maat and enlivening humans is recounted. According to CT 80, in the beginning of time Atum wanted to separate himself from the chaotic waters of Nun so as to create the living world. He is ordered to kiss, smell, and even eat Maat.[146]

With navigating the heaven comes the enlivening of humans, as well as the defeat of the enemies. Both the Berlin Papyrus 3055 and one of the unidentified blocks found among fragments of doorways erected by officers of the garrison of Hibis[147] share this thought. The block depicts four standing baboons in front of a solar barque containing the eye of Horus and a scarab inside a sun disk. The line of text gives the name *ꜥtt* for the barque's name and records the statement *wḏꜣ.k pt rꜥ nb ḫftyw.k ḫri*, "while you cross the heaven every day, your enemies are defeated." This statement, together with the name of the barque as *ꜥdt*, , occurs in the Papyrus Berlin: *ḫftyw.k ḫri wḏꜣ.k ḥr pt m ꜥnḫ wꜣs*

141 For comments on Maat as a life-giving force, and its relation to the sun god in particular, see Assman, "Gott," p. 759; idem, *Der König als Sonnenpriester*, pp. 63ff. For Maat's role in the rising of the sun, see Westendorf, "Ursprung und Wesen der Maat, der altägyptischen Göttin des Rechts, der Gerechtigkeit und der Weltordnung," pp. 201–225, esp. p. 203.

142 This transfiguration, or *sꜣḫw*, is a very important term and has received much discussion. The corpus of the *Sꜣḫw* or "glorification" spells mainly concerns the "transition" into an eternal state of being through the reviving of the body and the merging into the cosmos; Smith, *The Liturgy of Opening the Mouth for Breathing*, pp. 6–7. In practice, they were recited in association with important rituals; Smith, *The Liturgy of Opening the Mouth for Breathing*, pp. 6–7; Asssmann, *Das Grab der Mutirdis*, pp. 101–102; idem, "Harfnerlied und Horussöhne," p. 57 with n. 17. Some of these rituals are apparent in Hibis, like the offering rituals (chapel complex E) and the embalming rituals (chapel complex H).

143 For this, see Assmann, *Liturgische Lieder an den Sonnengott*, pp. 210, 219.

144 Shirun-Grumach, "Remarks on the Goddess Maat," pp. 176–179.

145 Moret, *Le rituel du culte divin journalier en Égypte*, p. 122.

146 *CT* 80 (I, 33–36). See also *PT* 627 on the birth of the king; Shirun-Grumach, "Remarks on the Goddess Maat," pp. 176–179.

147 Winlock, *The Temple of Hibis*, Part 1, pl. LI.

snb ḥb.k pt m ꜥḏt, "...your enemies are defeated. While you cross the heaven in life and dominion, while you make festive the heaven in your barque Adit...."[148]

The socle underneath the figure of Osiris on the west wall of chapel E1 is decorated with seven ambiguous signs:

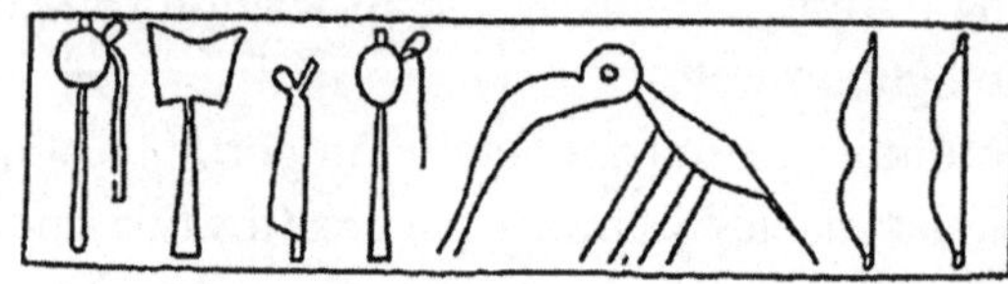

With the exception of the fifth sign from the left, they are all well preserved. Drioton[149] identified them as cryptograms with each reflecting one phonetic value. He proposed the first sign to be , reflecting *w* as in *wḏ*; the second to be , reflecting *s* as in *sꜣb*; the third , reflecting *r* as in *rsi*; the fourth as , reflecting *m* as in *mnw* (*Wb* II, p. 72, 3); the fifth troublesome sign to be reflecting *r*, for unknown reasons; then follows , reflecting the sign *s* as in *sty* (*Wb*. IV, p. 327, 8) and finally the other similar sign, reflecting *d*, from *dwn* (*Wb* V, p. 431, 1). These signs were grouped to form the phrase *ws(ỉ)r m r(ꜣ) st (ꜣw)*, "Osiris in Rosetau," .

Probable faults in the methodology concerning the identification of these signs are that despite the similarity of the fourth sign to the first sign, and the last two signs to each other, Drioton proposed different interpretations and values for each. The identification of the second sign as and the third as , forming the title *sꜣb šwty*, "variegated of feathers," a common epithet for Horus Behdet, is more plausible; however, the suggestion of Rosetau is not completely without reason.[150] Geographically, Rosetau is associated with the necropolis in the area of Memphis, but according to the funerary books (PT and the Book of the Two Ways), it is an intermediate place in the horizon, an *axis mundi* separating death and rebirth.[151] The term is also found within a solar context,[152] thus reflecting the solar/Osirian aspect of this room. In the Coffin Texts, Rosetau is associated with the circle of Osiris:

148 Moret, *Le rituel du culte divin journalier en Égypte d'après les papyrus de Berlin et les textes du temple de Séti Ier, à Abydos*, p. 137.

149 Drioton, "Une Erreur Antique de Déchiffrement," pp. 27–31. On the use of acrophony in Ancient Egyptian texts, see Fairman, "Notes on the Alphabetic Signs – 3. Acrophony," pp. 298–305.

150 For Rosetau, see Spiegelberg, "Zu *Rꜣ-stꜣ.w* 'Nekropolis,'" pp. 159–160; Zivie-Coche, "Aux Marges de Memphis: Giza," pp. 113–122. For Rosetau's connection to Osiris in a solar context, see Zivie, "Bousiris du Létopolite," pp. 91–107, and Zivie, "Encore Ro-setaou," p. 145. See Hawass, "The Discovery of the Osiris Shaft at Giza," pp. 390–392, with references, for Rosetau as a place of the underground burial of Osiris.

151 Spiegelberg, "Zu *Rꜣ-stꜣ.w* 'Nekropolis,'" pp. 159–160; DuQuesne, *Jackal at the Shaman's Gate*, pp. 12ff; Assmann, *Ägypten. Theologie und Frömmigkeit einer frühen Hochkultur*, pp. 39–43; Lesko, *The Ancient Egyptian Book of Two Ways*, pp. 1–6.

152 Zivie, "Encore Ro-setaou," p. 145, where a Ramesside text mentions Osiris with Re Horakhty, in Ro-Setau, as one entity; Zivie, "Bousiris du Létopolite," pp. 91–107, especially section 4.

> I was born in Rosetau of the horizon and the horizon was granted to me by the lord of the horizon. My dignified state is in Buto like the purification of Osiris (My) glorification in Rosetau is the guidance of the gods of the paths in the circle/entourage that surrounds Osiris, and I am one of those who guide them.[153]

Similar groups of these signs are attested in other texts that are funerary in nature, such as in the tombs of Psusennes and Shoshenq in Tanis and in Papyrus Salt 825.[154] In the sanctuary of the Temple of Hibis, some of the figures of Osiris have similar signs underneath the funerary bed or on the base of the statue.[155] A closer look at these examples reveals that they are mostly royal regalia: either groups of different crowns and wigs or different kinds of scepters or staffs. In the Papyrus Salt example are the nine bows, as in the Hibis example, and the Sema-Tawey sign. They are all connected with royal regalia and reserved for the image of Osiris as a reminder of his ancient regal rights. In fact, the fifth unusual sign in our socle could be interpreted as a combination of the two signs of the *atef* crown and the flagellum 𓋚/𓋭. A slight erosion of the wall could have led to the deformed shape seen in the outline. Such royal regalia can explain the existence of the last two signs that represent the bow, an important icon for the traditional enemies of Egypt. They are common features on the base of royal statues, symbolically trampled by the king's feet. As Osiris is considered the king of the dead, and since his own resurrection signifies the birth of his son Horus, the rightful heir to the throne, these symbols would stimulate the process of his resurrection. The interpretation of these groups of signs, decorating the socle underneath the statue of Osiris in the west wall, collectively as "Rosetau" or individually as royal regalia shows their primary function as amulets protecting Osiris during his resurrection.

THE NORTH AND SOUTH PILASTERS

Two of the three faces of each of the north and south pilasters in chapel E1 are decorated with purification scenes. One side has a figure of a priest, while the other side has a smaller-scale figure of a divinity pouring libation water from a *hes* vessel. The north pilaster has the Purification priest and Thoth. The south pilaster has the Iunmutef priest and Horus, son of Isis. The text surrounding these scenes invokes a purification of Geb and Duenanwey. Since his earliest attestation, this latter god, whose name probably means "spreader of wings/arms,"[156] was represented as the guardian of Osiris; in Edfu, he guards

---

153 *CT* VII 500. See also the similar spell *CT* VII 289, which mentions Re Horakhty.

154 Derchain, *Le papyrus Salt 825*, fig. IX, C, p. 94, n. 78; Montet, *Les constructions et le tombeau de Chéchanq III à Tanis*, p. 68, pl. XXX; Montet, *Les constructions et le tombeau de Psousennès à Tanis*, pl. XCIV. See also the stela of the Saite–Persian Period in Edwards, "The Shetayet of Rosetau,"pp. 27–36.

155 See, for example, Davies, *The Temple of Hibis*, Part 3, pl. 3, register II, figures 5 and 6; pl. 4, register V, figure 12; register VI, figure 21, register VIII, figure 17.

156 *Wb.* V, p. 432, 16.

Osiris in the Sokar-chapel.[157] He was the god of the 18th Upper Egyptian nome and lord of the east.[158] He is also represented in many solar contexts.[159] He plays an important role in the purification rituals, together with Horus, Seth, and Thoth, and this is also the case in the present chapel.[160] Both the textual and the iconographical evidence of the decorations of the pilasters clarify the use and function of chapel E1, if not the whole chapel complex E.

Textually, the purification scenes on the pilasters of chapel E1 are related to a group of very similar texts mentioned by Christophe.[161] In his selection, Christophe said that he only chose those that had "les prières de la transfiguration."[162] Beside the Hibis roof, his chosen texts come from Salle V of the Temple of Gurna, the tomb of Rekhmire, the sarcophagus of Butehamon of the 21st dynasty,[163] and the papyrus of the lady called Sayt from the Roman Period.[164] The beginning of the text according to the Gurna version, absent in the Hibis version, states: "Making incense offerings to Re as his beloved son, lord of the two lands (…) giving *s3ḫ* in his temple west of Thebes."[165] Impressively, these texts contain the Litany of Re with the offering of Maat that is depicted nearby on the west wall of chapel E1 in Hibis.[166] In parts C and D of Christophe's texts, which are absent from chapel E1, Iunmutef gives *msi* (rebirth) to the king, who is identified as Osiris and performs an Opening of the Mouth.[167] Based on these selected texts, Christophe concludes that through this tableau of "baptême solaire," the dead king is joined with both Amun Re and Osiris and that the mummy of the king must have been purified in Salle

157 *E* I, p. 198, 12; Wilson, *Lexicon*, p. 1188.

158 Kees, "Anubis, Herr von Sepa und der 18. Oberägyptische Gau," pp. 79–101; *PT* 1098a; 2078; 27–28; Vandier, *Papyrus Jumilhac*, pp. 28ff; Westendorf, "Dunanui," cols. 1152–1153.

159 Egberts, *In Quest of Meaning*, I, p. 294 n. 10.

160 Altenmüller-Kesting, *Reinigungsriten im ägyptischen Kult*, pp. 61–64; Gardiner, "The Baptism of Pharaoh," pp. 9ff

161 Christophe, "La salle V du temple de Séthi Ier à Gournah," pp. 117–180

162 Christophe, "La salle V du temple de Séthi Ier à Gournah," p. 120, n. 1. For the *s3ḫw* or "transfiguration" spells, see footnote 142.

163 The tomb of Rekhmire provided the oldest illustrated model for the Opening of the Mouth ritual; Otto, *Das Ägyptische Mundöffnungsritual* II, pp. 8ff, pl. 1. The coffin of Butehamon (coffin number 2236-7 in the Turin museum) provides much detailed textual information on the different episodes of the Opening of the Mouth ritual (Otto, *Das Ägyptische Mundöffnungsritual* I, Text 4, p. 173). However, this important coffin needs a new individual treatment as it is only described in general details in Marro, "Ernesto Schiaparelli 1856–1928," pp. 39–42. For pictures of the coffin and its different sides, see Donadoni Roveri, *Dal museo al museo: passato e futuro del Museo egizio di Torino*, plates on pp. 56–62; Vassilika, *Art Treasures from the Museo Egizio*, catalogue no. 58.

164 Christophe, "La salle V du temple de Séthi Ier à Gournah," pp. 120ff.

165 Christophe, "La salle V du temple de Séthi Ier à Gournah," p. 129.

166 Christophe, "La salle V du temple de Séthi Ier à Gournah," pp. 130–138.

167 Christophe, "La salle V du temple de Séthi Ier à Gournah," pp. 161–167. For the role of Iunmutef during the Opening of the Mouth ritual, see Rummel, *Untersuchungen zum Gott Iunmutef vom Alten Reich bis zum Ende des Neuen Reiches*, pp. 159–181.

V before the final burial at the tomb.[168] While the connection with the Opening of the Mouth in chapel complex E is evident from the nearby chapel E2, the association with Osiris is not at once clear; that might be explained by the fact that the Osiris episodes were reserved for the arrangement of the adjacent chapel complex H. However, a closer look at the scenes in E1 reveals many features of Osirian connection inside chapel complex E.

The elaborate image on the third side of each pilaster represents the emblem of Wepwawet, supported by two images of the king over a portable shrine (see figs. 37 and 38). The formula *(w)ʿbw.k (w)ʿbw dwn ʿnwy ṯs pẖr*, "Your purification is the purification of Duenanwey and vice-versa," has almost exact parallels in the tombs of Ramesses VII[169] and Ramesses IX.[170] This image, together with the purification of Duenanwey, appears to be borrowed from the iconography of the Ramesside Period. Inside the tomb of Ramesses IX is a similar motif in a purification ritual by an Iunmutef priest who is reciting similar passages of the purification of Duenanwey. The emblem in that scene incorporates two images of the king, once with Horus and once with Seth, seated on either side of the staff. On top is a *bnw* bird with his elaborate crown, seated on a floral bush on one side, while on the other side is a ram with two horns, two tall feathers, and a sun disk between. Both the images of the bird and the ram are placed on top of a sledge with a curved end.[171] Inside the Temple of Abydos, the Osiris chapel of king Seti I contains a very similar procession with standards like those in chapel E1. At the center is the emblem of Osiris over a shrine, at the top of which stand two images of the king on both sides.[172] In the Khonsu Temple, the king, accompanied by Isis, anoints the Osiris emblem that has at its base two identical figures of a king. This scene is preceded by a bull standard and rows of guardians with knives.[173] In the Libyan and Kushite Periods, it was common practice to represent this decorative motif of different standards on a portable sledge flanked by symmetrical images of the king and adored by Horus and Thoth opposite to the image of the adoration of the Ptah–Sokar–Osiris barque being adored by Isis and Nephthys.[174]

At the ends of both walls of the corridors in the tombs of Ramesses VII and IX an almost identical purification scene is shown on both sides, depicting the purification of the king as Osiris by the divine priest Iunmutef, which Hornung described as a new

168 Christophe, "La salle V du temple de Séthi Ier à Gournah," pp. 177ff. He calls the appearance of Amun-Re with the king during the purification ceremony an extraordinary occurrence. See also Naville, *La litanie du soleil*, pp. 6ff.

169 Hornung, *Zwei Ramessidische Königsgräber: Ramses IV. und Ramses VII.*, pp. 59–60, pl. 104.

170 Guilmant, *Le tombeau de Ramsès IX*, pp. 20, 9, pl. 85; *CT* IV, 402b; VI, 120c.

171 See Guilmant, *Le tombeau de Ramsès IX*, pl. LXXXV.

172 Otto, *Ancient Egyptian Art. The Cult of Osiris and Amon*, pl. 13. For a thourough study of the Abydos standard, see Coulon, "Les uræi gardiens du fétiche abydénien. Un motif osirien et sa diffusion à l'époque saïte," pp. 85–108.

173 *PM* II 2 p. 241 (102); Degardin, "Correspondances osiriennes entre les temples d'Opet et de Khonsou," fig. 7.

174 Both images appear on opposite sides of the Block Statue CG 42226; Fazzini, *Egypt Dynasty XXII–XXV*, p. 22, pl. XXII; Jansen-Winkeln, *Ägyptische Biographien der 22. und 23. Dynastie* I, pp. 136–149; II, pp. 506–514, pls. 30–33.

motif for a royal tomb:[175] "…in dieser Form ist die Szene des Königsgrabs neu, wird aber von Ramses IX. nochmals aufgegriffen und bildet wohl einen gewissen Ersatz für die zuletzt bei Ramses IV. verwendete Szene des Königs vor Osiris im Schrein in der oberen Pfeilerhalle."[176] The inscription of Iunmutef states that the purification of the Osiris-king is that of Horus, Seth, Thoth, and Duenanwey; his censing is in the heaven like Re and in earth like Geb. The continued inscription states that the purifications with incense and natron are those of Horus, Seth, Thoth, and Duenanwey *and vice versa*.[177] It is interesting that in this corridor the inscription designates the king on the left with Re and on the right as Osiris.[178] An offering of Maat seems to have been represented in this corridor, as the remaining inscriptions say *di f Mꜣꜥt rꜥw nb*, "may he give Maat every day."[179] Hornung recognized the solar/Osirian influence as a development from the earlier Sun-god/Osiris connections on the corridor of Ramesses IV:

> Sie folgt nicht mehr dem alten Schema mit einer Anrufung des Sonnengottes links und des Osiris rechts, ist aber auch keine bloße Titulaturzeile, wie bei Ramses IV., sondern scheint eine eigenwillige Lösung zu verwirklichen, wobei die linke Zeile wieder eher "solar" und die rechte "osirianisch" bestimmt ist.[180]

These previous examples associate this particular iconography of the pilaster decoration with the solar/Osiris connections. Beside the role of Wepwawet in the leading of processions and as opener of the ways during the Osirian ceremonies, the emblem also refers to the gathering of the limbs of Osiris during the same rituals. Inside the sanctuary of Hibis is a similar image of two kings on a sledge, tying an emblem inside which there is clearly a human leg, referring to the ritual of collecting the limbs of Osiris as part of his mysteries.[181] This emblem is thus assimilated into the so called "Osiris fetish" that seems to have represented the main reliquary of Osiris.[182] The standard representation of this fetish is composed of a long pole resting on the base of a shrine or a portable barque and flanked by the two images of the king.[183]

It is equally important that the Osiris fetish reflects the solar association. On the south wall of the Osiris barque chapel in the Temple of Seti I, as well as in the vignette of Book

175 Hornung, *Zwei Ramessidische Königsgräber: Ramses IV. und Ramses VII.*, pp. 52–63.

176 Hornung, *Zwei Ramessidische Königsgräber: Ramses IV. und Ramses VII.*, p. 58.

177 Hornung, *Zwei Ramessidische Königsgräber: Ramses IV. und Ramses VII.*, p. 60.

178 Hornung, *Zwei Ramessidische Königsgräber: Ramses IV. und Ramses VII.*, pp. 52ff.

179 Hornung, *Zwei Ramessidische Königsgräber: Ramses IV. und Ramses VII.*, p. 54

180 Hornung, *Zwei Ramessidische Königsgräber: Ramses IV. und Ramses VII.*, p. 58.

181 Davies, *The Temple of Hibis*, Part 3, pl. 4, register I; Beinlich, *Die "Osirisreliquien." Zum Motiv der Körperzergliederung in der altägyptischen Religion*, p. 213.

182 Eaton-Krauss, "The Festival of Osiris and Sokar in the Month of Khoiak: The Evidence from the Ninteenth Dynasty Royal Monuments at Abydos," pp. 84ff; Beinlich, *Die "Osirisreliquien." Zum Motiv der Körperzergliederung in der altägyptischen Religion*, pp. 17–42.

183 According to the images inside the Osiris hall and the Osiris Barque chapel of the Temple of Seti I; Eaton-Krauss, "The Festival of Osiris and Sokar in the Month of Khoiak: The Evidence from the Ninteenth Dynasty Royal Monuments at Abydos," pp. 84ff.

of the Dead chapter 138, the strong solar association is expressed by the decoration of the base of the emblem with the image of Aker.[184] The aim of such scenes on the pilasters of chapel E1 seems to be the eventual enlivening of the king's divine powers. Two scenes on the exterior walls of Hibis represent similar images of the emblem of Wepwawet with the two kings tying the knot around a column associated with giving the king the emblems of life and victory.[185]

THE ASTRONOMICAL LISTS ON THE NORTH AND SOUTH WALLS

The rows of deities depicted on the north and south walls of chapel E1 of Hibis are recognized as deities of the dual year.[186] Parker first coined this term;[187] in his explanation, he used examples from lists pertaining to an assembly of approximately 59 deities. He explained that 48 of these deities represented, on the one hand, the 36 weeks of the civil year plus 12 pseudo- or new decans added with a ratio of one per every group of three.[188] On the other hand, these 48 deities correspond to the lunar weeks, one god per each quarter of the lunar month. The remaining 11 gods, sometimes called those of the Epacts (from Greek: *epaktai hèmerai* = added days), consist of the five epagomenal (out of time/ intercalary) days plus 6 lunar days. They are a quantification of the difference between the lunar year of 354 days and the civil or solar year of 365 days.[189]

The list of deities in Hibis adds 6 more figures to the usual 57–59 previously-discussed deities of the dual year.[190] These deities are perhaps better regarded as representations of an almanac of stellar gods. Unfortunately, they bear hardly any labels that identify them with greater certainty.[191] The majority can be identified as decan gods, each representing the ancient Egyptian week of 10 days. A total of 56 figures remain on both walls. According to the reconstructions discussed above,[192] the number can amount to 66 or 64

184 Eaton-Krauss, "The Festival of Osiris and Sokar in the Month of Khoiak: The Evidence from the Ninteenth Dynasty Royal Monuments at Abydos," pp. 85–88, figs. 5, 6; Caulfield, *The Temple of the Kings at Abydos*, pl. II. Other solar motifs shown in connection with the Osiris fetish are the souls of Pe and Nekhen who greet the sun by performing the *hnw* jubilation and are associated with the divine kingship; see Eaton-Krauss, "The Festival of Osiris and Sokar in the Month of Khoiak," pp. 86–87 with references.

185 Davies, *The Temple of Hibis*, Part 3, pl. 47.

186 Davies, *The Temple of Hibis*, Part 3, p. 18; Cruz-Uribe, *Hibis Temple Project I*, p. 185.

187 Parker, *The Calendars of Ancient Egypt*, §§ 273–281.

188 These pseudo-decans, to this author's knowledge, are still lacking a satisfactory analysis.

189 Parker, *The Calendars of Ancient Egypt*, §§ 273–281; *EAT* III, p. 133; Clagett, *Ancient Egyptian Science*, II, p. 477. For the origin of the lunar and civil calendars, see Wells, "Re and the Calendars," pp. 1–37.

190 There are few examples of lists with the exact number of 59 gods, especially in the later lists. In Dendera the number is 57; Parker, *The Calendars of Ancient Egypt*, §§ 274.

191 The first decan, Sopdet, has traces of inscription above her figure on the north wall; small traces of a corner of the mouth (*r*) and a little notch at the top can perhaps suggest the combination sign 𓂋, used in the common title of Sopdet as *Nbt rnpw*. The god Ptah at the end of the first row of the south wall has the title *it nṯrw*, "the father of the gods."

192 See pp. 156ff.

figures. These are reconstructed as follows: 36[193] or 35 decan deities, 12 or 11 pseudo-deities (identified by the letter [*a*] next to their numbers), 11 gods of the epact, and finally 6 unidentified figures depicted toward the end of each row on the south wall.

Although some decans names appear in the Pyramid Texts, the first appearance of the decans lists is on the so-called "diagonal star calendars" of the Middle Kingdom coffins.[194] In the New Kingdom, decans were usually depicted on the ceilings of certain royal funerary temples and tombs. In the Late Period, decans began to appear on other media such as naoi,[195] stelae, sarcophagi,[196] amulets, bases and sides of statues, and various kinds of jewelry.[197] The tableau of the decans in Hibis can thus be considered as their first reappearance on temples after the New Kingdom, linking the ancient decanal tradition of the Middle Kingdom coffins and the funerary temples of the New Kingdom on the one hand, with the later Ptolemaic temples on the other.

Unfortunately this assembly of decans in Hibis was not discussed in *EAT*.[198] Even more puzzling is that this list was not mentioned by either Bull or Brugsch, who both published a treatise on astronomy and were involved directly in works about Hibis as well.[199] Kákosy was the first to mention the list among other astronomical examples of decan constellations and to add them to the sources from *EAT*.[200] Parker divided the

---

193 This number of 36 decans corresponding to the 36 weeks of the year is rather ideal; for example, the decans appearing on the New Kingdom astronomical diagrams never have an exact number of 36; Symons, "A Star's Year: The Annual Cycle in the Ancient Egyptian Sky," p. 10.

194 *EAT* I, p. vii; Parker, *The Calendars of Ancient Egypt*, §§273ff; A good review of the star clocks and their functionality is provided by Depuydt, "Ancient Egyptian Star Clocks and Their Theory," pp. 6–44. See also Leitz, *Altägyptische Sternuhren*; Symons, "A Star's Year: The Annual Cycle in the Ancient Egyptian Sky," pp. 1–33.

195 Habachi and Habachi, "The Naos with the Decades (Louvre D 37)," pp. 251–263. Other fragments of this naos were discovered recently by the Spanish mission; see Bomhard, *The Naos of the Decades: From the Observation of the Sky to Mythology and Astrology*.

196 Gundel and Schot, *Dekane und Dekansternbilder: Ein Beitrag zur Geschichte der Sternbilder der Kulturvölker*, pl. 8, for the example of the Bubastis stela in Cairo, and pl. 9 for Nektanebo's Sarcophagus in Berlin.

197 Kákosy, "Decans in Late-Egyptian Religion," pp. 163ff.

198 *EAT* I, II, III. Neither is discussed in Parker, *The Calendars of Ancient Egypt*. Even though Parker states that the Persian Period "must have stimulated the flow of Babylonian concepts into Egypt" (*EAT* I, p. vii), he ignored the only astronomical representation on a monument that could be dated to that period.

199 Bull, "An Ancient Egyptian Astronomical Ceiling-Decoration," pp. 283–286; Brugsch's pioneering work on Egyptian Astronomy, "Astronomische und astrologische Inschriften Altaegyptischer Denkmaeler;" idem, *Matériaux pour servir à la reconstruction du calendrier des anciens égyptiens: partie théorique*.

200 Kákosy, "Decans in Late-Egyptian Religion," p. 179. Davies briefly remarked that these figures "resemble those found in the lists of the fifty-nine deities of the dual year, though the number here is not certain," but did not discuss them any further; Davies, *The Temple of Hibis*, Part 3, p. 18.

decanal list into six different families, each with a number of examples and subgroups. The example at Hibis seems to have a strong association with the family of Seti I B.[201]

The decans began to appear in the distinctive form of snake and lion or lioness-headed deities from the time of Osorkon II, as is evident by the bracelets found in his tomb at Tanis.[202] Yet, the gesture of the king offering to them is an unusual motif. In front of the king the inscription reads: "presenting the field to his father, Amun of Hibis." Is this simply one of the cases noticed by Ludlow Bull as being "full of mistakes,"[203] or are these deities a cosmic aspect of the god Amun of Hibis? The latter suggestion seems to be in accord with Kákosy, who commented that the priests of the temple may have viewed them as "heavenly manifestation of Amun's universal might."[204] Since the initial appearance of the decanal lists on the Middle Kingdom coffins, they were associated with the funerary liturgy/offerings for the deceased.[205] The Hibis decans list is divided into two sections on the north and south wall. The north has decans 1–18, while the south wall starts with the decan numbers 19–36. This same division is found among many of the Middle Kingdom coffins.[206] The decan's rather complicated yet eternal cycle of appearance and disappearance in the sky might have been the reason for their attachment to the funerary realm. In the 70-day period when they were invisible, the ancient Egyptians assumed they disappeared into the underworld and associated them with the funerary rites and mummification period of 70 days after which the Opening of the Mouth is conducted on the corpse of the deceased or his statue.[207] After the period of invisibility, they first appear in the eastern heaven for 80 days; then they "work"[208] for 120 days and later appear in the western heaven for 90 days before they die again.[209] It is safe to assume that such decanal representations evoked in the Egyptians an obvious association with the cycle of resurrection and rebirth and, more importantly, an iterative eternal reoccurrence.

The important element of the king offering to each row of gods is a rather uncommon feature in the decanal representations. Gundel mentions one example of the king offering to the decans[210] from the Temple of Kom Ombo, where the decans are associated

---

201 Cruz-Uribe, *Hibis Temple Project I*, p. 185; *EAT*, III, pp. 105–152.

202 Kákosy, "Decans in Late-Egyptian Religion," pp. 163–164. However, one can argue that the transformation into the new shapes began earlier in the time of Psusennes, or even earlier during the time of Amenhotep III. The coffins of Psusennes and Harendotes were decorated with the astral figures that appear in much abbreviated outlines, almost taking the shape of snakes. On the inside of the coffin of Harendotes, there are some early images of the snake figures of the gods associated with the decan representations; see *EAT* III, pl. 16.

203 Bull, "An Ancient Egyptian Astronomical Ceiling-Decoration," p. 286

204 Kákosy, "Decans in Late-Egyptian Religion," p. 179.

205 *EAT* I, pp. 1–22

206 See example of the diagonal star clocks in *EAT* I, fig. 1, p. 1.

207 Shore, "Human and Divine Mummification," pp. 226ff; Goyon, *Rê, Maât et pharaon: ou le destin de l'Égypte antique*, p. 148.

208 Clagett (*Ancient Egyptian Science*, II, p. 57) defines "work" as the time that these decan stars are used as "transit-clock."

209 Ibid.

210 Gundel and Siegfried, *Dekane und Dekansternbilder: Ein Beitrag zur Geschichte der Sternbilder der Kulturvölker*, pp. 13–14.

with the main cities of the Egyptian nomes. According to Gundel, the inscriptions give the names of the decans, the number of stars relating to them, and the city where they receive their offerings.[211] The first decans are associated with Letopolis, Buto, and This.[212] These cities showed great dedication to the worship of Osiris and played a part in the mystery of gathering up the different parts of the body of Osiris.[213] References to these cities are found in the Osiris chapels on the roof of Dendera,[214] as well as in the roof chapel H2 of Hibis.

The first instance of the decanal gods in the form of snake- or lion-headed deities inside the tomb of Osorkon II at Tanis has special relevance. The inscription on one of the two bracelets of Prince Hornakht reads: "Words spoken by the gods and goddesses of the heaven, the earth and the underworld: what we are making is protection over you. Their arrows are defending your body in life and rule. The mother of god will be a shield behind you, if you get among the antelopes and wild fowls…."[215] The first phrase points to the three levels of the protection of heaven, earth, and the underworld, similar to the emphasis of the inscription in the doorway to E in Hibis. The second part of the bracelet inscription refers to the preceding rituals of the protection of the body of the deceased. As Osiris, his body is protected by the "mother of god," either referring to Isis or Nut, who will shield his body from the dangers connected with this stage. The word *sšrw*, "arrows," may refer to the important rituals of the protection of the body in the embalming chamber against enemies at each of the four cardinal points. This last part of the inscription is clearly reflected in the H complex of Hibis via the rituals of "throwing the four balls," as discussed earlier. On the naos of Saft el Henna, "the naos of the decades," dating to the time of Nectanebo I, the decans are similarly associated with the three domains of "heaven, earth, and underworld."[216]

An important document pertaining to the ritual of embalming provides further evidence for the role played by these astral figures in Hibis between chapel complexes E and H of the roof. The text reads:

> Your journey to the heaven will not be opposed. You assume your form of a divine falcon, you climb into the heaven as an august scarab…the amulets of the gods of

211 Gundel and Siegfried, *Dekane und Dekansternbilder: Ein Beitrag zur Geschichte der Sternbilder der Kulturvölker*, p. 14

212 Gundel and Siegfried, *Dekane und Dekansternbilder: Ein Beitrag zur Geschichte der Sternbilder der Kulturvölker*, p. 14.

213 Beinlich, *Die "Osirisreliquien." Zum Motiv der Körperzergliederung in der altägyptischen Religion*, pp. 314–315, 320–321.

214 Cauville, *Le temple de Dendara: les chapelles, osiriennes [2] Commentaire*, pp. 369, 380, 383–384.

215 Translation after Kákosy, "Decans in Late-Egyptian Religion," pp. 164–165, fig. 1; Montet, *Les constructions et le tombeau d'Osorkon II à Tanis*, p. 68, fig. 22.

216 This naos is currently preserved in two locations: in the Greco-Roman Museum at Alexandria and at the Louvre Museum; Habachi and Habachi, "The Naos with the Decades (Louvre D 37)," pp. 251–263. Leitz published some parts of the naos for the first time in Leitz, *Altägyptische Sternuhren*. See also Bomhard, *The Naos of the Decades*, p. 54.

> Upper and Lower Egypt are entering you. You are going with them as an excellent Ba. You will do in the heaven whatever you wish, being together with the stars. Your Ba belongs to the 36 stars....[217]

The text explains the process of inserting the amulets of the decans inside the bandages of the mummy and their symbolic significance. They will facilitate the advancement of the rising, when the Ba of Osiris will join the Ba of the sun god and enable him to rule the world. Later the text instructs: "Make 36 knots of it, and put it to his left hand, because there are 36 gods with whom his Ba goes to the heaven. There are 36 nomes in which the rituals are performed to Osiris according to the former (usage) of the nomes."[218]

Although I disagree with Cruz-Uribe in identifying the first figure on the south wall as Sakhmet, understanding the last female figure in the last register on the south wall as Sakhmet is a logical conclusion.[219] This goddess was closely associated with such lists. She is followed by a figure who is most probably Re Horakhty, seated on a low-backed throne.[220] On the astronomical ceiling of the Ramesseum, the stars of the southern sky declare that Re Horakhty will allow the rise of the Sothis star in the heaven at the dawn of New Year's Day, so that she and the other decades will give the king millions of years, Sed festivals, and long lifetime.[221] In the Late Period, amulets with the decans, usually associated with statues or statuettes of the leonine goddesses Sakhmet and Bastet, evoke the protection of the decan deities during every day of the year but especially during New Year's Day.[222] In the Walters Art Museum, an amulet on the throne of a Bastet is decorated with the decanal figures, and the inscriptions mention the protection of the New Year.[223] However, it seems that such decan lists were not only associated with the protection of the New Year but also had a more general purpose with regard to the resurrection and rebirth of Osiris and the sun god, especially when they are represented as part of the temple decoration.

The analysis of the other unidentified figures on the south wall is interesting. As noted before, at least six figures do not belong to the decan lists or the list of the Epacts. In the first register, the last figure of Ptah can be identified as Qd decan 28, but that conclusion is based on meager evidence.[224] The following register depicts a more likely

217 Kákosy, "Decans in Late-Egyptian Religion," p. 183; Sauneron, *Rituel de l'Embaumement*, pp. 28ff (8, 11–13)

218 Translation after Kákosy, "Decans in Late-Egyptian Religion," p. 183; Sauneron, *Rituel de l'Embaumement*, pp. 24ff; Töpfer, *Das Balsamierungsritual: Eine (Neu-)Edition der Textkomposition Balsamierungsritual*, pp. 163, 184, 282, 356.

219 Cruz-Uribe, *Hibis Temple Project I*, pp. 189–190.

220 Especially since his name is mentioned on the west wall without his image.

221 Kákosy, "Decans in Late-Egyptian Religion," p. 187; *EAT* III, pls. 4–5.

222 Bryan, "The Statue Program for the Mortuary Temple of Amenhotep III," pp. 60ff; Yoyoytte, "Une monumentale litanie de granit: les Sekhmet d'Aménophis III et la conjuration permanente de la déesse dangereuse," pp. 63–64.

223 Steindorff, *Catalogue of the Egyptian Sculpture in the Walters Art Gallery*, pl. xcii; Kákosy, "Decans in Late-Egyptian Religion," pp. 166–167.

224 The identification of Ptah and decan 28 is attested only once; *EAT* III, p. 146.

figure for this decan; moreover, the inscription above his head clearly names him "Ptah, father of the gods," thus giving him a different status from the rest of the surrounding figures. The second register has a figure of a coiled snake with an erect head. He lies on top of a pedestal with a shrine façade. He is identified, in other instances, as a star in the southern constellation Leo.[225] If this last hypothesis is true, then it is conceivable to view the other figures as other constellations or planets.[226] The following unidentified figure at the end of the third register confirms this idea. It takes the form of a human deity assimilated to Osiris and wearing the white crown of Upper Egypt. He holds the *was* scepter and the *ankh* sign and is identified with the southern constellation Orion.[227] Orion's heliacal rising occurred a few weeks before the appearance of Sirius and the Nile flood,[228] and that is probably why their association is equated with the close relationship between Isis and Osiris.

The order of the figures in the Hibis astronomical list suggests a close spatial relationship between the selected decans and constellations such as Leo and Orion. Orion is also associated with Taurus and Gemini, as they are among the prominent constellations of winter.[229] More significantly, in the Zodiacs of Esna, Orion occurs properly between Taurus and Gemini.[230] Could the preceding and the following unidentified figures of Orion be identified with Taurus and Gemini, respectively? The last figure on the fourth register is shown as a four-headed snake with his tail behind him. It is not clear whether the heads depicted are human or animal. The duality aspect is certainly implied by the quadracephalic head of the god. The first unidentified figure of Ptah offers a more likely relationship to Taurus. In general, Ptah is particularly associated with the bull. The relationship between the bull and Taurus was established early in the history of Babylonia.[231] In the Temple of Opet at Karnak, Ptah appears among many astronomical figures as the ithyphallic Min with the legend that identifies him with the bull: "the bull who raises his arm, who engenders the gods, Ptahtatenen, in the southern district."[232] In the Late Period especially, Apis bull worship was centered at Memphis where the priesthood of Ptah was responsible for the burial of the Apis bull.[233] The domain where the Apis lived,

225 Cruz-Uribe, *Hibis Temple Project I*, p. 187; Kákosy, "The Astral Snakes of the Nile," pp. 255–260, no. 25; *EAT* III, p. 202, n. Aa and pl. 42.

226 The only star that is identified with great certainty is Sothis, but scholars have made associations between other Egyptian constellations and actual stars, groups of stars, or planets like Orion, Leo, and Venus; Wells, "Astronomy," pp. 145–151.

227 Cruz-Uribe, *Hibis Temple Project I*, p. 188, Cruz-Uribe further mentions that in the Edfu A list the three figures *Wʿrt*, *Ṯpy-ʿ-spdt*, and Orion occur in the same order as in Hibis; *EAT* III, p. 201, n. P.

228 Krupp, *Echoes of the Ancient Skies*, p. 22.

229 Krupp, *Echoes of the Ancient Skies*, p. 9; Gallant, *The Constellations, How They Came to Be*, pp. 117ff.

230 Clagett, *Ancient Egyptian Science*, II, p. 479.

231 Jensen, *Die Kosmologie der Babylonier*, pp. 62–64. For the twin constellation with Gemini, see ibid, pp. 64–65. See also Hunger, *Astral Sciences in Mesopotamia*, pp. 271, 276.

232 *Opet* I, p. 154; II, pl. 8; III, p. 86.

233 Vercoutter, "The Napatan Kings and Apis Worship," pp. 62–76.

died, and was embalmed lies within the Temple of Ptah.[234] The Apis bull may even be identified with Ptah himself in the form of Ptah-Hephaestus.[235]

If this association of Taurus and Gemini is valid, then the list can be considered the earliest evidence for their attestation in Egypt, predating their confirmed appearance in the round Zodiac of Dendera by about five centuries.[236] It is widely accepted that the style of Egyptian astronomy in the Greco-Roman temples was influenced by the Hellenistic culture that in turn adapted the long tradition of Babylonia. However, astronomical knowledge from Babylonia to Greece might have been transported late in the 6th century BCE, when both Babylonians and Asiatic Greeks were under Persian control.[237] Certainly some of this knowledge must have traveled to Egypt as well, especially during the Persian time when omens in the Babylonian style were also introduced to Egypt.[238] Standing at the fringes of this list, these figures might express how the Hibis theologians incorporated such new ideas about the cosmos into their traditional astronomical setting.

Beside the suggested association with Gemini, the four-headed deity could also be related to other theologies. It could have been an influence of the Theban theology of the four Mins and four Montus who are an aspect of the cosmic and fertility god Amun-Min.[239] The four-headed creatures find a good analogy in the depiction of the gods of the winds. For example, on obelisk fragment BM EA 1512, the god of the North Wind is depicted as a ram with four heads and two wings.[240] In that context, he is connected with raising one of the four Bas of the sun-god to the sky to be united with the stars.[241] Within the astronomical representations, a two-human-headed god appears as the planet Venus.[242]

In the Osiris chapels of Dendera are many depictions of creatures with multiple heads. A four-ram-headed god appears among the "Génies de Pharbaïtos," and he is called *Ḥtyt mrt Mꜣꜥt*.[243] A four-falcon-headed god with a *udjat* eye on top of the four heads is seated

234 Dimick, "The Embalming House of the Apis Bulls," pp. 183–189.

235 Griffiths, "Lycophron on Io and Isis," pp. 472–477.

236 For the Zodiac of Esna and Dendera, see Cauville, *Le zodiaque d'Osiris*; Aubourg, "La date de Conception du Zodiaque du temple d'Hathor à Dendera," pp. 1–10; Cauville and Aubourg, "En ce matin du 28 décembre 47...." pp. 767–772.

237 Huxley, *The Interaction of Greek and Babylonian Astronomy*, p. 4.

238 Parker, *A Vienna Demotic Papyrus on Eclipse- and Lunar-Omina*; Hunger, *Astral Sciences in Mesopotamia*, p. 31.

239 Quaegebeur, "Les quatre dieux Min," pp. 253–268.

240 Woodhouse, "The Sun God, his Four Bas and the Four Winds in the Sacred District at Sais: The Fragment of an Obelisk (BM EA 1512)," pp. 137ff. For the iconography of the wind gods, see Gutbub, "Über die vier Winde in Ägypten," pp. 328–353.

241 Woodhouse, "The Sun God, his Four Bas and the Four Winds in the Sacred District at Sais: The Fragment of an Obelisk (BM EA 1512)," p. 140.

242 Brugsch, "Astronomische und astrologische Inschriften altaegyptischer Denkmaeler," table on page 68; Cauville, *Le zodiaque d'Osiris*, p. 30.

243 In chapel E2 of the Osiris chapels on the roof of Dendera; Cauville, *Le temple de Dendara: les chapelles, osiriennes [2] Commentaire*, p. 60; Cauville, *Le temple de Dendara. Vol. X/2 Les Chapelles osiriennes (Plates)*, X45; Cauville, *Le temple de Dendara: les chapelles, osiriennes [1] Transcription et traduction*, p. 59.

on a socle and identified as "Re Horakhty who takes place in Heliopolis of numerous appearance and different forms."[244] A three-serpent-headed goddess on one of the mounds is a protectress entity for Osiris.[245] Khnum also appears as a four-ram-headed god.[246] Beside these examples from the later Ptolemaic Period, earlier examples also associate the multiple-headed deities with both the sun god and Osiris. A four-ram-headed sun god in the tomb of Ramesses IX[247] is described as being Osirian.[248] This god is in front of Meret Segert, the goddess of the necropolis. The inscription reads: *Mry ꞽImn Rꜥ ḥrw ꜣḫt bꜣ šf(y)t ḥry-ib ꜣḫt*, "beloved of Amun Re Horakhty respected Ba, who dwells in the horizon." It includes this interesting statement: *bꜣ imntt ḥrw iꜣbtt*, "Ba of the West, Horus of the East."[249] The Ba of the West may refer to the Ba of the god of the west, that is, Osiris and at the same time Re, since the Ba of Osiris is Re.[250] The second phrase, "Horus of the East," may refer to the rule of Horus as the royal inheritor of the power of the combined deities. The scene is repeated in the tomb of Ramesses XI as well.[251]

The specific iconography of the decan gods as lions or lioness-headed figures and snakes reflects their solar symbolism as well. According to the Books of the Dead, the Amduat, and the astronomical vignettes in general, serpents represented vehicles for spatial or temporal relocations. They were usually depicted separating fields or delineating spaces and might even indicate sequence or orientation. Some snake figures in the Hibis list have their tails turned to the front, while others have their tails behind them. This perhaps indicates the orientation of the star orbit inside the celestial realm, which is constantly challenged by the adversarial Apophis snake as he tries to stop the orderly path of the sun god. The snake figures as astral representations later became very popular inside and outside Egypt.[252] Within the Hibis astronomical list may have been a hierarchy in the representations of the different gods. The gods with lion or lioness heads take precedence over the more "popular" representations of the snake deities. A higher status is reserved for the important lioness-headed seated Sothis star. The spacing between the figures varies in each register, and some figures are even separated from each other by vertical space dividers that seem to be placed with no apparent logical order. As mentioned earlier, this list is uniquely arranged and does not seem to have been slavishly

244 Cauville, *Le temple de Dendara. Vol. X/2 Les chapelles osiriennes (Plates)*, p. 201; Cauville, *Le temple de Dendara: les chapelles, osiriennes [1] Transcription et traduction*, p.199.

245 Cauville, *Le temple de Dendara. Vol. X/2 Les chapelles osiriennes (Plates)*, p. 203.

246 *Cauville, Le temple de Dendara. Vol. X/2 Les chapelles osiriennes (Plates)*, p. 202.a.

247 Hornung, *Knowledge for the Afterlife: The Egyptian Amduat – a Quest for Immortality*, fig. 41; Bács, "Amun-Re-Harakhti in the Late Ramesside Royal Tombs," fig. 1 on p. 46.

248 Bács, "Amun-Re-Harakhti in the Late Ramesside Royal Tombs," p. 47.

249 For the scene of Ramesses IX with the aforementioned four ram-headed gods in front of the goddess Meret Segert, see Bács, "Amun-Re-Harakhti in the Late Ramesside Royal Tombs," p. 51; Hornung, *Zwei Ramessidische Königsgräber: Ramses IV. und Ramses VII*, pls. 100 and 109.

250 See footnote 281, below.

251 Bács, "Amun-Re-Harakhti in the Late Ramesside Royal Tombs," fig. 3 on p. 48.

252 Egyptians influenced models appearing as far as Carthage in the east and Meroe in the south; Kákosy, "Decans in Late-Egyptian Religion," pp. 168–169; Vercoutter, *Les objets égyptiens et égyptisants du mobilier funéraire carthaginois*, pp. 317–37, figs. 30–36, pl. xxix.

copied from any of the comparable decanal families. It might have been adopted from another list that was compiled based on actual astronomical observation made at Hibis. The roof naturally provides the necessary space for such operations.

Astronomical allegorical representations are an important component of ancient Egyptian religion and mythology. Actual sightings of stars and other astronomical observations may well have taken place during important ceremonies, most naturally during ceremonies on the temple roof.[253] Many temples have been linked to an actual alignment toward the winter or summer solstice, such as the Temple of Satet at Elephantine[254] and the chapel of Re Horakhty at Abu Simbel.[255] In Dendera, the participants in the New Year ritual on top of the roof of the temple could have observed the heliacal rising of Sirius from the open kiosk on the roof.[256] Even though the Temple of Hibis does not appear to be astronomically aligned,[257] its astronomical list might have expressed astronomical sightings at the temple or at the time it was built. The ancient Egyptians likely experienced many astronomical phenomena such as conjunctions, comets, occultations, and solar and lunar eclipses; a solar eclipse may have happened about the time the Hibis Temple was built,[258] and at least two lunar eclipses were recorded during the reign of Darius I.[259]

The representations of the decan gods can also possibly refer to the feast of the decade of Amun that was associated with the rituals of the Mound of Djeme popular at Thebes and practiced until the 1st–2nd century CE.[260] The Mound of Djeme is associated with a cenotaph for primordial deities of creation and is identified with Amun as well as Osiris.[261] The visit to the Mound of Djeme incorporated the feast of the decade of Amun

253 Cf. Dieleman, "Claiming the Stars: Egyptian Priests Facing the Sky," p. 278.

254 Wells, "Sothis and the Satet Temple on Elephantine: An Egyptian "Stonehenge"?," pp. 105–115; Wells, "Sothis and the Satet Temple on Elephantine," pp. 255ff.

255 See Krupp, "Egypt. Astronomy: Temples, Traditions, Tombs," pp. 317ff.

256 Krupp, "Egypt. Astronomy: Temples, Traditions, Tombs," pp. 310; Krupp, *Echoes of the Ancient Skies*, pp. 248–258.

257 According to personal communication from Dr. Krupp, the azimuth (orientation with respect to true cardinal north) of Hibis Temple is non solstitial, that is, not aligned with either the summer or winter solstice. The Egyptian-Spanish mission on Egyptian archaeoastronomy conducted an investigation of nearly sixty temples and chapels in the oases of the Western desert in 2005 and concluded that astronomy played a major role in the orientation of such places away from the river Nile. The mission also suggested the possibility that many of these temples were aligned to either sunrise or sunset at the first day of the first month of the flood season (Akhet), that is, the New Year's Eve; Belmonte and Shalltout, "On the Orientation of Ancient Egyptian Temples. 2) New Experience at the Oases of the Western Desert," pp. 173–192, esp. table 2, pp. 182ff.

258 Parker, *A Vienna Demotic Papyrus on Eclipse- and Lunar-Omina*, p. 21 and n. 10 (Text A, col. IV, line 10).

259 Hunger, *Astral Sciences in Mesopotamia*, p. 157.

260 Herbin, "Une liturgie des rites décadaires de Djemê. Papyrus Vienne 3865," pp. 105–126.

261 Fazzini, "Some American Contributions to the Understanding of Third Intermediate and Late Period Egypt," p. 113 and n. 22; Traunecker, Le Saout and Masson, *La chapelle d'Achôris à Karnak. II. Texte [et] Documents*, esp. pp. 130–148.

that theoretically was supposed to be conducted every ten days, aimed at the renewal of his divine power as well as that of the royal figure.[262]

CHAPEL E2

On the decoration of the east wall, the only remaining wall of chapel E2, two main features are clear: the elaborate offering liturgy and the rubric of the Opening the Mouth and Eyes in the House of Gold. These features are not anomalous in themselves. Although the offering list does not belong to one of the known groups of offering lists described by Barta, it does have some parallels.[263] The Opening of the Mouth ceremony and the ritual of purification are very common episodes. They form an essential part of nearly every major ancient Egyptian religious rite; however, their immediate locations within the composition of the roof chapels, as well as general representations among the temple decorations, reveal more pertinent information.

The Opening of the Mouth is a ritual aimed primarily at reanimating the sensory potential of any corporeal object. It can be applied to human and animal bodies, statuary, and coffins.[264] The ritual is also depicted among the decoration of temples. A complete set of tools for the Opening the Mouth was part of the temple equipment.[265] Their occurrence inside temples has been interpreted as a ritual involving the animation of the two-dimensional representations of the gods and goddesses on the walls to protect the temple.[266] However, rarely do the Opening of the Mouth scenes inside temples show the Opening of the Mouth "proper" (scenes 26–27).[267] The scenes are generic and indicate the symbolic nature of the ritual as a means of resurrection. The term "House of Gold" certainly developed a deeper ritualistic purpose than simply a storeroom and was associated with the Opening of the Mouth since at least the Pyramid Texts.[268] Whether in temples or tombs, the House of Gold was associated with the place of resurrection and rebirth.[269]

---

262 Fazzini, "Some American Contributions to the Understanding of Third Intermediate and Late Period Egypt," p. 113 and n. 22; Traunecker, Le Saout and Masson, *La chapelle d'Achôris à Karnak. II. Texte [et] Documents*, pp. 130ff. See also Doresse, "Le dieu voilé dans sa châsse et la fête du début de la décade," in *RdE* 31 (1979), pp. 36–65; *RdE* 25 (1973), pp. 92–135; *RdE* 23 (1971), pp. 113–136.

263 Barta, *Die altägyptische Opferliste von der Frühzeit bis zur griechisch-römischen Epoche*, p. 151.

264 Bjerke, "Remarks on the Egyptian Ritual of 'Opening the Mouth' and its Interpretation," p. 203; Finnestad, "The Meaning and Purpose of Opening the Mouth in Mortuary Contexts," pp. 118–119.

265 Quirke, *Ancient Egyptian Religion*, p. 93 (according to inscription of the time of Amenemhat II)

266 Blackman and Fairman, "The Consecretion of an Egyptian Temple according to the Use of Edfu," pp. 75–91.

267 Bjerke, "Remarks on the Egyptian Ritual of 'Opening the Mouth' and its Interpretation," p. 206. One should add scene 37 to that "proper" corpus of the ritual.

268 Wilkinson, "Evidence for Osirian Rituals in the Tomb of Tutankhamun," pp. 329, 336–337.

269 Wilkinson, "Evidence for Osirian Rituals in the Tomb of Tutankhamun," pp. 328–329. See also Schott, "Goldhaus," col. 739.

The Opening of the Mouth usually followed the embalming ritual; therefore, in Hibis this ceremony was conveniently placed near chapel H2 where the embalming rituals occurred. The Osirian character of the ritual helps "transfer the vital powers from the god to the king."[270] The Opening of the Mouth ceremony together with the elaborate offering liturgy are important aspects of the Osiris rituals in Philae, Edfu, and Dendera.[271] The ceremony likely took place during the later phase of the Osiris rituals. Both the rising of Re/Horakhty and the declaration of the royalty and crowning of Horus follow the more intimate episodes of the Khoiak rituals of Osiris, usually taking place during the procession of the *Matin divine* after the night of the 25th or 26th day of the Khoiak.[272] Assmann emphasized the solar aspect of the Opening of the Mouth ceremony, performed in the open courts of the New Kingdom tombs, and considers it a forerunner to the *ẖnm itn* ceremony of the later periods.[273] In Hibis, the Opening of the Mouth is thus associated with the solar rising of the god as a subsequent phase of the Osiris resurrection.

In fact, it is safe to say that the sun's daily and nocturnal journeyings are symbolically spread between chapel complexes E and H, respectively. The *dwat* domain of Osiris is accentuated in the Osiris suites of chapel complex H, where he is constantly awakened and protected from the rebels. In chapel complex E, the solar aspect takes precedence. Cruz-Uribe noted that in all parallels to the hymn of Re on the west wall of E1, the texts end with the proclamation: "I have come in order to protect you (i.e., Re) throughout the times of the year."[274] It is only logical to understand that the god in this early stage is Re in his early rising as a child, when he is most vulnerable and thus needing the king's protection, and when the purification and Opening of the Mouth ceremony is most befitting.

A comparison of the textual and decorative components of the Hibis roof with the Book of Nut confirms the same symbolic imagery. Beside the similar decan representations,

270 Bjerke, "Remarks on the Egyptian Ritual of 'Opening the Mouth' and its Interpretation," p. 215.

271 For example, the "offering of the dates" in the House of Gold, as well as the different types of cakes, play an important part in the rejuvenation process of Osiris; Cauville, "Une offrande spécifique d'Osiris: le récipient de dattes (*mʿḏ3 n bnr*)," pp. 51–52, 57–59, 61; Centrone, "Corn Mummies, Amulets of Life," p. 39. See also Cauville, *Le temple de Dendara: les chapelles osiriennes [2] Commentaire*, pp. 156ff and fig. 15.

272 Cauville, *Le temple de Dendara: les chapelles osiriennes [2] Commentaire*, p. 23, where she says, "Cette transmission est, bien sûr, partie intégrante des cérémonies de khoiak où la mort du vieux roi (Sokar) prélude à la royauté du faucon (Horus/ Harsiesis), en l'absence de toute rupture ou d'un espace laissé aux forces séthiennes. Cet épisode avait lieu dans la nuit du 25 au 26, avant la grande procession du 'matin divin'." The divine morning no doubt refers to the birth and early rising of the solar god that is also closely associated with the crowning of the pharaoh. See also Goyon, "La fête de Sokaris à Edfou à la lumière d'un texte liturgique remontant au Nouvel Empire," pp. 426–427.

273 Assmann, "The Ramesside Tomb of Nebsumenu (TT 183) and the Ritual of Opening the Mouth," pp. 53–60; Assmann, *Ägypten. Theologie und Frömmigkeit einer frühen Hochkultur*, p. 55; Asmann, "Neith spricht als Mutter und Sarg (Interpretation und metrische Analyse der Sargdeckelinschrift des Merenptah)," pp. 126f; Assmann, *Das Grab des Amenemope TT 41*, p. 7, n. 3.

274 Cruz-Uribe, *Hibis Temple Project I*, pp. 190–191.

celestial terms such as the *dwat* and *msqt,* and the mention of the embalming process, it also emphasized the eventual rising of Re upward from the *dwat*, and finally the association of the sun rays with humankind. The Book of Nut comes from three main sources: the west half of the roof of the sarcophagus chamber of the Osireion at Abydos,[275] the south half of the ceiling of Hall E of the tomb of Ramesses IV,[276] and Papyrus Carlsberg I.[277] The studies of the first two earlier sources are usually viewed through the analysis of the later Papyrus Carlsberg I, since the latter represents a model copy or an "archetype" enriched by the comments of the scribe.[278] This book begins with the text on the origin and the rising of the sun, when "Re goes forth as a child of increasing strength" and "the sun rises upward from the *dwat*."[279] Then the text describes the moment of this exit from the *dwat*, the realm of Osiris, when his father Osiris pushes him to make him rise from the Nun. The inscription states (Text D, 43–44):

> [he (Re) is purified in the] arms of his father, Osiris. He is purified by the hand of his father, Osiris-that is to say, he is accustomed to do it. It is the water from which he rises. [he lives], he is glorious, when ‹ his father › has put himself under him. He lives, he is beautiful in his rising from it- that is to say, the water.[280]

So the hands of Osiris here are assimilated to the Nun.[281] Then the *msqt* region is mentioned, also within the context of this important meeting point between Osiris and Re. The three sources of the Book of Nut point to the location of *msqt* as a place directly related to the exit from the *dwat*: "it is from the *dwat* that the majesty of this god goes forth and in the *msqt* region that these stars go forth with him. He is reared and revived in the *msqt* region. It is the door of the *dwat*."[282] The following line repeats that "He (the sun god/Re) was glorious in the arms of his father, Osiris, in *tꜣ wr*—he was beautiful in the hand of his father Osiris, in the underworld—that is to say, it was in the underworld

---

275 Frankfort, *The Cenotaph of Seti I at Abydos*, I, pp. 72–86, and II, pls. LXXXI–LXXXV; *EAT* I, pp. 30–33, 44–54

276 Champollion, *Monuments de l'Égypte et de la Nubie*, III, pls. CCLXXV, CCLXXVI; Daressy, "Une ancienne liste des decans," pp. 84–87; *EAT* I, pp. 34–35, 44–51.

277 Neugebauer, *Papyrus Carlsberg no. I: Ein hieratisch-demotischer-kosmologischer Text*; *EAT* I, pp. 36–42; Barta, "Zum Buch von der Himmelsgöttin Nut im Papyrus Carlsberg I," pp. 7–12; Quack, "Kollation und Korrekturvorschläge zum Papyrus Carlsberg 1," pp. 165–171; Von Lieven, *Grundriss des Laufes der Sterne.*

278 *EAT* I, p. 38.

279 *EAT* I, pp. 43–47, pl 44; Von Lieven, *Grundriss des Laufes der Sterne*, pp. 49–50, 53.

280 *EAT* I, pp. 47–49, pls. 44–45; Von Lieven, *Grundriss des Laufes der Sterne*, p. 55.

281 In the Coffin texts *CT* IV, 62 b–c, Re is described as "the Ba that came forth from Nun." *CT* IV 63 says "the Ba 'which Nun created'." One may thus understand that at the time of rising, Osiris creates the Ba of Re and at the time of the setting, Re creates the Ba of Osiris. In the Louvre stela C 286, lines 2 and 9, Osiris inherits the throne of Geb and Re and becomes "Ba of Re, his own body;" Moret, "La légende d'Osiris à l'époque thébaine d'après l'hymne à Osiris du Louvre," pp. 729, 737.

282 *EAT* I, p. 50; Von Lieven, *Grundriss des Laufes der Sterne*, pp. 55ff.

that he was. That is the water from which Re rises."[283] The use of *msqt* in this specific context is similar to that of *msqt* mentioned on the doorway to chapel complex E in that it refers to an intermediate region where the sun and the stars pass through from the *dwat* into daylight between the domains of Osiris and the sun god. The following text puts forward the goal of this withdrawal (Papyrus Carlsberg I [text J, line 9—Text K, line 19]): "the order comes that he withdraws toward mankind…He sees Geb. His sight is at the earth, when the rising which he makes is complete. His sight is at his rays on the earth."[284] This perhaps refers to the concluding parts of the ritual when the aim was the ultimate protection of the king and his subjects by the text on the doorway to E, "your rays reach the faces." Parker noted that the sun here plays the role of Horus or Horakhty, the son of Osiris.[285] These texts subsequently mention the mysteries of Osiris, the decans, and the 70 days of the revivication of Osiris.[286]

Other liturgical works give a similar purpose and content to the decorative and textual components of the Hibis roof. Both the important corpus of liturgy called the *s3ḫw* as well as the later Demotic version of the Opening the Mouth for Breathing share many characteristics.[287] These characteristics are featured similarly in the decorations of the roof of Hibis. In Papyrus Berlin, whose title is *wpy.t-r3 n snsn*, "Opening the Mouth for Breathing," the rite appears in close connection with the solar and Osirian cycles. This is manifested by the existence of both the morning and evening barques of the sun god and the *hnw* barque of Osiris.[288] According to Mark Smith, the papyrus has a tripartite theme. First is the reawakening of the deceased by "his beloved son," and the reanimation of his limbs involves singing by Isis and Nephthys so as to enable the deceased to "rise up from the underworld and travel to the earth daily," as well as the mummification by Anubis. Second is the presentation of offerings of food and clothing and, finally, the integration of the individual into the cosmos, acceptance by the gods and blessed spirits, and the "journeyings throughout the sky, earth and underworld."[289]

It is noticeable that the mortuary liturgy is used significantly inside the Temple of Hibis. Thus, the temple could potentially provide more precise meanings for how these funerary liturgies have been interpreted and understood within the temple theology. The depiction of the Opening of the Mouth ritual on the roof of Hibis, the version of chapter 15 of the Book of the Dead in hypostyle hall M, and the use of a feminine pronoun in chapter 146w of the Book of the Dead on the staircase to chapel K1 were understood as indications of direct relation to the corpus of the New Kingdom funerary rites.[290] Despite the apparent distinction between the decoration programs of tombs and temples, some-

283 *EAT* I, p. 50; Von Lieven, *Grundriss des Laufes der Sterne*, p. 55.

284 *EAT* I, pp. 50–51; Von Lieven, *Grundriss des Laufes der Sterne*, pp. 56–57.

285 *EAT* I, p. 49, n. 43.

286 *EAT* I, pp. 80ff, as well as 42 and 73; Von Lieven, *Grundriss des Laufes der Sterne*, pp. 70ff.

287 Smith, *The Liturgy of Opening the Mouth for Breathing*, pp. 6–7.

288 Smith, *The Liturgy of Opening the Mouth for Breathing*, p. 16, n. 96–97 (P. Berlin 8351 II, 13 and 19 [episode 59C], III, 20, IV, 4, V, 4, 6 [episode 73]).

289 Smith, *The Liturgy of Opening the Mouth for Breathing*, pp. 7–8.

290 Cruz-Uribe, "Opening of the Mouth as Temple Ritual," pp. 63–73.

times the influence of one is seen in the other, especially in the Late Period.[291] Evidence for the use of temple liturgies of Osiris particularly in tombs comes from different periods in Egyptian history[292] and continued until Ptolemaic times.[293] This is reasonable because the tomb was regarded as a temple of Osiris.[294] In the meantime, any temple of Osiris was also considered a tomb.[295] It is not surprising to see the embalming ritual and the Opening of the Mouth ritual as the two most important sepulchral activities depicted at the temple.

Although the corpus of funerary books seems to have been commonly used in Late Period temple rituals,[296] the funerary rites in temples did not quite have the same function as in tombs. Even if slavishly copied from tomb sources, their status at once changed from protection and the return of life of one or more persons to statewide protection. They help emphasize the theology of the space within which they are placed. While the scenes of chapel E1 on the west wall and the pilasters can be seen as episodes of the Opening of the Mouth ceremony,[297] the meaning and purpose of this ritual inside the temple varied from the meaning and purpose of the funerary rite of the same name inside the tomb. In Hibis, these funerary rites help the eternal activation of the resurrection of the cosmos. On a number of representations the temple was viewed as a place of resurrection and "earthly reproductions of the kingdom beyond."[298]

Chapels E1 and E2 in Hibis seem to reflect that the second half of the Osirian rituals revolved around his association with "rising" and the solar god. Perhaps such rituals should be referred to as "the Osiris-Solar" ceremony. The concluding "second phase" of the ceremony took place inside chapels E1 and E2; it concerned the unification of the sun god with Osiris and the confirmation of the king's power so as to guarantee prosperity for all Egypt. Toward the end of the ceremony of Khoiak in the Middle Kingdom and the Sokar version of the New Kingdom, the rituals involved aspects of "rising" via

291 For mortuary texts inside temples, see Kákosy, "Temples and Funerary Beliefs in the Graeco-Roman Epoch," pp. 117–127; also Cruz-Uribe, "Opening of the Mouth as Temple Ritual," pp. 63–73.

292 Burkard, *Spätzeitliche Osiris-Liturgien im Corpus der Asasif-Papyri. Übersetzung, Kommentar, formale und inhaltliche Analyse.*

293 Assmann, "Egyptian mortuary liturgies," pp. 1–45.

294 Finnestad, "The Meaning and Purpose of Opening the Mouth in Mortuary Contexts," p. 128.

295 Plutarch recounts that, according to the priests he consulted, the bodies of Osiris and Apis were buried inside temples; Griffiths, *Plutarch's De Iside et Osiride*, p. 21.

296 Manassa, *The Late Egyptian Underworld: Sarcophagi and Related Texts from the Nectanebid Period*, I, pp. 468–475.

297 According to Otto, *Das ägyptische Mundöffnungsritual*, p. 161, the censing and the presenting of the offering table along with the hymn to Re-Horakhty belongs to episode 71. See also Cruz-Uribe, "Opening of the Mouth as Temple Ritual," pp. 70ff., who also equates the purification scenes to episodes 2 and 3 (Otto, *Das ägyptische Mundöffnungsritual*, pp. 37–44.) However, one hesitates to agree with him in attributing the decan representations on the north and south walls to scene 59D where there is no mention of any astronomical association but rather a very general invocation of gods to protect the deceased. (Otto, *Das ägyptische Mundöffnungsritual*, p. 137).

298 Kákosy, "Temples and Funerary Beliefs in the Graeco-Roman Epoch," pp. 127.

the accession toward the heaven in the Henu-barque, where Osiris or Sokar would rule alongside Re Horakhty. At a cultic level, this was translated by the offering of onions, for example during the 26th day of Khoiak, to enable the joining of Osiris and the sun god and his resurrection.[299] In Hibis this was similarly manifested through the elaborate offering liturgy, the decanal representations, and the Opening of the Mouth ceremony as vehicles for this transformation.

299 Graindorge, "Les oignons de Sokar," pp. 87–105. See also Goyon, "La fête de Sokaris à Edfou à la lumière d'un texte liturgique remontant au Nouvel Empire," pp. 415–438, for the ceremonies of the early morning of the Sokar procession during the episodes of the 26th of the Khoiak.

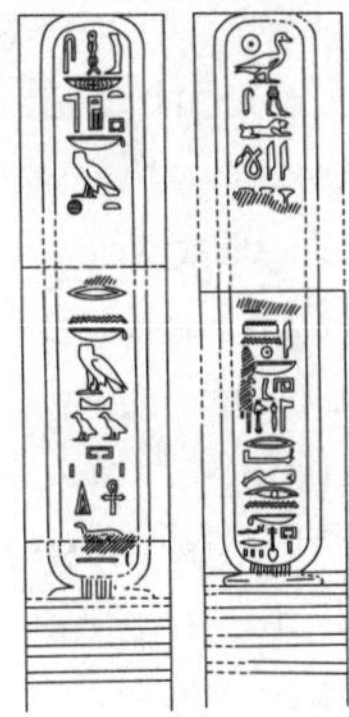

6
Conclusion

In essence, the chapels analyzed in this study functioned as secondary sanctuaries that were usually reserved as guest houses or residence halls for the *theoi synnaoi* or secondary deities who inhabited the temple together with the main lord, Amun of Hibis. While a single wall of the theological handbook of the sanctuary might express more than a hundred divinities and a dozen regional theologies, the images of these chapels illustrate a "zoom-in" of a few vignettes from the main sanctuary and explore them in further details. Conceptually, the secondary rooms of Hibis serve as a complementary appendix to the main sanctuary.

Yet each cultic room formed a coherent self-contained unit. The wall decoration of the studied chapels proved to be informative formulae; their scenes were carefully organized into one or more registers that, in turn, described certain rituals. Frequently, the ritual belonged to a specific regional liturgy. Whether stated or omitted in the hieroglyphic texts, references to a specific focus can be defined through the different attributes, iconographic details, rituals, or ceremonies. Some chapels contain what have been generally called "offering scenes," where no one suspected any deeper meaning. Cruz-Uribe stated that besides chapel L of the divine kingship, "no other room has this synthesis. The others contain disparate scenes, mainly offerings to a variety of deities...unlike Ptolemaic temples, none of these scenes appear to have any connection with scenes nearby[1] ... [Also there is a] lack of any effort to represent any 'myth' in the temple. No attempts are made to tell any religious saga."[2] However, through the analysis of the many levels of connection between the represented figures with their epithets, iconography, and cultic relationship on the different chapel walls, these seemingly disparate scenes exhibit meaningfully related episodes. Analyzing the scenes in each of these rooms provides continuous evidence for this theory.

The decoration of chapels G and F and the other chapels surrounding the sanctuary focus on a few theological topographies where the decorators incorporated their main deities, local manifestations, religious concepts, ceremonies, or rituals. This reflects similar theological principles that existed inside the sanctuary.[3] In chapel F, the religious doctrines of Memphis and Heliopolis and the solar theology are prominently displayed.

1 Cruz-Uribe, "The Hibis Temple Project. 1984–1985 Field Season, Preliminary Report," p. 166.
2 Cruz-Uribe, "The Hibis Temple Project. 1984–1985 Field Season, Preliminary Report," p. 165.
3 Sternberg-El-Hotabi, "Die 'Götterliste' des Sanktuars im Hibis-Tempel von El-Chargeh," pp. 240ff.

The east wall illustrates important aspects of the Memphite theology. The south wall incorporates Heliopolitan ideas and concepts, while the west wall is a summary of both the Memphite and Heliopolitan regional theological topographies. References to these regions are mentioned on the north wall of the main sanctuary, on registers IV, V, and VI.[4]

The decoration on the south and east walls of chapel F alludes to what happened in Memphis and Heliopolis during the royal coronation ceremony. The doctrines of these two regions seem to have had major roles in the local cult topography of the southern oasis in general. Kaper revealed the importance of these two theologies in the Dakhla Oasis and suggested that the establishment of the cult there may reach back as far as the Ramesside Period.[5] The coronation of the king and the writing of his name in Heliopolis are represented on the south wall of chapel F, atop other scenes confirming his legitimation to the throne, such as the receiving of the scimitar from Montu. On the east wall, the king is conducted into the presence of Ptah who accepts and praises the king's monument. Several elements indicate a Memphite location to this ritual; among them are the titles of Ptah and Hathor and the connection to the paired deities Hw and Sia and Iry and Sedjem, represented on the bottom register.

Also a part of the king's legitimating efforts is the idea of the "temple conception" gleaned from the east wall of chapel F and reinforced by the relationship with the other walls. Erecting, equipping, and renewing monuments went far beyond the king's mere religious obligation. Temple construction was an important and vital task of every king to guarantee his acceptance in both the divine and mortal worlds. This must have been especially important for foreign kings to legitimate their rule and guarantee its stability. In the Persian Period, the inscriptions of the naophorous statue of Udjahorresnet refer to the restoration of the Temple of Neith at Sais by the Persian kings.[6]

Finally, the west wall represents two of the main deities in Hibis Temple: Amun Re and Osiris, or one of the latter's hypostases, Heryshef. As the apparent custom in the temple's hierarchical arrangement dictated, Amun takes the upper register while Osiris takes the lower one. Each god is followed by one or two of their immediate companions. In the first register, Amun Re is followed by Mut and Khonsu; in the second register, Osiris is followed by Hathor of Heracleopolis. Each register is terminated by one or two gods relating to the main theological regions in this chapel: Sakhmet of Memphis is represented at the end of the first register, Nebet Hetepet and Iusaas of Heliopolis are represented at the end of the second register.

The wide range of deities represented inside the Temple of Hibis may indicate that it was intended to be a national temple, comparable with the Temple of Karnak. The Theban influence on the Temple of Hibis is evident from the gods worshipped there. The triad of Thebes is prominently displayed throughout Hibis Temple, indicating the continuation

4 Davies, *The Temple of Hibis*, Part 3, pl. 3; Cruz-Uribe, *Hibis Temple Project I*, Table 2.

5 Kaper, "A Painting of the Gods of Dakhla in the Temple of Ismant el-Kharab," pp. 213–214. In a recent article, Cauville discusses the importance of Thebes, Heliopolis, and Memphis in the decoration of major temples; Cauville, "Les trois capitales – Osiris – le roi," pp. 1–42.

6 Posener, *La première domination Perse en Égypte*, pp. 1–26; Baines, "On the Composition and Inscriptions of the Vatican Statue of Udjahorresne," pp. 83–92; Harari, "Fondation des temples," pp. 44–47.

of the theological and political relationship between the Kharga Oasis and the Theban region during that time period and encouraging statements describing the temple as "a Saite–Persian period Theban temple transplanted to the oasis."[7] However, the temple has its own distinctive character that is apparent from the unique choices of the decorators, especially regarding the selection of deities related to its geographical location.

On observing the gods in chapel G, one sees that many of the deities on both the east and west walls are rarely attested in other temples—for example, Iaqs, Merymutef, Isdes, Shesmu, and Hedjhotep. In fact, some deities are pictorially represented starting only from Hibis. Not only were the representations of such gods uncommon, but also some of their titles were not attested outside the parameter of this chapel. Despite the paucity of information about these gods in the scholarly literature and their rare attestation, it is possible to thoroughly analyze the forms, texts, and the intermingled theology among them. Each deity has a few traceable associations with specific locations or general attributions that enabled tracing the reasons behind their grouping. Each god functioned primarily as a protective entity and was associated with a specific place related to the roads of the western desert. Investigating the scenes of chapel G helps explain the symbolic use of the chapel as a place for celebrating the mountainous regions and the divinities of the wild.

The listing of this group of deities is based on more than just theological associations. The king is dedicating offerings to the divine lords of the territorial towns that were set at the foot of the cliffs at the eastern edge of the western desert. Here is found detailed mention of the cities en route to the oasis from the Nile River, perhabs delineated as stopping points of Amun's itinerary (or his *pẖr*). On the west wall, Ha was not only the god of the desert and wasteland but also resided at the Oxyrhynchite nome which dominates the western road to Bahariya Oasis that extends southward toward Farafra Oasis, Dakhla Oasis, and finally ends at the Kharga Oasis. Iaqs, who appears on the second register of the west wall, was known as the god of the mouth of the Nile and was titled "Lord of Thinis." Thinis, which was once the capital of the nome under which the Kharga Oasis was attached, is probably modern Girga or el Birba; it governed the shortest road to Kharga from the Valley of the Nile.

On the east wall, one reads Geb's unique title of *nb šmꜣyw*, or "Geb of the Place of Wilderness," beside depictions of Merymutef, who was known as the "Lord of Khayet," which is located in modern Manqabad found at the head of the northernmost direct road to the Kharga Oasis. On the south wall the text mentions a direct road to Kharga, using the specific term *m ḫnt wꜣst*, repeated as *ḫnty wꜣst*, "in front of/south of Thebes," thus stressing that the traveling began by going south or opposite of Thebes. This is in fact how the known southern road to Kharga from the Valley of the Nile begins. Slightly south of Thebes, a road known as Esna-El-Rezeigat diverts westward to the northern end of Darb el Arbaeen, south of the Hibis Temple (see pls. 19 and 20).

This network of places may be an itinerary of the god's *pẖr*, "circuit," to the *ḏw*, "mountains" or "oasis," which warranted the protection of the different gods who had power over the arid and desert areas. The Temple of Douch, about 80 km south of Hibis, was

7 Cruz-Uribe, "Opening of the Mouth as Temple Ritual," p. 69.

dedicated to Osiris Ipwy (*Osiris-Welcome!*) and Isis of Kouch (i.e., Douch).[8] And just like the temple of Douch, the Temple of Hibis might have functioned as a protective cult center for desert travelers.[9] Besides protecting desert travelers, Osiris was associated with religious rituals performed in desert locations,[10] such as the celebration of "Spending the Day," which is also connected with the desert locales from at least the Middle Kingdom onwards.[11]

Because this chapel indicates a trip into the wild, the ancient Egyptians sought the help of national gods famous for their powerful protective roles in the arid areas, notably, Geb, Nut, Shu, Tefnut, and Sakhmet, who played important roles in the local theology of the visited domains. The Egyptians requested their blessings in scenes depicting specific offerings known for their calming attributes and appeasing nature: milk, wine, linen, and the *wensheb* symbol. The decoration of chapel G is a miniature representation of the ancient Egyptian view of the desert geography and arid areas, which is in turn a copy of their two-faceted view of every part of the cosmos—both beneficial and frightening. These roads represented the gates to the western oasis, the dangerous places, where the ancient Egyptians obtained wealth and riches but sometimes encountered harshness and mischief. The products of the desert included gold, gemstones, and different types of building stones that certainly adorned the structures and artifacts of the temples. The west and east reveals to chapel G clearly refer to the making of the temple and its adornment by King Darius after going to the mountains or perhaps, more specifically, to the oasis.[12] The harsh desert climate and its unpredictable nature still represented an obstacle to the river-faring Egyptians. They used the three-hills of *Khaset* sign interchangeably to refer to the desert and foreign lands. This must have easily directed them toward contouring different theologies for the desert and arid regions, attaching different forms to their deities, paying homage to their gods, respecting their rituals, and presenting offerings to appease them. It is worth mentioning, though, that a similar chapel with such a grouping of deities does not exist elsewhere, at least not to this writer's knowledge; however, it is intriguing to find that most of the gods of chapel G, notably those of the places of the wild, appear together in other similar environmental terrains—Sinai, Nubia, and the eastern desert. The deities of such environments are represented likewise inside the

8 Vernus, "Douch arraché aux sables," pp. 7–10, 12, fig. 1. See also Leclant, "Isis au pays de Koush," pp. 37–59.

9 Valloggia, "Les Routes du Désert dans l'Egypte Ancienne," p. 168, n. 21–22. In note 23, the author takes notes of similar cult centers that were "reserved" for the protection of travelers, like the sanctuaries of Min at Coptos, governing the road to Wadi Hammamat, that of Sopdu at Saft el Henna, en route to Wadi Toumilat, and Seth at Oxyrhynchos, on the way to Bahariya Oasis.

10 Darnell et al., *Theban Desert Road Survey in the Egyptian Western Desert*, pp. 132–133; Darnell, "The Deserts," p. 48.

11 Darnell et al., *Theban Desert Road Survey in the Egyptian Western Desert*, pp. 129–138; Darnell, "The Deserts," p. 46. For another important ritual connected with the visitation of desert locations, see Verhoeven and Derchain, *Le voyage de la déesse libyque: Ein Text aus dem 'Mutritual' des Pap. Berlin 3053*, pp. 69–76.

12 See p. 71, footnote 26.

main sanctuary of the temple of Hibis. For example, they appear on the west wall, second register, figure 4; north wall, third register, figure 15; and among the figures at the end of the south wall, first register.[13]

The decoration of nearby chapel J exhibits similar features to the decoration of chapels F and G, especially in its single focus on one theological region. It is dedicated to the Ogdoad of Hermopolis. Beside the expected appearance of the common gods, Amun Re, Mut, and Khonsu in the upper register on the north wall and Ba-neb-Djed, a hypostasis of Osiris, on the lower register of the west wall,[14] the east and north wall mostly focus on the Ogdoad theology. In the upper register of the north wall, the king consecrates the white bread to "his fathers, the eight gods" (*sḳr ḥḏ t n itw.f ḫmnw*).[15] These gods are represented by snake-headed deities: Amun, Great God of the Ogdoads (*nṯr nfr n ḫmnw*), and Amunet, who "goes forth together with the Ogdoad" (*pri ḥnʿ ḫmnw*), Nun and Naunet. In the lower register of the east wall, the king offers ointment to "the divine Ogdoad, together with the divine Ennead" (*n ḫmnw ḥnʿ psḏwt*), represented by Kek, Keket, Gereh, and Gerehet. Inside the sanctuary, in the south wall's fifth register, is found the concentration of the Hermopolitan deities.[16]

The roof chapels of the Temple of Hibis are the earliest decorated roof chapels with explicit Osirian rituals. The analysis of the chapel complex H on top of the roof of Hibis revealed, among other observations, the distinctive use of chapel H2 as most probably a *štyt ḥrt*, "an upper chamber" or a temporary depository for an Osiris figurine where the embalming, resurrection, and above all the protection episodes were performed on the mummy of Osiris from at least the twenty-first of the month of Khoiak.[17] Most of the represented deities inside chapel H2 played prominent roles during the *Stundenwachen*, or the hourly vigil of Osiris, and especially during the night at the end of the embalming ritual.[18] In the Osiris chapels in the Temple of Dendera, these hourly vigils involved eight goddesses who "enter and mourn, two at a time" and who "stand inside the door of the court (with) the divine Ennead" (*ʿḥʿ ḫr.sn m-ḫnw sbꜣ n wsḫt (m) ʿb psḏt*).[19] This reflects the similar presentation of the eight goddesses at each corner of chapel H2. This ritual of protection against another attack by Seth was supposed to continue until the sun rose,[20] symbolizing the trajectory point of the myth when Re joined Osiris.

The textual and iconographical evidence of the pilasters' decoration of chapel E1, the Maat offering and hymn on the west wall of E1, as well as the offering list and Opening of the Mouth liturgies of chapel E2, concerned most importantly the Osiris–solar transformation that brings with it the reactivation of the king's powers, the protection of the

13 Davies, *The Temple of Hibis*, Part 3, pls. 2–5.

14 Davies, *The Temple of Hibis*, Part 3, pl. 21; Cruz-Uribe, *Hibis Temple Project I*, pp. 90–93.

15 The word *ḫmnw* is written as *ssnw* throughout the chapel; see Cruz-Uribe, *Hibis Temple Project I*, n. 356 on p. 91.

16 Davies, *The Temple of Hibis*, Part 3, pl. 4; Kessler, "Hermopolitanische Götterformen im Hibis-Tempel," pp. 211–223.

17 See p. 143, footnote 248.

18 Assmann, *Death and Salvation in Ancient Egypt*, pp. 260–261.

19 Cauville, *Le temple de Dendara: les chapelles osiriennes [1] Transcription et traduction*, p. 69.

20 Assmann, *Death and Salvation in Ancient Egypt*, pp. 263ff.

cosmos, and the prosperity of humans.[21] The doorway inscriptions on both the jambs and reveals clearly express these connotations. Their many ramifications to the themes that played important roles in the decorative program of the roof have been mentioned earlier.[22]

As stated before, chapel complex E is where, most likely, the concluding parts of the Osiris ceremonies from death to resurrection took place, as manifested by the various rituals. While the rituals of the chapel complex H revolved around the protection of the embalmed Osiris, especially at night, those of the chapel complex E represented the reviving rituals, especially by daylight. Both chapel complexes E and H demonstrate many similarities to the more developed roof chapels of Ptolemaic temples, as well as the Osiris–solar components of the New Kingdom funerary temples. Moreover, this overarching relationship between the two complexes consequently allows for more exciting conclusions regarding the other chapels surrounding the sanctuary—such as L, I, and K (1–2)—and the functions they might have had in relationship to these roof rituals. The first that should be considered is the possible function of chapel complex E.

The astronomical list and the inclusion of Sakhmet in particular suggest a strong link to the New Year celebration, where Sakhmet guaranteed a smooth transition from year to year.[23] Furthermore, Osing suggested that the complex E1–E2 accommodated the *ẖnm ꞽItn*, or "union with the sun disk," celebrations, where the statues of the gods were brought to the roofs of the temples to sunbathe, enabling them to symbolically recharge and regenerate the power of the gods within.[24] Considering the immediate and broader context of the astronomical list has shown other pertinent associations. In addition to the association with the specific New Year celebration, the depiction of such decan lists as well as the other representations in chapels E1–E2, evoke the timeless resurrection and rebirth cycle that expands the use of this complex into a year-round multipurpose room. It must be noted that Sakhmet appeared not only during the New Year but also at every significant moment in the year.[25] The *ẖnm ꞽItn* was neither confined to the New

---

21 After the first study of the Osiris mysteries of the Khoiak by Chassinat (*Le mystère d'Osiris au mois de Khoiak*), Derchain, who later treated the Khoiak mysteries in *Le papyrus Salt 825 (B.M. 10051)*, concluded that the interpretation of the ritual signifies the maintenance of the whole cosmos and not just the Osiris rejuvenation and resurrection. See also Goyon, "La fête de Sokaris à Edfou à la lumière d'un texte liturgique remontant au Nouvel Empire," pp. 415–438. The same conclusion has been reached on studying the "solar mysteries" by Assmann (*Solar Religion in the New Kingdom: Re, Amun and the Crisis of Polytheism*, p. 36), who stated that the function of the "solar mysteries" is to "keep the solar journey going, which was the same as preserving both cosmic order and the life of the king and mankind."

22 For these inscriptions, see figs. 35–36 and pp. 176ff.

23 Cruz-Uribe, *Hibis Temple Project I*, pp. 188–191.

24 Osing, "Zur Anlage und Dekoration des Tempels von Hibis," p. 763. See also Meeks, *Daily Life of the Egyptian Gods*, pp. 193ff; Alliot, *Le culte d'Horus à Edfou au temps des Ptolémées*, pp. 273–274, 303ff, and 325ff; Cauville, *Essai sur la théologie du temple d'Horus à Edfou*, pp. 47, 52, and 90.

25 Bryan, "The Statue Program for the Mortuary Temple of Amenhotep III," pp. 59–60; Germond, *Sekhmet et la protection du monde*, pp. 119ff and 194–224; Yoyotte, "Une monumentale litanie de granit: les Sekhmet d'Aménophis III et la conjuration permanente de la déesse dangereuse," pp. 63ff.

Year's celebration nor to the roof of temples.[26] In fact, the so-called New Year's celebration was celebrated not only on New Year's day or the "opening of the year's day," also called "the birth of Re," it also involved a series of stages that culminated on New Year's day. Usually the celebration began toward the end of the last month of the old year and ended at the last epagomenal day (Thoth).[27] What has been discussed as the "New Year celebration" seems to have been an amalgam of these later rituals as well as other rituals, the contents of which differed according to the individual character of each temple.[28] Even the later Ptolemaic New Year's court and the *wabet* chapel were used for different occasions throughout the year and were not limited to the New Year festivities.[29]

In general, chapel complex E hosted first and foremost the concluding celebrations of the Osiris–solar rituals which seem to have been designed—even if only theoretically—around the New Year.[30] These rituals concerned the confirmation of the royal power that formed in itself an episode also revolving around the New Year Day when the king's power was threatened by the forces of evil.[31] An important ritual embedded in the context of these celebrations involved a sophisticated offering of cloth, during which Tait, patroness of weaving and textiles, played a great role. During the ritual of the confirmation of the royal power—after the coronation—the king proceeded to another location where he was anointed and dressed.[32] He first received red linen and later several ointments, each protecting an aspect of his kingship, most important of which was the one that enabled him "to manifest himself like the sun emerging at dawn from the Osirian world."[33] In Edfu liturgy, the New Year's celebration featured a six-day-long "clothing festival," where Horus acquired new clothes for the whole year.[34] This "clothing ritual" seems to have developed from the earlier ritual of the New Kingdom when the

26 In Edfu, the ritual of the *ẖnm itn* was performed on the roof of the temple or in an open court inside the temple; Alliot, *Le culte d'Horus à Edfou au temps des Ptolémées*, p. 827; Žabkar, *A Study of the Ba Concept in Ancient Egyptian Texts*, p. 40. In Esna, this ritual was performed before the entrance to the hypostyle hall; *Esna V*, pp. 57 and 123; Žabkar, *A Study of the Ba Concept in Ancient Egyptian Texts*, p. 40. Cf. Waitkus, "Zum funktionalen Zusammenhang von Krypta, Wabet und Goldhaus," p. 287.

27 Goyon, *Confirmation du pouvoir royal au nouvel an*, pp. 41–46; Alliot, *Le culte d'Horus à Edfou au temps des Ptolémées*, pp. 303ff.

28 Daumas, "Neujahr," col. 470.

29 Coppens, "The Wabet and New Year's Court of the Temple of Shenhur," p. 92. For discussion of the *wabet* in relation to chapel E1, see pp. 213ff.

30 It was not the specific "date" of the New Year's Day that mattered but rather its symbolic nature of a "new beginning," making any cyclic transformation eternal and timeless.

31 See Goyon, *Confirmation du pouvoir royal au nouvel an*, pp. 29ff.

32 Meeks, *Daily Life of the Egyptian Gods*, pp. 188ff; Goyon, *Confirmation du pouvoir royal au nouvel an*, pp. 19, 34.

33 Meeks, *Daily Life of the Egyptian Gods*, p. 189; Goyon, *Confirmation du pouvoir royal au nouvel an*, p. 58 (II, 11–12).

34 Meeks, *Daily Life of the Egyptian Gods*, pp. 193ff; Alliot, *Le culte d'Horus à Edfou au temps des Ptolémées*, pp. 273–274, 303ff, 325ff; Cauville, *Essai sur la théologie du temple d'Horus à Edfou*, pp. 47ff, 90.

offerings of boxes of textiles were celebrated mainly in connection with the renewing of royal and Osirian regeneration powers.[35]

In Hibis, the clothing rituals are manifested clearly in the existence of one particular chapel that seems to have been dedicated wholly to this ritual, that is, chapel I on the ground floor of Hibis Temple. Backes suggested that chapel G in Hibis functioned as a precursor example to the treasury rooms and magazines—located inside the temples of Edfu and Dendera—that should be called "cloth rooms."[36] He based his theory partly on the presence of Shesmu and Hedjhotep among the wall decorations.[37] However, the absence of any offerings of linen or textiles throws much doubt on this theory. Chapel I on the ground floor of the Temple of Hibis was actually more likely a storeroom or linen treasury. It is different from the surrounding chapels because it is completely undecorated. The scenes surrounding its entrance doorway are of paramount importance. Not only does the goddess Tait appear, but also the hieroglyphic inscriptions prove very helpful, clearly spelling out the room's purpose more than once. At the lintel of the door leading to this room are these words: "Words spoken by Amun of Hibis, Geat God, the son of Re (…)¦, living forever, (who) gives to you your storehouse together with beautiful offerings?"[38]

Then the inscriptions continue to the right:

> Come that you may see the splendid temple, the clo[th] of beauty and linen. Your cloth is upon the arms of the two crocodiles of Tait…after you…your terror with Horus. May she be free from your enemies; may she be free from rebels.[39]

The lintel scene has Tait offering the linen and two figures of the king flanking the door and inviting only the purified ones to enter the room. The inscription follows:

> Words spoken to Amun of Hibis, Great God, powerful of strength. May Amun of Hibis take his bandages being as ritual red linen. The two arms of Tait are towards you. Demy will be the god who bandages the gods. May their spittle wash Hapy.[40]

The following part of the inscriptions associates the linen rituals with the rituals on the roof:

---

35 Ryhiner, *La Procession des Etoffes et l'union avec Hathor*, pp. 52–54.

36 Backes, *Rituelle Wirklichkeit: Über Erscheinung und Wirkungsbereich des Webergottes Hedjhotep und den gedanklichen Umgang mit einer Gottes-Konzeption im Alten Ägypten*, pp. 33–36.

37 Backes, *Rituelle Wirklichkeit: über Erscheinung und Wirkungsbereich des Webergottes Hedjhotep und den gedanklichen Umgang mit einer Gottes-Konzeption im Alten Ägypten*, pp. 33ff. For more details, see the section on chapel G, above.

38 Cruz-Uribe, *Hibis Temple Project I*, p. 50; Davies, *The Temple of Hibis*, Part 3, pl. 9.

39 Cruz-Uribe, *Hibis Temple Project I*, pp. 50–52; Davies, *The Temple of Hibis*, Part 3, pl. 9.

40 Cruz-Uribe, *Hibis Temple Project I*, p. 51, pl. 9; Davies, *The Temple of Hibis*, Part 3, p. 15.

> May it gladden your face through sun rays. May the cloth which is on your face be as what Isis wove and Nephthys spun, for they make the bright-colored cloth of Re. O, Amun of Hibis, may you be justified over your enemies for Re acts (as) lord of the two lands.[41]

Returning to the function of the chapel complex E, Waitkus, who was following up on his dissertation work on the most-developed decorated crypts of Dendera,[42] published an important article that revealed a functional coherence of the temple's crypts, the *wabet*, and the Gold House in the Ptolemaic temples.[43] To achieve this connection in the Temple of Hibis, he suggested that chapel E1 functioned as the *wabet*, conveniently located opposite to chapel E2 which, according to the inscription, is a "House of Gold" and not far from the crypts located at the entrance of stairway E.[44] However, the decoration evidence does not provide a similarly strong addition to his architectural evidence. He mainly relayed that the purification scene is similar to the ones inside the *wabet* of the Temples of Dendera and Edfu.[45] In his brief overview of the decoration on the walls of chapel E1, Coppens does not support the identification of chapel E1 as a *wabet*, based on its remaining decorative program.[46] He rather suggested that chapel E1 more likely functioned as a kiosk, as on the roofs of Edfu and Dendera, rather than as a *wabet*.[47]

It seems that the *wabet* was not yet in full form in Hibis Temple. In fact, the most distinguished features of the decorations of a *wabet* complex as a place of embalming, purification, and clothing or anointing[48] seem to be distributed in Hibis among several locations. Chapel complex K, together with H, served predominately as places of embalming. Chapel E1 was concerned, among other things, with the purification rituals, and chapel I functioned as the linen or clothing room. According to the revealing inscription on the north jamb of the door to stairway E, the Egyptians most probably named this chapel complex E "Wadjet,"[49] a term given to structures with columns.[50] But in the

41 Cruz-Uribe, *Hibis Temple Project I*, pp. 51–52, pl. 9; Davies, *The Temple of Hibis*, Part 3, p. 15.

42 Later published as Waitkus, *Die Texte in den unteren Krypten des Hathortempels von Dendera: Ihre Aussagen zur Funktion und Bedeutung dieser Räume.*

43 Waitkus, "Zum funktionalen Zusammenhang von Krypta, Wabet und Goldhaus," pp. 283–303.

44 Waitkus, "Zum funktionalen Zusammenhang von Krypta, Wabet und Goldhaus," pp. 290–292.

45 Waitkus, "Zum funktionalen Zusammenhang von Krypta, Wabet und Goldhaus," pp. 191–192, esp. n. 60.

46 Coppens, *The Wabet: Tradition and Innovation in Temples of the Ptolemaic and Roman Period*, pp. 219–221.

47 Coppens, *The Wabet: Tradition and Innovation in Temples of the Ptolemaic and Roman Period*, p. 221.

48 Coppens, *The Wabet: Tradition and Innovation in Temples of the Ptolemaic and Roman Period*, pp. 57ff, 175ff, also 195–208.

49 Davies, *The Temple of Hibis*, Part 3, pl. 7.

50 Spencer, *The Egyptian Temple. A Lexicographical Study*, pp. 68–71. See also p. 178, above.

temple of Dendera, this term designates its roof kiosk and not its *wabet*.[51] This yields another example showing that the Temple of Hibis stands at the perfect midpoint in the development of such structures.

In Hibis, the different episodes of the Osiris mysteries, the Opening of the Mouth ritual, the clothing rituals, etc., were closely connected with each other via the cyclic transformation of resurrection, regeneration, and rebirth in order to maintain the cosmic balance and the king's dominance, which subsequently guaranteed life and prosperity of Egypt and the Egyptians. One can generally distinguish three main parts of the Osiris mysteries or, better, the Osiris–solar rituals. First is the mystery itself that combined the sophisticated episodes of making, embalming, and protecting the Osiris effigy. Second is the reviving process when Osiris was enlivened by/as Re. Third is the materializing of this Osiris–solar journey by its association with the confirmation of the king's power that was renewed by numerous offerings, purification, and clothing rituals. This conveniently finds roots in the Middle Kingdom, as old as the earliest record of the Osiris mysteries of Abydos themselves.[52] Different parts of the temple seem to have emphasized one or more aspects of these various rituals.

Important chapels that should be considered at this point are the lower Osiris chapels, chapel complex K. The east reveal of chapel K contains a cartouche with a long inscription inside clearly stating that this suite is a temple for Osiris: "Millions of things in all life, stability and dominion for the temple of his father, Osiris, foremost of the westerners, Great God who dwells in Hibis…"[53]

According to the important inscription in the second register of the east wall of chapel K, the Khoiak ceremonies celebrated at Hibis Temple most probably began on day twelve of the fourth month of the inundation. On the east wall of chapel K, in the second register, the inscription reads:

> Fourth month of inundation, day 1[2][54] the goddess Djedit, ///speaking about it: being satisfied because of the entering of the musicians to the *pr ꜥnḫ irw*, in order to place seed grain upon water. D[jedit] places Lower Egyptian grain upon water/// in the garden (*ḥspt*), 12 cubits wide.[55] …[presentation] of the king when he offered incense and cool water to his par[ents, Osiris, Nu]t, Heqat and Shentyt. Hail to you, eldest one, august mummy (*sꜥḥ šps*), for your father Geb has created you and your mother Nut has borne you///.[56]

This perhaps suggests that these chapels contained the *ḥsp*, or the "basin/gardin," where the actual manufacture of the Osiris figurines took place, probably from day twelve to

51 *Dendera* VII, pp. 143, 3; 145, 8 and 15; Coppens (*The Wabet: Tradition and Innovation in Temples of the Ptolemaic and Roman Period*, pp. 67–68) suggests that both terms *wadjet* and *wabet* are synonymous.

52 Lichtheim, *Ancient Egyptian Autobiographies Chiefly of the Middle Kingdom*, pp. 99ff.

53 Cruz-Uribe, *Hibis Temple Project I*, p. 93; Davies, *The Temple of Hibis*, Part 3, pl. 22.

54 For the restoration of this number, see p. 144.

55 Davies, *The Temple of Hibis*, Part 3, pl. 22; Cruz-Uribe, *Hibis Temple Project I*, pp. 94–95.

56 Davies, *The Temple of Hibis*, Part 3, pl. 22, Cruz-Uribe, *Hibis Temple Project I*, p. 95.

day twenty-one, encompassing the nine days of watering mentioned by Plutarch,[57] after which the procession climbed up to chapel complex H to continue with the protection rituals of the manufactured mummy.

Besides the reference to the beginning of the Osiris ceremonies, the decoration of chapels K and K2 emphasizes the establishment of the kingship of Horus. On the west wall of chapel K2, Thoth, Isis, and Nephthys confirm the succession of Horus to the throne and his unification of the two parts of the country. The main inscription says:

> Words spoken by Isis and Nephthys as protection for the weary of heart: his son Horus replied. May Horus seize the white crown, being united with the red crown, for he has unified the double crown in peace, in order to drink the waters of the Khenwr. May I jubilate in his name, for he is a strong ruler. May the two arms be raised as Re comes to the offices of which he has spoken. O Wennefer, may the south, its north wind and the great green be given to him. May he shine forth. May the light illuminate his west. May he propitiate them with his strong arm forever and ever, because Horus, the son of Isis, the son of Osiris, he has seized the double crown.[58]

The king is represented on the east wall of chapel K, followed by his Ka, and burning incense to his father Osiris, and Nut, Heqat, and Shentyt.[59] The Ka of the king, which manifested the divine royal power that legitimized his accession to the throne,[60] was also the outcome of the complex theological system of the roof ritual. In the Temple of Edfu, after the ritual of purification, the Ba of the god joins his image, and the Ba is adored together with his Ka.[61] The purification and the joining of the Ba then indicated the performance of the *ẖnm ʾItn* during which the sun rays joined the Ba of the divinity to its statue and "imbued it with a renewed divine substance. The cult statue became ba-full."[62]

These features of the divine kingship may indicate that these chapels were revisited after the rituals were concluded on the roof chapels and prior to entering the following chapel L that functioned as the room of the *Kultstätten des Königs*, or "chapel of the royal cult."[63] The scenes of chapel L consistently represent the different features of divine kingship: the unification of the two lands, the offering of the crowns and *Heb Sed* symbols to the king, creating the image of the king on the potter's wheel of the god Khnum, and

57 Chassinat, *Le mystère d'Osiris au mois de Khoiak*, I, pp. 53–54, 69–73, Griffiths, *Plutarch's De Iside Et Osiride*, pp. 181ff. See pp. 136 and 142ff, above.

58 Davies, *The Temple of Hibis*, Part 3, pl. 24; Cruz-Uribe, *Hibis Temple Project I*, p. 103.

59 Davies, *The Temple of Hibis*, Part 3, pl. 22. For the role of the goddess Shentyt in the Osiris mysteries, see Cauville, "Chentayt et Merkhetes, des avatars d'Isis et Nephtyhs," pp. 24–27.

60 Bell, "Luxor Temple and the Cult of the Royal Ka," esp. pp. 256–261. See also Bell, "The New Kingdom 'Divine' Temple: The Example of Luxor," p. 131ff.

61 Alliot, *Le culte d'Horus à Edfou au temps des Ptolémées*, pp. 349–350; Žabkar, *A Study of the Ba Concept in Ancient Egyptian Texts*, pp. 39–40.

62 Žabkar, *A Study of the Ba Concept in Ancient Egyptian Texts*, p. 40.

63 For this term, see Arnold, *Wandrelief und Raumfunktion in Ägyptischen Tempeln des Neuen Reiches*, p. 57.

the suckling of the king by the goddess Neith (see pls. 39 and 40).[64] On the south jamb of the door to chapel L, it is written: "Hail to you Horus, for you have ruled this earth and all that exists through the inher[itance of your father].[65] May you rule the land…."

On the north jamb, the inscription states:

> Hail to you. May one rejoice over the throne,[66] protector of the king of Lower Egypt, for you have united the two lands together. You have hacked up the lands,[67] for the greatness of your strength.[68]

As in the Temples of Edfu and Dendera, the crowning scenes of chapel L occur near the Osiris Khoiak ceremonies represented in chapel complex K, as pointed out by Cauville.[69] It is thus through the death of Osiris that Horus ascends to the throne.

Cauville continues:

> Cette transmission est, bien sûr, partie intégrante des cérémonies de Khoiak où la mort du vieux roi (Sokar) prélude à la royauté du faucon (Horus/Harsiesis), en l' absence de toute rupture ou d'un espace laissé aux forces séthiennes.[70]

A hypothetical procession of the rituals might have started at chapel complex K and then moved to the chapel complexes H and E on the roof. After completing the roof rituals, the procession might have moved back downstairs to chapel I, revisited chapel complex K, and then ended at chapel L.

Even though some of the distinguished Osirian and solar scenes appear in different parts of the ancient Egyptian temples, the well-defined Hibis roof division—an Osirian unit on one hand and the solar unit on the other, yet still spatially and ritualistically connected—may have developed from similarly semi-isolated complexes like that of the Osireion in Abydos whose decorations express reciprocal ideas and layout.[71] While the

---

64 Davies, *The Temple of Hibis*, Part 3, pls. 26–27.

65 *Ỉmy*[*.t pr n it.k*].

66 Reading *mnbit* (spelled here as *mn.t-bi*), see *Wb.* II, pp. 63, 3–5, and De Meulenaere, " Notes ptolémaïques," pp. 108–110.

67 Instead of *bꜣ n.k idbw*, "you hacked up the lands," it could be read as *bꜣ*(*k*) *n.k idbw*, "the shores/banks serve you;" *Wb.* I, p. 427, 1–3.

68 Davies, *The Temple of Hibis*, Part 3, pl. 8; Cruz-Uribe, *Hibis Temple Project I*, p. 48. See also the inscription on the lintel to the door where the king makes offerings to the Osiris triad (Davies, *The Temple of Hibis*, Part 3, pl. 8; Cruz-Uribe, *Hibis Temple Project I*, pp. 47–48) and the numerous texts inside the chapel itself that emphasize the different aspects of kingship (Davies, *The Temple of Hibis*, Part 3, pls 26–27; Cruz-Uribe, *Hibis Temple Project I*, pp. 104–112).

69 Cauville, *Le temple de Dendara: les chapelles osiriennes [2] Commentaire*, p. 23, n. 59

70 Cauville, *Le temple de Dendara: les chapelles osiriennes [2] Commentaire*, pp. 23, 262ff, 265; Cauville, *La théologie d'Osiris à Edfou*, pp. 1–60; Cruz-Uribe, *Hibis Temple Project I*, p. 102; Calverley and Gardiner, *The Temple of King Sethos I at Abydos*, III, pls. 11–16;.

71 In fact, the main features of the Osireion appear to be part of the decoration program inside the underground chapels of the Edifice of Taharqa. Goyon associated the "mound of

roof decorations can be a reflection of the Osireion of Abydos, those of chapel complex K exhibit an almost direct relationship to the Osiris complex of Abydos. Several similarities exist between these two "temples of Osiris" in Abydos and Hibis. Cruz-Uribe and Cauville have pointed out the similarity of the scenes on the north and south walls of chapel K2 with scenes inside the first Osiris Hall of the Abydos Temple of Seti I.[72]

Among the approximately 200 temples of ancient Egypt, few still preserve their complete roofs. However, a comprehensive study that focuses on temple roofs is greatly needed.[73] The roof chapels of Dendera are the most cited and the only roof complex adequately published.[74] In the commentary volume of the Osiris chapels, Cauville briefly compared the Osirian chapels of Dendera with similar ones in other temples.[75] In that comparison, the Osiris representations on the walls of the main sanctuary M and chapel complex K on the ground floor of Hibis were compared with only few references to the contents of the chapel complex H on the roof and not a single mention of the chapels E1 and E2 nearby.[76] The following discussion aims at providing a more inclusive, yet brief comparison of the two important roof compositions in the Hibis and Dendera Temples.

The roof chapels of Dendera consist of six chapels, three on the east side, labeled E1–E3, and three on the west side, labeled W1–W3. In comparison with the Dendera roof chapels, the Hibis chapels convey a much-reduced version of similar cultic composition. The north wall of chapel H2 of Hibis reflects a summary of the detailed episodes of at least four chapels—E3, W1, W2, and W3—of the Temple of Dendera. Chapel H2 of Hibis, similar to chapels E3 and W3 of Dendera, represents the innermost space. These

---

Osiris" in chapel E of the Edifice of Taharqa to the Osireion at Abydos (Parker et al., *Edifice of Taharqa*, p. 62, n. 10, and pl. 25). That in turn has many theological similarities to the Hibis material. It is interesting to note that the three subterranean chapels (D, E, and F) seem to have similar elements to the Hibis roof complex, for example, the depiction of the spell of the revealing of the four balls on the lintel of the door in the east wall of room E (Parker et al., *Edifice of Taharqa*, pls. 24–25, 28–29). The underground chapels of the Edifice of Taharqa also bear similarities to the Chapel of Re at Medinet Habu as noted by Goyon (*Edifice of Taharqa*, IX).

72 Cruz-Uribe, *Hibis Temple Project I*, p. 102; Calverley and Gardiner, *The Temple of King Sethos I at Abydos*, III, pls. 11–16; Cauville, *Le temple de Dendara: les chapelles osiriennes [2] Commentaire*, pp. 262ff.

73 Beside the *LÄ* entry by Helck, "Tempeldach," col. 377, only one article treats the Egyptian temple roof structures in general: Kees, "Dach II (Religionsgeschichtlich)," pp. 536–540. See also an architectural treatment by Arnold, "Holzdächer spätzeitlicher ägyptischer Tempel," pp. 107–115.

74 Cauville, *Le temple de Dendara: les chapelles osiriennes*, Volumes 1-5.

75 Cauville, *Le temple de Dendara: les chapelles osiriennes [2] Commentaire*, pp. 257–276.

76 Cauville, *Le temple de Dendara: les chapelles osiriennes [2] Commentaire*, pp. 261–265. In her remarks about the different vignettes of the decoration of the north wall, she points to their associations with the different locales; for example, she takes the scene of the running Apis bull together with the Sokar chapel as a reference to Memphis.

chapels are protected by the many genies or guardian deities depicted especially on the preceding antechambers: H1 in Hibis and E2 and W2 in Dendera.[77]

In general, both features of the solar and Osirian episodes appear in each of the six chapels at the roof of the Temple of Dendera. However, some chapels concentrate more specifically on one of the two episodes. The features of the solar episodes with the amalgam of the confirmation of the royal power appear more focused on the eastern chapels, especially E1 and E2. E3 shares some of the Osirian episodes. It thus links the opposite, western chapels. In chapels W1, W2, and W3 the funerary aspect of the Osirian episodes appears more frequently. Sometimes the representations within a single chapel follow a similar pattern of distribution; for example, in Dendera's chapel E1, the west side depicts the funerary aspect of Osiris while the east shows the solar aspect.[78] In chapel E3, the day barque is represented on the east and the night barque on the west. Osiris is called Orion on the east and King of the Necropolis on the west.[79]

The eastern chapels of Dendera's roof depict the important scene of releasing the four birds, a rite that confirms royal power.[80] This scene, completely absent from the western chapels of Dendera,[81] is represented in the third register of the northeast side of chapel E1 and in the third register of the northwest side.[82] The birds are represented between the enthroned Horus, son of Isis, and the standing figure of Re Horakhty, who declares that he gives his own royalty (*nswyt*) to Horus, son of Isis, in the "place where Horus becomes the king of Upper and Lower Egypt (*St di ḥr m nswt n Šmˁ Mḥw*)."[83] The following scenes engage with bringing the symbols of power to the now-king Horus. This episode is being witnessed by the priests and the deities representing the different parts of Egypt, who are gathered to witness the transmission of power to Horus.[84]

Other scenes of the solar episodes that are likewise confined to the eastern chapels are the priestly procession of the New Year and the famous ceiling decoration of the Zodiac.[85] On the east side of chapel E1, the first and second registers show episodes XXIII–XXIV

77 For H1 of Hibis, see Davies, *The Temple of Hibis*, Part 3, pl. 19. For Dendera, see Cauville, *Le temple de Dendara. Vol. X/2 les chapelles osiriennes (Planches)*, pls. 47–48, 177–179. See also Cauville, *Le temple de Dendara: les chapelles osiriennes [2] Commentaire*, fig. 16 of the "disposition des forces protectrices."

78 Cauville, *Le temple de Dendara: les chapelles osiriennes [2] Commentaire*, pp. 28ff.

79 Cauville, *Le temple de Dendara: les chapelles osiriennes [2] Commentaire*, p. 126.

80 See Meeks, *Daily Life of the Egyptian Gods*, pp. 191ff; Goyon, *Confirmation du pouvoir royal au nouvel an*, pp. 30–32.

81 One should note that in chapel W1, south side, are representations of birds, but they are not being offered or released—they are still sitting on trees; Cauville, *Le temple de Dendara. Vol. X/2 les chapelles osiriennes (Planches)*, pls. 159 and 171.

82 Cauville, *Le temple de Dendara. Vol. X/2 les chapelles osiriennes (Planches)*, pls. 6, 16, and 32. The four birds are called the four sons of Horus: Hapy, Douamutef, Amset, and Kebehsenouef. They are considered as messengers who declare the pharaoh's accession to the throne to the four cardinal points, as well as the resurrection of Osiris; Cauville, *Le temple de Dendara: les chapelles osiriennes [2] Commentaire*, pp. 24–26.

83 Cauville, *Le temple de Dendara: les chapelles osiriennes [1] Transcription et traduction*, p. 31.

84 Cauville, *Le temple de Dendara: les chapelles osiriennes [2] Commentaire*, pp. 23–26, 209.

85 Cauville, *Le temple de Dendara. Vol. X/2 les chapelles osiriennes (Planches)*, pp. 9–14, 60, 86.

and XLIII–XLIV of the Opening of the Mouth ritual.[86] Chapel E1 in Dendera also evokes many solar aspects of Osiris.[87] The 159 columns of inscriptions, comprising the best extended version of the Khoiak rituals, are represented on chapel E1. Yet, as Cauville noted, several aspects of the ritual are found on the western chapels.[88]

The western chapels of Dendera reflect the *domaine funéraire d'Osiris* with secluded places of Osiris in the kingdom of the dead, with gates and portals protected by deities, and versions of the chapters 144–146 and 149 of the Book of the Dead.[89] The most important of these are the representations inside chapels E3 and W3, "the most sacred of the six chapels."[90] The central theme of these two Dendera chapels is expressed in chapel H2 of Hibis: the embalming and protection process of Osiris. Eight goddesses are assigned to the protection of Osiris, most important of which are Sakhmet, Bastet, Wadjet, and Shesemtet,[91] the other members of the "divine retinue," and the divine standards of the various sites aiding in the protection and the *Stundenwachen* of Osiris. The texts of the bandeau of chapels W2 and W3 clearly express these specific ceremonies relating to those of the twenty-fourth and twenty-fifth days of the Khoiak ritual.[92] The central scene in the east chapel 3 is the gestation of Osiris,[93] which further confirms the relation between these ceremonies and the manufacture of the Osiris effigies, especially the corn mummies. Cauville reported: "c'est le moment critique où l'on change les figurines d'une année sur l'autre; il s'y déroule d'autres part diverses processions."[94] Cauville later added the sound suggestion that chapel W3 functioned as a "tombeau transitoire qui correspond a la chapelle haute *štyt ḥrt*."[95]

Scenes of the various local deities that played important roles in the Osirian rituals in the roof chapels, especially in chapel H2, are represented in few of the sanctuary registers. The left sides of registers III, IV, and V of the south wall of the sanctuary show similar representation to the vignette of chapel H2 with slight variation, reflecting the different cult centers of Osiris.[96] The absence of any representation of the king in chapel

86 Cauville, *Le temple de Dendara: les chapelles osiriennes [2] Commentaire*, p. 20.

87 Cauville, *Le temple de Dendara: les chapelles osiriennes [2] Commentaire*, pp. 28ff.

88 Cauville, *Le temple de Dendara: les chapelles osiriennes [2] Commentaire*, pp. 17–19.

89 Cauville, *Le temple de Dendara: les chapelles osiriennes [2] Commentaire*, pp. 166–175; Cauville, *Le temple de Dendara. Vol. X/2 les chapelles osiriennes (Planches)*, pls. 192–195, 196–203.

90 Cauville, *Le temple de Dendara: les chapelles osiriennes [2] Commentaire*, pp. 210–212. Chapel E3 as "Zone de défense," Cauville, *Le temple de Dendara: les chapelles osiriennes [2] Commentaire*, pp. 107ff.

91 Cauville, *Le temple de Dendara: les chapelles osiriennes [2] Commentaire*, p. 98; Cauville, *Le temple de Dendara. Vol. X/2 les chapelles osiriennes (Planches)*, p. 97.

92 Cauville, "Les mystères d'Osiris à Dendera. Interprétation des chapelles osiriennes," pp. 23–36, esp. 30ff and fig.4; Cauville, *Le temple de Dendara: les chapelles osiriennes [2] Commentaire*, pp.17–19, 175, 203ff.

93 Cauville, *Le temple de Dendara: les chapelles osiriennes [2] Commentaire*, pp. 96–101; Cauville, *Le temple de Dendara. Vol. X/2 les chapelles osiriennes (Planches)*, p. 96.

94 Cauville, *Le temple de Dendara: les chapelles osiriennes [2] Commentaire*, pp. 17–19.

95 Cauville, *Le temple de Dendara: les chapelles osiriennes [2] Commentaire*, p. 212.

96 Davies, *The Temple of Hibis*, Part 3, pl. 4.

H2 might be because the chapel solely focuses on the Osirian rituals and the related divinities associated with them. These Osirian rituals certainly played a paramount role in the theology of the Temple of Hibis. The sanctuary expands the list to about ten of the sacred cult places that accommodated statues of the mummified Osiris.[97]

The scenes and inscriptions at the nearby Temple of Qasr el-Zayyan, 30 km south of the Temple of Hibis, present theological observations that are similar to those in both chapel G and the roof of Hibis Temple. Even though no formal example of "cult topographical texts" is found inside Hibis Temple,[98] the inscription of a cult topographical text at Qasr el-Zayyan gives significant insight into the local theology of the Temple of Hibis itself. The text dates to the time of Antoninus Pius (about 140 CE.) and is preserved in two versions, one on the door to the pronaos and one on the door to the naos.[99] The text reads:

> As for Hibis, it is Re who was there, while he was King of Upper and Lower Egypt, making pronouncements throughout the whole land. The same was the case after he was buried in Mendes: His majesty loved to "roam the marshes" upon this mountain. Isis would seek out the Ba of Osiris, in all places he might be.
>
> They would hear s[upplications(?)…] upon this mountain,[…] while every god therein was concealed of corpse […], in order to hide Isis[…] Lord of Appearances, Caesar, may he live eternally.[100]

This text is important in discussing both the theology of the roof of Hibis as well as the cosmography of chapel G. It represents the primary gods of Hibis as the sun god Re, followed by Osiris and suggests a unification of the two gods through the mention of Mendes, the theology of which powerfully reflects the association of the two divinities.[101] The text continues the emphasis on the Osirian mysteries and the role of Isis in finding

---

97 Davies, *The Temple of Hibis*, Part 3, pl 4/ VI, VIII, IX; Cauville, *Le temple de Dendara: les chapelles osiriennes [2] Commentaire*, pp. 114, 261–262.

98 Klotz, "The Cult Topographical Text of Qasr el-Zayyan," pp. 20–21. However, Klotz refers to few etymological examples in Hibis, giving theological evidence for the Hibis toponym and suggesting that the Persian Period understood the area as "the Temple of the Ram of the desert;" Klotz, "The Cult Topographical Text of Qasr el-Zayyan," pp. 21–22. These texts usually come from Graeco-Roman temples and they describe the mytho-historical background of the area of the individual temple; Gutbub, *Textes fondamentaux de la théologie de Kom Ombo*, pp. 502–521; Leitz, *Quellentexte zur ägyptischen Religion. Die Tempelinschriften der griechisch-römischen Zeit 1*, pp. 63–67. Cult topographical texts appear in the Dakhla Oasis and they associate the area with the "Osirian cycle via puns on the names of the Oasis temples;" Klotz, "The Cult Topographical Text of Qasr el-Zayyan," pp. 21ff. See also Kaper, "How the God Amun-Nakht Came to Dakhleh Oasis," pp. 151–156; Kaper, "Egyptian toponyms of Dakhla Oasis," pp. 124–129.

99 Klotz, "The Cult Topographical Text of Qasr el-Zayyan," pp. 23ff.

100 Translation after Klotz, "The Cult Topographical Text of Qasr el-Zayyan," pp. 24ff.

101 Willems, *Chests of Life: A Study of the Typology and Conceptual Development of Middle Kingdom Standard Class Coffins*, pp. 153ff.

his scattered limbs. The text ends, as Klotz noted, with a reference to the living pharaoh which "concludes the cyclical generational history of Hibis," starting with the solar god as king of Upper and Lower Egypt, followed by Osiris, and ending with the actual representation of Horus on earth.[102]

The text of Qasr el-Zayyan contains an important statement connected with this cycle: the "roaming of the marshes upon this mountain" performed by "his majesty." Klotz provides ample evidence that this example of "roaming of the marshes" does not denote the usual sexual reference, but rather indicates an actual marshy environment.[103] The designation of "*ḥm.f*," usually attributed to royal figures, appears in this example with the determinative of a seated god with a falcon head and wearing the solar disk. This determinative is similarly used as determinative for the name of the god Re at the beginning of the text. This majesty may also refer to Osiris, since "roaming the marshes" is reported after the mention of the burial in Mendes. Thus this "majesty" that loves to "roam the marshes upon the mountain" may refer to the Osirian–solar aspect of the king which is strongly reflected in the theology of the roof chapels of Hibis.[104]
Beside the religious nature of this roaming in the desert, the scene from the rear wall of the sanctuary of Qasr el-Zayyan corresponds with the other main idea—also reflected in chapel G of Hibis Temple—that the mountains are sources of treasures that the king offers to Amun of Hibis. In the scene at the rear wall of the sanctuary of Qasr el-Zayyan, the pharaoh says to Amun of Hibis:

> *Ii. n.i ḫr.k it.i Imn [Rꜥ nb] Hb nṯr ꜥꜣ wsr ḫpš ḥnk.i n.k mnty ḫr imy.sn*
> That I have come before you, my father, Amun Re, lord of Hibis, Great God, mighty of strong arm is so I might offer to you the plateaus bearing what is in them.[105]

For political and ideological reasons, the temple predominantly displayed the representation of the royal persona. In general, the choice of the particular deities or theologies to be represented usually followed the political ideology of the time. The decorators preferred to represent scenes that best reflected the unification of the country, the king's power and dominance, and, above all, his legitimacy to the throne. The celebration of the king's coronation, divine birth, and his *Heb Sed* celebration were among the common themes and motives in the earlier part of the temple. Both the Temple of Hibis and the famous Egyptian-made statue of King Darius found at Susa have unique titles emphasizing the authority of the king.[106] But instead of using royal propaganda based

102 Klotz, "The Cult Topographical Text of Qasr el-Zayyan," p. 33.

103 Klotz, "The Cult Topographical Text of Qasr el-Zayyan," note e on pp. 27–30.

104 See commentary of chapel complex E and chapel complex H, above.

105 Klotz, "The Cult Topographical Text of Qasr el-Zayyan," pp. 22ff and n. 43. See also Kaper, "How the God Amun-Nakht Came to Dakhleh Oasis," p. 151, and Guermeur, *Les cultes d'Amon hors de Thèbes: recherches de géographie religieuse*, pp. 446–447.

106 Davies, *The Temple of Hibis*, Part 3, pl. 29 (north reveal of doorway to Hypostyle B); Cruz-Uribe, *Hibis Temple Project I*, p. 114, following the interpretation of this cryptographic inscription by Drioton, "Recueil de Cryptographie Monumentale," pp. 360–377. The latter

on military achievements, the Temple of Hibis features royal propaganda stemming from numerous cultic actions. One immediately notices the absence of the smiting scenes usually decorating the façades of the traditional pharaonic temples. The other monuments of Darius, such as his statue found at Susa and the canal stelae, offer even more dignified representations of the subjected people. The conquered are shown exhibiting gestures of adoration instead of being portrayed as bound prisoners, which is the traditional guise.[107] References on the Persian monuments to acts of humiliation and subjugation might have been absent because the Egyptians, who were most probably responsible for erecting and decorating these monuments, avoided representations that would inherently allude to themselves.[108]

The supremacy of the king inside the Temple of Hibis is based on his close relationship with the gods, sometimes even embodying the gods themselves. On the gateway to hypostyle hall M, two images show the king represented as a complete falcon given the *ankh* sign of life by Montu on the left side and Amun Re of Hibis on the right (see pl. 41).[109] These scenes are above other icons of the king's legitimization. On the left, the king is represented as a young boy wearing the side-lock of hair and being suckled by Mut. On the right side, he is represented as wearing the blue crown and being embraced in Amunet's arms. This assimilation of the falcon image, no doubt referring to Horus, the legitimate inheritor of the throne of Egypt, is repeated on another important stela of Persian date, belonging to Padiusirpare, mentioned by Sternberg-El-Hotabi.[110] The owner of this stela is offering to King Darius, represented as a complete falcon. The inscription behind the falcon reads: "The good god, lord of the two lands, Darius." The scene is topped by the winged solar disk with two uraei.

In the Temple of Hibis, the king is also assimilated to Thoth. On the west wall of chapel E1 on the roof of Hibis, the king recites the hymn of Maat in which he declares that he is in fact Thoth who came forth from Hermopolis to protect the solar god.[111] A naos from Tuna el-Gebel, the cemetery of ancient Hermopolis and the main cult center for Thoth, is painted with an image of Darius, whose name is written inside a cartouche. Darius is represented assuming the role of Thoth in offering the *udjat* eyes to a falcon-headed god identified as "Horus the avenger of his father."[112] An unusual figure of Thoth as a

gives the translation "There is not another great sovereign like the king of Upper and Lower Egypt, son of Re, Darius, ruler of all the rulers and [all] foreign lands." The statue of Darius found at Susa gives the famous Persian title "King of the Kings;" Yoyotte, "Les inscriptions hiéroglyphiques égyptiennes de la statue de Darius," pp. 256–259.

107 Myśliwiec, *The Twilight of Ancient Egypt*, pp. 150–151; Root, *The King and Kingship in Achaemenid Art*, pp. 62–72, 142, pls. 9–11.

108 However, one must note that the cuneiform inscription gives a more cruel image of the ruler; Myśliwiec, *The Twilight of Ancient Egypt*, p. 151.

109 Davies, *The Temple of Hibis*, Part 3, pl. 39.

110 Sternberg-El-Hotabi, "Der Raum M im Hibistempel von el Charga," pp. 599–600, pl. 9; Borchardt, "Datierte Denkmäler der Berliner Sammlung aus der Achämenidenzeit," p. 71, pl. VIII.1.

111 See p. 168, above.

112 Myśliwiec, *The Twilight Of Ancient Egypt*, pp. 144–146.

human with a disk head that has an *udjat* eye inside appears on one loose block in the courtyard of Hibis and twice in the sanctuary of the temple.[113] The king might have been equated with the image of Seth fighting Apophis on the exterior wall of hypostyle hall M. This scene would have suitably substituted for the traditional scene of the pharaoh smiting his enemies on the pylons of temples, especially since the wall of hypostyle hall M functioned as a façade to the earlier Temple of Hibis.[114]

Many places in the Temple of Hibis show that the scenes are distributed according to symmetrical analogy—especially on the door lintels, where the pharaoh's crowns are distributed following the temple's cardinal directions; the king wears the white crown of Upper Egypt on either the south or west side of the temple and the red crown of Lower Egypt on the north or east side.[115] The decoration of hypostyle hall B seems to have been executed with attention to the contents of the secondary chapels, and perhaps its scheme was done after that of these nearby chapels. The west section of the south wall of hypostyle hall B, in particular, is interesting in this correlation.[116] The right side of its decoration is depicted on top of the door to chapel F, while the left side of the decoration is depicted on top of the door to chapel G (see pl. 42). The right side of the decoration (register I) shows the only depiction of Ptah of Memphis in hypostyle hall B. He is followed by his consort Sakhmet. The main inscription in this register mentions both Ptah and the great Ennead in the great temple in Heliopolis.[117] The left side of the decoration on the south wall, west section, of hypostyle hall B (registers I and II) shows Tefnut and Sakhmet who are represented inside chapel G. In register I, left side, Onuris Shu is shown receiving wine from the king. This god is associated with the myth of the wandering leonine "Eye of Re" and is equated with the god Shu, who is represented inside chapel G.[118] Furthermore, the left side of the second register shows Wepwawet, whose name means the "opener of the way." He is closely associated with leading the ritual processions of the kings and is also the main god of the Asyiut region.[119] This connection to Asyiut is confirmed by the representation of the unique goddess behind him. The inscription above her states,

113 Cruz-Uribe, "The Hibis Temple Project:" 1984–1985 Field season, preliminary report," pp. 161–162, fig. 6.

114 Sternberg-El-Hotabi, "Der Hibistempel in der Oase el Charga: Architektur und Dekoration im Spannungsfeld Ägyptischer und Persischer Interessen," p. 542. In the city of Bubastis, King Darius may have assimilated himself to the god Mahes, the son of Bastet, who was the main deity of the city, according to a tablet found by Naville (Naville, *The Festival-Hall of Osorkon II*, p. 62). The inscription on the statue of Darius found at Susa suggests that the statue was made to recall the image of the god Atum himself; Myśliwiec, *The Twilight of Ancient Egypt*, pp. 151–152.

115 See Davies, *The Temple of Hibis*, Part 3, pls. 7, 9, 10, 12, 39.

116 Davies, *The Temple of Hibis*, Part 3, p. 12.

117 For this inscription, see Cruz-Uribe, *Hibis Temple Project I*, pp. 62–63.

118 Christophe, "Onouris et Ramsès IV," pp. 33–40; Endrödi, "Statue de bronze d'Onouris et de Mekhit," pp. 9–16; Junker, *Die Onurislegende*.

119 Graefe, "Upaut," cols. 862–864; DuQuesne, "Votive Stelae for Upwawet from the Salakhana Trove," pp. 9–12.

"Words spoken by she of Shenakhen (*šnʿ ẖn*), Mistress of the 16, Hathor of Medjed."[120] These epithets associate her with the Asyiut region,[121] the region that is connected with the representation of Merymutef and Herwer in the first register of the east wall of chapel G and also with the important Mankabad–Asyiut road to Kharga.

Several other examples exist of this coherent relationship between the decoration of hypostyle hall B and the nearby secondary chapels. For example, the scene of the temple foundation, where Seshat plays an important role, is placed on the east wall, close to the door of chapel F.[122] Surrounding the doorway to the chapels of Osiris (K–K2) are scenes of the guardian deities wielding knives, famous for protecting Osiris in particular.[123] The elaborate offering list on top of the roof decorating the east wall of chapel E2 is repeated with slight modification on the south wall, east section, of hypostyle hall B, atop the doorway H that leads to the roof chapels.[124] Also depicted on the right side of this doorway is the scene of the running of the living Apis bull that is mentioned on the north wall of chapel H2 on the roof.[125] According to Sternberg-El-Hotabi, the analysis of the decoration of hypostyle hall M shows a variety of celebrations, including the Osiris ceremonies.[126] One is inclined to see that the episodes of the latter ceremony depicted inside this hall concerned the "external public displays" of the ceremonies, rather than the more intimate or private aspects of the rituals that are represented inside the innermost chapels.[127]

The analysis of the chapels and hypostyle halls surrounding the main chapels under discussion in this work points to only a few of the apparent connections to the overall theology of the temple. Those chapels undoubtedly are worthy of further investigation.

In the end it seems appropriate to quote Sternberg-El-Hotabi in her summary of the article mentioned above: "Und zum Schluß stellt sich die Frage, ob man den Hibis-Tempel überhaupt noch als einen Tempel im landläufigen Sinne bezeichnen darf."[128]

The Temple of Hibis has been shown to be unique, a temple where old traditions were treated in new and innovative ways. Although the scenes might seem puzzling, they are in no way uninformative stock formulae. The Temple of Hibis has provided very rich material resources, not only because of the numerous preserved texts with detailed descriptions and elaborate epithets, or its myriad of divine representations with unlimited iconographic repertoire and nontraditional forms. In addition, the temple contains a wide range of both ancient and new theological and artistic conventions; it carries both the fruits of previously developed ideas and the seeds of future innovative praxis.

---

120 Cruz-Uribe, *Hibis Temple Project I*, p. 63; DuQuesne, "The Great Goddess and her Companions in Middle Egypt," p. 5.

121 Leitz, *Lexikon der ägyptischen Götter und Götterbezeichnungen*, VII, p. 100; Yoyotte, "Études géographiques I," pp. 87–92. For the importance of Hathor of Medjed in Asyiut, see DuQuesne, "The Great Goddess and her Companions in Middle Egypt, pp. 1–26.

122 Davies, *The Temple of Hibis*, Part 3, pl. 13; see p. 42, above.

123 Davies, *The Temple of Hibis*, Part 3, pl. 10.

124 Davies, *The Temple of Hibis*, Part 3, pl. 11.

125 Davies, *The Temple of Hibis*, Part 3, pl. 11.

126 Sternberg-El-Hotabi, "Der Raum M im Hibistempel von el Charga," pp. 603ff.

127 Gaballa and Kitchen, "The Festival of Sokar," pp. 36, 74 and figs 1–3.

128 Sternberg-El-Hotabi, "Der Raum M im Hibistempel von el Charga," p. 606.

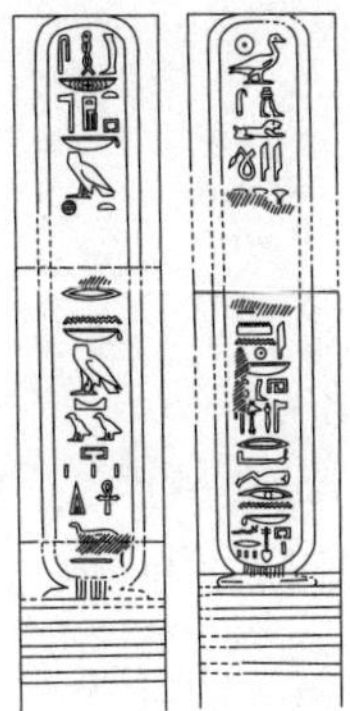

Bibliography

Abdel-Rahman, S. Y.

2011 "Amun-nakht Fighting against an Enemy in Dakhla Oasis: A Rock Drawing in Wadi al-Gemal," *BIFAO* 111: 13–22.

Allam, S.

1963 *Beiträge zum Hathorkult (bis zum Ende des Mittleren Reiches)*. MÄS 4. Berlin: Verlag Bruno Hessling.

Allen, J.

1949 "Some Egyptian Sun Hymns," *JNES* 8: 349–355.

1988 *Genesis in Egypt. The Philosophy of Ancient Egyptian Creation Accounts.* YES 2. New Haven: Yale University.

1989 "The Cosmology of the Pyramid Texts." In J. Allen, J. Assmann, A. Lloyd, R. Ritner, D. Silverman (eds.), *Religion And Philosophy In Ancient Egypt*: 1–28. New Haven: Yale University.

1997 "The Celestial Realm," In D. Silverman (ed.), *Ancient Egypt*: 114–131. New York: Oxford University Press.

Alliot, M.

1949 *Le culte d'Horus à Edfou au temps des Ptolémées.* BdE 20. Cairo: IFAO.

Altenmüller, B.

1977 "Harsaphes," *LÄ* 2: cols. 1015–1018. Wiesbaden: Harrassowitz Verlag.

Altenmüller, H.

1975 "Djed-Pfeiler," *LÄ* 1, cols. 1100–1105. Wiesbaden: Harrassowitz Verlag.

2009 "Die Wandlungen des Sem-Priesters im Mundöffnungsritual," *SAK* 38: 1–32.

Altenmüller-Kesting, B.

1968 *Reinigungsriten im ägyptischen Kult.* Dissertation zur Erlangung der Doktorwürde der Philosophischen Fakultät der Universität Hamburg. Hamburg: Lüdke bei der Uni.

Aly, M., Abdel-Hamid, F. and Dewachter, M.

1967 *Le temple d'Amada*, cahier IV: *dessins, index, tables de concordances.* Cairo: Centre de documentation et d'études sur l'ancienne Égypte.

Arafa, N.

2005 "Le dieu Igay," *DE* 63: 11–22.

Arnold, D.

1962 *Wandrelief und Raumfunktion in ägyptischen Tempeln des Neuen Reiches.* MÄS 2. Berlin: Verlag Bruno Hessling.

1999 *Temples of the Last Pharaohs.* New York: Oxford University Press.

2001 "Holzdächer spätzeitlicher ägyptischer Tempel." In M. Bietak (ed.), *Archaische griechische Tempel und Altägypten*: 107–115. Untersuchungen der Zweigstelle Kairo des Österreichischen Archäologischen Instituts 18. Vienna: Verlag der Österreichischen Akademie der Wissenschaften.

Assmann, J.

1969 *Liturgische Lieder an den Sonnengott. Untersuchungen zur altägyptischen Hymnik* I. MÄS 19. Berlin: B. Hessling.

1970 *Der König als Sonnenpriester. Ein kosmographischer Begleittext zur kultischen Sonnenhymnik in thebanischen Tempeln und Gräbern.* ADAIK 7. Glückstadt: Verlag J. J. Augustin.

1972 "Neith spricht als Mutter und Sarg. Interpretation und metrische Analyse der Sargdeckelinschrift des Merenptah," *MDAIK* 28: 115–139.

1973 *Das Grab des Basa (Nr. 389) in der thebanischen Nekropole.* Archäologische Veröffentlichungen (Deutsches Archäologisches Institut. Abteilung Kairo) 6. Mainz am Rhein: Verlag Philipp von Zabern.

1975 *Ägyptische Hymnen und Gebete. Eingeleitet, übersetzt und erläutert.*München: Artemis Verlag.

1977 "Gott," *LÄ* 2, cols. 756–786. Wiesbaden: Harrassowitz Verlag.

1977 *Das Grab der Mutirdis.* Archäologische Veröffentlichungen (Deutsches Archäologisches Institut. Abteilung Kairo) 13. Mainz am Rhein: Verlag Philipp von Zabern.

1979 "Harfnerlied und Horussöhne. Zwei Blöcke aus dem verschollenen Grab des Bürgermeisters Amenemhēt (Theben Nr. 163) im Britischen Museum," *JEA* 65: 54–77.

1983 *Re und Amun. Die Krise des polytheistischen Weltbilds im Ägypten der 18.-20. Dynastie.* Orbis biblicus et orientalis 51. Göttingen: Vandenhoeck & Ruprecht.

1983 *Sonnenhymnen in thebanischen Gräbern.* Theben 1. Mainz am Rhein: Verlag Philipp von Zabern.

1984 *Ägypten: Theologie und Frömmigkeit einer frühen Hochkultur.* Berlin: Verlag W. Kohlhammer.

1990 "Egyptian Mortuary Liturgies." In S. Israelit-Groll (ed.), *Studies in Egyptology presented to Miriam Lichtheim*: 1–45. Jerusalem: Magnes Press, Hebrew University.

1991 *Das Grab des Amenemope TT 41.* Theben 3. Mainz am Rhein: Verlag Philipp von Zabern.

1995 *Egyptian Solar Religion in the New Kingdom: Re, Amun and the Crisis of Polytheism.* Studies in Egyptology. London: Kegan Paul International.

2001 *The Search for God in Ancient Egypt.* Ithaca: Cornell University Press.

2001 *Tod und Jenseits im Alten Ägypten.* Munich: Beck.

2002 "Magic and Theology in Ancient Egypt," *Studies in the History of Religions* 75: 1–18.

2003 "The Ramesside Tomb of Nebsumenu (TT 183) and the Ritual of Opening the Mouth." In N. Strudwick and J. Taylor (eds.), *The Theban Necropolis: Past, Present, and Future*: 53–60. London: British Museum Press.

2005 *Death and Salvation in Ancient Egypt*. Ithaca: Cornell University Press,.

Assmann, J. and Bommas, M. (eds.)

2002 *Ägyptische Mysterien?* Munich: Fink.

Aubourg, É.

1995 "La date de conception du zodiaque du temple d'Hathor à Dendera," *BIFAO* 95: 1–10.

Aufrère, S.

1991 *L'univers minéral dans la pensée égyptienne*. 2 vols. BdE 105. Cairo: IFAO.

1998 "Religious Perceptions of the Mine in the Eastern Desert in Ptolemaic and Roman Times." In O. E. Kaper (ed.), Life on the Fringe: Living in the Southern Egyptian Deserts during the Roman and early-Byzantine Periods: 5–19. CNWS 71. Leiden: Research School CNWS, School of Asian, African, and Amerindian Studies.

Aufrère, S., Golvin, J.-C. and Goyon, J.-C.

1994 *L'Egypte restituée*. Tome II: *Sites et temples des déserts, de la naissance de la civilisation pharaonique à l'époque gréco-romaine*. Paris: Editions Errance.

Ayad, M.

2007 "Towards a Better Understanding of the Opening of the Mouth Ritual." In J.-C. Goyon and C. Cardin (eds.), *Proceedings of the Ninth International Congress of Egyptologists, Actes du neuvième Congrès international des égyptologues, Grenoble 6–12 September 2004*:109–116. OLA 150/1. Leuven: Peeters.

Backes, B.

2001 *Rituelle Wirklichkeit: Über Erscheinung und Wirkungsbereich des Webergottes Hedjhotep und den gedanklichen Umgang mit einer Gottes-Konzeption im Alten Ägypten*. Rites Egyptiens 9. Brussels: Fondation Égyptologique Reine Élisabeth.

Bács, T. A.

1992 "Amun-Re-Harakhti in the Late Ramesside Royal Tombs." In U. Luft (ed.), *The Intellectual Heritage of Egypt: Studies Presented to László Kákosy*: 43–54. Studia Aegyptiaca 14. Budapest: La chaire d'Egyptologie (ELTE).

Baines, J.

1972 "R. T. Rundle Clark's Papers on the Iconography of Osiris," *JEA* 58: 286–295.

1985 *Fecundity Figures. Egyptian Personification and the Iconology of a Genre*. Warminster: Aris & Phillips Publishers.

1996 "On the Composition and Inscriptions of the Vatican Statue of Udjahorresne." In P. Der Manuelian (ed.), *Studies in Honor of William Kelly Simpson*, 1: 83–92. Boston: Museum of Fine Arts.

Ballet, P.

2000 *Coptos: L'Egypte antique aux portes du désert*. Lyon: Musée des beaux-arts.

Baly, C.

1930 "Notes on the Ritual of Opening the Mouth," *JEA* 16: 173–186.

Barguet, P.

1962 "Une liste des Pehou d'Égypte sur un sarcophage du Musée du Louvre," *Kêmi* 16: 7–20.

1962 *Le temple d'Amon-Rê à Karnak: essai d'exégèse*. Recherches d'archéologie de philologie et d'histoire 21. Cairo: IFAO.

Barta, W.

1963 *Die altägyptische Opferliste von der Frühzeit bis zur griechisch-römischen Epoche*. MÄS 3. Berlin: Verlag Bruno Hessling.

1973 *Untersuchungen zum Götterkreis der Neunheit*. MÄS 28. Munich: Deutscher Kunstverlag.

1983 "Zum Buch von der Himmelsgöttin Nut im Papyrus Carlsberg I," *GM* 63: 7–12.

Barucq, A. and Daumas, F.

1980 *Hymnes et prières de l'Égypte ancienne*. Paris: Les Éditions du Cerf.

Bastin, D.

1992 "De la fondation d'un temple: 'Paroles dites par Seshat au Roi Sethi Ier.'" In M. Broze and P. Derchain (eds.), *L'atelier de l'orfèvre. Mélanges offerts à Ph. Derchain*: 9–24. Leuven: Peeters.

Beadnell, H. J. L.

1909 *An Egyptian Oasis: An Account of the Oasis of Kharga in the Libyan Desert, with Special Reference to Its History, Physical Geography, and Water-Supply*. London: J. Murray.

Beckerath, J. von

1984 *Handbuch der ägyptischen Königsnamen*. MÄS 20. Munich: Deutscher Kunstverlag.

Beinlich, H.

1976 *Studien zu den "Geographischen Inschriften" (10.-14. o. äg. Gau)*. Bonn: in Kommission bei Rudolf Habelt Verlag GmbH.

1984 *Die "Osirisreliquien:" Zum Motiv der Körperzergliederung in der altägyptischen Religion*. Ägyptologische Abhandlungen 42. Wiesbaden: Harrassowitz Verlag.

Bell, L.

1985 "Luxor Temple and the Cult of the Royal Ka," *JNES* 44: 251–294.

1997 "The New Kingdom 'Divine' Temple: The Example of Luxor." In B. E. Shafer (ed.), *Temples of Ancient Egypt*: 127–184. London: Tauris Publishers.

Belmonte, J. A. and Shaltout, M.

2006 "On the Orientation of Ancient Egyptian Temples. Part 2. New Experiments at the Oases of the Western Desert," *Journal for the History of Astronomy* 37: 173–192.

Bénédite, G.

1893–1895 *Le temple de Philæ*. Paris: Leroux.

Berlandini, J.

1985 "Varia Memphitica VI. La stèle de Parâherounemyef," *BIFAO* 85: 41–62.

1995 "Ptah-démiurge et l'exaltation du ciel," *RdE* 46: 9–41.

Billing, N.
2002 *Nut, The Goddess of Life: In Text and Iconography*. Uppsala Studies in Egyptology 5. Uppsala: Uppsala University.

Bilolo, M.
1996 "La notion du 'progrès historique' au cours du IIIe millénaire: Contribution à la philosophie pharaonique de l'histoire," *Studia Africana* 7: 87–100.

Bjerke, S.
1965 "Remarks on the Egyptian Ritual of 'Opening the Mouth' and its Interpretation," *Numen* 12: 201–216.

Blackman, A. M.
1913 *The Temple of Derr*. Les temples immergés de la Nubie. Cairo: IFAO.

Blackman, A. M. and Fairman, H. W.
1946 "The Consecration of an Egyptian Temple according to the Use of Edfu," *JEA* 32: 75–91.

Bleeker, J.
1956 *Die Geburt eines Gottes. Eine Studie über den ägyptischen Gott Min und sein Fest*. Leiden: E. J. Brill.
1967 *Egyptian Festivals, Enactments of Religious Renewal*. Leiden: E. J. Brill.
1973 *Hathor and Thoth. Two Key Figures of the Ancient Egyptian Religion*. Leiden: E. J. Brill.

Bomhard, A.-S. von
2007 "Le livre du ciel: de l'observation astronomique à la mythologie." In J.-C. Goyon and C. Cardin (eds.), *Proceedings of the Ninth International Congress of Egyptologists, Actes du neuvième Congrès international des égyptologues, Grenoble 6–12 September 2004*: 195–205. OLA 150/1. Leuven: Peeters.
2008 *The Naos of the Decades: From the Observation of the Sky to Mythology and Astrology*. Oxford Centre for Maritime Archaeology Monograph 3. Oxford: Oxford Centre for Maritime Archaeology.

Bonnet, H.
1952 *Reallexikon der ägyptischen Religionsgeschichte*. Berlin: De Gruyter.

Borchardt, L.
1907 *Das Grabdenkmal des Königs Ne-user-re*. Leipzig: J. C. Hinrichs.
1981 *Das Grabdenkmal des Königs S'aꜣḥu-reʿ*, II. Osnabrück: Otto Zeller.

Boylan, P.
1922 *Thoth, the Hermes of Egypt: A Study of Some Aspects of Theological Thought in Ancient Egypt*. London: Oxford University Press.

Breasted, J. H.
1901 "The Philosophy of a Memphite Priest," *ZÄS* 39: 39–54.
1906–1907 *Ancient Records of Egypt: Historical Documents from the Earliest Times to the Persian Conquest*, 4. Chicago: University of Chicago Press.

Bresciani, E.

2005 "Sobek, Lord of the Land of the Lake." In S. Ikram (ed.), *Divine Creatures: Animal Mummies in Ancient Egypt*: 199–206. Cairo: American University in Cairo Press.

Briant, P.

1996 *Histoire de l'Empire Perse: De Cyrus à Alexandre*. Paris: Fayard.

Brovarski, E.

1984 "Sokar," *LÄ* 5, cols. 1055–1074. Wiesbaden: Harrassowitz Verlag.

Brugsch, H.

1864 *Matériaux pour servir à la reconstruction du calendrier des anciens égyptiens*. Leipzig: Hinrichs.

1879 *Dictionnaire géographique de l'ancienne Égypte, contenant par ordre alphabétique la nomenclature comparée des noms propres géographiques qui se rencontrent sur les monuments et dans les papyrus, notamment les noms des préfectures et de leurs chefs-lieux, des temples et sanctuaires, etc*. Leipzig: Hinrichs.

1883 "Astronomische und astrologische Inschriften altaegyptischer Denkmaeler." In *Thesaurus Inscriptionum Aegyptiacarum. Altaegyptische Inschriften, gesammelt, verglichen, übertragen, erklärt und autographiert*, 1. Leipzig: Hinrichs.

1921 *Reise nach der grossen Oase El Khargeh in der libyschen Wüste: Beschreibung ihrer Denkmäler und wissenschaftliche Untersuchungen über das Vorkommen der Oasen in den altägyptischen Inschriften auf Stein und Papyrus*. Leipzig: Hinrichs.

Brunner-Traut, E.

1965 *Spitzmaus und Ichneumon als Tiere des Sonnengottes*. Nachrichten der Akademie der Wissenschaften in Göttingen. I. Philologisch-Historische Klasse 7. Göttingen: Vandenhoeck & Ruprecht.

1977 "Der Sehgott und der Hörgott in Literatur und Theologie." In J. Assmann, E. Feucht, and R. Grieshammer (eds.), *Fragen an die altägyptische Literatur*: 125–145. Wiesbaden: Dr. Ludwig Reichert Verlag.

1982 "Neunheit," *LÄ* 4, cols. 473–479. Wiesbaden: Harrassowitz Verlag.

Bryan, B. M.

1991 *The Reign of Thutmose IV*. Baltimore: The Johns Hopkins University Press,.

1997 "The Statue Program for the Mortuary Temple of Amenhotep III." In S. Quirke (ed.), *The Temple in Ancient Egypt, New Discoveries and Recent Research*: 57–81. London: British Museum Press.

Budde. D.

2000 *Die Göttin Seschat*. Konobos 2. Leipzig: Verlag Helmar Wodtke und Katharina Stegbauer.

Budde, D., Sandri, S. and Verhoeven, U. (eds.)

2003 *Kindgötter im Ägypten der griechisch-römischen Zeit: Zeugnisse aus Stadt und Tempel als Spiegel des interkulturellen Kontakts*. OLA 128. Leuven: Peeters.

Budge, E. A. W.

1909 *The Book of the Opening of the Mouth, the Egyptian Texts with English Translations*, I. London: K. Paul, Trench, Trübner & Co.

1911 *Osiris and the Egyptian Resurrection: Illustrated after Drawings from Egyptian Papyri and Monuments*, I–II. London: Putnam.

Buhl, M.-L.

1959 *The Late Egyptian Anthropoid Stone Sarcophagi*. Kopenhagen: Nationalmuseet.

Bull, L. S.

1923 "An Ancient Egyptian Astronomical Ceiling-Decoration," *The Metropolitan Museum of Art Bulletin* 18/12/1: 283–286.

Burchardt, M.

1911 "Datierte Denkmäler der Berliner Sammlung aus der Achämenidenzeit," *ZÄS* 49: 69–80.

Burkard, G.

1995 *Spätzeitliche Osiris-Liturgien im Corpus der Asasif-Papyri. Übersetzung, Kommentar, formale und inhaltliche Analyse*. Ägypten und Altes Testament 31. Wiesbaden: Harrassowitz Verlag.

Cailliaud, F.

1822 *Travels in the Oasis of Thebes, and in the Deserts Situated East and West of the Thebaid, in the Years 1815, 16, 17, and 18*. New Voyages and Travels 7. London: R. Phillips & Co.

Calverley, A. M. and Gardiner, A. H.

1933 *The Temple of King Sethos I at Abydos*, I–IV. London: Egypt Exploration Society.

Caminos, R. A.

1974 *The New-Kingdom Temples of Buhen*, II. London: Egypt Exploration Society.

Carter, H.

1904 *The Tomb of Thoutmôsis IV*. Westminster: Constable.

Caton-Thompson, G.

1952 *Kharga Oasis in Prehistory*. London: University of London.

Caulfeild, A. T. S., Christie, H. L., and Petrie, W. M. F.

1902 *The Temple of the Kings at Abydos*. Egyptian Research Account 8. London: Quaritch, reprint 1989.

Cauville, S.

1980 "Une offrande spécifique d'Osiris: le récipient de dattes (*mʿḏꜣ n bnr*)," *RdE* 32: 47–64.

1981 "Chentayt et Merkhetes, des avatars d'Isis et Nephtyhs," *BIFAO* 81: 21–40.

1983 "Une règle de la grammaire du temple," *BIFAO* 83: 51–84.

1983 *La théologie d'Osiris à Edfou*. Cairo: IFAO.

1987 "A propos des désignations de la palette de scribe," *RdE* 38: 185–187.

1987 *Essai sur la théologie du temple d'Horus à Edfou*, I–II. BdE 102. Cairo: IFAO.

1988 "Les mystères d'Osiris à Dendera, interprétation des chapelles osiriennes," *BSFE* 112: 23–36.

1990 "Les inscriptions dédicatoires du temple d'Hathor à Dendera," *BIFAO* 90: 83–114.

1997 *Le temple de Dendara*, Vol. X, Part 1: *Les chapelles osiriennes. (Inscriptions).* Cairo: IFAO.

1997 *Le temple de Dendara*, Vol. X, Part 1: *Les chapelles osiriennes. (Planches).* Cairo: IFAO.

1997 *Le temple de Dendara: Les chapelles osiriennes*, I: *Transcription et traduction*, BdE 117. Cairo: IFAO.

1997 *Le temple de Dendara: Les chapelles osiriennes*, II: *Commentaire*. BdE 118. Cairo: IFAO.

1997 *Le temple de Dendara: Les chapelles osiriennes*, III: *Index*. Cairo: IFAO.

1997 *Le zodiaque d'Osiris: Le Zodiaque de Dendara au musée du Louvre*. Leuven: Peeters.

2010 "Les trois capitales – Osiris – le roi," *RdE* 61: 1–42.

Cauville, S. and Aubourg, É.

1998 "En ce matin du 28 décembre 47…" In W. Clarysse, A. Schoors, and H. Willems (eds.), *Egyptian Religion, The Last Thousand Years. Studies Dedicated to the Memory of Jan Quaegebeur*: 767–772. OLA 85. Leuven: Peeters.

Cauville, S. and Devauchelle, D.

1985 *Le temple d'Edfou*, XV. MMAF 32. Cairo: IFAO.

Centrone, C. M.

2004 "Corn-Mummies: A Case of 'Figuring it out.'" In J.-C. Goyon and C. Cardin (eds.), *Proceedings of the Ninth International Congress of Egyptologists, Actes du neuvième Congrès international des égyptologues, Grenoble 6–12 September 2004*: 293–301. OLA 150/1. Leuven: Peeters.

2005 "This is the form of […] Osiris of the mysteries, who springs from the returning waters." In A. Amenta, M. M. Luiselli, and M.N. Sordi (eds.), *L'acqua nell'antico Egitto: vita, rigenerazione, incantesimo, medicamento: Proceedings of the First International Conference for Young Egyptologists: Italy, Chianciano Terme, October 15–18, 2003*: 355–360. Rome: L'Erma di Bretschneider.

2006 "Corn Mummies, Amulets of Life." In K. Szpakowska (ed.), *Through a Glass Darkly: Magic, Dreams and Prophecy in Ancient Egypt*: 33–46. Swansea: The Classical Press of Wales.

Champollion, J.-F.

1827 *Notice descriptive des monuments égyptiens du Museé Charles X*, I. Paris: Impr. de Crapelet.

1970 *Monuments de l'Égypte et de la Nubie. Réduction photographique de l'édition originale*, I–IV (Geneva: Éditions de Belles-Lettres, 1970).

Chassinat, É.

1918–1928 *Le temple d'Edfou*, II–XIV. MMAF 11 and 20–31. Cairo: IFAO.

1939 *Le Mammisis d'Edfou*. MIFAO 16. Cairo: IFAO.

1952 *Le temple de Dendera*, I–V. Temples 1. Cairo: IFAO.

1966 *Le Mystère d'Osiris au mois de Khoiak*. Cairo: IFAO.

Chassinat, É. and Daumas, F.
1965–1978 *Le temple de Dendera*, VII–IX. Temples 7–9. Cairo: IFAO.

Chauveau, M.
1996 "Les archives d'un temple des oasis au temps des Perses," *BSFE* 137: 32–47.

Christophe, L. A.
1950 "La salle V du temple de Séthi Ier à Gournah," *BIFAO* 49: 117–180.
1957 "Onouris et Ramsès IV," *MDAIK* 15: 33–40.

Ciccarello, M.
1977 "Shesmu the Letopolite." In J. Johnson (ed.), *Studies in Honor of George R. Hughes*: 43–54. SAOC 39. Chicago: Oriental Institute of the University of Chicago.

Clagett, M.
1989 *Ancient Egyptian Science: A Source Book*, 3 vols. Memoirs of the American Philosophical Society 184, 214, 232. Philadelphia: American Philosophical Society.

Clark, R. T. R.
1959 *Myth and Symbol in Ancient Egypt*. London: Thames and Hudson.

Clère, P.
1961 *La Porte d'Évergète à Karnak*. MIFAO 84. Cairo: IFAO.

Collier, S. A.
1996 *The Crowns of Pharaoh: Their Development and Significance in Ancient Egyptian Kingship*. PhD Dissertation, University of California, Los Angeles.

Coppens, F.
1999 "Wabet and New Year's Court of the Temple of Shenhur," *GM* 171: 87–92.
2007 *The Wabet: Tradition and Innovation in Temples of the Ptolemaic and Roman Period*. Prague: Charles University of Prague.

Corthals, A.
2005 "The Procession of the New Year in the Staircases at Edfu and Dendera." In A. Amenta, M. Sordi, and M. Luiselli (eds.), *L'acqua nell'Antico Egitto: vita, rigenerazione, incantesimo, medicamento. Proceedings of the First International conference for Young Egyptologists, Italy, Chainciano Terme, October 15–18, 2003*: 211–219. Rome: L'Erma di Bretschneider.

Coulon, L.
2011 "Les uræi gardiens du fétiche abydénien. Un motif osirien et sa diffusion à l'époque saïte." In D. Devauchelle (ed.), *La XXVIe dynastie, continuités et ruptures: Actes du Colloque international organisé les 26 et 27 novembre 2004 à l'Université Charles-de-Gaulle–Lille 3*: 85–108. Paris: Cybèle.

Cruz-Uribe, E.
1986 "The Hibis Temple Project: 1984–1985 Field Season, Preliminary Report," *JARCE* 23: 157–166.
1987 "Hibis Temple Project: Preliminary Report, 1985–1986 and Summer 1986 Field Seasons," *VA* 3: 215–230.

1988 *Hibis Temple Project I: Translations, Commentary, Discussions and Sign-List.* San Antonio: Van Siclen Books.

1992 "The Writing of the Name of King Darius," *Enchoria* 19/20: 5–10.

1994 "The Demotic Graffiti from Gebel Teir," *EVO* 17: 79–86.

1999 "Opening of the Mouth as Temple Ritual." In E. Teeter and J. Larson (eds.), Gold of Praise: Studies on Ancient Egypt in Honor of Edward Wente: 69–73. SAOC 58. Chicago: Oriental Institute of the University of Chicago.

2005 "The Ancient Reconstruction of Hibis Temple." In P. Jánosi and D. Arnold (eds.), *Structure and Significance; Thoughts on Ancient Egyptian Architecture*: 247–262. Vienna: Verlag der Österreichischen Akademie der Wissenschaften.

2008 "The Foundation of Hibis Temple." In S. H. d'Auria (ed.), *Servant of Mut: Studies in Honor of Richard Fazzini*: 73–82. Probleme der Ägyptologie 28. Leiden: Brill.

2008 *Hibis Temple Project III: The Graffiti from the Temple Precinct.* San Antonio: Van Siclen Books.

Daressy, G.

1900 "Une ancienne liste des decans," *ASAE* 1: 84–87.

1919 "Décret d'Amon en faveur d'Osiris," *ASAE* 18: 218–224.

Darnell, J. C.

1997 "The Apotropaic Goddess in the Eye," *SAK* 24: 35–48.

2002 "Opening the Narrow Doors of the Desert: Discoveries of the Theban Desert Road Survey." In R. Friedman (ed.), *Egypt and Nubia: Gifts of the Desert*: 132–155. London: British Museum Press.

2007 "The Antiquity of Ghueita Temple," *GM* 212: 29–40.

2007 "The Deserts." In T. A. H. Wilkinson (ed.), The Egyptian World: 29–48. London: Routledge.

2004 The Enigmatic Netherworld Books of the Solar-Osirian Unity: Cryptographic Compositions in the Tombs of Tutankhamun, Ramesses VI and Ramesses IX. OBO 198. Fribourg: Academic Press.

Darnell, J. C. and Darnell, D.

2002 *Theban Desert Road Survey in the Egyptian Western Desert.* OIP 119. Chicago: Oriental Institute of the University of Chicago.

Daumas, F.

1959 *Les Mammisis de Dendera.* Cairo: IFAO.

1982 "Neujahr," *LÄ* 4, cols. 466–472. Wiesbaden: Harrassowitz Verlag.

David, R.

1973 *Religious Ritual at Abydos (c. 1300 B.C.).* Modern Egyptology. Warminster: Aris & Phillips.

1981 *A Guide to Religious Ritual at Abydos.* Modern Egyptology. Warminster: Aris & Phillips.

2002 *Religion and Magic in Ancient Egypt.* London: Penguin Books.

Davies, N. de Garis

1943 *The Tomb of Rekh-Mi-Rē at Thebes*. Publications of the Metropolitan Museum of Art Egyptian Expedition 11. New York: The Plantin Press.

1953 *The Temple of Hibis in El Khargeh Oasis, Part 3: The Decoration*. Publications of the Metropolitan Museum of Art Egyptian Expedition 17. New York: The Metropolitan Museum of Art.

De Buck, A.

1938 "The Building Inscription of the Berlin Leather Roll." In A. M. Blackman, E. Otto, J. Vandier, and A. de Buck, *Studia Aegyptiaca I*: 48–57. Analecta Orientalia 17. Rome: Institutum Pontificum Biblicum.

De Buck, A. and Gardiner, A. H.

1935–1961 *The Egyptian Coffin Texts*, I–VII. OIP 34. Chicago: The University of Chicago Press.

De Cenival, F.

1988 *Le mythe de l'œil du soleil. Translittération et traduction avec commentaire philologique*. Demotische Studien 9. Sommerhausen: Gisela Zauzich Verlag.

Degardin, J.-C.

1985 "Correspondances osiriennes entre les temples d'Opet et de Khonsou," *JNES* 44: 115–131.

De Meulenaere, H.

1953 "Notes ptolémaïques," *BIFAO* 53: 108–110.

Depuydt, L.

1998 "Ancient Egyptian Star Clocks and Their Theory," *BiOr* 55: 6–44.

Derchain, P.

1952 "Bébon, le dieu et les mythes," *RdE* 9: 23–47.

1962 "Un manuel de géographie liturgique à Edfou," *CdÉ* 37, no. 73: 31–65.

1965 *Le papyrus Salt 825 (B.M. 10051): Rituel pour la conservation de la vie en Égypte*. Brussels: Palais des Académies.

1966 "Réflexions sur la décoration des pylônes," *BSFE* 46: 17–24.

1972 *Hathor Quadrifrons. Recherches sur la syntaxe d'un mythe égyptien*. Istanbul: Nederlands Historisch-Archeologisch Instituut in het Nabije Oosten.

2004 "Review of C. Thiers, Tôd. Les inscriptions du temple ptolémaïque et romain, II: Textes et scènes nos 173–329," *BiOr* 61: 542–544.

Derchain-Urtel, M.-T.

1981 *Thot à travers ses épithètes dans les scènes d'offrandes des temples d'époque gréco-romaine*. Rites Egyptiens 3. Brussels: Fondation Égyptologique Reine Élisabeth.

1991 "Die Bild und Textgestaltung in Esna eine 'Rettungsaktion.'" In P. Derchain, U. Verhoeven, and E. Graefe (eds.), *Religion und Philosophie im Alten Ägypten. Festgabe für Philippe Derchain zu seinem 65. Geburtstag am 24. Juli 1991*: 107–121. OLA 39. Leuven: Department Orientalistiek.

Desroches Noblecourt, C.

1985 "Les zélateurs de Mandoulis et les maitres de Ballana et de Qustul." In P. Posener-Kriéger (ed.), Mélanges Gamal Eddin Mokhtar I: 199–218. BdE 97. Cairo: IFAO.

Dewachter, M.

1981 "Nubie-Notes diverses (III). § 9 à 11." In *Bulletin du centenaire, Le Caire, Institut français d'archéologie orientale*: 3–10.

Di Cerbo, C. and Jasnow, R.

1996 "Five Persian Period Demotic and Hieroglyphic Graffiti from the Site of Apa Tyrannos at Armant," *Enchoria* 23: 32–38.

Dieleman, J.

2003 "Claiming the Stars: Egyptian Priests Facing the Sky." In S. Bickel and A. Loprieno (eds.), *Basel Egyptology Prize, 1. Junior Research in Egyptian History, Archaeology, and Philology*: 277–289. Aegyptiaca Helvetica 17. Basel: Schwabe.

Dils, P.

1993 "Wine for Pouring and Purification in Ancient Egypt." In J. Quaegebeur (ed.), *Ritual and Sacrifice in the Ancient Near East*: 107–123. OLA 55. Leuven: Peeters.

Dimick, J.

1958 "The Embalming House of the Apis Bulls," *Archaeology* 11: 183–189.

Donadoni Roveri, A. M.

1989 *Dal museo al museo, passato e futuro del Museo egizio di Torino. Archivi di archeologia*. Turin: U. Allemandi.

Doresse, M.

1971 "Le dieu voilé dans sa châsse et la fête du début de la décade," *RdE* 23: 113–136.

1973 "Le dieu voilé dans sa châsse et la fête du début de la décade," *RdE* 25: 92–135.

1979 "Le dieu voilé dans sa châsse et la fête du début de la décade," *RdE* 31: 36–65.

Dorman, P.

1991 *The Tombs of Senenmut: The Architecture and Decoration of Tombs 71 and 353*. Publications of the Metropolitan Museum of Art Egyptian Expedition 24. New York: Metropolitan Museum of Art.

Dorman, P. and Bryan, B.

2007 *Sacred Space and Sacred Function in Ancient Thebes*. SAOC 61. Chicago: Oriental Institute of the University of Chicago.

Drioton, É.

1926–1927 *Rapport sur les fouilles de Médamoud: les inscriptions*. FIFAO 4.2. Cairo: IFAO.

1933 "Un oudja à représentation hermopolitaine," *RdE* 1: 81–85.

1940 "Recueil de cryptographie monumentale," *ASAE* 40: 305–427.

1960 "Une erreur antique de déchiffrement," *RdE* 12: 27–31.

Dunand, F.
1991 "Le Babouin Thot et la Palme. A propos d'une terre cuite d'Égypte," *CdÉ* 66: 341–348.

DuQuesne, T.
1991 *Jackal at the Shaman's Gate. A Study of Anubis Lord of Ro-Setawe, with the Conjuration to Chthonic Deities.* Oxfordshire Communications in Egyptology 3. Thame Oxon: Darengo.
2000 "Votive Stelae for Upwawet from the Salakhana Trove," *DE* 48: 5–47.
2002 "Effective in Heaven and on Earth." In J. Assmann and M. Bommas (eds.), *Ägyptische Mysterien?*: 37–46. Munich: Fink.
2008 "The Great Goddess and her Companions in Middle Egypt." Tn B. Rothöhler and A. Manisali (eds.), *Mythos and Ritual: Festschrift für Jan Assmann zum 70. Geburtstag*: 1–26. Münster: Lit.

Eaton, K.
2007 "Memorial Temples in the Sacred Landscape of Nineteenth Dynasty Abydos: An Overview of Processional Routes and Equipment." In Z. Hawass and J. E. Richards (eds.), *The Archaeology and Art of Ancient Egypt: Essays in Honor of David B. O'Connor, Volume 1*: 231–250. Supplément aux ASAE 36. Cairo: American University in Cairo Press.

Eaton-Krauss, M.
2006 "The Festival of Osiris and Sokar in the Month of Khoiak: The Evidence from the Ninteenth Dynasty Royal Monuments at Abydos," *SAK* 35: 75–101.

Edel, E.
1955 "Inschriften des Alten Reiches. V. Die Reiseberichte des *ḥrw-ḫwjf* (Herchuf)." In O. Firchow (ed.), *Ägyptologische Studien, Hermann Grapow zum 70. Geburtstag gewidmet*: 51–75. Berlin: Akademie-Verlag.

Edwards, I. E. S.
1986 "The Shetayet of Rosetau." In L. Lesko (ed.), *Egyptological Studies in Honor of Richard A. Parker: Presented on the Occasion of his 78th Birthday, December 10, 1983*: 27–36. Hanover: University Press of New England.

Egberts, A.
1995 *In Quest of Meaning. A Study of the Ancient Egyptian Rites of Consecrating the Meret-Chests and Driving the Calves*, I–II. Egyptologische Uitgaven 8. Leiden: Nederlands Instituut voor het Nabije Oosten.

Eigner, D.
1984 *Die monumentalen Grabbauten der Spätzeit in der thebanischen Nekropole, Mit einem Beitrag von Josef Dorner*. Denkschriften der Gesamtakademie 8. Vienna: Verlag der Österreichischen Akademie der Wissenschaften.

Einaudi, S.
2007 "The 'Tomb of Osiris:' An Ideal Burial Model?" In J.-C. Goyon and C. Cardin (eds.), *roceedings of the Ninth International Congress of Egyptologists, Actes du neuvième Congrès international des égyptologues, Grenoble 6–12 Septembre 2004*: 475–485. OLA 150/1. Leuven: Peeters.

El-Adly, S. A.

1981 *Das Gründungs-und Weiheritual des Ägyptischen Tempels von der frühgeschichtlichen Zeit bis zum Ende des Neuen Reiches*. PhD Dissertation, Eberhard-Karls-Universität, Tübingen.

1984 "Die Berliner Lederhandschrift (pBerlin 3029)," *Die Welt des Orients* 15: 6–18.

El-Banna, E.

1989 "A propos des aspects héliopolitains d'Osiris," *BIFAO* 89: 101–126.

1991 "Une stèle inédite d'un prêtre-ouâb d'Hathor-Nébet-Hétépet," *GM* 124: 7–20.

El-Kordy, Z.

1982 "Deux études sur Harsomtous," *BIFAO* 82: 171–186.

El-Saady, H.

1994 "Reflections on the Goddess Tayet," *JEA* 80: 213–217.

El-Sabban, S.

2000 T*emple Festival Calendars of Ancient Egypt*. Liverpool: Liverpool University Press.

El-Sharkawy, A.

1997 *Der Amun-Tempel von Karnak, Die Funktion der Grossen Säulenhalle, erschlossen aus der Analyse der Dekoration ihrer Innenwände*. Wissenschaftliche Schriftenreihe Ägyptologie 1. Berlin: Verlag Dr. Köster.

Endrödi, J.

1980 "Statue de bronze d'Onouris et de Mekhit," *Bulletin du Musée Hongrois des Beaux Arts* 55: 9–16.

Engelbach, R.

1934 "A Foundation Scene of the Second Dynasty," *JEA* 20: 183–184.

Erichsen, W.

1933 *Papyrus Harris I: hieroglyphische Transkription*. Bibliotheca Aegyptiaca 5. Brussels: Fondation Égyptologique Reine Élisabeth.

Erman, A. and Golenishchev, V.

1994 *Hymnen an das Diadem der Pharaonen: aus einem Papyrus der Sammlung Golenischeff*. Buchholz-Sprötze: LTR-Verlag.

Erman, A. and Grapow, H.

1926–1931 *Wörterbuch der ägyptischen Sprache*, 5 vols. Berlin: Akademie-Verlag.

Evelyn White, H. G. and Oliver, J. H.

1938 *The Temple of Hibis*, Part 2, *The Greek Inscriptions*. Metropolitan Museum of Art Egyptian Expedition 14. New York: Arno Press.

Fairman, H. W.

1943 "Notes on the Alphabetic Signs Employed in the Hieroglyphic Inscriptions of the Temple of Edfu," *ASAE* 43: 191–318.

1945 "An Introduction to the Study of Ptolemaic Signs and their Values," *BIFAO* 43: 51–138.

Fakhry, A.

1942 *Bahria Oasis*. Egyptian Deserts. Cairo: Government Press.

1951 "The Rock Inscriptions of Gabal el-Teir at Kharga Oasis," *ASAE* 51: 401–434.

1951 *The Necropolis of El-Bagawāt in Kharga Oasis*. Egyptian Deserts. Cairo: Government Press.

1974 *The Oases of Egypt,* Vol. 2, *Bahriyah and Farafra Oases*. Cairo: American University in Cairo Press.

Faulkner, R. O.

1933 *The Papyrus Bremner-Rhind (British Museum no. 10188)*. Bibliotheca Aegyptiaca 3. Brussels: Fondation Égyptologique Reine Élisabeth, 1933).

1934 "The Lamentations of Isis and Nephthys," *Mélanges Maspero* 1: 337–348. Cairo: IFAO.

1958 *An Ancient Egyptian Book of Hours*. Oxford: Griffith Institute at the University Press.

1969 *The Ancient Egyptian Pyramid Texts*. Oxford: Clarendon Press.

2004 *The Ancient Egyptian Coffin Texts*. Oxford: Aris & Phillips.

Faulkner, R. O., Goelet, O., von Dassow, E., and Wasserman, J.

1994 *The Egyptian Book of the Dead: The Book of Going Forth by Day; Being the Papyrus of Ani (Royal Scribe of the Divine Offerings)*. San Francisco: Chronicle Books.

Fazzini, R. A.

1988 *Egypt, Dynasty XXII–XXV*. Iconography of Religions 10. Leiden: Brill.

1996 "Some American Contributions to the Understanding of Third Intermediate and Late Period Egypt." In N. Thomas and J. P. Allen (eds.), *The American Discovery of Ancient Egypt*: 111–130. Los Angeles: Los Angeles County Museum of Art.

Feder, F.

1998 "Das Ritual sꜥḥꜥ *kꜣ sḥn.t* als Tempelfest des Gottes Min." In R. Gundlach and M. Rochholz (eds.), Ägyptologische Tempeltagung, 4, Köln, 10–12 Oktober 1996: Feste im Tempel: 31–54. ÄAT 33. Wiesbaden: Harrassowitz, 1998.

Finnestad, R. B.

1978 "The Meaning and Purpose of Opening the Mouth in Mortuary Contexts," *Numen* 25: 118–134.

Fischer, H. G.

1957 "A God and a General of the Oasis on a Stela of the Late Middle Kingdom," *JNES* 16: 223–235.

1984 "Qus," *LÄ* 5, cols. 71–73. Wiesbaden: Harrassowitz.

Fischer-Elfert, H.-W.

1998 *Die Vision von der Statue im Stein: Studien zum altägyptischen Mundöffnungsritual*. Schriften der Philosophisch-historischen Klasse der Heidelberger Akademie der Wissenschaften 5. Heidelberg: Universitätsverlag.

in progress "Verben der Bewegung in altägyptischer Erklärung."

Fox, M. V.
1977 "A Study of Antef," *Orientalia* 46: 393–423.

Frankfort, H., De Buck, A., and Gunn, B. G.
1933 *The Cenotaph of Seti I at Abydos*, I–II, Memoir of the Egypt Exploration Society 39. London: Egypt Exploration Society.

Gaballa, G. A. and Kitchen, K. A.
1969 "The Festival of Sokar," *Orientalia* 38: 1–76.

Gabolde, M.
1994 "La statue de Merymaât gouverneur de Djâroukha (Bologne K.S. 1813)," *BIFAO* 94: 261–275.
1995 "L'inondation sous les pieds d'Amon," *BIFAO* 95: 235–258.

Galán, J. M.
1995 *Victory and Border: Terminology Related to Egyptian Imperialism in the XVIIIth Dynasty*. HÄB 40. Hildesheim: Gerstenberg.

Gallant, R. A.
1979 *The Constellations, How They Came to Be*. New York: Four Winds Press.

Gardiner, A. H.
1915 "Some Personifications," *PSBA* 37: 253–262.
1916 "Some Personifications," *PSBA* 38: 43–54.
1917 *The Inscriptions of Sinai*, I–II. Memoir of the Egypt Exploration Fund 36. London: Egypt Exploration Fund.
1943 "The God Semseru," *JEA* 29: 75–76.
1944 "Horus the Behdetite," *JEA* 30: 23–60.
1947 *Ancient Egyptian Onomastica II*. Oxford: Oxford University Press.
1948 *The Wilbour Papyrus II*. Oxford: Oxford University Press.
1950 "Onnouphris," *Miscellanea Academica Berolinensia*: 44–53. Berlin: Akademie Verlag.
1950 "The Baptism of Pharaoh," *JEA* 36: 3–12.

Gauthier, H.
1911 *Le temple de Kalabchah*. Les temples immergés de la Nubie. Cairo: IFAO.
1913 *Le temple d'Amada*. Les temples immergés de la Nubie. Cairo: IFAO.
1925–1931 *Dictionnaire des noms géographiques contenus dans les textes hiéroglyphiques*, I-VII. Cairo: Société Royale de Géographie d'Égypte.

George, B.
1974 "Eine Stockholmer Statuette des Gottes Osiris-Min," *Medelhavsmuseet Bulletin* 9: 3–18.

Germer, R.
1980 "Die Bedeutung des Lattichs als Pflanze des Min," *SAK* 8: 85–87.

Germond, P.
1981 *Sekhmet et la protection du monde*. Aegyptiaca Helvetica 9. Geneva: Éditions de Belles-Lettres.

Gestermann, L.

1984 "Hathor, Harsomtus und *Mnṯw-ḥtp.w II*." In F. Junge (ed.), *Studien zu Sprache and Religion Ägyptens. Zu Ehren von Wolfhart Westendorf überreicht von seinen Freunden and Schülern*, II: 763–776. Göttingen: Hubert & Co.

Giddy, L. L.

1987 *Egyptian Oases. Bahariya, Dakhla, Farafra and Kharga during Pharaonic Times*. Warminster: Aris & Phillips.

Gillam, R. A.

2005 *Performance and Drama in Ancient Egypt*. London: Duckworth.

Giveon, R.

1984 "Sopdu," LÄ 5, cols. 1107–1110. Wiesbaden: Harrassowitz.

Goff, B. L.

1979 *Symbols of Ancient Egypt in the Late Period: The Twenty-First Dynasty*. The Hague: Mouton.

Götte, K.

1986 "Eine Individualcharakteristik Ptolemäischer Herrscher anhand der Epitheta Sequenzen beim Weinopfer," *RdE* 37: 63–80.

Goyon, G.

1957 *Nouvelles inscriptions rupestres du Wadi Hammamat*. Paris: Imprimerie Nationale. Librairie d'Amérique et d'Orient Adrien-Maisonneuve.

Goyon, J.-C.

1968 "Le cérémonial pour faire sortir Sokaris. Papyrus Louvre I. 3079, col. 112–114," *RdE* 20: 63–96.

1968 "Les cultes d'Abydos à la Basse Époque d'après une stèle du musée de Lyon," *Kêmi* 18: 29–44.

1969 "Textes mythologiques, I. 'Le livre de protéger la barque du dieu,'" *Kêmi* 19: 23–64.

1971 "Un parallèle tardif d'une formule des inscriptions de la statue prophylactique de Ramsès III au Musée du Caire (Papyrus Brooklyn 47.218.238, col. X + 13, 9 à 15)," *JEA* 57: 154–159.

1974 *Confirmation du pouvoir royal au nouvel an (Brooklyn Museum 47.218.50)*. Wilbour Monographs 7. Cairo: IFAO.

1975 "Textes mythologiques. II. 'Les révélations du mystère des quatre boules,'" *BIFAO* 75: 349–399.

1978 "La fête de Sokaris à Edfou à la lumière d'un texte liturgique remontant au Nouvel Empire," *BIFAO* 78: 415–438.

1985 *Les dieux-gardiens et la genèse des temples: d'après les textes égyptiens de l'époque gréco-romaine: les soixante d'Edfou et les soixante-dix-sept dieux de Pharbaethos*. BdEs 93. Cairo: IFAO.

1999 *Le Papyrus d'Imouthès fils de Psintaes au Metropolitan Museum of Art de New-York (Papyrus MMA 35.9.21)*. New York: Metropolitan Museum of Art.

Goyon, J.-C. and Kurz, M.

1998 *Rê, Maât et pharaon: ou le destin de l'Égypte antique*. Collection Egyptologie. Lyon: Editions A.C.V.

Graefe, E.

1982 "Oxyrhynchos," *LÄ* 4, cols. 638-639. Wiesbaden: Harrassowitz.

1984 "Das Ritualgerät *šbt/wnšb/wtṯ*." In F. Junge (ed.), *Studien zu Sprache and Religion Ägyptens. Zu Ehren von Wolfhart Westendorf überreicht von seinen Freunden and Schülern*, II: 895–905. Göttingen: Hubert & Co.

1986 "Upaut," LÄ 6, cols. 862–864. Wiesbaden: Harrassowitz.

1993 "Die Deutung der sogenannten 'Opfergaben' der Ritualszenen ägyptischer Tempel als 'Schriftzeichen'." In J. Quaegebeur (ed.), Ritual and Sacrifice in the Ancient Near East: 143–156. OLA 55. Leuven: Peeters.

Graindorge, C.

1992 "Les oignons de Sokar," *RdE* 43: 87–105.

1994 *Le dieu Sokar à Thèbes au Nouvel Empire*, I-II. Göttinger Orientforschungen 28. Wiesbaden: Harrassowitz.

1996 "La quête de la lumière au mois de Khoiak: Une histoire d'oies," *JEA* 82: 83–105.

Grandet, P.

1994 *Le Papyrus Harris I, BM 9999*. BdE 109.Cairo: IFAO.

Grapow, H.

1915 *Religiöse Urkunden*. Leipzig: J.C. Hinrichs.

Grdseloff, B.

1947 "Notice sur un monument inédit appartenant à Nebwa', premier prophète d'Amon à Sambe (det)," *BIFAO* 45: 175–183.

Grieshammer, R.

1980 "Isden," *LÄ* 3, cols. 184–185. Wiesbaden: Harrassowitz.

Griffith, J. G.

1970 *Plutarch's De Iside et Osiride*. Cardiff: University of Wales Press.

1977 "Hakerfest," *LÄ* 2, cols. 929–931. Wiesbaden: Harrassowitz.

1986 "Lycophron on Io and Isis," *Classical Quarterly* 36: 472–477.

Guermeur, I.

2005 *Les cultes d'Amon hors de Thèbes: Recherches de géographie religieuse*. BEHE Sciences Religieuses 123. Turnhout: Brepols.

Gugliemi, W.

1982 "Personifikationen," *LÄ* 4, cols. 978–987. Wiesbaden: Harrassowitz.

Guilhou, N. and Aufrère, S.

1999 "Génies funéraires, croque-mitaines ou anges gardiens? Étude sur les fouets, balais, palmes et épis en guise de couteaux." In *Encyclopédie religieuse de l'Univers végétal. Croyances phytoreligieuses de l'Égypte ancienne*, 1: 365–417. Orientalia Monspeliensia 10. Montpellier: Université Paul Valéry-Montpellier III.

Guilmant, F.
1907 *Le tombeau de Ramsès IX*. MIFAO 15. Cairo: IFAO.

Gundel, W. and Schott, S.
1936 *Dekane und Dekansternbilder: Ein Beitrag zur Geschichte der Sternbilder der Kulturvölker*. Studien der Bibliothek Warburg 19. Glückstadt: J.J. Augustin.

Gundlach, R.
1995 "Das Dekorationsprogramm der Tempel von Abu Simbel und ihre kultische und königsideologische Funktion." In D. Kurth, W. Waitkus, and S. Woodhouse (eds.), *3. Ägyptologische Tempeltagung. Hamburg, 1.–5. Juni 1994. Systeme und Programme der ägyptischen Tempeldekoration, Akten der Ägyptologischen Tempeltagungen* 1: 47–71. Wiesbaden: Harrassowitz.

Gutbub, A.
1962 "Remarques sur les dieux du nome tanitique à la Basse Époque," *Kêmi* 16: 42–75.
1973 *Textes fondamentaux de la théologie de Kom Ombo*, I–II. BdE 47. Cairo: IFAO.
1985 "Remarques sur quelques règles observées dans l'architecture, la décoration et les inscriptions des temples de Basse Epoque." in W. Y. Adams, F. Geus, and F. Thill (eds.), *Mélanges offerts à Jean Vercoutter*: 123–136. Paris: Editions Recherche sur les civilisations.
1995 "Über die vier Winde in Ägypten." In O. Keel (ed.), *Jahwe-Visionen und Siegelkunst. Eine neue Deutung der Majestätsschilderungen in Jes. 6, Ez 1 und 10 und Sach 4*: 328–353. Stuttgart: Verlag Katholisches Bibelwerk.
1995 *Kôm Ombo*, I. Cairo: IFAO.

Habachi, L.
1955 "Preliminary Report on Kamose Stela and other Inscribed Blocks Found Reused in Foundations of Two Statues at Karnak," *ASAE* 53: 195–202.
1957 *Tell Basta*. Supplément aux ASAÉ 22. Cairo: IFAO.
1969 "Divinities Adored in the Area of Kalabsha, with a Special Reference to the Goddess Miket," *MDAIK* 24: 169–183.

Habachi, L. and Habachi, B.
1952 "The Naos with the Decades (Louvre D 37) and the Discovery of another Fragment," *JNES* 11: 251–263.

Handoussa, T.
1979 "A propos de l'offrande *šbt*," *SAK* 7: 65–74.
1987 "The Goddess Mikt," *ASAE* 71: 101–105.

Hannig, R.
1995 *Grosses Handwörterbuch Ägyptisch-Deutsch (2800–950 v. Chr.): Die Sprache der Pharaonen*. Kulturgeschichte der Antiken Welt 64. Mainz: P. von Zabern.

Harari, I.
1989 "Fondation des temples," *DE* 14: 37–48.

Hawass, Z.
2007 "The Discovery of the Osiris Shaft at Giza." In Z. Hawass, J. E. Richards

(eds.), *The Archaeology and Art of Ancient Egypt. Essays in Honor of David B. O'Connor*, I: 390–392. Supplément aux ASAÉ. Cairo: IFAO.

Helck, W.
1958 "Ramessidische Inschriften aus Karnak. I. Eine Inschrift Ramses IV.," *ZÄS* 82: 98–140.
1963 *Materialien zur Wirtschaftsgeschichte des Neuen Reiches*, IV. Mainz: Akademie der Wissenschaften und der Literatur, in Kommission bei F. Steiner.
1982 "Merimutef," *LÄ* 4, col. 96. Wiesbaden: Harrassowitz.
1982 "Tempeldach," *LÄ* 4, col. 377. Wiesbaden: Harrassowitz.
1987 *Untersuchungen zur Thinitenzeit*. Ägyptologische Abhandlungen 45. Wiesbaden: Harrassowitz.

Herbin, F. R.
1984 "Une liturgie des rites décadaires de Djemê. Papyrus Vienne 3865," *RdE* 35: 105–126.
1994 *Le livre de parcourir l'éternité*. OLA 58. Leuven: Peeters.

Hoenes, S.-E.
1976 *Untersuchungen zu Wesen und Kult der Göttin Sekhmet*. Habelts Dissertationsdrucke: Reihe Ägyptologie, Heft 1. Bonn: Habelt.

Hofmann, I.
1977 "Miszellen zu einigen meroitischen Götterdarstellungen," *GM* 24: 41–49.

Holmberg, M. S.
1946 *The God Ptah*. Lund: C.W.K. Gleerup.

Hornung, E.
1967 *Einführung in die Ägyptologie. Stand. Methoden. Aufgaben*. Altertumswissenschaft. Darmstadt: Wissenschaftliche Buchgesellschaft.
1976 *Das Buch der Anbetung des Re im Westen (Sonnenlitanei). Nach den Versionen des Neuen Reiches*. Teil II: *Übersetzung und Kommentar*. Aegyptiaca Helvetica 2. Geneva: Éditions de Belles-Lettres.
1977 "Hedjhotep," *LÄ* 2, col. 1078. Wiesbaden: Harrassowitz.
1979 *Das Totenbuch der Ägypter*. Bibliothek der alten Welt. Zurich: Artemis.
1990 *Zwei Ramessidische Königsgräber: Ramses IV und Ramses VII*. Mainz am Rhein: Verlag Philipp von Zabern.
1996 "Götterworte im Alten Ägypten," *Eranos* 4: 159–186.
1997 *Altägyptische Jenseitsbücher: Ein einführender Überblick*. Darmstadt: Primus Verlag.
1999 *The Ancient Egyptian Books of the Afterlife*. Ithaca: Cornell University Press.
2003 *Knowledge for the Afterlife: The Egyptian Amduat, A Quest for Immortality*. Zurich: Living Human Heritage Publications.

Hornung, E. and Abt, T.
2007 *The Egyptian Amduat: The Book of the Hidden Chamber*. Zurich: Living Human Heritage Publications,.

Hornung, E. and Staehelin, E.
2006 *Neue Studien zum Sedfest*. Aegyptiaca Helvetica 20 (Basel: Schwabe, 2006).

Hoskins, G. A.
1837 *Visit to the Great Oasis of the Libyan Desert; With an Account, Ancient and Modern, of the Oasis of Amun, and the Other Oases Now Under the Dominion of the Pasha of Egypt*. London: Longman, Rees, Orme, Brown, Green & Longman.

Hunger, H. and Pingree, D. E.
1999 *Astral Sciences in Mesopotamia*. Handbook of Oriental Studies. Section 1 The Near and Middle East 44. Leiden: Brill.

Huxley, G.
1964 *The Interaction of Greek and Babylonian Astronomy*. New Lecture Series 16. Belfast: Queen's University.

Ismail, F.
2015 "A Brief Investigation of the God Iaqs." In R. Jasnow, K. M. Cooney (eds.), *Joyful in Thebes: Egyptological Studies in Honor of Betsy M. Bryan*: 233–237. Material and Visual Culture of Ancient Egypt 1. Atlanta: Lockwood Press.

Jansen-Winkeln, K.
1985 *Ägyptische Biographien der 22. und 23. Dynastie*, I–II, ÄAT 8. Wiesbaden: Harrassowitz.

Janssen, J.
1997 "The Daily Bread. A Contribution to the Study of the Ancient Egyptian Diet," *BES* 13: 15–38.

Jasper, K.
2016 "Did the Ancient Egyptian Traveller Consider Ha, god of the Western Desert, while Traversing his Domain?" in C. Alvarez, A. Belekdanian, A. Gill, and S. Klein (eds), *Current Research in Egyptology 2015: Proceedings of the Sixteenth Annual Symposium; University of Oxford, United Kingdom, 15–18 April 2015*: 62–73. Philadelphia: Oxbow Books.
2017 "Will the Hunger be Repelled in the End? Notes on Scribal Solutions and Textual Transmission – the Case of PT 204, § 119b," *GM* 251: 47–70.

Jensen, P.
1890 *Die Kosmologie der Babylonier: Studien u. Materialien*. Strassburg: Trübner.

Jéquier, G.
1936–1940 *Le monument funéraire de Pepi II*, I–III. Cairo: IFAO.

Junge, F.
1994 "Mythos und Literarizität: Die Geschichte vom Streit der Götter Horus und Seth." In H. Behlmer (ed.), *Quaerentes scientiam. Festgabe für Wolfhart Westendorf zu seinem 70. Geburtstag überreicht von seinen Schülern*: 83–101. Göttingen: Seminar für Ägyptologie und Koptologie.

Junker, H.
1917 *Die Onurislegende*. Vienna: Hölder in Komm.

Kákosy, L.
1981 "The Astral Snakes of the Nile," *MDAIK* 37: 255–260.

1982 "Decans in Late Egyptian Religion," *Oikumene* 3: 163–191.

1982 "Phoenix" *LÄ* 4, cols. 1030–1039. Wiesbaden: Harrassowitz.

1982 "Temples and Funerary Beliefs in the Graeco-Roman Epoch." In *L'Égyptologie en 1979, axes prioritaires de recherches*, vol. 1: 117–127. Paris: Éditions du Centre National de la Recherche Scientifique.

1984 "Solar Disk or Solar Globe?" in F. Junge (ed.), *Studien zu Sprache and Religion Ägyptens. Zu Ehren von Wolfhart Westendorf überreicht von seinen Freunden and Schülern*: 1057–1067. Göttingen: Hubert & Co.

1998 "A New Source of Egyptian Mythology and Iconography." In C. Eyre (ed.), *Proceedings of the Seventh International Congress of Egyptologists, Cambridge, 3–9 September 1995*: 619–624. OLA 82. Leuven: Peeters.

1999 *Egyptian Healing Statues in Three Museums in Italy: Turin, Florence, Naples.* Catalogo del Museo egizio di Torino 9. Turin: Ministero per i beni e le attività culturali, Soprintendenza al Museo delle antichità egizie.

Kamal, A.

1902 "Le Pylône de Qous," *ASAE* 3: 215–235.

1911 "Rapport sur les fouilles exécutées dans la zone comprise entre Déîrout, au nord, et Déîr-el-Ganadlah, au sud," *ASAE* 11: 3–39.

Kamal, M.

1938 "The Stela of [hieroglyphs] in the Egyptian Museum," *ASAE* 38: 265–283.

Kaper, O. E.

1987 "How the God Amun-Nakht Came to Dakhleh Oasis," *JSSEA* 17: 151–56.

1992 "Egyptian Toponyms of Dakhla Oasis," *BIFAO* 92: 117–132.

1997 "A Painting of the Gods of Dakhla in the Temple of Ismant el-Kharab." In S. Quirke (ed.), *The Temple in Ancient Egypt: New Discoveries and Recent Research*: 204–215. London: British Museum Press.

Karlshausen, C.

1992 "Une perruque divine du Nouvel Empire: la coiffure à volants." In C. Obsomer and A. Oosthoek (eds.), Amosiades, Mélanges offerts au Professeur Claude Vandersleyen par ses anciens étudiants: 153–173. Louvain-la-Neuve: Université Catholique de Louvain, Institut Catholique, Collège Erasme.

Kaufmann, C. M.

1902 *Ein altchristliches Pompeji in der libyschen Wüste: Die Nekropolis der "Grossen Oase;" Archaeologische Skizze*. Mainz: F. Kirchheim.

Kees, H.

1915 "Nachlese zum Opfertanz des ägyptischen Königs," *ZÄS* 52: 61–72.

1923 "Anubis, Herr von Sepa und der 18. Oberägyptische Gau," *ZÄS* 58: 79–101.

1929–1942 "Kulttopographische und mythologische Beiträge," *ZÄS* 64 (1929): 99–112; 65 (1930): 83–84; 71 (1935): 150–155; 77 (1942): 24–27.

1930 "Göttinger Totenbuchstudien: Ein Mythus vom Königtum des Osiris in Herakleopolis aus dem Totenbuch Kap. 175," *ZÄS* 65: 65–83.

1954 "Ein Herrschaftsspruch aus den Pyramidentexten des A.R. und Sopdu der smsrw," *ZÄS* 79: 36–40.

1956 "Dach II (Religionsgeschichtlich)," *Realexikon für Antike und Christentum*: 536–540.

1958 "Der Gau von Kynopolis und seine Gottheit," *MIO* 6: 157–175.

1961 *Ancient Egypt. A Cultural Topography*, translated from German by I. F. D. Morrow, edited by T. G. H. James. Chicago: The University of Chicago Press.

Kessler, D.

2003 "Hermopolitanische Götterformen im Hibis-Tempel." In N. Kloth, K. Martin, E. Pardey, and H. Altenmüller (eds.), *Es werde niedergelegt als Schriftstück: Festschrift für Hartwig Altenmüller zum 65. Geburtstag*: 211–223. SAK Beihefte 9. Hamburg: Buske.

Kienitz, F. K.

1953 *Die politische Geschichte Ägyptens vom 7. bis zum 4. Jahrhundert vor der Zeitwende*. Berlin: Akademie-Verlag.

Kitchen, K. A.

1975–1996 *Ramesside Inscriptions. Translated & Annotated. Translations*, I–VIII. Oxford: Blackwell Publishers.

1991 "Towards a Reconstruction of Ramesside Memphis." In E. Bleiberg and R. Freed (eds.), *Fragments of a Shattered Visage: The Proceedings of the International Symposium on Ramesses the Great*: 87–104. Monographs of the Institute of Egyptian Art and Archaeology 1. Memphis: Memphis State University.

Klotz, D.

2006 *Adoration of the Ram: Five Hymns to Amun-Re from Hibis Temple*. YES 6. New Haven: Yale Egyptological Seminar.

2009 "The Cult Topographical Text of Qasr el-Zayyan," *RdE* 60: 17–39.

Kockelmann, H. and Pfeiffer, S.

2009 "Betrachtungen zur Dedikation von Tempeln und Tempelteilen in ptolemäischer und römischer Zeit." In R. Eberhard and B. Kramer (eds.), *"... Vor dem Papyrus sind alle gleich:" Papyrologische Beiträge zu Ehren von Bärbel Kramer*: 93–104. Archiv für Papyrusforschung und verwandte Gebiete, Beiheft 27. Berlin: Walter de Gruyter.

Koemoth, P.

1993 "Le rite de redresser Osiris." In J. Quaegebeur (ed.), *Ritual and Sacrifice in the Ancient Near East*: 157–174. OLA 55. Leuven: Peeters.

1994 *Osiris et les arbres: contribution à l'étude des arbres sacrés de l'Egypte ancienne*. Ægyptiaca Leodiensia 3. Liège: C.I.P.L.

Kruchten, J.-M.

1989 *Les Annales des Prêtres de Karnak (XXI–XXIIImes dynasties) et autres textes contemporains relatifs à l'initiation des prêtres d'Amon*. OLA 32. Leuven: Peeters.

Krupp, E. C.

1983 *Echoes of the Ancient Skies: The Astronomy of Lost Civilizations*. New York: Harper & Row.

1984 "Egypt. Astronomy: Temples, Traditions, Tombs." In E. C. Krupp (ed.), *Archaeoastronomy and the Roots of Science*. AAAS Selected Symposium 71. Boulder: Westview Press.

Kuhlmann, K. P.

1977 *Der Thron im alten Ägypten. Untersuchungen zu Semantik, Ikonographie und Symbolik eines Herrschaftszeichens*. ADAIK, Ägyptologische Reihe 10. Glückstadt: Verlag J. J. Augustin.

Kurth, D.

1977 "Haroëris," *LÄ* 2, cols. 999–1003. Wiesbaden: Harrassowitz.

1982 "Nut," *LÄ* 4, cols. 535–541. Wiesbaden: Harrassowitz.

1983 *Die Dekoration der Säulen im Pronaos des Tempels von Edfu*. Göttinger Orientforschungen, IV. Reihe, Ägypten 11. Wiesbaden: Harrassowitz, 1983.

Labrique, F.

1992 *Stylistique et théologie à Edfou. Le rituel de l'offrande de la campagne: Étude de la composition*. OLA 51. Leuven: Peeters.

Lacau, P.

1902 "La déesse [hieroglyphs]," *RecTrav* 24: 198–200.

Lacau, P. and Chevrier, H.

1977 *Une chapelle d'Hatshepsout à Karnak*, I. Cairo: IFAO.

Larson, J.

1981 "The Heb-Sed Robe and the 'Ceremonial Robe' of Tut'ankhamun," *JEA* 67: 180–181.

Laskowska-Kusztal, E.

1988–1991 "Imhotep d'Elephantine." In S. Schoske (ed.), *Akten des vierten Internationalen Ägyptologen Kongresses, München 1985*: 281–287. SAK Beihefte 1. Hamburg: Helmut Buske Verlag.

Lavier, M.-C.

1988–1991 "Les mystères d'Osiris à Abydos d'après les stèles du Moyen Empire et du Nouvel Empire." In S. Schoske (ed.), *Akten des vierten Internationalen Ägyptologen Kongresses, München 1985*: 289–295. SAK Beihefte 1. Hamburg: Helmut Buske Verlag.

Leclant, J.

1950 "Quelques données nouvelles sur 'l'édifice dit de Taharqa', près du Lac Sacré à Karnak," *BIFAO* 49: 181–192.

1951 "Le rôle du lait et de l'allaitement d'après les Textes des Pyramides," *JNES* 10: 123–127.

1965 *Recherches sur les monuments thébains de la XXVe dynastie dite éthiopienne*. BdE 36. Cairo: IFAO.

1981–1982 "Isis au pays de Koush," *Annuaire. École Pratique des Hautes Études. Ve section – Sciences Religieuses* 90: 37–59.

Lecoco, F.

2005 "Les Sources égyptiennes du mythe du phénix." In J. Leclant and F. Lecoco (eds.), *L'Égypte à Rome: Actes du colloque de Caen des 28–30 Sept. 2002*: 211–264. Caen: Université de Caen.

Lefebvre, G.

1903 "Sarcophages égyptiens trouvès dans une nécropole gréco-romaine à Tehneh," *ASAE* 4: 227–231.

Legrain, G.

1901 "Le temple et les chapelles d'Osiris à Karnak," *RecTrav* 23: 65–75, 163–172.

1915 "La litanie de Ouasit," *ASAE* 15: 273–283.

Leitz, C.

1994 "Auseinandersetzungen zwischen Baba und Thoth." In H. Behlmer (ed.), *Quaerentes scientiam: Festgabe für Wolfhart Westendorf zu seinem 70. Geburtstag überreicht von seinen Schülern*: 103–117. Göttingen: Seminar für Ägyptologie und Koptologie.

1995 *Altägyptische Sternuhren*. OLA 62. Leuven: Peeters.

2002–2003 *Lexikon der Ägyptischen Götter und Götterbezeichnungen*. OLA 110–116, 129. Leuven: Peeters.

2004 *Quellentexte zur ägyptischen Religion Die Tempelinschriften der griechisch-römischen Zeit*, I. Münster: Lit, 2004.

Lepsius, R.

1897–1913 *Denkmäler aus Aegypten und Aethiopien*, Text edited by E. Naville, I–V. Leipzig: Hinrichs.

Lesko, L.

1972 *The Ancient Egyptian Book of Two Ways*. Berkeley: University of California Press.

Lesko, L. and Lesko, B. S.

2002 *A Dictionary of Late Egyptian*, 2nd edition, I–II. Providence: B.C. Scribe.

Lichtheim, M.

1973 *Ancient Egyptian Literature: A Book of Readings*, I–III. Berkeley: University of California Press.

1988 *Ancient Egyptian Autobiographies Chiefly of the Middle Kingdom: A Study and an Anthology*. OBO 84. Göttingen: Vandenhoeck & Ruprecht.

von Lieven, A.

2007 *Grundriss des Laufes der Sterne: Das Sogenannte Nutbuch*, I–II. Carlsberg Papyri 8, CNI Publications 31. Copenhagen: The Carsten Niebuhr Institute of Near Eastern Studies, University of Copenhagen.

Lloyd, A.

2007 "Darius I in Egypt: Suez and Hibis." In C. Tuplin (ed.), *Persian Responses: Political and Cultural Interaction with(in) the Achaemenid Empire*: 99–115. Swansea: Classical Press of Wales.

Lorton, D.

1994 "The Invocation Hymn at the Temple of Hibis," *SAK* 21: 159–217.

Louant, E.

2003 "Harsomtus the Child, Son of Horus of Edfu, and the Triple Confirmation of the Royal Power." In D. Budde, S. Sandri, and U. Verhoeven (eds.), *Kindgötter im Ägypten der griechisch-römischen Zeit: Zeugnisse aus Stadt und Tempel als Spiegel des interkulturellen Kontakts*: 225–250. OLA 128. Leuven: Peeters.

Lubicz, R. A. Schwaller de

1999 *The Temples of Karnak*. London: Thames & Hudson.

Mahmud, A. El-Sayed

1978 *A New Temple for Hathor at Memphis*. Warminster: Aris & Phillips.

Málek, J.

1997 "The Temples at Memphis: Problems highlighted by the EES survey." In S. Quirke (ed.), *The Temple in Ancient Egypt, New Discoveries and Recent Research*: 90–101. London: British Museum Press.

Manassa, C.

2007 *The Late Egyptian Underworld: Sarcophagi and Related Texts from the Nectanebid Period*. ÄAT 72. Wiesbaden: Harrassowitz.

Marchand, S., Coulon, L., and Leclère, F.

1995 "'Catacombes' Osiriennes de Ptolémée IV à Karnak: Rapport préliminaire de la campagne de fouilles 1993," *Karnak* 10: 205–251.

Mariette, A.

1869 *Abydos. Description des fouilles exécutées sur l'emplacement de cette ville*. Paris: Imprimerie nationale.

1870–1875 *Dendérah: Description générale du grand temple de cette ville, Ouvrage publié sous les auspices de s.a. Ismail-pacha, khédive d'Egypte,* I–VI. Paris: A. Franck.

1892 *Monuments divers recueillis en Égypte et en Nubie*. Paris: Vieweg.

Marro, G.

1929 "Ernesto Schiaparelli 1856–1928," *BSPABA* 13: 39–42.

Martin, K.

1992 "Einige magische Kleindenkmäler griechisch-römischer Zeit im Übersee-Museum zu Bremen, in U. Luft (ed.), *The Intellectual Heritage of Egypt: Studies Presented to László Kákosy*: 411–421. Studia Aegyptiaca 14. Budapest: La chaire d'Egyptologie (ELTE).

Maspero, G.

1915 "Les Monuments Égyptiens du Musée de Marseille," *RecTrav* 37: 1–16.

Massart, A.

1957 "The Egyptian Geneva Papyrus MAH 15274," *MDAIK* 15: 172–185.

Meeks, D.

1972 *Le grand texte des donations au temple d'Edfou*. BdE 59. Cairo: IFAO.

Meeks, D. and Favard-Meeks, C.

1996 *Daily Life of the Egyptian Gods*. Ithaca: Cornell University Press.

Meyer, C.
1986 "Toilettengeräte," *LÄ* 6, cols. 625–627. Wiesbaden: Harrassowitz.

Minas-Nerpel, M.
2006 *Der Gott Chepri: Untersuchungen zu Schriftzeugnissen und ikonographischen Quellen vom Alten Reich bis in griechisch-römische Zeit*. OLA 154. Leuven: Peeters.

Mokhtar, G.
1991 "Relations between Ihnasya and Memphis during the Ramesside Period." In E. Bleiberg and R. Freed (eds.), *Fragments of a Shattered Visage: The Proceedings of the International Symposium on Ramesses the Great*: 105–107. Monographs of the Institute of Egyptian Art and Archaeology 1. Memphis: Memphis State University, 1991, pp. 105–107.

Montet, P.
1947 *Les constructions et le tombeau d'Osorkon II à Tanis*. Paris: Jourde et Allard.
1951 *Les constructions et le tombeau de Psousennès à Tanis*. Paris: J. Dumoulin.
1960 *Les constructions et le tombeau de Chéchanq III à Tanis*. Paris: Jourde et Allard.
1964 "Le rituel de fondation des temples égyptiens," *Kêmi* 17: 74–100.

Morenz, S. and Schubert, J.
1954 *Der Gott auf der Blume. Eine ägyptische Kosmogonie und ihre weltweite Bildwirkung*. Artibus Asiae 12. Ascona: Verlag Artibus Asiae.

Moret, A.
1902 *Le rituel du culte divin journalier en Égypte d'après les papyrus de Berlin et les textes du temple de Séti Ier, à Abydos*. Paris: Leroux.
1913 *Mystères égyptiens*. Paris: A. Colin, 1913.
1931 "La légende d'Osiris à l'époque thébaine d'après l'hymne à Osiris du Louvre," *BIFAO* 30: 725–750.

Morgan, J. de
1895–1909 *Kom Ombos: Catalogue des monuments et inscriptions de l' Egypte antique*, V. Vienna: Adolphe Holzhausen.

Morkot, R.
1996 "The Darb el-Arbain, the Kharga Oasis and its Forts, and other Desert Routes." In D. M. Bailey (ed.), *Archaeological Research in Roman Egypt*: 82–94. Journal of Roman Archaeology Supplement 19. Ann Arbor: Journal of Roman Archaeology.

Munro, I.
1983 *Das Zelt-Heiligtum des Min. Rekonstruktion und Deutung eines fragmentarischen Modells (Kestner-Museum 1935.200.2500)*. MÄS 41. Munich: Deutscher Kunstverlag.

Münster, M.
1968 *Untersuchungen zur Göttin Isis, vom Alten Reich bis zum Ende des Neuen Reiches*. MÄS 11. Berlin: B. Hessling.

Myśliwiec, K.

1979 *Studien zum Gott Atum*. Band II: *Name – Epitheta –Ikonographie*. HÄB 8. Hildesheim: Gerstenberg Verlag.

1985 *Eighteenth Dynasty before the Amarna Period*. Iconography of Religions XVI.5. Leiden: E.J. Brill.

1991 "Ramesside Traditions in the Arts of the Third Intermediate Period." In E. Bleiberg and R. Freed (eds.), *Fragments of a Shattered Visage: The Proceedings of the International Symposium on Ramesses the Great*: 108–126. Monographs of the Institute of Egyptian Art and Archaeology 1 Memphis: Memphis State University.

2000 *The Twilight of Ancient Egypt: First Millennium B.C.E.* Ithaca: Cornell University Press.

Naville, É.

1875 *La litanie du soleil: inscriptions recueillies dans les tombeaux des rois à Thèbes*. Leipzig: Engelmann.

1885–1887 *The Shrine of Saft el Henneh and the Land of Goshen*. MEEF 5. London: Egypt Exploration Fund.

1886 *Das ägyptische Todtenbuch der XVIII. bis XX. Dynastie*, I–III. Berlin: Asher.

1887–1889 *The Festival-Hall of Osorkon II in the Great Temple of Bubastis*. MEEF 10. London: K. Paul, Trench, Trübner.

Naville, É. and Somers Clarke, G.

1894 *The Temple of Deir El Bahari*, I–VII. MEEF 12–14, 16, 19, 27, 29. London: Egypt Exploration Fund.

Nelson, H. H.

1936 *Reliefs and Inscriptions at Karnak*, I–II. OIP 25. Chicago: University of Chicago Press.

1981 *The Great Hypostyle Hall at Karnak*, I, Part 1: *The Wall Reliefs*, ed. by W. G. Murnane. OIP 106. Chicago: University of Chicago Press.

Neugebauer, O. and Lange, H. O.

1940 *Papyrus Carlsberg no. I: Ein hieratischdemotischer-kosmologischer Text*. Copenhagen: Munksgaard.

Neugebauer, O. and Parker, R. A.

1960 *Egyptian Astronomical Texts I. The Early Decans*. Brown Egyptological Studies 3. London: Lund Humphries.

1964 *Egyptian Astronomical Texts II. The Ramesside Star Clocks*. Brown Egyptological Studies 5. London: Lund Humphries.

1969 *Egyptian Astronomical Texts. III. Decanṣ, Planets, Constellations and Zodiacs*. Brown Egyptological Studies 6. Providence: Brown University Press.

Newberry, P. E.

1932 *"Šsm.t." Studies presented to F. L. Griffith*. London: Egypt Exploration Society.

Osing, J.

1982 "Die beschrifteten Funde." In J.Osing (ed.), *Denkmäler der Oase Dachla. Aus dem Nachlass von Ahmed Fakhry*: 18–41. Archäologische Veröffentlichungen 28. Mainz am Rhein: Verlag Philipp von Zabern.

1986 "Zu den Osiris-Räumen im Tempel von Hibis." In H. Altenmüller (ed.), *Hommages à François Daumas*: 511–516. Montpellier: Université de Montpellier.

1990 "Zur Anlage und Dekoration des Tempels von Hibis." In S. Israelit-Groll (ed.), *Studies in Egyptology Presented to Miriam Lichtheim*, II: 751–767. Jerusalem: The Magnes Press, the Hebrew University.

Otto, E.

1938 "Die Lehre von den beiden Ländern Ägyptens in der ägyptischen Religionsgeschichte." In A. M. Blackman and H. Stock (eds.), *Studia Ægyptiaca*: 10–16. Analecta Orientalia 17. Rome: Pontificium Institutum Biblicum.

1960 *Das ägyptische Mundöffnungsritual*, I–II. Ägyptologische Abhandlungen 3. Wiesbaden: Harrassowitz.

1963 "Altägyptischer Polytheismus. Eine Beschreibung," *Saeculum: Jahrbuch für Universalgeschichte* 14: 249–285.

1967 *Ancient Egyptian Art: The Cults of Osiris and Amon*. New York: Abrams.

1975 "Augensagen," *LÄ* 1, cols. 562–567. Wiesbaden: Harrassowitz.

Panagiotis, K.

2007 "Some Remarks on the Ritual of 'Striking the Ball' in the Liturgical Environment of the Ptolemaic Temples." In H. Beinlich, R. Gundlach, and D. Kurth (eds.). *Ägyptologische Tempeltagung 6: Funktion und Gebrauch altägyptischer Tempelräume: Leiden, 4–7. September 2002*: 153–166. Königtum, Staat und Gesellschaft früher Hochkulturen 3. Wiesbaden: Harrassowitz.

Panofsky, E.

1939 *Studies in Iconology: Humanistic Themes in the Art of the Renaissance*. New York: Oxford University Press.

Parker, R. A.

1941 "Darius and his Egyptian Campaign," *AJSL* 58: 373–377.

1950 *The Calendars of Ancient Egypt*. SAOC 26. Chicago: University of Chicago Press.

1959 *A Vienna Demotic Papyrus on Eclipse and Lunar Omina*. Brown Egyptological Studies 2. Providence: Brown University Press, 1959.

Parker, R. A., Leclant, J., and Goyon, J.-C.

1979 *The Edifice of Taharqa by the Sacred Lake of Karnak*. Brown Egyptological Studies 8. Providence: Brown University Press.

Pécoil, J.-F.

1993 "Les sources mythiques du Nil et le cycle de la crue," *BSEG* 17: 97–110.

Perrin, Y.

1982 "Néron et l'Egypte, Une stèle de Coptos montrant Néron devant Min et Osiris (Musée de Lyon)," *Revue des Études Anciennes* 84: 117–131.

Peterson, B. J.

1964 "Der Gott Schesemu und das Wort *mḏd*," *Orientalia Sueca* 12: 83–88.

Petrie, W. M. F.

1896 *Koptos*. London: Quaritch.

1917 *Tools and Weapons, illustrated by the Egyptian Collection in University College*. Publications of the Egyptian Research Account and British School of Archaeology in Egypt 30. London: British School of Archaeology in Egypt.

Piankoff, A.

1942 *Le Livre du Jour et de la Nuit*. BdE 13. Cairo: IFAO.

1944 "Le Livre des Quererts," *BIFAO* 42: 1–62.

1954 *The Tomb of Ramesses VI*. Bollingen Series 40.1. New York: Pantheon Books.

1955 *The Shrines of Tut-Ankh-Amun*. Bollingen Series 40.2. New York: Pantheon Books.

1964 *The Litany of Re. Texts Translated with Commentary*. New York: Bollingen Foundation.

Piccato, A.

1997 "The Berlin Leather Roll and the Egyptian Sense of History," *LingAeg* 5: 137–159.

Pinch, G.

2004 *Egyptian Mythology: A Guide to the Gods, Goddesses, and Traditions of Ancient Egypt*. Oxford: Oxford University Press.

Poncet, C. J.

1709 *A Voyage to Æthiopia, Made in the Years 1698, 1699, and 1700, Describing Particularly That Famous Empire; As Also the Kingdoms of Dongola, Sennar, Part of Egypt, With the Natural History of Those Parts*. London: Printed for W. Lewis.

Poo, M.

1995 *Wine and Wine Offering in the Religion of Ancient Egypt*. London and New York: Kegan Paul International.

Porter, B., Moss, R. L. B., and Málek, J.

1962–1999 *Topographical Bibliography of Ancient Egyptian Hieroglyphic Texts, Reliefs, and Paintings*, I–VIII. Oxford: Griffith Institute, Ashmolean Museum.

Posener, G.

1936 *La première domination Perse en Egypte: recueil d'inscriptions hiéroglyphiques*. BdE 11. Cairo: IFAO.

1969 "Sur l'emploi euphémique de *ḫftj(w)* 'ennemi(s),'" *ZÄS* 96: 30–35.

Quack, J. F.

1989 "Sur l'emploi euphémique de *ḫft* "ennemi" en démotique," *RdE* 40: 197–198.

1992 "Philologische Miszellen 1," *LingAeg* 2: 151–153.

1999 "Der historische Abschnitt des Buches vom Tempel." In J. Assmann and E. Blumenthal (eds.), *Literatur und Politik im pharaonischen und ptolemäischen Ägypten: Vorträge der Tagung zum Gedenken an Georges Posener 5–10. September 1996 in Leipzig*: 267–278. BdE 127. Cairo: IFAO.

2000 "Das Buch vom Tempel und verwandte Texte: Ein Vorbericht," *Archiv für Religionsgeschichte* 2: 1–20.

2000 "Die Rituelle Erneuerung der Osirisfigurinen," *Die Welt des Orients* 31: 5–18.

2000 "Kollation und Korrekturvorschläge zum Papyrus Carlsberg 1." In Paul J. Frandsen and Kim Ryholt (eds.), *A Miscellany of Demotic Texts and Studies*: 165–171. The Carlsberg Papyri 3. Copenhagen: Museum Tusculanum Press,.

Quaegebeur, J.

1986 "Thot-Hermès, le dieu le plus grand!" In H. Altenmüller (ed.), *Hommages à François Daumas*: 525–544. Montpellier: Université de Montpellier.

1991 "Les quatre dieux Min." In P. Derchain, U. Verhoeven, and E. Graefe (eds.), *Religion und Philosophie im Alten Ägypten. Festgabe für Philippe Derchain zu seinem 65. Geburtstag am 24. Juli 1991*: 253–268. OLA 39. Leuven: Peeters.

1991 "Somtous l'Enfant sur le lotus," *CRIPEL* 13: 113–121.

Quirke, S.

1992 *Ancient Egyptian Religion*. London: British Museum Press.

Raven, M.

1982 "Corn Mummies," *OMRO* 63: 3–38.

1997 "Four Corn Mummies in the Archaeological Museum at Cracow," *Materialy Archeologiczne* 30: 5–11.

Recklinghausen, D. von and Stadler, M. A.

2011 *Kultorte: Mythen, Wissenschaft und Alltag in den Tempeln Ägyptens*. Berlin: Manetho.

Refai, H.

2000 *Untersuchungen zum Bildprogramm der grossen Säulensäle in den thebanischen Tempeln des Neuen Reiches*. Beiträge zur Ägyptologie 18, Veröffentlichungen der Institute für Afrikanistik und Ägyptologie der Universität Wien 91. Vienna: Afro-Pub.

2001 "Nebet-Hetepet, Iusas und Temet, Die Weiblichen Komplemente des Atum," *GM* 181: 89–94.

Reymond, E. A. E.

1969 *The Mythical Origins of the Egyptian Temple*. Manchester: Manchester University Press.

1972 "The *sʿḥ* 'Eternal Image,'" *ZÄS* 98: 132–140.

Ringgren, H.

1947 *Word and Wisdom: Studies in the Hypostatization of Divine Qualities and Functions in the Ancient Near East*. Lund: H. Ohlssons Boktryckeri.

Ritner, R. K.

1993 *The Mechanics of Ancient Egyptian Magical Practice*. SAOC 54. Chicago: Oriental Institute of the University of Chicago.

Roberts, A.

1995 *Hathor Rising. The Serpent Power of Ancient Egypt*. Totnes: Northgate Publishers.

Rochemonteix, Le Marquis de
1897 *Le temple d'Edfou I.* MMAF 10. Cairo: IFAO.

Roeder, G.
1914 *Naos, Catalogue général des antiquités égyptiennes 70001–70050.* Leipzig: Breitkopf & Härtel, 1914.

Rohlfs, G., Ascherson, P., Jordan, W., and von Zittel, K. A.
1875 *Drei Monate in der libyschen Wüste.* Cassel: T. Fischer.

Root, M. C.
1979 *The King and Kingship in Achaemenid Art. Essays on the Creation of an Iconography of Empire.* Acta Iranica 19. Leiden: E.J. Brill.

Roth, A. M.
2002 "Magical Bricks and the Bricks of Birth," *JEA* 88: 121–139.

Rummel, U.
2003 *Untersuchungen zum Gott Iunmutef vom Alten Reich bis zum Ende des Neuen Reiches.* PhD Dissertation, Universität Hamburg.

Rusch, A.
1922 *Die Entwicklung der Himmelsgöttin Nut zu einer Totengottheit.* Mitteilungen der Vordersiatisch-Ägyptischen Gesellschaft 22. Leipzig: Hinrichs.

Sambin, C.
1988 *L'offrande de la soit-disant "clepsydre." Le symbole Šbt / wnšb / wtṯ.* Budapest: Université Eőtvős Loránd.

Sander-Hansen, C. E.
1937 *Die religiösen Texte auf dem Sarg der Anchnesneferibrê.* Copenhagen: Levin & Munksgaard, 1937.

Sauneron, S.
1952 *Rituel de l'Embaumement. Pap. Boulaq III. Pap. Louvre 5.158.* Cairo: Imprimerie Nationale.
1962 *Les fêtes religieuses d'Esna aux derniers siècles du paganisme.* Esna 5. Cairo: IFAO, 1962.
1963–1975 *Le temple d'Esna*, II-IV. Cairo: IFAO.

Schott, E.
1977 "Goldhaus," *LÄ* 2, col. 739. Wiesbaden: Harrassowitz.

Schott, S.
1938 "Das blutrünstige Keltergerät," *ZÄS* 74: 88–93.
1953 *Das schöne Fest vom Wüstentale. Festbräuche einer Totenstadt.* Wiesbaden: Verlag der Akademie der Wissenschaften und der Literatur in Mainz.
1965 "Nut spricht als Mutter und Sarg," *RdE* 17: 81–87.
1968 "Falke, Geier und Ibis als Krönungsboten," *ZÄS* 95: 54–65.

Schulman, A. R.
1994 "Take for Yourself the Sword." In B. Bryan and D. Lorton (eds.), *Essays in Egyptology in Honor of Hans Goedicke*: 265–295. San Antonio: Van Siclen Books.

Schumacher, I. W.

1988 *Der Gott Sopdu, der Herr der Fremdländer*. OBO 79. Göttingen: Vandenhoeck & Ruprecht.

Schweinfurth, G. A.

1875 "Notizen zur Kenntniss der Oase El-Chargeh," *Petermann's geographische Mittheilungen* 10: 384–393.

Seele, K.

1959 *The Coregency of Ramses II with Seti I and the Date of the Great Hypostyle Hall at Karnak*. SAOC 19. Chicago: University of Chicago Press.

1959 *The Tomb of Tjanefer at Thebes*. OIP 86. Chicago: The University of Chicago Press.

Sethe, K.

1902 *Imhotep: Der Asklepios der Aegypter, Untersuchungen*. Untersuchungen zur Geschichte und Altertumskunde Aegyptens 2. Leipzig: Hinrichs, reprint 1964.

1910 "Untersuchungen über die ägyptischen Zahlwörter," *ZÄS* 47: 1–41.

1928 *Dramatische Texte zu altägyptischen Mysterienspielen*. Untersuchungen zur Geschichte und Altertumskunde Aegyptens 10. Leipzig: Hinrichs.

1935 *Übersetzung und Kommentar zu den altägyptischen Pyramidentexten*, I–IV. Leipzig: Hinrichs.

1960 *Die altägyptischen Pyramidentexte, nach den Papierabdrücken und Photographien des Berliner Museums, neu herausgegeben und erläutert*, I–III. Hildesheim: Georg Olms Verlagsbuchhandlung.

Shirun-Grumach, I.

1985 "Remarks on the Goddess Maat." In S. Israelit-Groll (ed.), *Pharaonic Egypt: The Bible and Christianity*: 176–179. Jerusalem: The Magnes Press, the Hebrew University.

Shore, A. F.

1992 "Human and Divine Mummification." In A. B. Lloyd (ed.), *Studies in Pharaonic Religion and Society in Honour of J. Gwyn Griffiths*: 226–235. Occasional Publications 8. London: The Egypt Exploration Society.

Smith, M.

1993 *The Liturgy of Opening the Mouth for Breathing*. Oxford: Griffith Institute.

2005 *Papyrus Harkness (MMA 31.9.7)*. Oxford: Griffith Institute.

2006 "The Great Decree Issued to the Nome of the Silent Land," *RdE* 57: 217–232.

2009 *Traversing Eternity: Texts for the Afterlife from Ptolemaic and Roman Egypt*. Oxford: Oxford University Press.

Spencer, A. J.

1978 "Two Enigmatic Hieroglyphs and their Relation to the Sed-Festival," *JEA* 64: 52–55.

Spencer, N. and Rosenow, D.

2006 *A Naos of Nekhthorheb from Bubastis: Religious Iconography and Temple Building in the 30th Dynasty*. London: British Museum.

Spencer, P.

1984 *The Egyptian Temple. A Lexicographical Study*. London: Kegan Paul International.

Spiegel, J.

1956 "Das Auferstehungritual der Unas-Pyramide," *ASAE* 53: 339–439.

Spiegelberg, W.

1924 "Zu *R3-št3.w* 'Nekropolis,'" *ZÄS* 59: 159–160.

Spieß, H.

1991 *Der Aufstieg eines Gottes. Untersuchungen zum Gott Thot bis zum Beginn des Neuen Reiches*. PhD Dissertation, Universität Hamburg.

Stadelmann, R.

1970 "Totentempel und Millionenjahrhaus in Theben," *MDAIK* 35: 303–321.

Steindorff, G.

1946 *Catalogue of the Egyptian Sculpture in the Walters Art Gallery*. Baltimore: Walters Art Gallery.

Sternberg-El-Hotabi, H.

1985 *Mythische Motive und Mythenbildung in den ägyptischen Tempeln und Papyri der griechisch-römischen Zeit*. Göttinger Orientforschungen, IV. Reihe, Ägypten 14. Wiesbaden: Harrassowitz.

1994 "Die 'Götterliste' des Sanktuars im Hibis-Tempel von El-Chargeh. Überlegungen zur Tradierung und Kodifizierung religiösen und kulttopographischen Gedankengutes." In M. Minas, Z. Jürgen (eds.), *Aspekte spätägyptischer Kultur. Festschrift für Erich Winter zum 65. Geburtstag*: 239–254. Mainz am Rhein: Verlag Philipp von Zabern.

2006 "Der Hibistempel in der Oase el Charga: Architektur und Dekoration im Spannungsfeld Ägyptischer und Persischer Interessen." In R. Rollinger, B. Truschnegg, and P. W. Haider (eds.), *Altertum und Mittelmeerraum: Die antike Welt diesseits und jenseits der Levante: Festschrift für Peter W. Haider zum 60. Geburtstag*: 527–547. Oriens et Occidens 12. Stuttgart: F. Steiner.

2006 "Der Raum M im Hibistempel von el Charga." In F. Junge, G. Moers (eds.), *Jn.t Dr.w: Festschrift für Friedrich Junge*, II: 597–623. Göttingen: Seminar für Ägyptologie und Koptologie.

Stricker, B. H.

1953 "Osiris en de obelisk," *OMRO* 34: 32–47.

Symons, S.

2007 "A Star's Year: The Annual Cycle in the Ancient Egyptian Sky." In J. M. Steele (ed.), *Calendars and Years: Astronomy and Time in the Ancient Near East*: 1–34. Oxford: Oxbow.

Teeter, E.

1997 *The Presentation of Maat: Ritual and Legitimacy in Ancient Egypt*. SAOC 57. Chicago: Oriental Institute of the University of Chicago.

The Epigraphic Survey

1930–1970 *Medinet Habu*. OIP 8, 9, 23, 51, 83, 84, 93, 94, 8 vols. Chicago: Oriental Institute of the University of Chicago.

Thiem, A.-C.

2000 *Speos von Gebel es-Silsileh: Analyse der architektonischen und ikonographischen Konzeption im Rahmen des politischen und legitimatorischen Programmes der Nachamarnazeit*. ÄAT 47. Wiesbaden: Harrassowitz.

Tolmachta, H. G.

2003 "A Reconsideration of the Benu-Bird in Egyptian Cosmogony." In Z. A. Hawass, L. P. Brock (eds.), *Egyptology at the Dawn of the Twenty-First Century: Proceedings of the Eighth International Congress of Egyptologists, Cairo, 2000*, II: 522–526. Cairo: American University in Cairo Press.

2004 "Ancient Egyptian Roots of the Phoenix Myth: On the History of the Problem." In A. Maravelia (ed.), *Europe, Hellas and Egypt: Complementary Antipodes during Late Antiquity. Papers from Session IV. 3, Held at the European Association of Archaeologists Eighth Annual Meeting, in Thessaloniki, 2002*: 93–98. Oxford: Archaeopress.

Töpfer, S.

2015 *Das Balsamierungsritual: Eine (Neu-)Edition der Textkomposition Balsamierungsritual (pBoulaq 3, pLouvre 5158, pDurham 1983.11 + pSt. Petersburg 18128)*. Studien zur spätägyptischen Religion 13. Wiesbaden: Harrassowitz.

Tooley, A. M. J.

1996 "Osiris Bricks," *JEA* 82: 167–179.

Traunecker, C.

1980 "Un document nouveau sur Darius Ier à Karnak," *Karnak* VI: 209–213.

1986 "Cryptes décorées, cryptes anépigraphes." In H. Altenmüller (ed.), *Hommages à François Daumas*: 571–577. Montpellier: Université de Montpellier.

1991 "De l'hiérophanie au temple. Quelques réflexions…" In U. Verhoeven and E. Graefe (eds.), *Religion und Philosophie im Alten Ägypten. Festgabe für Philippe Derchain zu seinem 65. Geburtstag am 24. Juli 1991*: 303–317. OLA 39. Leuven: Peeters.

1991 "Observations sur le Décor des temples Égyptiens." In F. Dunand, J. Spieser, and J. Wirth (eds.), *L'image et la production du sacré*: 77–102. Paris: Geuthner.

1992 *Coptos. Hommes et dieux sur le parvis de Geb*. Leuven: Peeters.

1994 "Cryptes connues et inconnues des temples tardifs," *BSFE* 129: 21–46.

1995 "Les ouabet des temples d'el Qal'a et de Chenhour. Décoration, origine et evolution." In D. Kurth, W. Waitkus, and S. Woodhouse (eds.), *Ägyptologische Tempeltagung. Hamburg, 1–5 Juni 1994. Systeme und Programme der ägyptischen Tempeldekoration*, III: 241–282. ÄAT 33. Wiesbaden: Harrassowitz.

Traunecker, C., Le Saout, F., and Masson, O.

1981 *La chapelle d'Achôris à Karnak. II. Texte [et] Documents*. Paris: Éditions A.D.P.F..

Ullmann, M.

2007 "Thebes: Origins of a Ritual Landscape." In P. Dorman and B. Bryan (eds.), *Sacred Space and Sacred Function in Ancient Thebes*: 3–25. SAOC 61. Chicago: Oriental Institute of the University of Chicago.

Valbelle, D.

1981 *Satis et Anoukis*. Mainz am Rhein: Verlag Philipp von Zabern.

Valloggia, M.

1981 "This sur la route des Oasis." In *Bulletin du centenaire*: 185–190. BIFAO Supplément 81. Cairo: IFAO.

1983 "Les routes du désert dans l'Égypte ancienne." In C. Yves (ed.), *Le désert, image et réalité. Actes du Collogue de Cartigny*: 165–171. Cahiers du Centre d'étude du Proche-Orient Ancien 3. Leuven: Peeters.

van den Broek, R.

1972 *The Myth of the Phoenix According to Classical and Early Christian Traditions*. Leiden: E. J. Brill.

van der Plas, D.

1994 "Tempel in Ägypten." In R. Gundlach and M. Rochholz (eds.), *Ägyptische Tempel – Struktur, Funktion und Programm. Akten der Ägyptologischen Tempeltagungen in Gosen 1990 und in Mainz 1992*: 239–254. HÄB 37. Hildesheim: Gerstenberg Verlag.

Vandier, J.

1956 "Quelques remarques sur le XVIIIe nome de Haute Égypte," *MDAIK* 14: 208–213.

1961 *Le Papyrus Jumilhac*. Paris: Centre National de la Recherche Scientifique.

1961 "Memphis et le taureau Apis dans le Papyrus Jumilhac." In *Mélanges Mariette*: 116–118. Cairo: IFAO.

1964 "Iousâas et (Hathor)-Nébet-Hétépet," *RdE* 16: 55–146.

1965 "Iousâas et (Hathor)-Nébet-Hétépet, Deuxième article," *RdE* 17: 89–176.

1966 "Iousâas et (Hathor)-Nébet-Hétépet, Troisième article," *RdE* 18: 67–142.

1968 "Iousâas et (Hathor)-Nébet-Hétépet. Quatrième article (additions)," *RdE* 20: 135–148.

Vassilika, E.

1989 *Art Treasures from the Museo Egizio*. Turin: Umberto Allemandi & Co.

1989 *Ptolemaic Philae*. OLA 34. Leuven: Peeters.

te Velde, H.

1977 "Geb," *LÄ* 2, cols. 427–429. Wiesbaden: Harrassówitz.

Vercoutter, J.

1945 *Les objets égyptiens et égyptisants du mobilier funéraire carthaginois*. Paris: Geuthner.

1960 "The Napatan Kings and Apis Worship," *Kush* 8: 62–76.

Verhoeven, U. and Derchain, P.
1985 *Le voyage de la déesse libyque. Ein Text aus dem 'Mutritual' des Pap. Berlin 3053*. Rites Egyptiens 5. Brussels: Fondation Égyptologique Reine Élisabeth.

Vernus, P.
1979 "Douch arraché aux sables," *BSFE* 85: 7–21.
1991 "Le mythe d'un mythe: la pretendue noyade d'Osiris; de la derive d'un corps à la derive du sens," *Studi di Egittologia e di Antichità Puniche* 9: 19–34.

Veryard, E., Favard-Meeks, C., Volkoff, O. V., and Pitts, J.
1981 *Voyages en Egypte pendant les années 1678-1701*. Cairo: IFAO.

Vivian, C.
2008 *The Western Desert of Egypt: An Explorer's Handbook*. Cairo: American University in Cairo Press.

Vittmann, G.
1996 "Zum Gebrauch des *kꜣ*-Zeichens im Demotischen," *Studi di Egittologia e di Antichità Puniche* 15: 1–12.

Wahlberg, N.
2003 "Representations of Hathor and Mut in the Hibis Temple." In R. Ives (ed.), *Current Research in Egyptology III: December 2001*: 69–75. BAR International Series 1192. Oxford: Archaeopress.

Waitkus, W.
1995 "Zum funktionalen Zusammenhang von Krypta, Wabet und Goldhaus." In D. Kurth, (ed.), *Ägyptologische Tempeltagung, 3. Ägyptologische Tempeltagung: Hamburg, 1.–5. Juni 1994: Systeme und Programme der ägyptischen Tempeldekoration*: 283–303. ÄAT 33. Wiesbaden: Harrassowitz.
1997 *Die Texte in den unteren Krypten des Hathortempels von Dendera. Ihre Aussagen zur Funktion und Bedeutung dieser Räume*. MÄS 47. Mainz: Verlag Philipp von Zabern.

Weill, R.
1948 "Notes sur l'histoire primitive des grandes religions égyptiennes," *BIFAO* 47: 59–150.

Weinstein, M.
1973 *Foundation Deposits in Ancient Egypt*. PhD Dissertation, University of Michigan, Ann Arbor.

Wells, R. A.
1985 "Sothis and the Satet Temple on Elephantine," *SAK* 12: 255–302.
1985 "Sothis and the Satet Temple on Elephantine: An Egyptian 'Stonehenge?'" in S. Schoske (ed.), *Akten des vierten Internationalen Ägyptologen Kongresses, München 1985*: 105–115. SAK Beihefte 1. Hamburg: Verlag Helmut Buske.
1994 "Re and the Calendars." In A. J. Spalinger (ed.), *Revolutions in Time: Studies in Ancient Egyptian Calendrics*: 1–37. San Antonio: Van Siclen Books.
2001 "Astronomy," in D. B. Redford (ed.), *The Oxford Encyclopedia of Ancient Egypt*, vol. 1: 145–151. Oxford: Oxford University Press.

Welvaert, E.

1996 "On the Origin of the Ished-Scene," *GM* 151: 101–107.

Werner, E.

1985 *The God Montu: From the Earliest Attestations to the End of the New Kingdom.* PhD Dissertation, Yale University, New Haven.

Westendorf, W.

1966 "Ursprung und Wesen der Maât, der altägyptischen Göttin des Rechts, der Gerechtigkeit und der Weltordnung." In W. Will (ed.), *Festgabe für Dr. Walter Will*: 201–225. München: Heymann.

1975 "Dunanui," *LÄ* 1, cols. 1152–1153. Wiesbaden: Harrassowitz.

Wiedemann, A.

1901 "Bronze Circles and Purification Vessels in Egyptian Temples," *PSBA* 23: 263–274.

Wijngaarden, V.

1954 "Der Hibistempel in der Oase El-Chargeh," *ZÄS* 79: 68–72.

Wildung, D.

1972 "Two Representations of Gods from the Early Old Kingdom." In *Miscellanea Wilbouriana 1*: 146–160. Brooklyn: The Brooklyn Museum.

1977 "Ha," *LÄ* 2, col. 923. Wiesbaden: Harrassowitz.

1977 *Imhotep und Amenhotep. Gottwerdung im Alten Ägypten.* MÄS 36. Munich: Deutscher Kunstverlag.

Wilkinson, A.

1985 "Evidence for Osirian Rituals in the Tomb of Tutankhamun." In S. Israelit-Groll (ed.), *Pharaonic Egypt: The Bible and Christianity*: 328–340. Jerusalem: The Magnes Press, the Hebrew University.

Wilkinson, R. H.

1994 *Symbol and Magic in Egyptian Art.* New York: Thames and Hudson.

2000 *The Complete Temples of Ancient Egypt.* New York: Thames and Hudson.

2003 *The Complete Gods and Goddesses of Ancient Egypt.* New York: Thames and Hudson.

Willeitner, J.

2002 *Die ägyptischen Oasen: Städte, Tempel und Gräber in der libyschen Wüste.* München: Philipp von Zabern.

Willems, H.

1988 *Chests of Life: A Study of the Typology and Conceptual Development of Middle Kingdom Standard Class Coffins.* Mededelingen en verhandelingen van het Vooraziatisch-Egyptisch Genootschap 25. Leiden: Ex Oriente Lux.

Wilson, P.

1997 *A Ptolemaic Lexikon: A Lexicographical Study of the Texts in the Temple of Edfu.* OLA 78. Leuven: Peeters.

Winlock, H. E.
1941 *The Temple of Hibis in El Khargeh Oasis*, Part I: *The Excavations*. The Metropolitan Museum of Art, Egyptian Expedition. New York: Publications of The Metropolitan Museum of Art.

Winter, E.
1987 "Weitere Beobachtungen zur 'Grammaire du Temple' in der griechisch-römischen Zeit." In W. Helck (ed.), *Tempel und Kult*: 61–76. Ägyptologische Abhandlungen 46. Wiesbaden: Harrassowitz.
1989 "A Reconsideration of the Newly Discovered Building Inscription on the Temple of Denderah," *GM* 108: 75–85.

de Wit, C.
1958–1968 *Les inscriptions du temple d'Opet, à Karnak*, I–III. Bibliotheca Aegyptiaca 11–13. Brussels: Fondation Égyptologique Reine Élisabeth.
1961 "Inscriptions dédicatoires du temple d'Edfou," *CdÉ* 36: 277–320.

Woodhouse, S.
1997 "The Sun God, his Four Bas and the Four Winds in the Sacred District at Sais: The Fragment of an Obelisk (BM EA 1512)." In S. Quirke (ed.), *The Temple in Ancient Egypt. New Discoveries and Recent Research*: 132–151. London: British Museum Press.

Wuttmann, M., Bousquet, B., Chauveau, M., Dils, P., Marchand, S., Schweitzer, A., and Volay, L.
1996 "Premier rapport préliminaire des travaux sur le site de 'Ayn Manawir (oasis de Kharga)," *BIFAO* 96: 385–451.

Yoyotte, J.
1953 "Pour une localisation du pays de Iam," *BIFAO* 52: 173–178.
1957 "Le Soukhos de la Maréotide et d'autres cultes régionaux du dieu-crocodile d'après les cylindres du Moyen Empire," *BIFAO* 56: 81–95.
1961 "Études géographiques I. La 'Cité des Acacias' (Kafr Ammar)," *RdE* 13: 71–105.
1973 "Les inscriptions hiéroglyphiques égyptiennes de la statue de Darius," *Comptes rendus de l'Académie des Inscriptions et Belles-Lettres* (1973): 256–259.
1977 "La cuve osirienne de Coptos. Tanis: problèmes, bilans et perspectives," *Annuaire. Ecole Pratique des Hautes Etudes, Ve section – sciences religieuses, Paris* 86: 163–172.
1979 "Textes relatifs au culte d'Osiris et de Sokaris," *Annuaire. Ecole Pratique des Hautes Etudes, Ve section - sciences religieuses, Paris* 88: 193–199.
1980 "Une monumentale litanie de granit: les Sekhmet d'Aménophis III et la conjuration permanente de la déesse dangereuse," *BSFE* 87–88: 46–75.
1981–1982 "Religion de l'Egypte ancienne," *Annuaire. Ecole Pratique des Hautes Etudes, Ve section - sciences religieuses, Paris* 90: 189–196.
1991–1992 "Recherches de géographie historique et religieuse: sources et méthodes," *Annuaire du Collège de France* (1991–1992): 625–645.

Žabkar, L. V.

1968 *A Study of the Ba Concept in Ancient Egyptian Texts*. SAOC 34. Chicago: University of Chicago Press.

1975 *Apedemak. Lion God of Meroe. A Study in Egyptian-Meroitic Syncretism*. Warminster: Aris & Phillips.

Zecchi, M.

1996 "In Search of Merymutef, 'Lord of Khayet,'" *Aegyptus. Rivista Italiana di Egittologia e di Papirologia, Milano* 76: 7–14.

Ziegler, C.

1979 "A propos du rite des quatre boules," *BIFAO* 79: 437–439.

Zivie, C. M.

1980 "Bousiris du Létopolite." In J. Vercoutter (ed.), *Livre du Centenaire 1880–1980*: 91–107. Cairo: IFAO.

1984 "Encore Ro-setaou," *JEA* 70: 145.

Zivie-Coche, C. M.

1988 "Aux Marges de Memphis: Giza." In A. P. Zivie (ed.), *Memphis et ses nécropoles au Nouvel Empire. Nouvelles données, nouvelles questions. Actes du colloque CRNS. Paris, 9 au 11 octobre 1986*: 113–122. Paris: Éditions du Centre National de la Recherche Scientifique.

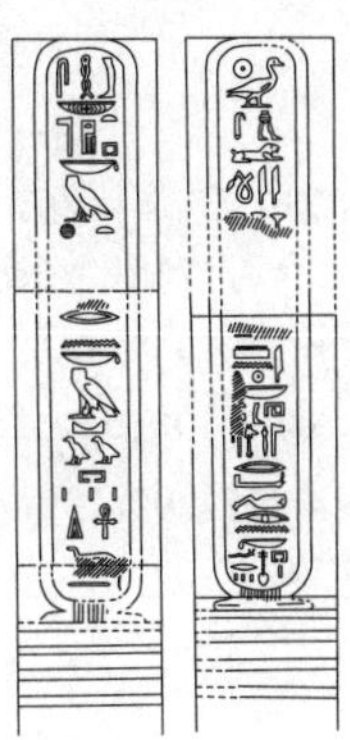

Index

DEITIES

WRITTEN SOURCES

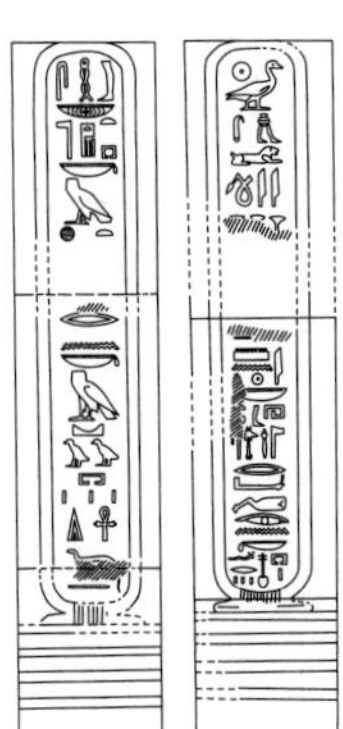

Plates

Plate 1: General view of the Temple of Hibis (photo taken by Fatma Ismail).

Plate 2: Aerial view of the site of the Temple of Hibis (photo after Willeitner, *Die ägyptischen Oasen: Städte, Tempel und Gräber in der libyschen Wüste*, fig. 26).

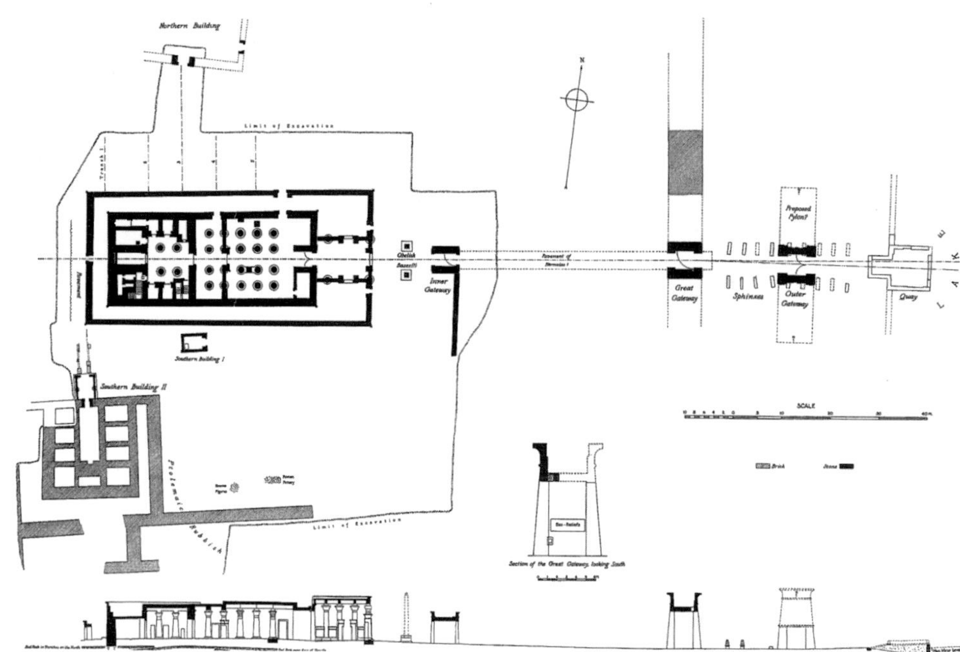

Plate 3: Plan of the Temple of Hibis (after Winlock, *The Temple of Hibis*, Part 1, plate XXX).

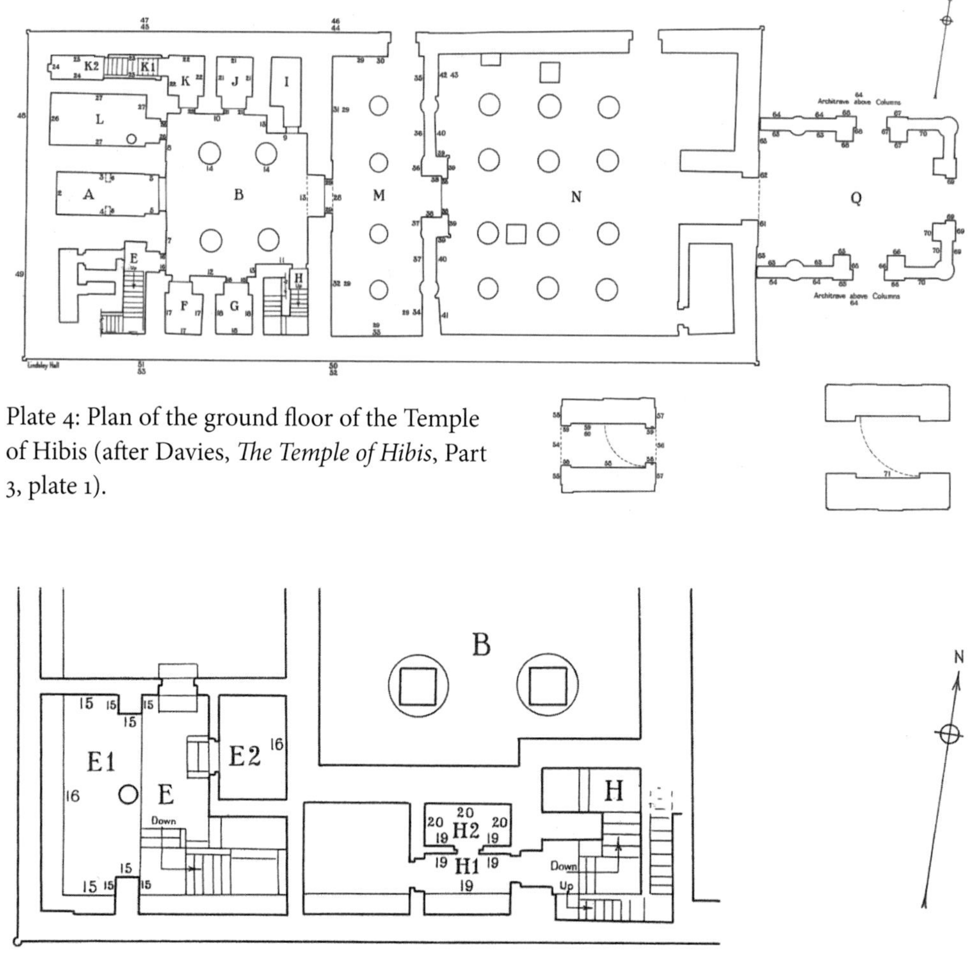

Plate 4: Plan of the ground floor of the Temple of Hibis (after Davies, *The Temple of Hibis*, Part 3, plate 1).

Plate 5: Plan of the upper floor of the Temple of Hibis (after Davies, *The Temple of Hibis*, Part 3, plate 1).

Plate 6: Line drawing of the scene of Seth slaying the Apophis snake (Davies, *The Temple of Hibis*, Part 3, plate 42).

Plate 7: Photo of the scene of Seth slaying the Apophis snake (photo taken by Fatma Ismail).

Plate 8: Line drawing of the south wall of the main sanctuary of the Temple of Hibis (Davies, *The Temple of Hibis*, Part 3, plate 4).

Plate 9: North wall of the main sanctuary of the Temple of Hibis (photo taken by Fatma Ismail).

Plate 10: View from the north side of hypostyle hall B, to the entrance doorways of the secondary chapels south of the main sanctuary A. From left to right, the photo shows the doorway to stairway H, the entrance doorway to chapel G, the entrance doorway to chapel F and the sunlit doorway to stairway E (photo taken by Fatma Ismail).

Plate 11: View westward from hypostyle hall M toward the main sanctuary A of the Temple of Hibis, across hypostyle hall B. Six side chapels are arranged around the south, west, and north walls of hypostyle hall B (photo taken by Fatma Ismail).

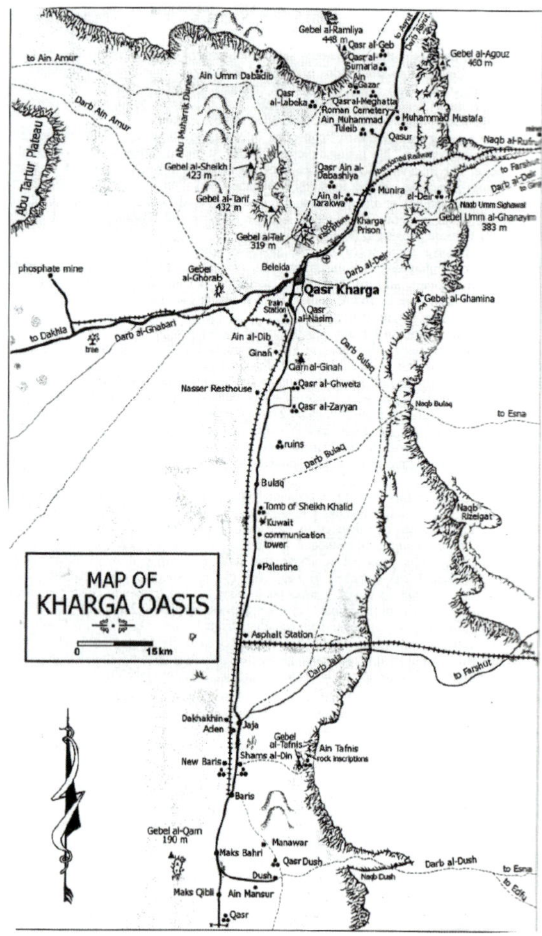

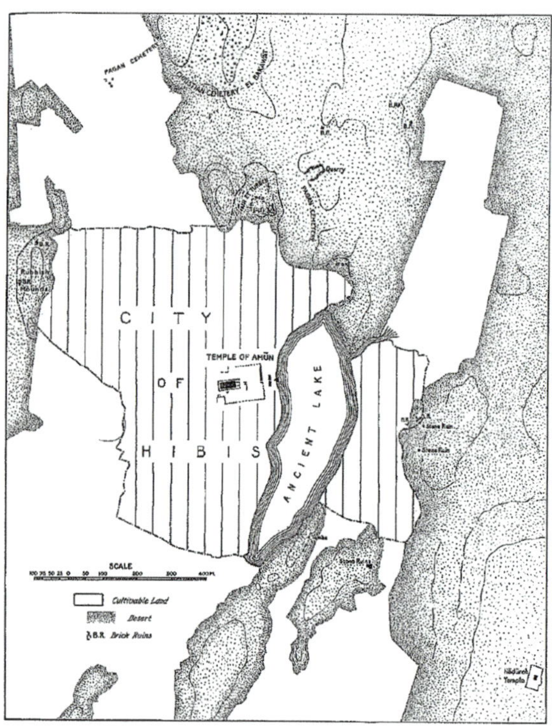

Plate 13: Map of the city of Hibis (after Winlock, *The Temple of Hibis*, Part 1, plate XXIX).

← Plate 12: Map pf Kharga Oasis (after Vivian, *The Western Desert of Egypt: An Explorer's Handbook*, 52).

Plate 14: A reused block discovered in the summer of 2007 by the SCA, among the foundation blocks in hypostyle hall M (photo taken by Fatma Ismail).

Plate 15: A reused block discovered in the summer of 2007 by the SCA, among the foundation blocks in hypostyle hall M (photo taken by Fatma Ismail).

Plate 16: A reused block discovered in the summer of 2007 by the SCA, among the foundation blocks in hypostyle hall M (photo taken by Fatma Ismail).

Plate 17: The doorway to stairway E, showing the two trap doors to the undecorated crypts (photo taken by Fatma Ismail).

Plate 18: First register of the west wall of chapel F (photo taken by Fatma Ismail).

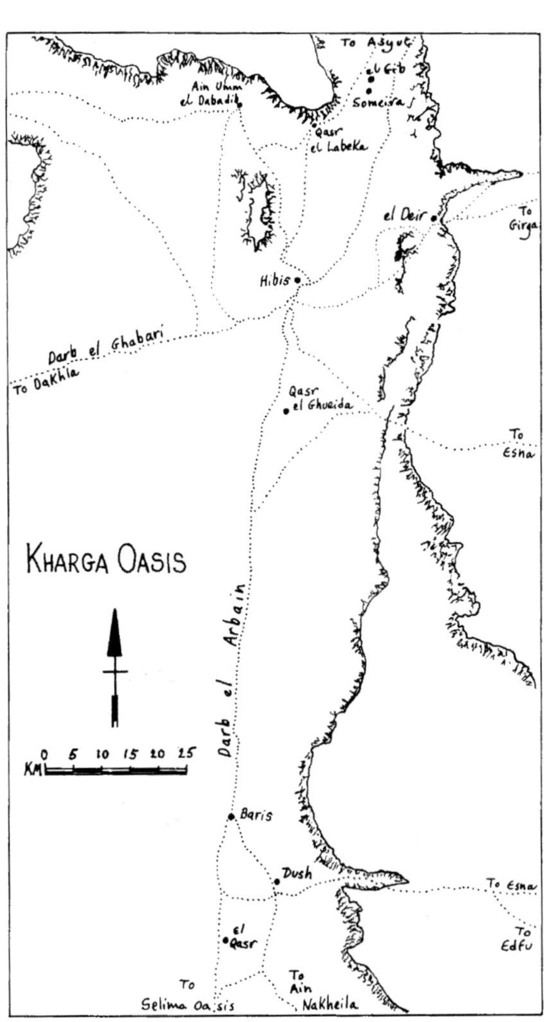

Plate 19: Sketch map of Kharga Oasis and its main desert roads (after Morkot, "The Darb el-Arbain, the Kharga Oasis and its Forts, and other Desert Routes," fig. 1).

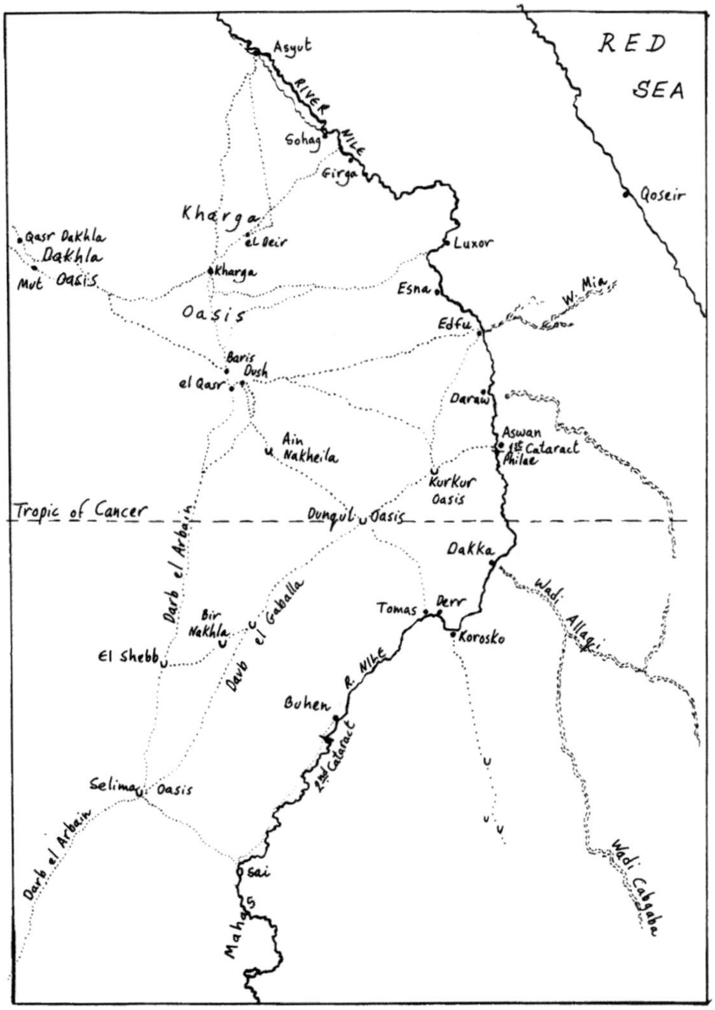

Plate 20: Sketch map of the main desert roads in the western desert (after Morkot, "The Darb el-Arbain, the Kharga Oasis and its Forts, and other Desert Routes," fig. 4).

Plate 21: The lion-headed god Shesmu on the stairway of the Temple of Dendera (photo taken by Fatma Ismail).

↓ Plate 22: The human-headed god Shesmu on the stairway of the Temple of Dendera (photo taken by Fatma Ismail).

Plate 23: View eastward into chapels H1 (to the right side) and H2 (to the left side). The dividing wall between the two chapels is now gone. The south wall of chapel H1 is the only remaining wall of the chapel. From chapel H2, one can still see the east wall and the north wall (photo taken by Fatma Ismail).

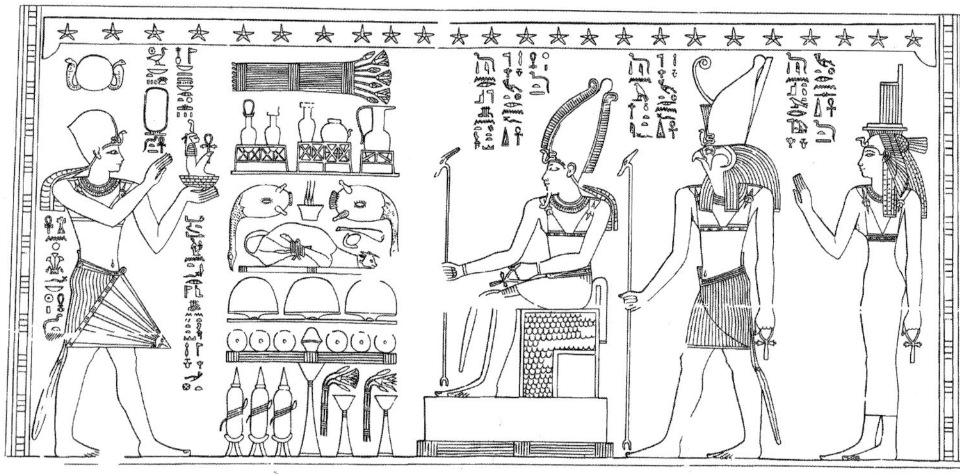

Plate 24: South and north walls of chapel H1 (after Davies, *The Temple of Hibis*, Part 3, detail from plate 19).

Plate 25: The south wall of chapel H1 (photo taken by Fatma Ismail).

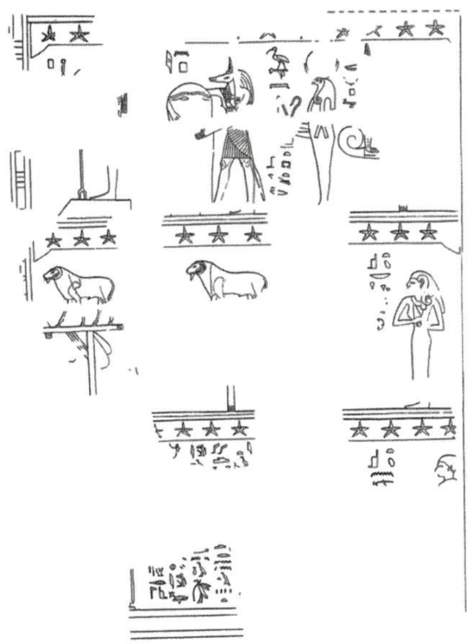

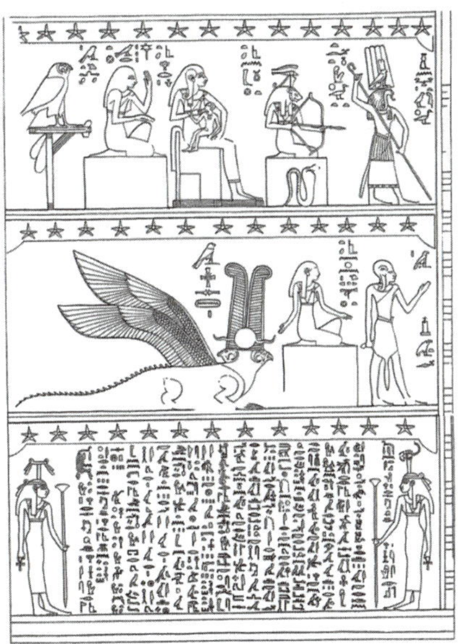

Plate 26: West and east walls of chapel H2 (after Davies, *The Temple of Hibis*, Part 3, detail from plate 20).

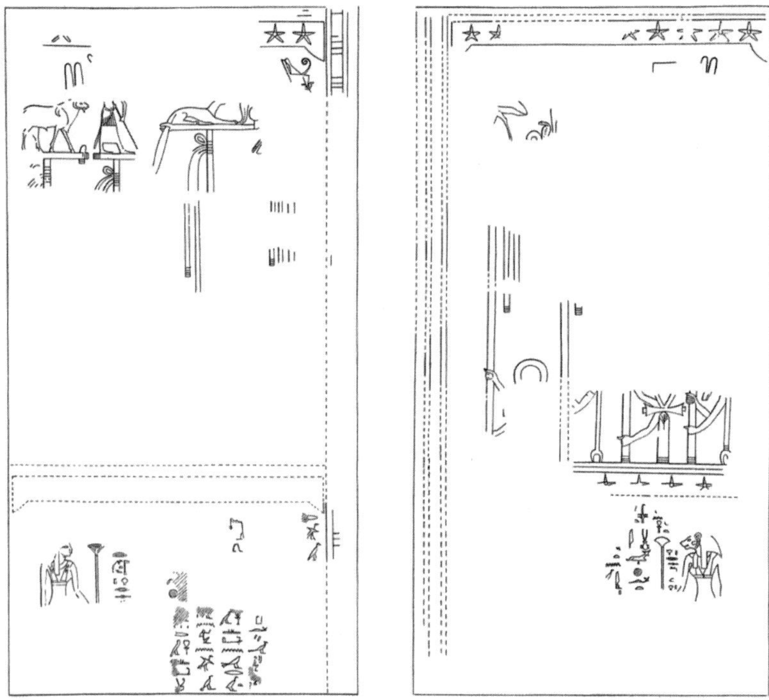

Plate 27: South wall of chapel H2 (after Davies, *The Temple of Hibis*, Part 3, detail from plate 19).

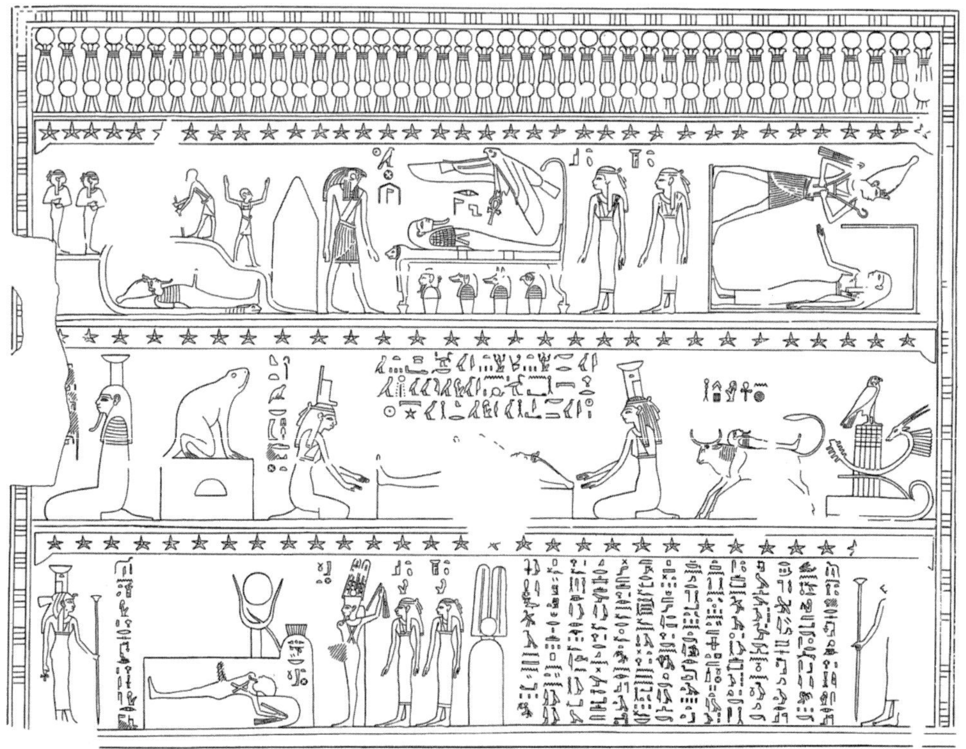

Plate 28: North wall of chapel H2 (after Davies, *The Temple of Hibis*, Part 3, detail from plate 20).

Plate 29: North wall of chapel H2 (photo taken by Fatma Ismail).

Plate 30: The goddess Nut with dwarfed legs inside a shrine on the left side, from the Temple of Dendera (after, Drioton, "Un oudja à representation Hermopolitaine," 82, fig. 3).

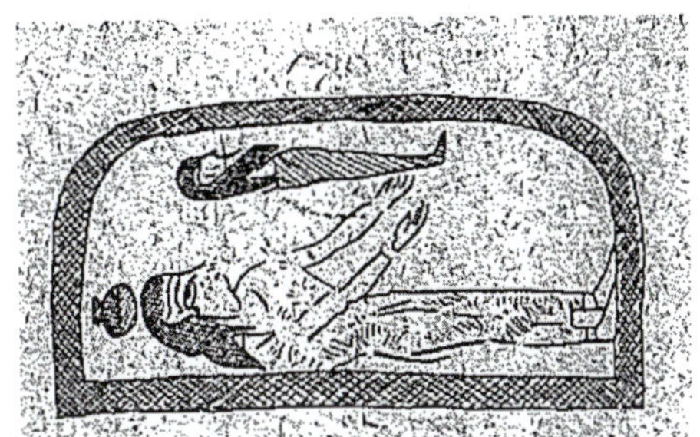

Plate 31: The goddess Nut, from Papyrus Rhind I (after Rusch, *Die Entwicklung der Himmelsgöttin Nut zu einer Totengottheit*, 37, fig. 4).

Plate 32: Scene from the Tomb of Amenhotep, Bahariya Oasis (after Billing, *Nut, the Goddess of Life: In Text and Iconography*, fig. C.55).

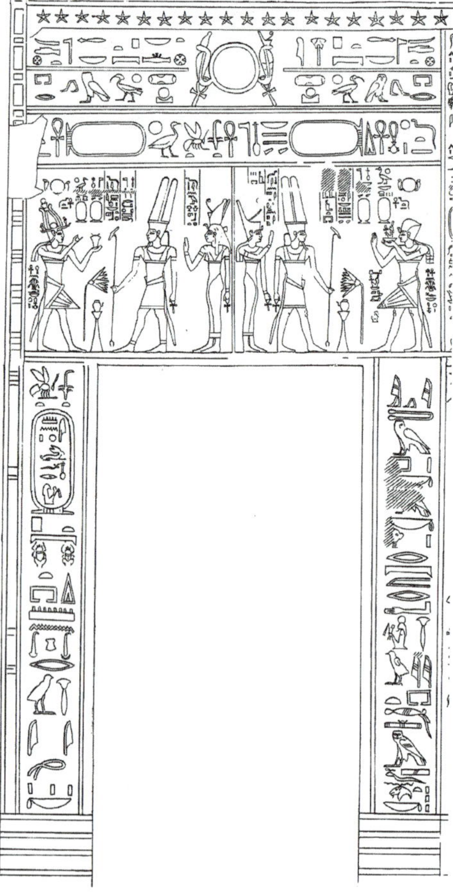

Plate 33: The doorway to stairway E, including the door lintel and the two jambs (after Davies, *The Temple of Hibis*, Part 3, detail from plate 7).

↓ Plate 34: View from chapel complex H into chapel E1, showing the north pilaster and wall to the right and the south pilaster to the left. The west wall is shown in the middle of the photo (photo taken by Fatma Ismail).

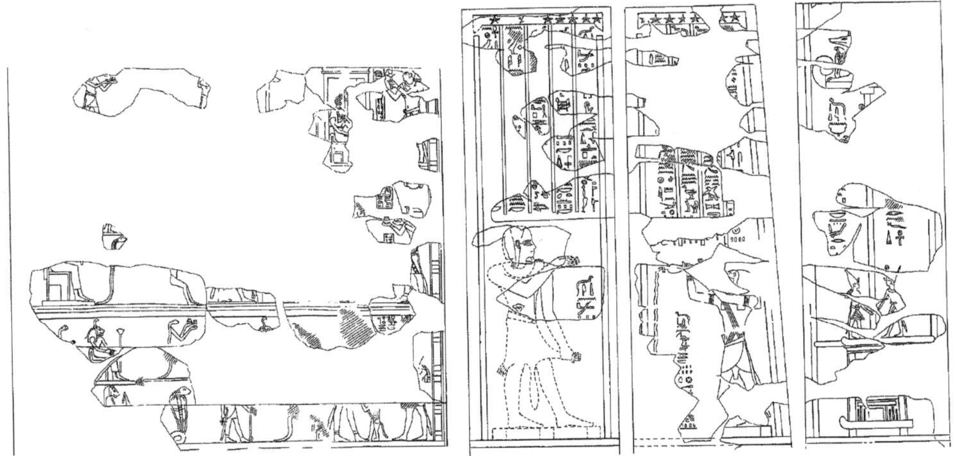

Plate 35: The north wall and north pilaster of chapel E1 (after Davies, *The Temple of Hibis*, Part 3, detail from plate 15).

Plate 36: The south wall and south pilaster of chapel E1 (after Davies, *The Temple of Hibis*, Part 3, detail from plate 15).

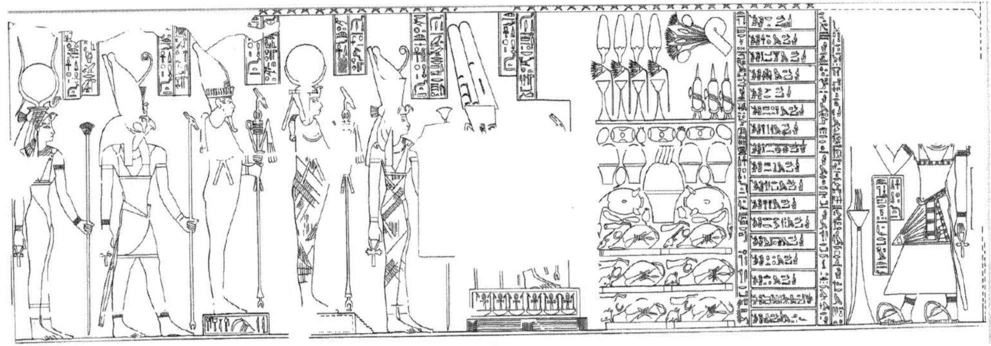

Plate 37: The west wall of chapel E1 (after Davies, *The Temple of Hibis*, Part 3, detail from plate 16).

Plate 38: View from chapel E1 to the east wall of chapel E2. Chapel complex H is shown to the right side (photo taken by Fatma Ismail).

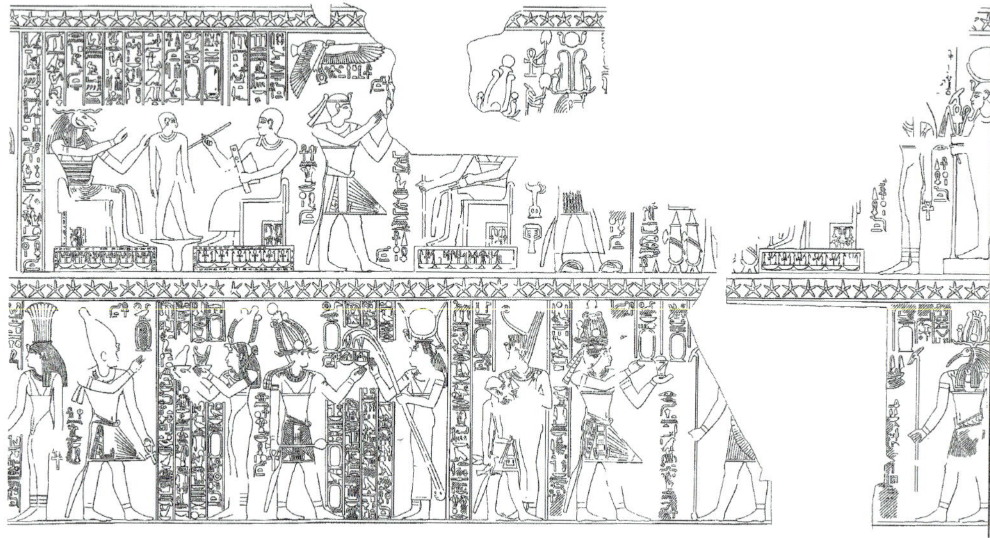

Plate 39: The south wall of chapel L (after Davies, *The Temple of Hibis*, Part 3, detail from plate 27).

Plate 40: The west wall of chapel L (after Davies, *The Temple of Hibis*, Part 3, detail from plate 26).

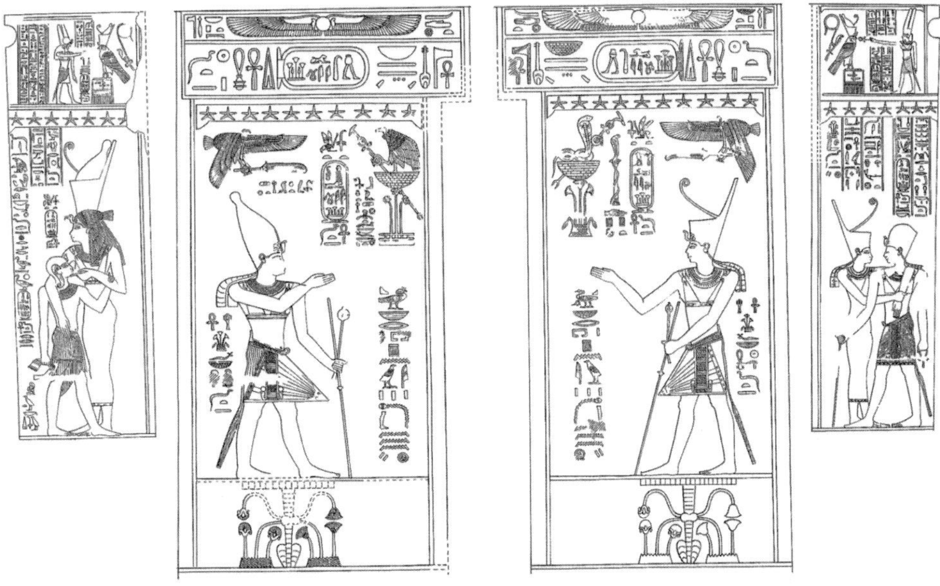

Plate 41: Hypostyle hall N, west wall, gateway to hypostyle hall M (after Davies, *The Temple of Hibis*, Part 3, plate 39).

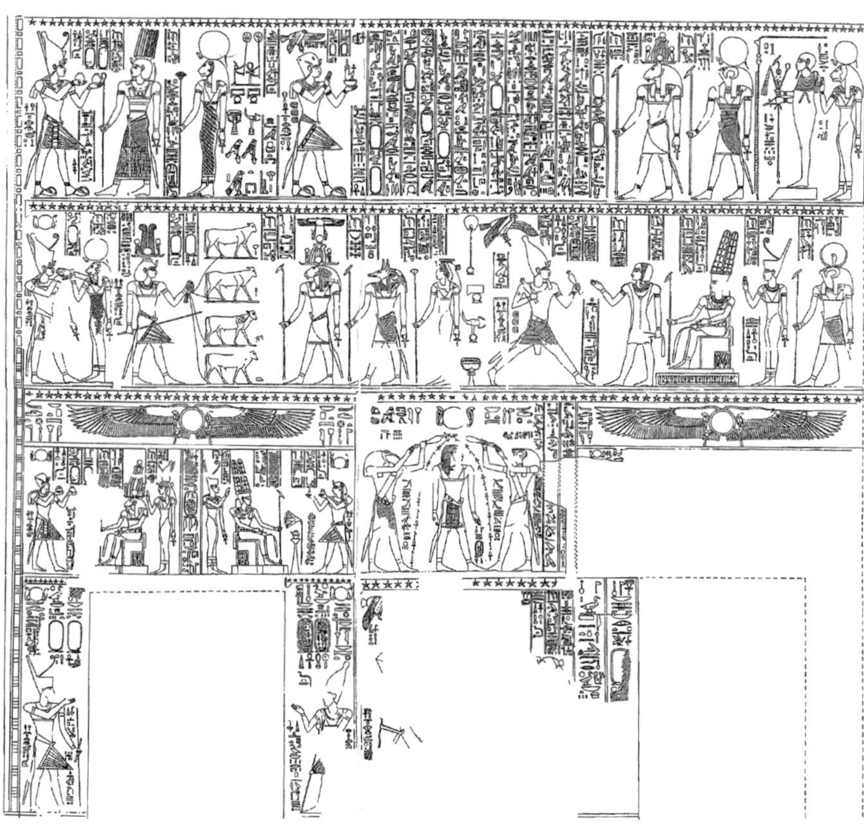

Plate 42: Hypostyle hall B, south wall, west section (after Davies, T*he Temple of Hibis*, Part 3, plate 12).